Franz M. Wittmann

Non-violent Education as a Children's Right – A Human Rights-based Response to Child Sexual Abuse in Educational Institutions

ReligionsRecht im Dialog
Law and Religion

herausgegeben von / edited by

Prof. Dr. Adrian Loretan
(Universität Luzern
University of Lucerne, Switzerland)

Band / Volume 35

LIT

Franz M. Wittmann

Non-violent Education as a Children's Right – A Human Rights-based Response to Child Sexual Abuse in Educational Institutions

LIT

This book is printed on acid-free paper.

Bibliographic information published by the Deutsche Nationalbibliothek
The Deutsche Nationalbibliothek lists this publication in the Deutsche Nationalbibliografie; detailed bibliographic data are available on the Internet at https://dnb.dnb.de.

ISBN 978-3-643-80418-1 (pb)
ISBN 978-3-643-85418-6 (PDF)
Zugl.: University College Cork, Diss., 2024

Flössergasse 10
CH-8001 Zürich
Tel. +41 (0) 78-307 91 24
E-Mail: zuerich@lit-verlag.ch https://www.lit-verlag.ch
Distribution:
In the UK: Global Book Marketing, e-mail: mo@centralbooks.com
In Germany: LIT Verlag Fresnostr. 2, D-48159 Münster
Tel. +49 (0) 2 51-620 32 22, Fax +49 (0) 2 51-922 60 99, e-mail: vertrieb@lit-verlag.de

Contents

Acknowledgements

This work was first elaborated as a PhD thesis for University College Cork and looks into an area of the law where international human rights and the canon law of the Catholic Church and Ireland's internal legal order intersect and partially overlap. None of these particular subject-matters was well known territory to me when I first came to the wider topic of children's rights in the Church; or rather, the topic came to me in the course of relocating as a family to Ireland at around the first decade of the 2000's. This study's focus is on children's rights as they were stipulated in the 1989 UN Convention on the Rights of the Child (CRC or 'the Convention') to which Ireland as well as the Holy See became a State Party; the earlier without any reservations added and the latter attaching an interpretive declaration as well as reservations to its formal act of ratification. In a similar way, my analysis was inspired by reception of the four major contemporary child abuse reports from Ireland captioned as *'Ferns'* (2005), *'Ryan'* (2009), *'Murphy'* (2009) and *'Cloyne'* (2010) respectively. These reports document institutional and structural features of child care and education deemed gravely abusive, in the State or in the Church. Therefore, making reality of children's rights following the Convention's coming into force, requires an act of implementation that starts from rights provisions to be transposed into state duties and obligations with the help of a tripartite typology of 'Respect', 'Protect' and 'Fulfil' (RPF). As a typology RPF has become an accepted framework for human rights analysis and the relevant chapters in this book fully explain and further elaborate on the methodological aspects with application to the right to non-violent education

Accordingly, as a matter of enormous gratitude my academic teachers deserve to find their names reproduced here (in order of appearance): Professor Adrian Loretan of University of Lucerne, Lucerne (Switzerland) whose never ending enthusiasm about children's human rights to be faithfully implemented into ecclesiastical contexts everywhere, helped to think big about the responsibility of office holders in the Church to liberate and expand their canon law conceptions and practice. Also, Professor Loretan helped to secure an important research grant from Swiss National Fund (SNF) which was indispensible at the outset in order to get the whole project started. Professor Ursula Kilkelly of University College Cork, one of the leading experts in the field of children's rights, was generous enough to accept me into her faculty's PhD programme; her wide-spread professional knowledge of children in conditions detrimental to their development prevented me from building upon false assumptions about children being best protected against violence and abuse within their families. With a certain measure of strictness in terms of rigorously following through with axiomatic principles built upon at the point of departure Professor Conor O'Mahony very patiently re-read my drafts which got much shorter by every round of re-reading and gained in clarity of expression at the same time. With a relentless sense of duty and responsibility for transposing many different legal aspects into one piece of synthesis he carried the main load of supervision during months and years. Professor Mary McAleese who came in as an external examiner for my viva, proved to be an enthusiastic advocate for taking children's rights seriously in all circumstances, where children who were or were not baptized into the Catholic Church profit from educational services as schoolchildren; her profound knowledge and expertise regarding the Holy See as a subject of international law brought great seriousness to the discussion. As an internal examiner for my viva Professor Aoife Daly of University College Cork read the final version of the work very diligently adding useful remarks where necessary; she certainly helped to bring the whole project across the finishing line, without undue delay.

Accordingly, what I had to explore was the extent to which the Holy See and Ireland have discharged their protective obligations emanating from that RPF scheme. Thus, an obligation of implementation falls on the Holy See as a State Party to the Convention, and some initial steps of legal reform in the interest of children and their rights were undertaken, in the domain of criminalization, mandatory reporting and investigation. In response to revelations about child abuse by clerics and in Catholic run institutions the *Pontifical Commission for the Protection of Minors* was set up, but its institutional independence within the Roman Curia network is not secured.

Finally, in order to avoid dangerous fragmentation of child-related services in the State it proved necessary to streamline the statutory regime under which child protection agencies and crime prevention organs presently co-operate, in the education sector, among others. As my analysis demonstrates, it might be helpful to consider an orientation for legislators, administrators and the judiciary along the lines of the right to non-violent education so as to prioritise children and their actual needs; they are, and must be seen to be independent holders of economic, social and cultural rights. May this work help schoolchildren and their educators everywhere to become ever more confident that the vast majority of educational institutions, be they state-owned or owned and managed by ecclesiastical bodies, shall be free, as a matter of course, from all forms of violence and abuse.

By way of dedication: *uxorem diligatam.*

Zurich/Switzerland, May 2025.

Introduction

From its origins in Latin a dissertation (the verb *'serere'* translates 'to bind together', 'to entwine') refers to a disentanglement of arguments which shall rather be presented in a well structured and properly sequenced manner; a legal dissertation, therefore, presents legal arguments in this way.

In terms of triggering curiosity and research this dissertation owes its emergence to momentous events that, in January 2014, fell into exactly the same week: one is the final judgment given by the Grand Chamber of the European Court of Human Rights in the case of *O'Keeffe v Ireland* by which the Court found that the structure of primary education in Ireland failed to protect a schoolgirl from sexual abuse by her teacher; another one is the issuance by the Committee on the Rights of the Child of their Concluding Observations on the second periodic report of the Holy See.[1] To this very day, these particular Observations document a wide rift of opinion as regards the legally obliging nature of the Holy See's commitment made by signature and ratification of the Convention on the Rights of the Child (CRC, or 'the Convention'). As the CRC Committee observed:

> *While welcoming the Holy See's approach to ensuring that the legislation of Vatican City State complies with the Convention, the Committee regrets that the same approach has not been followed in relation to its internal laws, including Canon Law.*[2]

From this observation it becomes obvious that canon law is a problem for monitoring the degree of the fulfilment of obligations under the Convention by the Holy See as a State Party to the Convention. For this context it seems fitting that, in 2010, I had obtained a 'Higher Diploma in Canon Law' issued by a Dublin based institution which was accredited by the National University of Ireland.

---

1 *O'Keeffe v Ireland* App no 35810/09 (ECtHR, 28 January 2014); CRC/C/VAT/CO/2 *Concluding Observations on the second periodic report of the Holy See* dated 31 January 2014.

2 CRC/C/VAT/CO/2 (2014) para 13.

While protecting schoolchildren from violence and abuse appears to be a matter of undisputable urgency in all circumstances, making progress in the achievement of non-violent education *via* an approach starting from children themselves and their human rights as they were stipulated in a binding treaty, proved to be a much more contentious subject. Adding to the complexity of the issue documentary materials reporting about child sexual abuse in an unprecedented mass of detail and global dispersion are demonstrating the need for comprehensive analysis. Sadly, Catholic run institutions are featuring prominently in many official reports.

Questions for Research

Initially, the following set of research questions emerged: First, which are the rights pupils and students attending Catholic educational institutions have for their protection against sexualised violence and abuse; second, which are the corresponding duties and obligations falling on States Parties to the Convention including the Holy See; and third, how effectively are duties and obligations stemming from the Convention discharged in practice by States Parties such as Ireland and the Holy See?

By means of researching these topics an attempt is made at overcoming what Ursula Kilkelly identified as *'the Convention's Achilles Heel'*, namely a lack of formal means by which binding international obligations can be translated into justiciable claims at national level.[3] Mainly through academic research other means were developed by which CRC obligations can be observed or the wider implementation of its principles and provisions promoted; those were designated as *'Children's Rights Auditing'* and *'Strategic Litigation'*.[4] My modest contribution to the field builds upon elaboration and adaptation of a typology of obligations widely accepted as a scheme of duties for States under international human rights law. Through scholarly writing and in the practice of UN treaty bodies a tripartite typology was adopted as a means of translating treaty-based abstract guarantees into clear-cut obligations encompassing obligations to respect, and obligations to protect and obligations to fulfil the human rights of children (*'Respect'*, *'Protect'*, *'Fulfil'*, 'RPF' for short).

---

3 U Kilkelly, 'Using the Convention on the Rights of the Child in Law and Policy: Two Ways to Improve Compliance' in A Invernizzi et al (eds), *The Human Rights of Children: From Visions to Implementations* (Ashgate 2012) 179, 185.

4 Ibid 185, 191.

Utilized as a rather formal, schematic algorithm of sorts this typology is easily transferable between jurisdictions seen as duty-bearers and thereby helps to gain comparative insights into the actual state of CRC standards being implemented. Thus, the actual state of implementation for which Ireland as a jurisdiction is held accountable may be assessed in comparison to other subjects of international law, including the Holy See as the centre of government of the worldwide Catholic Church. Since the Roman Catholic Church is the world's largest non-governmental provider of educational and welfare services to children, selecting the Holy See – an early CRC signatory – as my second comparator jurisdiction proved to be especially relevant.[5]

As to its compatibility with CRC standards Ireland's internal legal order based on the 1937 Constitution of Ireland comes to be assessed, and exactly the same needs to be done in respect of the internal legal order of the Catholic Church, codified in its *Codex Iuris Canonici,* also known as the 1983 Code of Canon Law. Unsurprisingly, at one stage during its decade-long discourse with representatives of the Holy See the CRC Committee found some of the provisions of canon law not to be in conformity with the provisions of the Convention, '... *in particular those relating to children's rights to be protected against discrimination, violence and all forms of sexual exploitation and sexual abuse'*.[6] This targeted observation may be read as an instance of children's rights auditing which requires more research and a deeper exploration into the extent of non-compliance regarding the body of canon law on the one hand and the Convention system of children's rights, on the other. For reasons of feasibility, however, my analysis here will focus on the risk of sexual abuse in Catholic schools and similar educational settings.

As Mary McAleese, in her seminal work *'Children's Rights and Obligations in Canon Law'* (2019) explains, the relationship between the CRC as an instrument of international public law and canon law as a source of rights and obligations impacting on children worldwide is uncertain and in dispute; any research into their interface of conflict and cooperation needs

---

5 Prior to this study, under the supervision of Prof Dr Adrian Loretan (chair of Canon Law at Universität Luzern, Lucerne/Switzerland) the role of the Holy See as a State Party to the Convention was researched, with an accent on Switzerland as a comparator jurisdiction.

6 Fn 2 above.

to be of an inter-disciplinary character accordingly.[7] Since this dissertation equally looks into both bodies of law separately as well as into their areas of overlapping, it also needs to be inter-disciplinary in character, building on insights drawn from disciplines such as international law, comparative law and canon law including their interpretive methods.

Legal Techniques and Disciplines

Primarily, for answering my research questions I had to do three things: First, to receive and interpret the Convention, its words and its spirit, as the most ratified human rights treaty comprising an array of rights and corresponding obligations; second, to develop a technique for determining the extent to which domestic laws, policies and practice are in compliance with CRC standards; and third, to come to an assessment about the fulfilment of obligations by way of comparative analysis regarding measures of implementation undertaken by Ireland or by the Holy See seen as duty-bearers under the Convention.

International human rights law is a body of law rich in substance on rights and freedoms primarily stipulated for the benefit of individuals, but no independent court (like the Strasbourg based European Court) empowered to authoritatively state a violation of rights was ever instituted for the CRC system of children's rights. As a discipline comparative law has a strong methodological component generating studies of meta-analysis treating the functional method of comparative law according to which an analysis of legal systems will be concerned about the law's functionality, its regulatory effects and contexts, rather than its peculiar nomenclature.[8] Especially for bringing out the criminal dimension of child sexual abuse regard must be had to starkly different approaches taken by either national or canon law systems for an effective prosecution of crimes perpetrated against minors. Since this study demonstrates that 'criminalization' is an obligation under CRC, how child victims or suspects of child sexual abuse were treated, and are being treated in practice, must not be left out of the comparative analysis picture. Other areas of the law, administrative in nature and application, are much less easy to understand and compare from a

7 M McAleese, *Children's Rights and Obligations in Canon Law: The Christening Contract* (Brill Nijhoff Leiden Boston 2019) 6.

8 R Michaelis, 'The Functional Method of Comparative Law' in M Reimann, R Zimmermann (eds) *The Oxford Handbook of Comparative Law* (OUP 2006) 339–381.

functionalist perspective; administrative investigations into complaints of child sexual abuse will serve as an example for this difficulty.

The Roman Catholic Church and its canon law-based internal legal order builds on almost 2000 years of procedural practice within this church and its institutions worldwide, but the codification of laws in a generally communicable legal language is a relatively recent development. Appearing at sessions sponsored by UN treaty monitoring bodies is not an easy routine for representatives of the Holy See where, in modern times, human rights have been a subject of preaching to the world at large but not for self-scrutiny.

Binding these disciplines together was made possible by the fact that the Holy See signed and ratified the CRC, not without attaching three reservations and a declaration to its act of ratification. Providing educational and welfare services to children worldwide the Catholic Church lawfully operates its institutions in many different jurisdictions which are also State Parties to the Convention; any such State must enforce their own rules and regulations in the field of child welfare and protection.[9] Children and their families living in these jurisdictions may well find themselves burdened by a multi-layered network of obligations and, to a lesser extent, empowered by rights. Thus it is not hard to see, how, in the field of school-based compulsory education, spheres of legal responsibility do intermingle and overlap; protecting schoolchildren from violence and abuse is no exception to this general observation, even if an obligation to provide effectively for this kind of protection is not disputed by anyone. Nevertheless, overlapping spheres of legal responsibility may become a cause for conflict and confusion requiring instead careful consideration of the applicability and scope of specified provisions or whole normative systems such as canon law or ECHR case-law. Regularly, this includes a disentanglement of concepts covering, among others, obligations of 'reporting', of 'investigation' or 'inspection' undertaken for the purpose of protecting children from violence.

As a consequence, binding legal disciplines together anew from a children's rights perspective was the main task of this study. If children's rights, such as the right to non-violent education, are taken seriously implementing measures must be effectively coordinated at the highest

[9] McAleese (n 7) 6.

national – and indeed international – level, and the child's best interests taken as a primary consideration in all action concerning public and private educational and social welfare institutions (Article 3 CRC). Using the tripartite typology of obligations for fleshing out in detail what this means in terms of international obligations falling on CRC State Parties effectively turning them into duty-bearers became a burdensome yet rewarding exercise.

Social Contexts

As a resource for reflection and analysis the Commission of Inquiry reports from Ireland constitute a foundation on which this study on children's right to protection from violence builds; four of them were selected for reasons of accessibility, and for their qualities in helping to identify issues and address relevant legal and social contexts. Equally, the UN commissioned *World Report on Violence against Children* (*'Pinheiro'*) had important contributions to make in terms of recommendations given for rights implementing legislation and for suggesting wide-spread reforms of domestic law, policy and practice. Given the fact that the CRC Committee played a decisive role in its genesis it does not come as a surprise to find the *World Report* taking children's rights seriously, not least the right to protection from violence and abuse (Article 19 CRC). Also, the 2012 report from the Office of the Special Representative of the Secretary General on Violence against Children (*'Tackling Violence in Schools: A global perspective'*) provided stimulus for bridging the gap between standards and practice. Here, children's education rights as specifically set out in Articles 28, 29 CRC served as a human rights framework into which drawing conclusions and recommending itemized measures may well be fitted.

In particular *'Ryan'* and *'Murphy'*, both from Ireland and published in the same year 2009, make for gruesome reading throughout; however, these reports, each according to the terms of its legal mandate, also display an enormous wealth of materials helpful for legal and even for canonical analysis.[10] Famously, in the ECHR case of *O'Keeffe v Ireland* the European Court even relied on evidence from official documents such as *'Ryan'* reporting on the incidence of sexual abuse of children in Ireland, and found that the risk of abuse occurring in schools was fore-

---

[10] For *'Ryan'* (2009) see Fn 64; for *'Murphy'* (2009) see Fn 65.

seeable.[11] The most recent of abuse reports, namely *'Cloyne'* published in the month of December 2010, exclusively received a formal response from the Holy See, diplomatically drafted in tone and substance.[12] Both documents – report and response – describe a web of historically grown canon law-based responsibilities which, in effect, helped to build up a blockage against fresh legislative measures initiated for the protection of children from violence and abuse in Ireland. Children and their human rights seemingly did not have any significance for ecclesiastic or government authorities dealing with the issue of clerical sexual abuse at the time.

Preview of Sections

This study has three main parts treating 'Rights and Freedoms' (*First Part*), 'Duties and Obligations' (*Second Part*) and 'Jurisdictions and Implementations' (*Third Part*) in sequence. Each of these main parts has two or three chapters sub-divided into sections and sub-sections where most of the detailed and itemized work of discussion and analysis may be found.

For the first part children's rights and freedoms, and the right to non-violent education in particular, come to the forefront. Both sets of rights, the right to freedom from all forms of violence (Article 19 CRC) and children's education rights (Articles 28, 29 CRC) are explained and interpreted in accordance with principles and rules distilled from the *Vienna Convention on the Law of Treaties* (VCLT).[13] Finally, the right to non-violent education is introduced as a synthesis of protective rights re-defined for interpreting them in conjunction with treaty-based education rights of the child.

The wording in Article 19(1) CRC 'any other person who has the care of the child' helps to broaden this protective obligation's application to include a wide variety of caregivers operating from a range of care settings situated beyond the child's family home. Consequently, these words taken from the core provision about the right to freedom from violence shall be interpreted as covering the personnel of both private and public institutions extending to services or facilities responsible for the care of children, including schools. Thereby, the right to non-violent education will be defined as a right to protection from violence particularly concerned about the risk

---

[11] *O'Keeffe v Ireland* (n 1) paras 75–84.

[12] For *'Cloyne'* (2011) see Fn 66.

[13] For VCLT see Fn 202.

of abuse as it manifests itself in a variety of school-like settings involving children who are enjoying their education rights.

Another ingredient going into the synthesis is coming from children's education rights which were extensively stipulated in two separate articles of the Convention demonstrating their overall importance for the development of the child's personality. Already, in its very first General Comment treating the aims of education the Committee found that

> *Children do not lose their human rights by virtue of passing through the school gates. Thus, for example, education must be provided in a way that respects the inherent dignity of the child … . Education must also be provided in a way that respects … and promotes non-violence in schools.*[14]

Accordingly, the Convention promotes a qualitative dimension of education which must be seen in conjunction with the substance of the child's right to freedom from all forms of violence, including violent or abusive behaviour originating from care-settings such as schools; taken together both aspects will result in accepting the child's right to non-violent education. Having this right as a fused version of children's rights *in* education gives a clearer profile to rights-bearing individuals of minor age who must not be forced to pick and choose their corresponding duty-bearers from a variety of government agencies each responsible for partial aspects of child protection; such is the added value of this right. Compared to freedom from violence as provided by Article 19 CRC the right to non-violent education is not limited to keeping possible perpetrators of violence away from children but empowers children to claim educational resources for themselves.

Internal Materials

Developed in clear correspondence to specified CRC provisions, duties and obligations falling on States Parties as a matter of international law make for the bulk of discussion and analysis throughout the second part. Here, the tripartite typology of obligations including its items of 'Respect', 'Protect' and 'Fulfil' are fully detailed and brought to application on the right to non-violent education as a children's right. The third part treating Ireland and the Holy See which are, individually and separately, States Parties to

[14] CRC/GC/2001/1 para 8.

the Convention, focuses on an assessment about their respective legal order's compatibility with CRC standards. While the Irish Government, over many years, became reasonably active drafting fresh legislation and reforming administrative structures for the benefit of children, the Holy See remains in a state of denial arguing against the legal character of its obligations under the Convention. It became necessary, therefore, to deeply look into the wording and content of reservations and an interpretive declaration entered by the Holy See when ratifying the Convention; again, the *Vienna Convention* containing international rules on the validity of reservations, had to be consulted for bringing the argument to a resolution.

In striking contrast to its negation of international obligations undertaken as a State Party to the Convention, the Holy See drafted fresh legislation dealing with specific aspects of criminalizing child sexual abuse which was re-framed as an offence against the child's human dignity (Apostolic Constitution *Pascite Gregem Dei*, 4 June 2021). Moreover, a clarification of existing legislation was articulated by the ecclesiastic legislator for removing ecclesiastic officeholders from office on grounds of a failure to start an investigation, to report and sanction cases of clerical child abuse (Apostolic Letter *Come una madre amorevole* 4 June 2016; Apostolic Letter *Vos estis lux mundi* 9 May 2019, Title II). And that same legislator acting for the Church worldwide even proceeded to setting up a system for the reporting of child sexual abuse as newly defined in canon law (Apostolic Letter *Vos estis lux mundi* 9 May 2019, Title I).

For Ireland, its written Constitution which has even been amended for the purpose of bringing children's rights to an exalted level of constitutional rights, receives some attention while highly complex legislation had to be analysed and critically reviewed. In essence, by virtue of the *Criminal Law (Sexual Offences) Act* 2017 and the *Criminal Justice (Victims of Crime) Act* 2017 the law of sexual offences is widely overhauled, both in terms of substance and procedure, with particular attention to minors as victims and witnesses of crime. A whole sequence of novel legislation starting from the *Criminal Justice (Withholding of Information against Children and Vulnerable Persons) Act* 2012 leading on to the *Children First Act* 2015 establishes a system for reporting violence against children not without leaving certain instances of non-reporting unsanctioned. This is not unproblematic, since an obligation to protect the child's right to non-violent education needs to widen its personal scope in order to prevent other children (beyond those victimized already) that are members of the same community from becoming victims of crime.

Handled by the Child and Family Agency/Tusla[15] an administrative practice of responding to complaints of child sexual abuse and starting inquiries that may lead to making findings and sharing information shall be described, analysed and critically reviewed from a children's rights perspective; therefore, an accent of analysis was laid on the *Child Care Act* 1991 including the question of its compatibility with higher ranking norms such as the Constitution or ECHR case law. Finally, for school inspections a highly elaborated rule-book issued by the Department of Education and Skills, and its practical applications posed a set of serious questions respecting professional responsibilities of registered teachers; naturally, their action or in-action plays a decisive role in securing children's right to non-violent education in practice.

Bringing the set of RPF-obligations to completion three important aspects of 'Fulfill' will be reviewed through the lens of the right to non-violent education, namely Inter-agency collaboration which is repeatedly addressed in Committee observations; and comprehensive sexuality education seen as a topic for the official curriculum that controls teaching in schools, and is an obligation under the Convention. Equally, human rights education and dissemination of the principles of the Convention will be mentioned because of their potential for children to be legally empowered; the latter being explicitly stipulated as an obligation in the Convention (Article 42 CRC).

Not fully explored in this study, the matter of Church-State relations in Ireland and how children are being affected by poorly demarcated spheres of legal responsibility will briefly be addressed; a Concordat-type of treaty between the Government and the Holy See treating the matter of education in Catholic or "National" schools will be recommended.

---

[15] For 'Tusla' as an acronym naming the Child and Family Agency (CFA), see Fn 858.

FIRST PART: Rights and Freedoms

Introduction

The history of children's rights owes much to the western philosophical tradition, to the teachings of the early and medieval Christian church and to interventions from a number of sources, Christian and non-Christian alike, all of which contributed to the development of a legal-doctrinal concept properly speaking; the use of international law instruments, however, to declare and assert individualised human rights, including rights specific to children, is a feature of the twentieth century.[16] Because of its near universal ratification the 1989 UN Convention on the Rights of the Child (CRC or "the Convention") stands out from this human rights context.[17] Following the Convention's coming into force on 2 September 1990, the American political scientist Lawrence J. Leblanc observed that this human rights treaty has become the most important legal instrument on the rights of the child; he found, it had also acquired considerable political importance, being repeatedly cited as the most authoritative standard-setting instrument on children's rights at conferences such as the World Summit for Children in 1990 and the UN World Conference on Human Rights in 1993.[18]

16 McAleese (n 7) 43.

17 GA resolution 44/25 of 20 November 1989 (1577 UNTS 3), entry into force on 2 September 1990; 140 Signatories, 196 Parties as of March 2016; UNTC chapter IV Nrs 11 (CRC), 11b (OPAC), 11c (OPSC), 11d (OPCP); there are three Optional Protocols (OPSC, OPAC, OPCP) supplementing and strengthening minimum standards as set out in the Convention; For this study no extra attention will be given to the content of these OP's, although some of their definitions will be referenced from time to time.

18 L J Leblanc, 'Reservations to the Convention on the Rights of the Child: A macroscopic view of state practice' (1996) 4 IJCR 357; UN World Conference on Human Rights, Vienna Declaration and Programme of Action (VDPA) adopted 25 June 1993 paras 45–53 (part II) 'The rights of the child'.

This observation may be corroborated by Ursula Kilkelly's statement made 15 years later that the terms of the Convention have become the common interdisciplinary language of those who work with and for children in a variety of settings; thus, the Convention's relevance to the study and implementation of children's rights in theory and in practice ranges from healthcare to education, from adoption and alternative care to children in conflict with the law.[19] Its comprehensive approach means that the CRC contains legal standards applicable to all areas of the child's life including school (Articles 28, 29) and the family (Articles 3, 5, 7, 9 and 18) as well as in specific settings of alternative care (Articles 20, 21) and youth justice (Articles 37, 40) for example.[20] Equally, the Convention makes provision for children's well-being in a variety of social contexts and, furthermore, makes detailed provision for children with disabilities (Article 23), children whose parents have separated (Articles 3, 9), children who were threatened with a risk of abuse or exploitation (Articles 19, 32–36, 39) and refugee children (Article 22).[21] Not surprisingly, given the extreme vulnerability of children in this regard, the issue of child sexual abuse is explicitly addressed at several locations in the Convention text: Article 9(1) CRC on 'separation from parents' considers a situation involving abuse or neglect of the child by the parents; Article 19(1) CRC on the child's right to protection from all forms of violence lists sexual abuse as a form of violence from which children must be protected; and Article 34(1) CRC on 'sexual exploitation of children' enunciates an undertaking by State parties to protect the child, especially at the level of international treaty-making, from all forms of sexual exploitation and sexual abuse. With respect to child sexual abuse, Article 19(1) CRC, therefore, takes an overarching approach to protection from all forms of violence regardless of its origin in familial or care situations traditionally thought to be immune from state intervention; legal protection is thus extended to both private and public institutions, services or facilities responsible for the care and protection of children, including schools. Without going into detail at this stage of the work, what must be introduced here is the concept of general principles developed from the following set of CRC articles: Article 2

19 U Kilkelly, 'The CRC at 21: assessing the legal impact' (2011) 62 NILQ, 143.

20 Kilkelly, 'Using the Convention' (n 3) 179, 180.

21 Ibid.

(Non-discrimination), Article 3 (Best interest), Article 6 (Life, Survival, Development) and Article 12 (Participation).[22]

In terms of implementation, by virtue of its Article 43 the Convention establishes an expert treaty body sponsored by the United Nations (CRC-Committee, or "the Committee"), which is to monitor compliance with obligations incurred under international law by States Parties to the treaty; as explicitly stated by Article 43(2) CRC the Committee's independent expert members, though elected by State Parties, serve in their personal capacity as experts in the fields of law or education. As a means of rights promotion several kinds of legally structured explanatory documents, General Comments and Concluding Opinions among them, are being issued by the Committee on a regular basis (Article 45 (d) CRC).[23]

Generally perceived to be the object and purpose of the Convention in its integrity are two equally important features of this document's provisions, namely making the child universally visible as an independent subject of both child-specific rights as well as fundamental freedoms; and also to provide, by means of obligating States Parties, for socio-legal empowerment of the child to be realized within his or her living context as an efficient instrument of control.[24] More specifically, the extent of children's rights to protection from abuse and neglect was perceived as an important area where children's rights have yet to be clarified; and that was in a 2006 publication with particular regard for children in the United States.[25] In a similar vein, building on his expertise as a CRC-Committee chairperson Jaap E. Doek in 2009 looked back over 20 years of having the CRC available as an international legal instrument and found that with regard to implementing children's rights the prevention of violence against children

---

22 CRC/GC/2003/5 para 12.

23 As of early 2022 the Committee issued 25 general comments covering many practical aspects; meanwhile, through hundreds of concluding observations, the Committee addressed country-specific issues dealt with in the course of State reporting cycles.

24 Fnn 35, 36 below with reference to writings by M Freeman and K Federle; as a third element, providing for a UN sponsored supervision machinery may be included.

25 B B Woodhouse, 'The Changing Status of the Child' in J Todres et al (eds), *The U.N. Convention on the Rights of the Child, An Analysis of Treaty Provisions and Implications of U.S. Ratification* (Transnational Publishers 2006) 51, 61; Having signed but not ratified the Convention itself the U.S. signed and ratified two Optional Protocols (OPAC, OPSC, Fn 17 above) and complies with its reporting and monitoring duties within this special framework.

was one major challenge; the other one being reduction and elimination of child poverty.[26]

Taking this brief general overview just sketched out as my principal frame of reference,[27] this first part of the dissertation is informed by one core research question: Does the UN Convention on the Rights of the Child provide a legal-doctrinal basis for the right to non-violent education as a human right for children that must be implemented by States Parties into their own internal legal order as a consequence? Having answered this question in the affirmative and also having proffered my legal reasoning for grounding this affirmation, a second part of the study will explore in detail what State duties and implementing obligations were found to be correspondent to the right to non-violent education as a children's right; and finally, two different subjects of international law (Ireland, Holy See) will come into focus for the third part of this thesis, and this is for a comparative review of their respective implementing efforts observable so far. Here, the aim of the exercise will be to formulate an assessment about the achievement of securing the right to non-violent education to each child within their jurisdiction.[28]

Such thing as an individualised children's right to non-violent education may be in existence already by virtue of a few national legal orders, such as German Family Law or the laws of some Nordic states, but that clearly is an altogether different thing, in theory as well as practice.[29] By

---

[26] J E Doek, 'The CRC 20 years: An overview of some of the major achievements and remaining challenges' (2009) 33 Child Abuse & Neglect 771, 781; G Lenzer, 'Violence against children' in W Vandenhole et al (eds) *Routledge International Handbook of Children's Rights Studies* (Routledge 2015) 276.

[27] Lenzer (n 26 above) 276.

[28] L Ferguson, 'Not merely rights for children but children's rights: The theory gap and the assumption of the importance of children's rights' (2013) 21 IJCR 177, 179.

[29] German Civil Code (BGB), §1631 (2) per December 2022; A Nolan, 'Litigating the Child's Right to a Life free from Violence: Seeking the Prohibition of Parental Physical Punishment of Children through the Courts' in: M Freeman, *Current Legal Issues: Childhood and Law Studies* (OUP 2012) 530 (reporting, at Fn 7, from Venezuela where national legislation includes non-violent education and upbringing as an element to the child's well-being); Similarly, the UK House of Lords, through the words of Baroness Hale, found that "... *if a child has the right to be brought up without institutional violence, as he does, that right should be respected whether or not his parents and teachers believe otherwise*", see M Freeman and B J Saunders, 'Can we Conquer Child Abuse' (2014) 22 IJCR 681, 697.

an act of special legislation the Republic of Austria, in 2011, even created the right to non-violent education (*Recht auf gewaltfreie Erziehung)* as a children's right to be inserted, among others, into the body of this jurisdiction's Federal Constitutional Law.[30] Again, this piece of legislation, its scope of application, cannot reach beyond the borders of the particular jurisdiction concerned.

This first part of this study is made up of three chapters, and I will first describe and analyse in general terms what I see as a challenge before me (*chapter 1 – The Challenge*); following this I will then take a deeper look into international law documents such as the UN Convention on the Rights of the Child but other treaties also (*chapter 2 – Express Provisions and Implied Terms*) and, lastly, I will make an attempt to demonstrate what exactly might be the legal meaning of any talk about the right to non-violent education when claimed as a children's right (*chapter 3 – The Right to Non-violent Education*).

Chapter 1 – The Challenge

First Section: Introduction

Anyone sifting through the actual text of the *International Bill of Human Rights* (UDHR, ICCPR, ICESCR) will have a problem finding anything like the right to non-violent education; and equally, anyone taking a diligent look at the Convention will face a similar problem: no such thing expressly stipulated in any of the substantive articles belonging to this instrument. Regarding the manifold sources of international law, this observation might seem to be either arbitrary or trivial, since among the plethora of actors in the field of international human rights law surely there must be one who had asserted already for children to be holders of a right to non-violent education, among others; or if, on the other hand, children's rights in education are fully protected as a matter of law, a right to non-violent education is not really needed by anyone.[31]

---

[30] *Bundesverfassungsgesetz über die Rechte von Kindern* vom 20.01.2011; see Fn 215 below and accompanying text.

[31] C Chinkin, 'Sources' *in* D Moeckli et al (eds) *International Human Rights Law* (3rd ed OUP 2018) 63, 65; C Grabenwarter, *European Convention on Human Rights, Commentary* (C.H. Beck 2014) 390 ("school education without violence").

In this piece of academic research, however, I am not pretending to invent or newly define another human right from afresh; rather, my ambition is much more moderate. Upon a close reading of contemporary violence-related reporting materials (of a mainly empirical character) on the one hand and existing legal documents on the other, I re-define and re-conceptualize existing human rights in order to make them more explicit and more inclusive and to extend their reach to children as a group in particular;[32] as an overall effort this intellectual exercise might be described as '*the refinement and extension of existing rights through treaty interpretation*'.[33] What will be needed, therefore, is a section on treaty interpretation for which the *Vienna Convention on the Law of Treaties* (VCLT) will come in as an international law framework to which fittingly enough both my comparator jurisdictions are States Parties.[34]

At the outset, however, what follows is a comprehensive review of mainly factual observations about violence as a reality in many children's lives already published in a multitude of reports. Building on and guided by this review, my legal-doctrinal analysis of core provisions taken from the Convention will follow and will then lead on to my synthesizing the right to non-violent education as an aggregate of special protection rights for children. As a consequence, the challenge I see before me will be circumscribed with manifold factual situations in mind where violence against children, and schoolchildren in particular, was clearly and hurtfully perceived as a problem for the life, survival and development of any individual child thus threatened or victimized (*Second Section: Interpersonal Violence as a Problem for Educational Institutions*).

A great many efforts have been undertaken, by legislators and educators alike, to eliminate or eradicate all violence from children's lives and from their schooling lives in particular. A general acknowledgement of children as independent holders of fundamental rights and freedoms seems to be the most promising of these efforts, as Michael Freeman with particular regard for children and their fundamental rights summarized, '*It is the rights thesis that protects the integrity of the person in leading his*

[32] T v Boven, 'Categories of Rights' in D Moeckli et al (eds), *International Human Rights Law* (n 31 above) 135, 147.

[33] Chinkin (n 31) 68; P Capps, *Human Dignity and the Foundations of International Law* (Hart 2010), 7, 210 (progressive interpretation).

[34] Fn 202 for detail.

or her life'.[35] Based on a similar concern for the place that rights do have in the lives of children Katherine Hunt Federle also found rights to have an important transformative aspect; and that is because of their potential to reduce victimization and dependence by changing the rights holder into a powerful individual who commands the respect of those in the legal system.[36] Accordingly, 'Freedom from violence' will thus be another intermediate step on my way towards the end of synthesizing the right to non-violent education as a children's right (*Third Section: Freedom from Violence as an Issue for Children's Rights*).

CRC-based Protection from Violence in Context

In the following, one main aspect of analysis is concerned about the sheer ubiquity worldwide of violence being perpetrated against and experienced by children, in families, in schools or similar educational institutions such as church dioceses and parishes as well as prisons or detention facilities (occasionally including school-like learning sessions) everywhere. Seen as a global problem for humanity it must be stated that reports of cruel and humiliating punishment, genital mutilation of girls, neglect, sexual abuse, homicide and other forms of violence against children have long been recorded, but the grave and urgent nature of this problem has only recently been revealed.[37] Admittedly, by reference to expert-led reporting such as the *World Report* I am according an enhanced evidential status to international documents such as this one, but this is consistent with a reflected understanding about the sources of international human rights law; by virtue of Article 38 ICJ-Statute the 'teachings of the most highly qualified publicists' as another subsidiary means for determining the law was fully accredited as belonging to the sources of international law.[38]

As a consequence, the next section following immediately is titled *"Interpersonal Violence as a Problem for Educational Institutions"* (*Second*

---

35 M Freeman, 'The Value and Values of Children's Rights' in: A Invernizzi et al (eds), *The Human Rights of Children: From Visions to Implementations* (Ashgate 2011) 21, 30.

36 K H Federle, *Children and the Law* (OUP 2013), 33; K H Federle, 'Rights flow downhill' (1994) 2 IJCR 343.

37 UN document A/61/299 para 24 *World Report on Violence against Children*, Fn 42 below and accompanying text; Lenzer (n 26) 278.

38 Article 38(1)(d) ICJ-Statute; Chinkin (n 31) 63, 78 (persuasiveness).

Section) and it will look at abstract definitions and concrete situations of violence against children as they were recently reported and documented, from Ireland but from other countries around the globe also.[39]

Second Section: Interpersonal Violence as a Problem for Educational Institutions

Proceeding on a predominantly factual level, this section will follow an inquiry into the actual state of the violence problem, including its nature and extent, its causes and consequences as comprehensively documented in the 2006 *World Report on Violence against Children*, but other reports also.[40] Accordingly, for the following two sub-sections this 2006 *World Report*, also known as *Pinheiro*-Report, as well as the four most prominent Abuse Reports from contemporary Ireland, also known as *Ferns-, Ryan-, Murphy-* and *Cloyne-Report* respectively, will be at the centre of attention.[41]

Sub-section (1) – The 2006 World Report

The first documentation revisited here is the 2006 *World Report*, published by the UN Secretary-General's Study on Violence against Children, also known as *Pinheiro*-Report; describing itself as the first comprehensive, global study conducted by the United Nations on all forms of violence against children.[42] The Study process included nine substantial regional

---

39 J Todres 'Taking Prevention Seriously: Developing a Comprehensive Response to Child Trafficking and Sexual Exploitation' 43 Vand J Transnat'l L. 1 (2010) 3.

40 J Tobin, 'Justifying Children's Rights' 21 IJCR (2013) 395, 413.

41 The Irish Government refers to *Ferns Inquiry Report* (2005), *Commission of Investigation-Dublin Archdiocese* (2009), *Commission to Inquire into Child Abuse* (2009) and *Report of Commission of Investigation into Catholic Diocese of Cloyne* (2011) characterising them as a set of four significant inquiries into child abuse in Ireland, see DCYA (2013), Ireland's Consolidated Third and Fourth Reports to the UN Committee on the Rights of the Child, para 399.

42 In 2001 the UN General Assembly requested the Secretary General to conduct an in-depth study on the question of violence against children and to put forward recommendations for consideration by Member States; The resulting "Report of the independent expert for the United Nations study of violence against children", prepared by Paulo Sérgio Pinheiro, provides an understanding of the nature, extent, causes and consequences of different forms of violence against children; On 29 August 2006, in the format of a UN document (A/61/299), this "Pinheiro-Report" (*'Pinheiro'*) was formally transmitted to the General Assembly.

consultations, a round of expert seminars, a detailed questionnaire sent to States by Professor Pinheiro and responded to by over 130 governments, as well as many submissions from organizations and individuals, including children themselves.[43] Simply and straightforwardly, the report's key message is *'No violence against children is justifiable; all violence against children is preventable'*.[44] As explained in its final report (transmitted to the UN General Assembly) this study profited from a close cooperation between the Committee and Professor Pinheiro who held regular consultations with Committee members but other experts also for the purposes of completing his study.[45]

This World Report was refocused and refined by a thematic report from the Office of the Special Representative of the Secretary General on Violence against Children titled *'Tackling Violence in Schools: A global perspective'*.[46] This report examined a number of elements that were found to be essential to the development of rights-based, violence-free schools and this examination gave rise to a number of recommendations for governments committed to eliminating violence from their school systems.[47] Thereby, this thematic report advanced the concept of a rights-based, child-friendly school as a means to reduce and eliminate violence against children in general.[48] For the sake of brevity and focus I will deal with both documents together.

The earlier 2006 *World Report* provides information on the incidence of various types of violence against children, and proposes recommendations to prevent and respond to this issue. It looks at the principal settings in which violence takes place, one of which being schools and educational settings (others are the family, care and residential institutions).[49] Along

---

43 A/61/299, paras 11–23 (contribution of "faith-based organizations" in paras 12, 21).

44 A/61/299, para 93 (Conclusions).

45 A/61/299 para 15; CRC/C/GC/13 paras 3, 15, 68, 75 (Committee referencing *'Pinheiro'*); Lenzer (n 26) 276, 278.

46 Office of the Special Representative of the Secretary General (SRSG) on Violence against Children, *Tackling Violence in Schools: A global perspective, Bridging the gap between standards and practice* (New York 2012), Marta Santos Pais acting as Special Representative; Doek (n 26) 771, 777.

47 *Tackling Violence in Schools* (n 46 above) 39.

48 Ibid.

49 A/61/299 paras 38–80.

these lines, in the introduction to its chapter on violence against children in schools and educational settings, this report explains:

> *Children spend more time in the care of adults in pre-schools, schools, vocational training centres and other places of learning than they do elsewhere outside of their homes. Like parents, the adults who oversee, manage and staff these places have a duty to provide safe and nurturing environments that support and promote children's education and development. They also have a duty to make sure such development prepares children for life as responsible adults, guided by the values of non-violence, gender equality, non-discrimination, tolerance and mutual respect. These are the values that Governments embrace when they ratify the Convention on the Rights of the Child (CRC) ... .*[50]

Normatively, in its section on violence in schools and other educational settings the *World Report* starts from a general reference to human rights instruments, such as Articles 28, 29 CRC on education rights and Article 19 CRC on the right to protection from all forms of violence.[51] Throughout the *World Report* four main forms of violence in schools are identified: bullying (1), sexual and gender-based violence (2), physical and psychological violence (3), and violence including a dimension external to schools, such as violence associated with gang culture, weapons and fighting (4).[52] Equally, this *World Report*, because it systematically refers to sexual violence and contextualises it in various settings, such as sexual abuse, sexual exploitation and sexual harassment, is credited for reinforcing at UN level the discourse on sexual violence against children.[53]

Definitions of Violence

As observed by Lenzer, the introduction (triggered by the Convention's coming into force) of the domain of 'violence against children' was a significant expansion in the perception of a real world problem; it must not be seen as a simple terminological change away from an earlier phra-

---

50 *World Report* (print version ISBN-10 92–95057–51–1) 111.

51 *World Report* (n 50 above) 113.

52 *Tackling Violence in Schools* (n 46) 5.

53 ECPAT International (Jaap E. Doek chairperson of the Interagency Working Group) *Terminology Guidelines for the Protection of Children from Sexual Abuse and Sexual Exploitation* (28 Jan 2016) 13.

seology gravitating around 'child abuse and neglect' in most legal, social science and policy discussions.[54] Regarding the definition of ' violence'presupposed for the *World Report* two different elements come in, one of which is an idea adopted from the listing in Article 19(1) CRC (physical or mental violence, injury or abuse, neglect or negligent treatment, maltreatment or exploitation, including sexual abuse) and the other is an understanding conceptualized earlier by the World Health Organization that defined as child-related violence '[T]*he intentional use of force or power, threatened or actual, against a child, by an individual or group, that either results in or has a high likelihood of resulting in actual or potential harm to the child's health, survival, development or dignity'*.[55]

The *World Report's* final recommendations are sub-divided into one section containing twelve overarching recommendations for States, such as 'Prohibit all violence against children' (Nr 2), 'Prioritize prevention' (Nr 3), 'Ensure participation of children' (Nr 7), 'Create accessible and child-friendly reporting systems and services' (Nr 8), 'Ensure accountability and end impunity' (Nr 9). Following after that, more setting-specific recommendations are targeting schools and other educational settings:

a) *Encourage schools to adopt and implement codes of conduct applicable to all staff and students that confront all forms of violence, taking into account gender-based stereotypes and behaviour and other forms of discrimination;*
b) *Ensure that school principals and teachers use non-violent teaching and learning strategies and adopt classroom management and disciplinary measures that are not based on fear, threats, humiliation and physical force;*
c) *Prevent and reduce violence in schools through specific programmes which address the whole school environment including through encouraging the building of skills such as non-violent approaches to conflict resolution, implementing anti-bullying policies and promoting respect for all members of the school community;*
d) *Ensure that curricula, teaching processes and other practices are in full conformity with the provisions and principles of the Convention*

54 Lenzer (n 26) 276, 278.

55 A/61/299 para 8 with reference to *World Report on Violence and Health* (Geneva, World Health Organization, 2002).

> *on the Rights of the Child, free from references actively or passively promoting violence and discrimination in any of its manifestations.*[56]

Here, the CRC as a whole including its principles and substantive provisions is expressly taken up as a primary point of normative reference for the implementation of education policies tackling violence in schools from a global perspective; this approach may justly be identified as a human rights-based approach to education.[57] Generally speaking a child rights approach is defined as one which furthers the realization of the rights of all children as set out in the Convention by developing the capacity of duty bearers to meet their obligations to respect, protect and fulfil rights, and the capacity of rights holders to claim their rights.[58] With particular regard for the right to freedom from violence the Committee found that a child rights-based approach to child caretaking and protection requires a paradigm shift towards respecting and promoting the human dignity and the physical and psychological integrity of children as rights-bearing individuals rather than perceiving them primarily as 'victims'.[59]

An element of particular interest to this dissertation involving Catholic schools is the description given in the World Report of the widespread sexual abuse of boys by male teachers (often clerics) in church-run schools.[60] With reference to the so-called *John Jay* study commissioned in 2002 by the US Conference of Catholic Bishops, the following figures were reproduced in '*Pinheiro*': nearly 4,400 priests (4% of all priests ministering during the period under observation) had been accused of sexually abusing nearly 10,700 children, in acts that took place between 1950 and 2002, and the vast majority of the children were boys.[61]

---

56 A/61/299 paras 28/9; *Tackling Violence in Schools* (n 46) 40 recommends to promote violence-prevention programmes (Nr 1), to secure children's legal protection from violence (Nr 2) and to ensure that children have access to confidential counselling, complaints and reporting mechanisms (Nr 3).

57 *Tackling Violence in Schools* (n 46) 39; UNICEF/UNESCO, 'A Rights-Based Conceptual Framework for Education' in *A Human Rights-Based Approach to Education for All* (2007), 27–37.

58 CRC/C/GC/13 para 59.

59 CRC/C/GC/13 para 3.

60 *World Report* (n 50) 119.

61 Ibid, 119; actually, both *John Jay* studies (2004, 2006) provide the best data available to date, see M Keenan, *Child Sexual Abuse and the Catholic Church, Gender, Power and Organizational Culture* (OUP 2012) 7.

As an element to the big picture about the nature and extent of a global violence problem these figures represent an incidence of considerable magnitude regarding abuse in organizations or institutions operating in the name of the Catholic Church. With my focus on Ireland as a jurisdiction I will not discuss those US related figures in more detail here.[62] What must be kept in mind, however, with regard to the Holy See and its universally claimed jurisdictional supremacy worldwide, are an overall responsibility for child sexual abuse perpetrated by adults in ecclesiastic positions of trust and authority; bishops and other church officials including Vatican-based clerical adjudicators, were subsequently covering-up abuse cases stemming from all over the world.

Sub-section (2) – Four Abuse Reports from Ireland

As an overview this sub-section will consider a selection of recently published reports produced on the basis of public and official inquiries into child abuse in Ireland, captioned as *Ferns* (2005),[63] *Ryan* (2009),[64] *Murphy* (2009)[65] and *Cloyne* (2011)[66] respectively. These reports provide an empirical foundation of some significance including conclusions and recommendations for fresh legislative and administrative measures. Being officially commissioned reports they will be helpful for identifying legal-constitutional issues to be addressed by legislators for purposes of implementing Convention rights in Ireland but other jurisdictions also.[67] Seen from an internal Church perspective, the Irish reports have also shown that what has been operated within this Catholic church (in Ireland) must be

---

62 S J Rosetti, 'Learning from our mistakes' in C J Scicluna et al (eds) *Towards Healing and Renewal* (Paulist Press 2012) 29, 40 (U.S. focus).

63 F D Murphy, H Buckley and L Joyce, *The Ferns Report, Presented by the Ferns Inquiry to the Minister for Health and Children* (Dublin, Government Publications, 2005), (*'Ferns'*).

64 *Report of the Commission to Inquire into Child Abuse* (Chair: Judge Séan Ryan) (2009), (*'Ryan'*).

65 *Commission of Investigation, Report into the Catholic Archdiocese of Dublin* (Chair: Judge Yvonne Murphy) (Dublin, Department of Justice and Law Reform, 2009), (*'Murphy'*).

66 *Commission of Investigation, Report into the Catholic Diocese of Cloyne* (Chair: Judge Yvonne Murphy) (Dublin, Department of Justice and Law Reform, 2011) (*'Cloyne'*).

67 U Kilkelly, 'Learning lessons from the Past: Legal Issues Arising from Ireland's Child Abuse Reports' (2012) 12 Ir J Appl Soc Stud 8.

described as a "blind zone" implying the idea of a space where certain relationship systems are widely regarded as normative and therefore not open to scrutiny.[68] Historically, State inquiries into the care of children in Ireland can be roughly divided into several periods and from the late 1990s onwards, a number of cases highlighted the vulnerability of children in environments traditionally considered safe such as orphanages, clubs and schools.[69] Against this broader historic background an astonishing sequence of high-profile inquiry reports concerned about institutional and clerical child abuse in Ireland have been published during the first decade of the 21st century which included the four reports mentioned above.

The first of these reports, the *Ferns Report*, investigated the handling of over 100 allegations of child sexual abuse against 21 priests in the diocese between 1996 and 2002; the date of the report's final publishing was October 2005. This report highlighted the failure of the Church, and diocesan bishops in particular, to respond to complaints about abuse, chiefly by non-removal of priests from active ministry and the non-reporting of complaints to the civil authorities. It also underlined the subsequent failure of state agencies, including the Gardaí (Irish police) and the health authorities, to investigate effectively and prevent the further abuse of victims. The final chapter in *'Ferns'* on conclusions and recommendations is full of detail and in a highly elaborated manner addresses issues such as mandatory reporting or inter-agency communication between State and Church authorities.[70]

This report was building on a very basic definition of ' abuse'although an inquiry into the actual occurrence of abuse was not within the remit of this commission; the definition presupposed reads *'Child sexual abuse occurs when a child is used by another person for his or her gratification or sexual arousal or that of others.'*[71] Although this definition was accompa-

68 McAleese (n 7) 18.

69 A-M McAlinden, 'An inconvenient truth: barriers to truth recovery in the aftermath of institutional child abuse in Ireland' 33 Leg Stud (2013) 189, 193; Kilkelly (n 67) 8, 9.

70 *'Ferns'* 183–198 with legal, regulatory and general recommendations at 195; treating a mandatory system of reporting at 196 (Nr 5); treating an 'Inter Agency Review Committee' at 196 (Nr 8); recommending the introduction of a new criminal offence of wanton or reckless endangerment at 197 (Nr 14); recommending the creation of an offence of child sexual abuse based on Art 19 CRC at 53.

71 *'Ferns'* 2, Terms of Reference (no explicit mandate to establish whether abuse occurred); *'Ferns'* 8 (definition); according to this definition examples of child sexual

nied in *'Ferns'* by an explanatory statement warning in broad terms against a reductionist understanding of child sexual abuse, it proves to be reductionist itself in that it focuses exclusively on external activities to be qualified as 'use'or 'abuse', and on the abuser's gratification or sexual arousal as an object and purpose of such use.[72] As far as canon law is concerned, *'Ferns'* focuses on the lack of clear and enforceable rules and procedures for the suspension of priest-suspects from active ministry; it recommends some legislative solution empowering the High Court to bar or otherwise restrain any person from having unsupervised access to children where reasonable grounds exist for the belief that the person has abused or has a propensity to abuse children.[73] Interestingly, *'Ferns'* reflects in a general manner about the authority and function of canon law within sovereign States such as Ireland and declares that canon law is recognised by the Irish legal system as a scientific legal system and body of law, both substantive and adjective.[74] Thus, the need for analysing the role of canon law in the emergence of clerical child abuse arises because of an exclusive power residing in ecclesiastic authority figures, such as bishops or Vatican officials, to remove an ordained cleric who came under suspicion of child maltreatment from his priestly office and its corresponding ministry in the Church.

Over the course of nine years, the *Commission to Inquire into Child Abuse* investigated the treatment of children in residential institutions run by Catholic religious orders, dating back to 1936. The publication of the five-volume *Ryan Report* in May 2009 generated widespread media coverage and public outcry throughout Ireland and beyond.[75] The Ryan Re-

abuse include the following: exposure of the sexual organs, intentional touching or molesting of the body of a child, masturbation in the presence of the child, sexual intercourse with the child, sexual exploitation of a child which by itself includes inciting, encouraging, propositioning, requiring or permitting a child to solicit for, or to engage in prostitution or other sexual acts.

72 *'Ferns'* 8, 9.

73 *'Ferns'* 197 (recommendation Nr 13); also explaining, at 35, with regard to 'The Framework Document' (Fn 92 below): " ... *Every person or organisation which employs or appoints an individual to a position which gives him or her unsupervised access to young people must have and exercise the power to suspend that individual from that employment if an allegation is made or reasonable suspicion arises that the individual has sexually abused a child".*

74 *'Ferns'* 30.

75 Keenan (n 61) 192; G Shannon, *Child Law* (2nd ed Thomson Reuters Dublin 2010) para 14–134.

port's significance lies in its concluding assessment that an abuse of children (physically, sexually, emotionally and through neglect) and the failure of Church and State authorities to adequately respond to disastrous situations, were widespread in Irish child care institutions; in this *'Ryan'* fully depicted the problem in its institutional and systemic proportions.[76] Expressly addressing the RCC's canon law this report identified 'a culture of silence' about the issue of sexual abuse by members of religious Orders when, in this kind of case, internal procedures and canon law were used to deal with the matter whereas lay perpetrators were reported effectively to the Gardaí (Irish police).[77] Given the mandate of the whole inquiry Ursula Kilkelly found it surprising that *'Ryan'* made so few recommendations concerning measures aimed at support for increased protection for the rights of children; in particular she observed that the Commission did not remark on whether Irish law was considered fit for the purpose of protecting children in care.[78] Equally, she found no consideration of whether legislative or even constitutional change was necessary to advance the goal of child protection.[79] As an observation regarding the qualities of the report this is absolutely correct. What I found remarkable in this context, however, is the point actually made by the Commission about the importance of existing rules and regulations being enforced, breaches being reported and sanctions applied.[80] From this perspective, not what was lacking in the laws and regulations actually in force at the time was a primary factor for

76 McAlinden (n 69) 189, 195; *'Ryan'* Vol IV para 6.02: "The *system of large-scale institutionalisation* ... outdated and incapable ... . The *defects of the system* ... exacerbated by the way it was operated ... "; para 6.03: "The deferential and submissive attitude of the Department of Education ... ."; para 6.04: "The capital and financial commitment made ... a major factor in prolonging the *system of institutional care* ... "; para 6.05: "The *system of funding* through capitation grants led to demands by ... "; para 6.06: "The *system of inspection* by the Department of Education ... fundamentally flawed and incapable of being effective." [my italics throughout].

77 *'Ryan'* Vol IV para 6. 29.

78 Kilkelly (n 67) 11; C O'Mahony and U Killkelly, 'O'Keeffe v Ireland and the duty of the state to identify and prevent child abuse' 36 J Soc Welf Fam L (2014) 320, 328.

79 Kilkelly (n 67) 11.

80 *'Ryan'* Vol IV para 7.10: " ... *cannot be explained by the absence of rules or any difficulty in interpreting what they meant. The problem ... in the implementation of the regulatory framework.* [...]."; para 7.11: "*A culture of respecting and implementing rules and regulations and of observing codes of conduct should be developed.*".

concern, but that legal-normative instruments existing at all levels were not applied properly by those who were responsible for child protection.

Throughout *'Ryan'* the expression 'abuse' was meant to refer to an understanding as statutorily defined for the purpose[81]; it includes

a) *The wilful, reckless or negligent infliction of physical injury on, or failure to prevent such injury, to the child;*
b) *the use of the child by a person for sexual arousal or sexual gratification of that person or another person;*
c) *failure to care for the child which results, or could reasonably be expected to result, in serious impairment of the physical or mental health or development of the child or serious adverse effects on his or her behaviour or welfare, or*
d) *any other act or omission towards the child which results, or could reasonably be expected to result, in serious impairment of the physical or mental health or development of the child or serious adverse effects on his behaviour or welfare, and cognate words shall be construed accordingly.*

For each of the lettered sub-categories above *'Ryan'* is captioning its definitions by the following terms: letter (a) translates into physical abuse, letter (b) into sexual abuse, letter (c) into neglect and letter (d) into emotional abuse.[82] Compared to *'Ferns'* this abuse definition as a whole is much wider, the element of sexual abuse as included here under letter (b) is the single one on which 'Ferns'was based whereas it figures as one element only among several others in *'Ryan'* here.[83] In that sense *'Ryan'* is not restricted to child sexual abuse *per se*, but follows a much more comprehensive approach encompassing physical, sexual and emotional abuse as well as abuse through neglect.

Another Commission of Investigation examined the handling of com-

---

81 *'Ryan'* Vol I para 1.06 with reference to section 1(i) of the *Commission to Inquire into Child Abuse Act* 2000 as amended by section 3 of the *Commission to Inquire into Child Abuse (Amendment) Act* 2005.

82 *'Ryan'* Executive Summary 3; on definitions of abuse as given in *Children First: National Guidance for the Protection and Welfare of Children* (2011) see E McPartland, *The Best Interests of the Child* (2nd ed. Gill & Macmillan 2013) 32.

83 Fn 71 and accompanying text.

plaints about child sexual abuse by Church and State authorities in the Archdiocese of Dublin from 1975 to 2004; their one-volume *'Murphy'* report was published a few months later in that same year 2009, following the publication of *'Ryan'*. While *'Ryan'* was concerned with establishing whether or not abuse had occurred and the nature and scale of that abuse, this inquiry had no such mandate.[84] Nor had it a specific remit to make recommendations regarding future legislation, but the Commission has given its views on a range of matters which it considered significant.[85] This report found that successive archbishops and bishops failed to report their concerns to the Gardaí, and often the suspected perpetrator was transferred to another parish or diocese where they continued to have access to minors and the opportunity to abuse repeatedly. Consequently, the Commission concluded that child sexual abuse was 'covered-up'within the Church during that period.[86] Moreover, there were inadequate communications between Church and State authorities in relation to the handling of abuse allegations.[87] The definition of child sexual abuse adopted by this Commission was the one which had already been adopted earlier by the Ferns Report.[88]

Finally, after two more years, in July 2011, the so-called *'Cloyne'-Report* covering the Catholic diocese of Cloyne and its child abuse activities was published in writing. The period examined ran from January 1996 until February 2009 and this historical remit is significant because a period in time is covered here for which the Catholic Church in Ireland had first put in place formalised procedures to deal with allegations of abuse. This temporarily and territorially limited inquiry examined, like *' Murphy'*, the handling of allegations and concerns about child sexual abuse, not the occurrences of such abuse in terms of their incidence or prevalence.[89] As a final conclusion, this report stated that the response of the Church

---

[84] *'Murphy'* paras 2.1–2.42 (overall mandate); para 2.2 (terms of reference); para 2.8 (interpretation of its terms of reference).

[85] *'Murphy'* para 1.7.

[86] *'Murphy'* para 1.35: *"Complainants were often met with ... and cover-up ... ."*; para 1.113: *"... clerical child sexual abuse was covered up by the Archdiocese of Dublin and other Church authorities ... ."*

[87] *'Murphy'* para 1.101: *"Such communications as took place between the Archdiocese and the Gardaí ... were largely inappropriate. ... ."*.

[88] *'Murphy'* para 2.9 citing literally from *'Ferns'* (n 63).

[89] *'Cloyne'* para 1.5 (Context), paras 2.1–2.27 (How the Commission conducted its investigation).

was 'inadequate and inappropriate'and that it had failed to carry out proper canonical investigations which are formal investigations internal to the Church and based on canon law provisions enforced as a matter of ecclesiastic discipline.[90] More points of concern to the commissioners were the non-reporting of complaints to the Gardaí (Irish police) or to public health authorities in Ireland and the non-implementation of an independent advisory panel which could be of assistance to Church authorities in taking action when an allegation of abuse was made.[91]

In their published reports both, *'Murphy'* as well as *'Cloyne'* , have almost identical paragraphs about the 'Framework Document' which was the core policy document for the handling of abuse complaints drafted, in 1996, under the auspices of the Irish Bishop's Conference; it aimed at the provision of some sort of general outline on the basis of which bishops (in Ireland) could fulfil their respective canon law obligations for their diocese. Instead of discussing it as an Irish aspect with relation to every single report separately I attach one conclusive observation on the Framework Document below.[92] Finally, this 2011 *Cloyne* Report received an express response from the Holy See in writing dated 3 September 2011 which was required, as this response sees it, by the Irish Government acting through its Deputy Prime Minister in the course of a meeting with the Apostolic Nuncio in Ireland.[93] As may be perceived from this, the content and value of the 1996 Framework Document for general purposes of child protection was uncontested between the Irish Government and the Holy See, whereas many more aspects regarding State-Church relations in general clearly are not.

Sub-section (3) – Itemized Conclusions

My review of this series of reports, documentary in character or fully State-sponsored as Commission of Inquiry Reports, leads me to a final formulation of the following observations concerned about violence, injury or abuse

[90] *'Cloyne'* paras 1.71, 1.72 (Adequacy and appropriateness of the response), paras 1.49–1.52 (Canonical investigations).

[91] *'Cloyne'* paras 1.73–1.78 (Conclusion).

[92] *'Murphy'* paras 7.1–7.57 (*The Framework Document*); *'Cloyne'* paras 4.10–4.41 (*The Framework Document 1996*); for details, see Fn 642 below and accompanying text.

[93] *Response* of the Holy See to the Government of Ireland regarding the Report of the Commission of Investigation into the Catholic Diocese of Cloyne (3 Sept 2011) 1, retrievable from https://www.gov.ie .

perpetrated against or experienced by children in a variety of settings, many of them apparently set up with a mandate to provide for their care and education. As seen in the reports, these settings may be kindergartens, orphanages or schools of all levels publicly or privately funded, owned and managed; or they may be faith-based establishments institutionally linked to dioceses, parishes or congregations situated in many different parts of the world.[94]

1. Systemic Abuse One overall important conclusion drawn by *'Ryan'* in particular, but by other reports in a similar manner, relates to the systemic nature of child abuse as prevalent throughout institutions and periods in time falling under the remit of that commission; equally seen as 'systemic' were the failures of all protective mechanisms already in existence at the time, such as those related to government inspections or complaints about individual perpetrators.[95] The report identified clear patterns of abuse implying a network of perpetrators and others, including persons in authority, who were aiding and abetting child sexual abuse in the State and in the Church; viewing individual perpetrators in isolation did not capture the essence of countless violations and infringements of rights.

As Anne-Marie McAlinden sees it, *'Ryan'* was clearly significant because it highlighted the fact that abuse of children (physically, sexually, emotionally and through neglect), and the failure of Church and State authorities to adequately respond to the problem was systemic in Irish child care institutions.[96] In a similar vein, supporting her argument for constitutional law reform, Ursula Kilkelly summarises *'Ryan'*s conclusions,

> [T]*hat physical and emotional abuse and neglect had been features of the institutions investigated, that sexual abuse had occurred in many of them and that schools were run in a severe, regimented manner that imposed oppressive discipline on children … the 'deferential and submissive attitude' of the*

---

94 Although one might argue that what is described as faith-based establishments here must come under the heading of "privately managed", this may not be taken for granted; see Fn 177 for details.

95 *'Ryan'* IV, chapters 6 and 7 and paras 6.02, 6.04–6.06, 6.09, 6.10, 6.15, 6.18, 6.23, 6.27, 6.40, 7.03, 7.07, 7.13 and para 7.18 in particular where "system(s), systematic or systemic" qualities or features and functionalities are explicitly mentioned; see also Fn 76 above.

96 McAlinden (n 69) 189, 195; C O'Mahony, 'State liability for abuse in primary schools: systemic failure and O'Keeffe v Hickey', 28 Ir Edu Stud (2009) 315, 321.

> *Department of Education towards the congregations who ran the institutions 'compromised its ability' to carry out its statutory duty of inspection and monitoring of the schools and indeed the system of inspection by the Department of Education was described as fundamentally flawed and incapable of being effective.*[97]

Operating on a different level in terms of history or geography, the 2006 *World Report* sees a clearer picture emerging of the magnitude and pervasive nature of the problem provided by a variety of initiatives such as international statistical analysis or action research at local level. These initiatives indicate that some violence may be unexpected and isolated, whereas the majority of violent acts experienced by children are perpetrated by people who are part of their lives: parents, schoolmasters, teachers, employers, boyfriends or girlfriends, spouses and partners.[98] With a different focus social sciences scholar Marie Keenan in 2012 published her comprehensive study titled *'Child sexual abuse and the Catholic Church'* with a focus on gender, power, and organizational culture.[99] Based on her extensive re-lecture of the four Abuse Reports from Ireland but on many other reports mainly from the US also, she presents her analysis of child sexual abuse occurring in different settings institutionally linked to the Roman Catholic Church (RCC). While acknowledging the role of individual agency in influencing behaviour, Keenan emphasizes institutional context and power structures within RCC in explaining the systemic implications of manifold 'bad judgements' made by perpetrators themselves, but also by those organisationally responsible for them.

Arguing from an analysis of organizational culture, the central thesis of her book is,

> [T]*hat just as clerical men who sexually abused minors were not in the main psychological or moral "deviants" who infiltrated the system, neither were the bishops who "erred" nonconforming deviants who did not obey the institution's roles. On the contrary, my argument is that both were rule-keepers in an organization whose very institutional condition gave shape to the contours of the problem.*[100]

---

[97] Kilkelly (n 67) 11.
[98] A/61/299 para 28.
[99] Keenan (n 61).
[100] Ibid 53.

Interestingly for my study here, Keenan's analysis also envisages the role of canon law as an important contributing factor, and I will come back to that in more detail when exploring canon law as the RCC's internal legislative order, controlled and administered by the Holy See.[101]

The systemic characteristics of child sexual abuse are widespread patterns of action and also failures to act regarding direct perpetrators on the one hand, and authorities for their supervision on the other. As the Human Rights Committee rightly stated, State Parties must respond appropriately to patterns of violence perpetrated against categories of victims, children among them.[102]

2. Dimensions of Abuse From the beginning of the public coverage of child sexual abuse cases stemming from institutionalised child care and education, it has become obvious that there are two dimensions to the problem: one is the actual perpetration of an act of child sexual abuse as a criminal offence by itself; the other is a response given by those in authority to the increasing number of abuse complaints brought to their attention.[103] The so-called "Brander" chapter in *'Ryan'* specifically dealt with the career of a serial sexual and physical abuser who taught children in the primary and secondary school sector in Ireland for 40 years;[104] at various times during Brander's career, parents attempted to challenge his behaviour but he was persistently protected by diocesan and school authorities. Complaints to the Department of Education were ignored or treated dilatorily and questions were raised about the bona fides of the complaint which did not even receive proper communication.[105] As a consequence, that *'Ryan'* report sees this case as an ample illustration about the ease with which sexual predators could operate within the educational system of the State without fear of disclosure or sanction.[106]

As regards clerical perpetrators of child sexual abuse (male adult Catholics brought into a permanent relationship of unconditional service to the Church by way of ordination), another dimension – international in

---

101 ibid 209.

102 UN Human Rights Committee, *General Comment* No. 35 (2014) para 9.

103 Keenan (n 61) 180.

104 *'Ryan'* Vol I paras 14.01–14.157.

105 *'Ryan'* Vol I paras 14.129 – 14.153.

106 *'Ryan'* Vol I para 14.157 (Conclusions); *O'Keeffe* v *Ireland* (n 1) para 79 referring to "the Brander-chapter".

scope and character – comes to bear on the final outcome of any abuse allegation.[107] Through several channels the Holy See as the central governing body of the RCC traditionally controlling the bulk of disciplinary matters in regard to its clerical personnel, gets formally involved as a matter of administrative routine. Without showing proper concern for the children abused locally this Vatican-based institution helps to make sure that perpetrators, in a number of cases, can evade from regular criminal investigation and prosecution in their state of residence. Recent revelations of abuse in Blackrock College (Dublin) from whence it was reported that children were abused, confirms this tendency; no formal inquiry has yet been established, let alone completed.

3. Rightless Children Seen from a viewpoint of having the CRC available as an international law instrument, the dominant impression gained from those four Irish abuse reports in particular, is a complete invisibility of individual rights to be claimed by children on their own behalf. Even for those who were mature enough to speak for themselves no legal help or support was practically available anywhere in the State. This state of almost complete rightlessness relates to statutory or non-statutory rights under then existing laws in Ireland, but also to fundamental rights and freedoms such as those globally proclaimed in international law documents such as the 1948 Universal Declaration of Human Rights or both International Covenants dating from 1966 (ICCPR, ICESCR).[108] True, from 1953 onwards the ECHR as an international law document was binding on Ireland; even the 1937 Constitution of Ireland made some cursory references to children's rights such as education rights according to Article 42. So children did have some rights, but not until much later did their understanding in terms of individualized legal entitlement (including mechanisms for application and enforcement) develop.

Lacking most fundamentally indeed was what in his writing about the value of having rights Michael Freeman conceptualised, with reference to Hannah Arendt, as the right to have rights.[109] As a matter of historical truth,

---

[107] Child Rights International Network (CRIN), *Child Sexual Abuse and the Holy See. The need for justice, accountability and reform* (UK, no date), especially 9–11, part II 'Mapping the Scale of the Abuse'.

[108] These documents taken together are addressed as "The International Bill of Human Rights".

[109] Freeman (n 35) 21, 23.

however, law creation and law enforcement machinery in Ireland was fully intact at the time and its mechanisms were running smoothly, as Diarmaid Ferriter summarised his study attached to *'Ryan'*.[110] It is just that as bearers of fundamental rights children themselves had absolutely no say in all of this; the child as an independently acting subject of rights and freedoms was totally ignored and disregarded by those in authority on behalf of the State as well as the Church.[111]

This is not to say that retrospectively no valid finding of children's human rights being violated were possible; what had happened in Irish mother and baby homes during the 1950s or the 1960s can, indeed must, be analysed through an ECHR lens which as a treaty became binding on Ireland from 1953 onwards.[112] However, for this study focusing on rights implementation as an international obligation under the Convention the approach is slightly different in that a primary aim of the exercise is to identify gaps and failures in the law itself. What is lacking in terms of children's rights being made accessible and available to children as legal subjects in their own rights must be made visible.

4. Canon Law The Roman Catholic Church (RCC) is a global, non-territorial, supranational spiritual community counting over one and a quarter billion individual members including millions of children distributed in a multitude of so-called Particular Churches across the globe.[113] As a source of laws the legislative authority of the Catholic Church provides for ecclesiastical laws on an ongoing basis. Those baptised in the Catholic Church (or received into it) who enjoy sufficient use of reason and have completed seven years of age are bound by merely ecclesiastical laws (can

---

[110] D Ferriter, *Report* (June 2006) attached to *'Ryan'* Vol. V after p 354.

[111] Freeman (n 35) 24 citing Baroness Hale in the House of Lords: *'This is, and always has been, a case about children, their rights and the rights of their parents and teachers. Yet there has been no one here to speak on behalf of the children. The battle has been fought on ground selected by the adults'*, with reference to *Williamson* v *Secretary of State for Education and Employment* [2005] 2 AC 246 at para 71.

[112] *Annual Report of the Special Rapporteur on Child Protection* 2021 (Prof Conor O'Mahony) 69–134.

[113] Membership in the Church is defined in canon law as follows: by baptism one is incorporated into the Church of Christ and is constituted a person in it with the duties and rights which are proper to Christians in keeping with their condition, insofar as they are in ecclesiastical communion and unless a legitimately issued sanction stands in the way, cann. 11, 96, 205–207, 219, 1331 CIC.

11 CIC). These laws are contained in the canon law of the Catholic church which is the body of universal law through which the Church organises itself worldwide upholding its own internal legal order.[114] For its *sui juris* Latin Church (the 'Western' as opposed to 'Eastern' churches) the Roman Catholic Church provides a separate Code of Canon Law (*Codex Iuris Canonici* or *1983 Codex*, for short) which was promulgated in 1983 by the Pope acting as a supreme legislator.

Church lawyers have ever been emphasising that sexual abuse of minors is not just a canonical delict or a breach of an internal code of conduct for the Church, but a serious crime punishable and prosecuted under criminal legislation in almost every of the world's jurisdictions.[115] Although this may be true from an abstract level of observation, from a victim's perspective the reality looks somewhat different since huge differences are being made if the person suspect of child abuse is an ordained cleric. It becomes obvious, from a re-lecture of official abuse reports, that canon law massively contributed to the problem by playing an active role in bringing about what was later, somewhat sweepingly, labelled as child sexual abuse within the Catholic Church. As Mary McAleese retrospectively observed from a canon law perspective

> *The Church's self-ideation as a bastion of children's rights has been damaged by revelations of physical and sexual abuse of children by clerics or in Church run institutions and the lack of effective action by Church authorities.*[116]

Marie Keenan's research, from a social sciences point of view, is equally helpful in this regard as it analyses both the role of canon law and also the role of Vatican institutions (operating under canon law norms) as they made their respective contributions to the handling of abuse complaints flooding in from all over the world.[117]

The core of the matter lies not in any sort of permission or licence to abuse a child that might somehow be retrievable from within a vast body of privileges, precepts or impediments to be categorized as belonging to the

---

[114] McAleese (n 7) 21; More detail on canon law will be provided in the third part of this study.

[115] C J Scicluna, 'The Quest for Truth in Sexual Abuse Cases' in C J Scicluna et al (eds) *Toward Healing and Renewal* (Paulist Press 2012) 47, 54.

[116] McAleese (n 7) 17.

[117] Keenan (n 61) 190, 209 ("The Role of Canon Law"); 214 ("The Role of the Vatican").

canon law of the RCC.[118] Rather, in respect of canon law the problematic aspects are twofold: first, that it was not helpful at all in bringing out the criminal parameters of child sexual abuse; and second, that once credible allegations about serious infringements of a child's personal integrity were made, canon law norms were used selectively to protect the good name of a clerical perpetrator and to protect the reputation of the Church as an organization, whereas valid interests of the child victim were completely disregarded or even ignored.

Canon Law Confidentiality

As indicated already under (2) above, canon law as a religious legal system played a role, first in letting happen what came to be designated as clerical sexual abuse, and second, in (selectively) analyzing who was legally responsible for what had happened and what needed to be done in order to avoid similarly abusive practices from occurring again in the future. Relating to this latter point, the dominant concern is about 'confidentiality' or a duty of confidentiality as understood and conceptualized for canon law purposes on the one hand, and the general maxim of modern rule of law concepts pertaining to the public administration of justice, on the other.[119] Traditionally, a very high value is placed on the overall secrecy of the canonical process which, as a legal-procedural principle, is in stark contrast to civil law which requires that justice be administered publicly implying that structures be in place for holding decision-makers accountable in the eyes of the public.[120] Historically, this kind of an individual obligation to secrecy or confidentiality on the part of participants in a canonical process ("code of silence") constituted an efficient inhibition on the reporting or disclosure of cases of child sexual abuse to civil authorities; no help from outside was therefore available for most of the child victims concerned.[121]

---

[118] The *Catechism of the Catholic Church* (CCC) which is not a legal document in the strict sense of the word, takes a somewhat ambiguous stance on the matter of corporal punishment of children; see CCC para 2223 where an Old Testament saying on "not spare the rod" is referenced without further exegesis.

[119] *'Murphy'* paras 4.82–4.86.

[120] This so-called "Pontifical Secrecy" was abolished, in 2019, for sexual abuse cases, see Fn 651 below.

[121] CRC/C/VAT/CO/2 para 43 (extract): *"Due to a code of silence … , cases of child sexual abuse have hardly ever been reported to the law enforcement authorities … "*.

From a perspective of scientific legal research one conclusion drawn by *'Murphy'* is predominant for this research context:

> *It is a basic feature of every coherent legal system that there is a firm, simple and unmistakeable procedure for the promulgation of a law. The absence of any such procedure within Church Law, in the Commission's view, makes that law difficult to access, and very difficult to implement and to monitor compliance.*[122]

Remarkably, it is not the legal-normative content of any specific canon found on the code-book that causes concern to the Commission; rather, it is the lack of precision and the difficulties of finding the exact content of almost any piece of canon law which the commissioners (led by an experienced High Court judge from Ireland) can hardly understand or accept. As a consequence, the Commission expressed its deep concern about the lack of precision in canon law as regards the power of bishops to exercise control over offending priests.[123]

To sum up, under four different headings I put together what I think are core issues when taking children's rights seriously for the protection from violence, neglect and abuse in any kind of educational context. Included are learning contexts provided by Catholic schools as a distinct set of educational institutions operating under a wider legal authority of the Holy See.[124] I make no claim that these are the only issues relevant for the purpose; what I am asserting here is their critical importance based on what was documented throughout the reports in terms of real-life situations containing an inherent risk of becoming abusive in character.

Third Section: Freedom from Violence as an Issue for Children's Rights

Introduction

As the core instrument on children's rights the CRC reasserts a set of traditionally acknowledged civil or political 'freedom'-rights, such as the

---

122 *'Murphy'* para 4.89.

123 *'Murphy'* para 4.91; similar concerns expressed in *'Ferns'* 30.

124 Although in an immediate sense a Catholic school may be legally owned and managed by a diocese, a parish, a congregation or a registered charity, the Holy See via its canonically claimed authority must be held co-responsible for much of the school's organizational structure and its behavioural practices; see Fn 678 below.

right to freedom of expression (Article 13), the right to freedom of thought, conscience and religion (Article 14) and the right to freedom of association and to freedom of assembly (Article 15). Article 19 CRC's right to freedom from all forms of violence, however, does not require the State to stay out of its (minor) citizens' private lives; exactly the opposite is intended: here is a requirement for State intervention which shall be encouraged for eliminating all forms of violence against children.[125] This right to protection from violence presents itself as an individualized human right to be free from all forms of violence, abuse and neglect; it is stated as a fundamental freedom of every single child to live, learn and develop his or her own personality in an environment of respect and non-violence. Accordingly, as the Committee sees it, a child rights-based approach to child protection requires a paradigm shift towards respecting and promoting the human dignity and the physical and psychological integrity of children as rights-bearing individuals rather than perceiving them primarily as 'victims'.[126] As a novelty the CRC, through one of its core protection rights, equally addresses violent or abusive situations of a hidden and quasi-private character from wherein the child is threatened by domestic and care-related violence.[127]

Such thing as a right to non-violent education, however, is nowhere explicitly mentioned throughout the text of the CRC, but there are other express provisions in the Convention to inspire the quest for a right to freedom from violence specifically adopted to cover situations of professional childcare and school-based education. As a whole the Convention outlines the duty of the State to protect children from exploitation and abuse in a way that covers a wide range of possibly life-threatening situations; the following Articles are listed for illuminating this instrument's overall object and purpose:

- Article 32 (right to protection from economic exploitation);
- Article 33 (right to protection from drug abuse);
- Article 34 (right to protection from sexual abuse);
- Article 35 (right to protection from abduction);

---

[125] L Bracken, *Child Law in Ireland* (Clarus Press 2018) 147.

[126] CRC/C/GC/13 para 3b.

[127] Article 19(1) CRC: "... *while in the care of parent(s), legal guardian(s) or any other person who has the care of the child*"; see Fn 134 below for details.

- Article 36 (protection from other forms of exploitation);
- Article 37 (protection from torture or other cruel treatment);
- Article 38 (protection from engagement in armed conflict).

As explained earlier with regard to the *World Report,* a more specific set of human rights was found to be most pertinent to the task of analyzing violence against children in schools and other educational settings, and they are the child's education rights on the one hand and his or her protection rights on the other.[128] Article 19 CRC seems to be particularly relevant stipulating what the Committee designated as the right of the child to freedom from all forms of violence.[129] Additionally, in Articles 28 and 29 CRC the Convention provides for the children's right to quality education captioning the access right to education provided for in Article 28 CRC as well as the aims of education listed in Article 29 CRC.[130]

Sub-section (1) – Text and Basic Content of Article 19 CRC

Situated among a sequence of family-related substantive provisions Article 19 CRC captioned 'Prevention of abuse and neglect' by the Convention's Legislative History,[131] refers, through its first paragraph to *'all forms of physical or mental violence, injury or abuse, neglect or negligent treatment, maltreatment or exploitation, including sexual abuse'*, and calls, through its second paragraph, for *'other forms of prevention and for identification, reporting, referral, investigation, treatment and follow-up of instances of child maltreatment described heretofore, and, as appropriate, for judicial involvement'*.

State Parties are seen to make a strong legal commitment to protect children against violence, abuse or neglect by which any particular child might be threatened while in the home or in a similar care setting, and pro-

---

128 Fn 51 above and accompanying text.

129 CRC/C/GC/13 *General comment No. 13 (2011), The right of the child to freedom from all forms of violence.*

130 C M Fiorvanti et al, 'Advancing Child Protection Through Respecting Children's Rights: A Shifting Emphasis for School Psychology' 43 School Psych Rev (2014) 349–366.

131 UN OHCHR *Legislative History* (Geneva 2011) 512; A different caption was used for the *Travaux Préparatoires*: 'Prevention of abuse by those having care', see S Detrick et al, *The UN CRC, A Guide to the "Travaux Préparatoires"* (Martinus Nijhoff 1992) Article 8 bis.

tective measures are spelled out with an accent on means of support to be attributed to the child and to caretakers involved. As a means of final resort judicial involvement is projected here supplementing earlier measures of official investigation and treatment which were dealing with concrete instances of child maltreatment identified by or reported to public authorities.

Indicating a seriousness of the underlying issues two special features in the wording of this article seem particularly noteworthy: an extensive list of protective measures as spelled out at the beginning of the article, and further detailed by a listing that fills the whole second paragraph. Equally, the Article's first paragraph unambiguously interlinks child sexual abuse as an issue to be subsumed under or included within 'all forms of physical or mental violence'.[132] In comparison to a more general article in the Convention such as Article 3 CRC, two more distinguishing features in the wording of Article 19 CRC are remarkable here: while the undertaking in Article 3(2) CRC in a more general manner relates to protection and care as necessary for the wellbeing of the child, protective measures as envisaged by Article 19 seem to be directed at protection from specified harm such as physical or mental violence against children.[133] Furthermore, as anticipated by Article 19(1) CRC several kinds of strongly personalized care settings, such as the one provided by the child's family, by parents, guardians or professional caretakers need to be kept under observation by the State, because of acts of inter-personal violence against the child that may occur, and remain covered-up in any such situation.

As understood by the Committee care settings are places where children spend time under supervision of their 'permanent' primary caregiver (such as a parent or guardian), or a proxy or 'temporary' caregiver (such as a teacher or youth group leader) for a defined period of time.[134] Thus, schools, classrooms and other educational locations typically count as a care setting, and the same is true for ecclesiastic locations and places of worship, as long as any kind of an authorized caregiver person (possibly

---

[132] *Terminology Guidelines* (n 53) 13, entry 'sexual violence against children'.

[133] CRC/C/GC/14 para 71 ("protection and care").

[134] CRC/C/GC/13 para 34 (care settings); periods of time defined for the duration of "temporary" care-giving may be short-term, long-term, repeated or once only.

turning violent in his behaviour towards children) is regularly present.[135] Since all forms of physical or mental violence are captured by the scope of Article 19 CRC there is not much space left for evasion in terms of violence against children that might seem acceptable from a legislator's point of view: the Convention in effect tolerates no form of violence, neglect or abuse towards a child who is in the care of a parent or another guardian.[136]

Sub-section (2) – Text and Basic Content of Articles 28, 29 CRC

Articles 28, 29 CRC captioned 'Education, including vocational training and guidance' and 'Aims of education' respectively[137] provide in Article 28 CRC, through its first paragraph, for access to several stages of education whereas conditions for the administration of school discipline are set out through its second paragraph. Article 29 CRC formulates a listing of educational aims and stipulates the freedom of education in Article 29(2) CRC.

Read together, as they indeed must be, both articles in conjunction constitute what has been termed the child's right to quality education when it is equally understood to be in the best interests of the child to have access to such quality education.[138] What is missing from the treaty text, however, is an open reference to the requirement for all education to be free from violence whereas the non-violent character of education generally features as an important quality aspect of school-based education. Two inter-dependent aspects of rights-based education might get lost as a consequence: schools are places of learning and social interaction that play a key role in the overall-prevention of violence, and violence can undermine education with both teachers and students suffering as a result.

---

[135] Ibid (situations envisaged for outside intervention); *Terminology Guidelines* (n 53) 78 ('children at risk' or 'children in vulnerable situations').

[136] J Tobin, 'Fixed Concepts but Changing Conceptions: Understanding the Relationship between Children and Parents under the CRC' in M D Ruck et al (eds) *Handbook of Children's Rights* (Routledge 2017) 53, 65.

[137] *Legislative History* (n 131) 632 (Article 28), *Legislative History* 653 (Article 29); Semi-official title given by UNICEF (R Hodgkin P Newell) *Implementation Handbook* (2007) 407 'Child's right to education' (Art 28) and 437 'The aims of education' (Art 29).

[138] M Verheyde, 'Article 28: The Right to Education' in A Alen et al (eds) *A Commentary on the United Nations Convention on the Rights of the Child* (Martinus Nijhoff 2007) 1; *Tackling Violence* (Fn 46) 1; CRC/C/GC/14 para 79.

While Article 28 CRC focuses upon obligations of States Parties in relation to the establishment of comprehensive educational systems and in ensuring access thereto, Article 29(1) CRC underlines the individual child's subjective right to a specific quality of education.[139] Thus Article 28 CRC sets out the basic right to education which is to be achieved *'progressively and on the basis of equal opportunity'*, whereas Article 29 CRC sets out the aims of a child's education, including the development of his or her personality; respect for human rights and fundamental freedoms; and the preparation of the child for responsible life in a free society, in the spirit of understanding, peace, tolerance, equality of sexes, and friendship among peoples.[140] As a comparatively new element that was lacking in earlier instruments Article 28(2) CRC includes an obligation to ensure that school discipline is administered in a manner consistent with the child's dignity, to be read as a prohibition of corporal punishment in accordance with the Committee's *GC 8*.[141] Not surpisingly, the Committee is grounding its argument for an overall prohibition of corporal punishment on, among others, Article 19 CRC's right to freedom from violence as this practice directly conflicts with the equal and inalienable rights of children to respect for their human dignity and physical integrity.[142] In consistency with legal guarantees similarly covering 'education' as a human right Article 29(2) CRC reiterates a prohibition on government interference with the private liberty

---

[139] CRC/GC/2001/1 para 9; F Coomans, 'Education and Work' in D Moeckli et al (eds), *International Human Rights Law* (3rd ed OUP 2018) 232, 236.

[140] S J Klees and N Thapliyal, 'The Right to Education: The Work of Katarina Tomasevski' 51 Comparative Education Review (2007) 497, 500 ('progressive realization'); F Coomans (n 139 above) 232, 236 (aims of education); U Khaliq and R Churchill, 'The protection of economic and social rights: a particular challenge?' In H Keller et al (eds), *UN Human Rights Treaty Bodies: Law and Legitimacy* (CUP 2012) 199, 224 ('holistic approach').

[141] CRC/C/GC/8 *General comment No. 8 (2006), The right of the child to protection from corporal punishment and other cruel or degrading forms of punishment (arts. 19; 28 para 2; and 37, inter alia)*; E/C.12/1999/10 para 41 (ESC-Committee); M Freeman and B J Saunders (n 29) 681.

[142] CRC/C/GC/8 para 21; defining "corporal" punishment the Committee refers to any punishment in which physical force is used and intended to cause some degree of pain or discomfort, see CRC/C/GC/13 para 24.

to establish and direct educational institutions, but this (parental) liberty is not without specific conditions attached.[143]

In respect of the right to education as comprehensively stated in Article 13 ICESCR to be 'the right of everyone' the monitoring body in charge circumscribed from a human rights perspective what 'education' was all about:

> *Education is both a human right in itself and an indispensible means of realizing other human rights. As an empowerment right, education is the primary vehicle by which economically and socially marginalized adults and children can lift themselves out of poverty and obtain the means to participate fully in their communities. Education has a vital role in empowering women, safeguarding children from exploitative and hazardous labour and sexual exploitation, promoting human rights and democracy, protecting the environment, and controlling population growth.*[144]

What I find remarkable in this general overview given by the ESC Committee is that a special role of education for safeguarding children from sexual exploitation was made visible in a document not even particularly concerned about children's rights. To protect children from all forms of violence occurring in a school setting therefore seems doubly important: for reasons pertaining to every individual child's personal integrity to be secured at all times, and also for reasons of keeping education, organized either publicly or privately, intact as an institutionalized service, including its stated aims such as the preparation of the child for responsible life in a free society.[145]

Chapter 2 – Express Provisions and Implied terms

This chapter attempts at a structured explanation of the scope and legal content of the right to freedom from violence as stipulated in Article 19 CRC, and of the right to quality education as provided for by Articles 28,

---

[143] Article 26 UDHR; Article 13(4) ICESCR is in its wording identical with Article 29(2) CRC.

[144] E/C.12/1999/10 para 1 ESC-Committee (1999) General comment No. 13, The right to education (Article 13 of the Covenant).

[145] Article 29(1)(d) CRC.

29 CRC. Both sets of rights – protection rights on the one hand and education rights on the other – will be expounded here in their human rights context as provided by the CRC, but by other treaties also.[146]

First Section: The Right to Freedom from Violence (Article 19 CRC)

Article 19 CRC requires that children be protected from 'all forms of physical and mental violence' while in the care of parents or others: the scope of this Article clearly targets what happens within the family home and within other 'caretaker' situations, such as foster care and day care, schools, all institutional settings and the like.[147]

Thus, the basic idea expressed in Article 19 CRC is twofold: children, free from discrimination, must be protected against violence, abuse, neglect and maltreatment wherever, in terms of practical life situations, they are being threatened by any such risk of ill-treatment; and State Parties are pledging to take the widest possible range of measures with the aim of making their protective efforts as effective as possible. This article's specific scope and content may be described in terms of its material scope covering both violence-related threats against children and also protective measures to stop that kind of threat from being carried out (*sub-section (1) below*). Its personal scope covers children to be protected against harm, but also parents, guardians and other individuals factually positioned in relation to the child so as to provide for an appearance of care-taking (*sub-section (2) below*).[148]

Sub-section (1) – Material Scope of Article 19 CRC

The material scope of Article 19 CRC can be ascertained from a perspective of specific risks, and from a perspective of protective measures that

---

[146] General comments given by the Committee treating 'Education' as a main topic: CRC/GC/2001/1 (Aims of Education), CRC/C/GC/8 (Corporal Punishment), CRC/C/GC/13 (Protection from Violence), CRC/C/GC/14 (Best Interests) and CRC/C/GC/20 (Adolescence); for protection from corporal punishment see also E/C.12/1999/10 *General Comment No. 13,* The right to education (Article 13 of the Covenant) – ESC-Committee.

[147] *Implementation Handbook* (n 137) 258.

[148] S Besson, 'The Principle of Non-discrimination in the Convention on the Rights of the Child' in M Freeman (ed), *Progress and Perspectives* (Mart Nijhoff 2011) 85, 103.

must be taken as a response to those same risks: '... *all appropriate legislative, administrative, social and educational measures* ... '.[149] In a similar fashion Article 19(1) CRC sets up a list of risks or threats against which the child must be protected: '... *all forms of physical or mental violence, injury or abuse, neglect or negligent treatment, maltreatments or exploitation, including sexual abuse'*. Here is a distinctive feature of protection and care as understood in this provision compared to the more general provision in Article 3(2) CRC;[150] by stating in detail what the child must be protected from the objective of Article 19 CRC is formulated in limited or negative terms, thus clarifying an obligation according to which any violent threat whatever its origin must be steered away from the child.

Defining Sexual Abuse

As spelled out in its first paragraph Article 19 CRC encompasses all forms of physical or mental violence, injury or abuse, neglect or negligent treatment as well as maltreatment or exploitation, including sexual abuse. None of these terms is specifically defined from a child rights perspective, not in this place or in any other part of the Convention.[151] Child sexual abuse as addressed in Article 19 CRC is conceptualized in close connection to exploitation:[152] Article 34 CRC dealing with sexual exploitation of children seems to use both terms 'sexual exploitation' and 'sexual abuse' as interchangeable and coterminous.[153] Indeed, as far as sexual abuse is concerned which Article 19 CRC links in to all forms of physical or mental violence, an overlap exists with another undertaking in the Convention to protect the child from all forms of sexual exploitation and sexual abuse as stipulated

---

[149] This set of measures reappears literally in Article 32(2) CRC dealing with protection from economic exploitation.

[150] Article 3(2) CRC reads (extract): '... *to ensure the child such protection and care as is necessary for his or her well-being*... '; CRC/C/GC/14 para 71 (care, protection and safety of the child).

[151] Tobin (n 40) 395, 417.

[152] For Articles 32, 34 and 36 CRC, see p 47; 'sexual abuse' from which the child must be protected is mentioned at only two locations, Articles 19 and 34 CRC.

[153] *Legislative History* (n 131) 713 captioning Article 34 CRC "Sexual exploitation and sexual abuse"; T Buck, *International Child Law* (3rd ed Routledge 2014) 353; CRC/C/GC/13 para 25; V Muntarbhorn, 'Article 34, Sexual Exploitation and Sexual Abuse' in A Alen et al (eds) *A Commentary on the United Nations Convention on the Rights of the Child* (Martinus Nijhoff Leiden Boston 2007) para 3.

in Article 34 CRC. As a harm done to children 'sexual abuse' is mentioned in Article 34 CRC, but an element of commercialism comes in at that stage where this kind of abuse is addressed as a problem of exploitation.[154]

However, from the list of threats provided in Article 34 CRC, against which preventive action must be taken an initial understanding may be acquired about elements defining sexual abuse as a legal-operational term: *the inducement or coercion of a child to engage in any unlawful sexual activity* (Art 34 CRC letter a), *the exploitative use of children in prostitution or other unlawful sexual practices* (letter b), *the exploitative use of children in pornographic performances and materials* (letter c). What 'child prostitution' or 'child pornography' means, can be gleaned from Article 2 OPSC defining child prostitution as meaning the use of a child in sexual activities for remuneration (letter b), and also defining child pornography as meaning any representation of a child engaged in real or simulated explicit sexual activities or any representation of the sexual parts of a child for primarily sexual purposes (letter c).

Here, as a key term 'sexual activity' appears for purposes of delineating sexualized violence against other forms of violence from which children must be protected. As the Committee understands it, 'sexual abuse' encompasses the inducement or coercion of a child to engage in any unlawful or psychologically harmful sexual activity; but this latter term's exact scope remains under-defined at an international law level.[155] Since this term is not defined at this location in the Convention or in the Protocol (OPSC) there might be damaging consequences by leaving a potential gap in international law with regard to sexual activities that would be considered to be 'non-explicit'.[156] Accordingly, in an Explanatary Report to *Lanzarote* the notion of 'sexually explicit conduct' or 'sexual activity' was set out to include

> *at least the following real or simulated acts: a) sexual intercourse, including* genital-*genital, oral-genital, anal-genital or oral-anal, between children, or between an adult and a child; b) bestiality; c) masturbation; d) sadistic or*

[154] Muntarbhorn (n 153) para 2 ('sexual abuse' linked with remuneration in cash or kind).

[155] Council of Europe, *Explanatory Report* – CETS 201 - *Protection of Children against Sexual Exploitation and Sexual Abuse*, para 127; CRC/C/GC/13 para 25 (reference to criminal law provisions rooted in national laws).

[156] *Terminology Guidelines* (n 53) 3.

masochistic abuse in a sexual context; or e) lascivious exhibition of the genitals or the pubic area of a child. It is not relevant whether the conduct depicted is real or simulated.[157]

Meanwhile, for all purposes of legislating measures of protection it is widely agreed that all forms of sexual conduct involving penetration should come within the scope of 'sexual activity', but legal definitions have also included masturbation and lascivious exhibition of children's genitals as a manifestation of sexually explicit conduct.[158] As evidenced by sexual abuse included within Article 19 CRC no restricted understanding about violence against children can be prevailing: there is, indeed, a growing recognition that violence against children often is of a psychological and sexual nature, and is not in fact limited to forms of physical violence.[159] Primarily subsuming a list of bodily activities this term of 'sexual violence' covers both, acts of commission as well as acts of omission, and may also be associated to physical or psychological violence.[160]

In conclusion, no element of exchange is required for the definition of child sexual abuse as a key term which will be fulfilled even if the mere purpose of an act is sexual gratification of the person committing the act.[161] Determining factors may be elements such as a position of authority, trust or control regularly given in the person of a headmistress, a schoolteacher or a religious leader. Child sexual abuse can be committed without an exhibition of external force or restraint, but there is no legal requirement to establish any of these elements if the child is below the age of sexual consent. In this case, the mere fact of sexual activity taking place in the presence of a child is sufficient to constitute abuse. Thus, child sexual abuse appears to be a broad category ("umbrella term") defining the harm caused to children by forcing or coercing them to engage in sexual activity, whether they are aware of what is happening or not.[162] Further

157 *Lanzarote* Explanatory Report (n 155) para 143, referenced by *Terminology Guidelines* (n 53) 3.

158 *Terminology Guidelines* (n 53) 3.

159 *Terminology Guidelines* (n 53) 13; Lenzer (n 26) 276, 292; Council of Europe, *Violence reduction in schools, how to make a difference* (C Gittins coordinating) 12 (definitions of violence).

160 *Terminology Guidelines* (n 53) 16.

161 Ibid 19 (child sexual abuse).

162 Ibid 20.

aspects of child sexual abuse relate to sexual activity between adults in the immediate presence of a child who is forced to observe passively what is happening without being actively involved; similarly, exposure of a child to pornographic material from which which the child cannot distance him- or herself implies a moment of coercion.

Preventing Harm

Given the object and purpose of the CRC which is about establishing the child as a subject, not an object, of rights it becomes evident that prevention against 'instances of child maltreatment' is a core aspect of freedom from violence as understood by Article 19 CRC. An understanding about protective measures that must be of a preventive character and must be implemented with the aim of hindering the child's victimization in the first instance is spelled out in Article 19(2) CRC. Here, protective measures are seen as including 'other forms of prevention' besides the establishment of social programmes to provide support for the child and for caregivers involved.[163]

The CRC's *travaux préparatoires* even show that it was generally felt that emphasis should be placed on preventive action which then led to the reference to 'social and educational measures' in Article 19(1).[164] Equally, the key message from the 2006 *World Report* ('All violence against children is preventable') is clearly corresponding with this reading of Article 19 CRC as a protection right of an essentially preventive character.[165] Another argument supporting this preventive lecture of Article 19 CRC builds on its contradistinction to Article 39 CRC where the child in his or her situation after the fact is clearly designated as 'child victim' for whom rehabilitative measures must be made available.[166]

Furthermore, there are good reasons for including 'sexual victimization', understood as an inter-personal encounter which is not accompanied by physical force or restraint but is nonetheless psychologically intrusive,

---

163 C M Fiorvanti et al (n 130) 349.

164 S Detrick, *A Commentary on the United Nations Convention on the Rights of the Child* (Martinus Nijhoff 1999) 323; *Legislative History* (n 131) 512 using 'Prevention of abuse and neglect' as a caption for Article 19 CRC.

165 Fn 44 and accompanying text.

166 Article 39 CRC deals with measures to promote physical and psychological recovery and social reintegration of a child victim of neglect, exploitation or abuse.

exploitative and traumatic, into child sexual abuse as mentioned in Article 19 CRC.[167] Envisaging spheres of naturally close relationships such as the family-home (or a classroom and a schoolhouse) child sexual abuse must not be seen from a reductionist perspective as a one-off act of violent behaviour but rather as an abusive relationship developing over time and including shorter or longer phases of 'grooming'; this was evidenced also by quite a few descriptions that went into official Abusc Reports analysing the systemic aspects of child abuse. And cases of clerical sexual abuse in particular can only be fully understood by including this kind of sexual victimization into the wider concept of child sexual abuse as developed for this CRC context.

Assuming that, without exception, every single case of child sexual abuse must be regarded as a severe case of child-related violence, this definition should be adopted for purposes of interpreting Article 19 CRC: *Child sexual abuse is any involvement of dependent, developmentally immature children and adolescents in sexual activities that they do not fully comprehend and to which they are unable to give informed consent or that violate the social taboos of family roles; sexual activities, for this context, must be defined (with reference to the definition suggested by Lanzarote) to include sexual intercourse, bestiality, masturbation, sadistic or masochistic abuse in a sexual context or lascivious exhibition of the genitals or the pubic area of a child.* As mentioned above this definition includes sexual victimization which is psychologically intrusive, exploitative and traumatic. Thus, involvement of the child into sexual activity may take the form of active bodily contacts but may also be passive in terms of forced observation or exposure to pornographic material.

Protective Measures

Protective measures as envisaged by Article 19 CRC encompass a wide range of legislative, administrative, social and educational measures, which must be of a general protective character, not limited to 'protection of the law' as seen in Article 16 CRC concerned about the child' s right to privacy. An additional feature of this range of protective measures is that they must be appropriate. The notion of ' appropriateness'is generally understood in international human rights law as allowing for an adaptation

[167] CRC/C/GC/13 para 25 ("sexual victimization").

of universally drafted treaty standards to local conditions for which every individual State can be held responsible, in a monitoring context, among others.[168] In comparison to a general obligation of implementation as enunciated in Article 4 CRC the listing of protective measures in Article 19 CRC explicitly mentions 'social and educational measures' (not just 'other measures') which, as explained earlier, is indicative of the emphasis on prevention as intended by the drafters of the Convention.[169]

Sub-section (2) – Personal Scope of Article 19 CRC

As explained earlier Article 19 CRC envisages as its main beneficiary 'the child' understood as every human being below the age of 18 years unless under the law applicable to the child, majority is attained earlier (Article 1 CRC). From a CRC perspective protective obligations do not abruptly end if an adolescent who, though being below 18 years of age, legally attains majority under his or her national laws. Article 19(1) CRC, furthermore, speaks about persons or groups of persons who, despite their appearance of being responsible for taking care of the child, are mainly seen here as contributing to the emergence of an abusive environment, namely parents, guardians and other caretakers.[170]

As envisaged by Article 19 CRC 'the child' means every single child living within the jurisdiction (Article 2 CRC) irrespective of his or her citizen-status held as a matter of that or any other State's internal laws. With respect to protection from sexual abuse being the object and purpose of the Convention and its Article 19 CRC in particular, it amounts to sheer arbitrariness if legal distinctions on the basis of a child's citizenship were made. Required by general principles of the Convention protective measures must be available to all children without discrimination (Article 2 CRC) and the views of the child should be respected (Article 12 CRC), for example in planning and implementing social programmes, as well as in individual cases whenever child protection mechanisms are activated.[171]

Since his or her family members as well as other relatives or caretakers are addressed as possible abusers acting in opposition to the child's best

---

[168] E/C.12/1998/24 Committee on Economic, Social and Cultural Rights, *Draft general comment No. 9* paras 1, 2.

[169] Fn 164 and accompanying text.

[170] Fn 134 and accompanying text.

[171] *Implementation Handbook* (n 137) 589 (commenting on Article 39 CRC).

interest, the child, looked upon through the lens of Article 19 CRC, features as an independent holder of protection rights to be claimed against abusive caretakers who started disregarding their duty of care. Thus, the child's autonomy regarding his or her Article 19 CRC protection rights becomes obvious from a comparative outlook on Article 39 CRC where, for purposes of recovery and reintegration the child is addressed as 'a child victim'.[172] As envisaged by Article 19 CRC the child to be protected must not be totally denigrated to a status of complete passivity which can be a consequence of such victimization.

In sum, Article 19 CRC including its overall protective mandate primarily covers the child at risk of harm even if the cause of harm is rooted in a situation externally characterizing as a care related one, such as a schoolhouse or parishbuilding; for triggering protective obligations on behalf of the State no prior proof is needed of violent behaviour authored by an identified individual and perpetrated against the child.

Second Section: The Right to Quality Education (Articles 28, 29 CRC)

In this section the child's right to quality education will be explored more deeply on the basis of Articles 28, 29 CRC, but more provisions taken from other international instruments, such as Article 26 UDHR or Articles 13, 14 ICESCR will be consulted for an integrated understanding about children as independent holders of educational rights. The quest is for the scope and substance of an individualized right to violence-free quality education in particular.[173]

Sub-section (1) – Material Scope of Articles 28, 29 CRC

The term education was not defined from a child's rights perspective, not in these articles or in any other article of the Convention, but – partly – through an early UNESCO instrument.[174] For an interpretation of Conven-

[172] Fn 166 for the content of Article 39 CRC.

[173] Article 26 UDHR proclaims for "everyone" a right to education whereas through Articles 13, 14 ICESCR the right to education takes a legally binding form.

[174] *UNESCO, Convention against Discrimination in Education, adopoted by the General Conference at its eleventh session,* Paris, 14 December 1960, Article 1 ("Education" including the standard and quality of education and the conditions under which it is given).

tion rights another definition of education developed by UNESCO seems to be fitting:

> [T]*he word "education" implies the entire process of social life by means of which individuals and social groups learn to develop consciously within, and for the benefit of, the national and international communities, the whole of their personal capacities, attitudes, aptitudes and knowledge. This process is not limited to any specific activities.*[175]

Similarly, it was found by the Committee that 'education' in a context of Convention-based aims of education *'goes far beyond schooling to embrace the broad range of life experiences and learning processes which enable children, individually and collectively, to develop their personalities, talents and abilities and to live a full and satisfying life within society.'*[176] Thus, defining education for a Convention context must not be limited to instruction delivered in the classroom but should also look at a range of extra-curricular activities such as faith-based activities including preparation for the reception of sacraments which must be legally structured so as to be CRC compliant too.

Articles 28, 29 CRC both explicitly reference, in Article 28(1)(e), 'regular attendance at schools', and, in Article 29(2), private 'educational institutions' which implies that most children will normally attend school.[177]

---

[175] UNESCO *Recommendation concerning Education for International Understanding* (1974) reproduced in *Implementation Handbook* (n 137) 411.

[176] CRC/GC/2001/1 para 2.

[177] Fn 139 and accompanying text; RCC canon law mainly envisages "Catholic Schools" as what is being designated a "Diocesan school" supervised by the diocesan bishop, and "Parish schools" under the supervision of the pastor who carries out his responsibilities under the authority of the diocesan bishop, J P Beal et al (eds) *New Commentary on the Code of Canon Law* (Paulist Press 2000) 957 (commenting on can 803 CIC); In this thesis I cannot deal with all relevant legal configurations or bodies corporate functioning as a possible vehicle for Catholic educational institutions anywhere in the world, such as "Trusts" or "registered charities" under UK Law. On Catholic schools from a social science perspective, see G Grace, *Catholic Schools: Mission, Markets and Morality* (Routledge/Falmer 2002); With special regard to the schools explored for his study the author explains (*Catholic Schools* xii*): "The Catholic secondary schools in London, Liverpool and Birmingham, … , are not private schools. Their formal status in England is that of 'voluntary-aided' schools, which means in practice that they are non-fee-paying institutions and an integrated part of the free secondary school system."* Whatever the particular legal format chosen for Catholic

At a somewhat hidden location in their body of general comments the Committee explains about 'the school' seen from a perspective of children's rights:

> [T]*he school plays an important role in the life of many adolescents, as the venue for learning, development and socialisation. Article 29 (1) CRC states that education must be directed to 'the development of the child's personality, talents and mental and physical abilities to their fullest potential'. In addition, General Comment Nr 1 on the aims of education states that "education must also be aimed at … . Basic skills should include … the ability to make well balanced decisions; to resolve conflicts in a non-violent manner; and to develop a healthy lifestyle [and] good social relationships … .*[178]

Thus, Article 29(1) CRC, setting out the agreed aims of education, not only adds a qualitative dimension to the rights of education recognized in Article 28, it also insists on the need for all education to be child-centred, child-friendly and child-empowering.[179] In this regard, Article 29 CRC requires the reworking of curricula as well as systematic revision of all teaching materials and changes to school policies including officially developed inspection regimes. In addition, the whole school environment must promote human rights: a school which allows bullying or other violent and exclusionary practices to occur, clearly is not in compliance with standards set by Article 29(1) CRC.[180] Accordingly, teaching human rights and non-violence as a subject matter for curricular instruction necessarily requires the establishment of an educational atmosphere that respects human rights and builds on non-violent teaching methods.

A Bundle of Educational Rights

In academic writing it has become common to refer to CRC-based educational rights as a collection of rights:[181] the right ' to'education in Article

---

schools under their respective domestic laws there can be no doubt that their activities are covered by "education" as understood by Articles 28, 29 CRC.

178 CRC/GC/2003/4 para 17 with reference to CRC/GC/2001/1 para 9.

179 CRC/GC/2001/1 para 2

180 CRC/GC/2001/1 paras 18, 19.

181 C Hamilton, 'Rights of the child: a right to education and a right in education' in C Bridge (ed) *Family Law Towards the Millenium: Essays for P M Bromley* (Butterworths London 1997) 201, 203; S J Klees and N Thapliyal, 'The Right to Education' (Fn 140) 497, 500.

28 CRC implying progressive access of all children without discrimination to basic education which is free and of good quality, expands on earlier treaty norms through an additional provision requiring States to encourage regular attendance at school and reduce drop-out rates (sub-paragraph e). This article, through its second paragraph, also addresses a significant aspect of children's rights 'in'education by requiring states to take measures ensuring a humane administration of school discipline. As a matter of principle respect for the views of the child and for the fundamental freedoms set out through Articles 12 to 16 CRC are equally included in this disciplinary maxim. Article 29 CRC, furthermore, expands on children's rights 'through' education by setting aims that include the development of the child's respect for different cultural identities, languages and values as well as the child's respect for the natural environment.[182] Thus, children's rights in education are not just about receiving some form of schooling but are wider than this and may accordingly be referenced as rights *to* education, rights *in* education and rights *through* education.[183]

In sum, rights-based education in all its forms and at all levels shall exhibit the following interrelated features drawn together by use of the so-called *'4-A-Scheme'* which was originally developed for economic, social and cultural rights in general.[184] According to this scheme functioning educational institutions and programmes have to be available in sufficient quantity, through a public educational system and also by allowing for private parties to establish non-public schools ('*Availability*'); educational institutions and programmes have to be accessible to everyone, without discrimination on any ground, equally implying the removal of physical and economic barriers ('*Accessibility*'); the form and substance of education, including curricula and teaching methods, have to be relevant, culturally appropriate, of good quality and in accordance with the best interests of the child; this includes a safe and healthy school environment ('*Acceptability*'); and education has to be flexible so it can adapt to the needs of changing societies and communities and respond to the needs of students within their specific social and cultural settings, including the evolving capacities

---

182 Hamilton (n 181 above) 203; L Lundy, 'Children's rights and educational policy in Europe, the implementation of the United Nations Convention on the Rights of the Child' (2012) 38 Oxf Rev Educ 393, 395.

183 Hamilton (n 181) 203 (emphasis in the original).

184 F Coomans (n 139) 232, 235.

of the child ('*Adaptability*').[185] Thus, a legal requirement for all education to be free from all forms of physical and mental violence appears to be an element of this education's acceptability as set out above.

What must be inserted here for keeping in mind that Catholic schools will be one of my specified objects of analysis is a short outlook on the freedom of education as mentioned in Article 29(2) CRC; here the liberty to establish and direct educational institutions is stipulated, subject to conditions such as conformity to officially defined minimum educational standards. Extending to 'bodies' which may be legal persons or entities such as a diocese or a parish, this liberty confers the right to establish and direct all types of educational institutions including nurseries or schools for children.[186] Whereas the agreed aims of education must be observed, an education given in this kind of independent institution must not disregard what was set as a minimum standard for all educational institutions by the government in terms of oversight and inspection.

Sub-section (2) – Personal Scope of Articles 28, 29 CRC

Every child must have access to school-based education as recognized by virtue of Article 28(1) CRC, and this approach focusing on the individual child is confirmed by the primary aim of all education as set out in Article 29(1)(a) CRC: the development of this child's personality, talents and mental and physical abilities to their fullest potential. On the basis of his or her fundamental right to life, survival and development (Article 6 CRC) the child typically aiming at development of his or her personality is equally valued here as a human being but also as a human 'in becoming'.[187] In a similar vein, Manfred Nowak when commenting on the children's right to development (Article 6 CRC) found that any development of the child to a large extent depends on his or her enjoyment of the right to education.[188] Laying an accent on infantile personality development in this way is incompatible with any allowance for powerful authority figures relying on

185 E/C.12/1999/10 para 6.

186 E/C.12/1999/10 para 30.

187 Freeman (n 35) 21, 26.

188 M Nowak, 'Article 6 The Right to Life, Survival and Development' in A Alen et al (eds), *A Commentary on the UN Convention on the Rights of the Child* (Leiden Boston 2005) para 77.

teaching methods that disregard the child's human dignity or violate his or her mental and bodily integrity.

Free and compulsory primary education of good quality for every single child is the most fundamental of all education rights as stipulated in Articles 28, 29 CRC; thus, it is in the best interests of the child (Article 3 CRC) to have access to quality education, including early childhood education, non-formal or informal education and related activities, free of charge.[189] The element of compulsion thereby included serves to insist that neither parents, nor guardians, nor the State are entitled to treat as optional the decision as to whether the child should have access to primary education.[190] Accordingly, parents find themselves under an obligation not only to abstain from any negative interference with the child's schooling life, but also to promote and encourage regular attendance at school, as envisaged in Article 29(1)(e) CRC.[191]

In conclusion, a children's right to be protected against sexual abuse as well as their right to quality education were stated through express provisions in the Convention. Furthermore, as an important aspect of quality education non-violence includes protection from sexual abuse at the hands of school personnel or caretakers engaged. Given as a treaty-based guarantee to children their rights must be realized by all authorized educators or carers irrespective of their employment status in the State or in the Church; measures must be taken by the State to ensure that all children, without discrimination, can enjoy their educational rights in an environment free from all forms of violence. Likewise, under CRC the State must make sure that disciplinary action which is inconsistent with the Convention does not occur in any public or private educational institution.[192]

Chapter 3 – The Right to Non-violent Education

Introduction

Having reviewed a set of rights closely related to protection from violence and to quality education as enunciated through specific provisions in the Convention, from here on I will proceed with a more ambitious project

---

189 CRC/C/GC/14 para 79.

190 E/C.12/1999/4 para 6, also referenced in E/C.12/1999/10 para 10.

191 Nowak (n 188 above) paras 59–61.

192 E/C.12/1999/10 para 41 (ESC Committee).

in mind. Here, the basic aim is to further interpret the Convention in a way that helps to develop a proper legal-normative response to manifold findings about conditions of child sexual abuse occurring within a relatively closed educational setting; in many cases this kind of abuse was wilfully ignored and tolerated, or even perpetrated, by authority figures such as patrons, school-managers, teachers, headmasters, school-staff and the like. Also, in a great number of cases, as documented by official abuse reports, any help from outside came much too late in the predatory process or did not arrive at all.

In terms of interpretive methodology my ambition is about a legal-doctrinal synthesis in the field of human rights for children.[193] From its roots in ancient Greek philosophy the value of synthesis lies in the proof that a coherently completed whole displays a greater epistemic value than would a mere collection of its constituent parts; thus, the importance of having the right to non-violent education will prove to be a higher one compared to just having a loosely combined collection of protection and education rights bound together *ad hoc*.[194] In particular, the right to non violent education allows for comprehensively articulating rights *in education* and *through education*which opens up further dimensions compared to just having access *to education* guaranteed as a human right.[195]

As was made fundamentally clear by the UNICEF/UNESCO *EFA* framework study in its introductory paragraph

> [T]*he development of a human rights-based approach to education requires a framework that addresses the right of access to education, the right to quality education and respect for human rights in education. These dimensions are interdependent and interlinked, and a rights-based education necessitates the realization of all three.*[196]

Taken as an illustration from the history of children's rights as they were first stipulated in the Convention (but in other instruments also), the ever widening ban on corporal punishment proves to be an interesting

[193] Fnn 32, 33 above.

[194] S Blackburn, *The Oxford Dictionary of Philosophy* (1994) entries 'analythic/synthetic', 'analysis', 'analytical philosophy'.

[195] Fn 183 above and accompanying text (dimensions of education).

[196] UNICEF/UNESCO (principally drafted by G Lansdown), *Education for All* (2007) 27.

example of successful treaty interpretation. As a legal document *GC 8* issued by the CRC-Committee fully demonstrated on the basis of Articles 19, 28 (2) and 37 CRC that, as a matter of international law, the child had a right to protection from corporal punishment and other cruel, inhuman or degrading forms of punishment extending to the school and to the home.[197] Along these lines and on a basis of sound interpretive methodology, I present my case by demonstrating that *GC 8* did in fact not go far enough, but unnecessarily limited its conceptual understanding about the child's right to liberty and security of person to a functional context of discipline in education or correction and punishment.[198] In my view, the Committee thus prematurely refrained from exhausting the potential transformative meaning of core provisions taken from the CRC.[199] Similarly, through its *GC 13* on freedom from violence the commentators strayed too far away from analyzing specific settings highly relevant in their specificity for the daily life of children, such as (compulsory) education and schooling.

The Effectiveness of Children's Rights

Although there is no express provision in the Convention text clearly stipulating a right to non-violent education, an interpretive effort will lead to the conclusion that the Convention itself, its Article 19 read in conjunction with Articles 28, 29 CRC, provide a treaty basis for the right to non-violent education as a human right of the child. Basically, my argument is that the principle of effectiveness requires that everywhere protection from violence as a children's right must be made fully effective while it cannot become effective as long as education, its value and function in the life of children and adolescents, is not specifically addressed as a legal issue. Seen from a perspective of children's rights the school and compulsory education in particular, has an important role to play in the life of all children as the venue for learning, development and socialisation.[200] Thus, an education free from all forms of violence is an indispensable precondition for what the CRC states as the aim of all education, '*the development of the child's personality, talents, and mental and physical abilities to their fullest poten-*

[197] CRC/C/GC/8 (Fn 141); v Boven (n 32) 135, 144.
[198] Freeman (n 35) 21, 23.
[199] J Arato, 'Treaty Interpretation and Constitutional Transformation: Informal Change in International Organizations' 38 Yale J Intern L (2013) 289, 291.
[200] Fn 178 and accompanying text.

tial and *the preparation of the child for responsible life in a free society'* (Article 29(1) CRC). In terms of children's protection rights, what seems to be particularly problematic about school-based education for children and adolescents is a routine of regular enforced separation from their primary caretakers (parents, other relatives or guardians) for long hours of the day. As an obligation protecting schoolchildren from all forms of violence must not end at the school-gates nor see education as a realm beyond the reach of child protection agencies lawfully operating in the State. This is especially true for faith-based educational institutions and other more private places of instruction which have a tendency to seclude themselves from the public eye.

Any such interpretive effort needs to be properly framed so as to ensure not only the final outcome's legitimacy but its plausibility and acceptability in terms of scientific legal research.[201] An interpretive technique has been sought here for ensuring that legal guarantees for children and their rights retain their relevance within a dynamic treaty system operating under international law.

First Section: The Vienna Convention as a Framework for CRC Interpretation

Serving as a framework to my interpretive effort the *1969 Vienna Convention on the Law of Treaties* (VCLT) is also known as a 'treaty for treaties' for its outstanding significance as an internationally applicable rule-work framing the interpretation of human rights treaties such as the UN Convention on the Rights of the Child.[202]

With respect to rule-based interpretation of human rights treaties Malgosia Fitzmaurice explains

> *Human rights treaties undoubtedly fall within the definition of a treaty for the purposes of the VCLT. Although most of them were concluded before the entry*

---

[201] H Keller and G Ulfstein, 'Introduction' in *UN Human Rights Treaty Bodies, Law and Legitimacy* (CUP 2012) 6; H Keller and L Grover, 'General Comments of the Human Rights Committee and their legitimacy' in H Keller and G Ulfstein, *UN Human Rights Treaty Bodies* ibid 116, 138; J Tobin, 'Seeking to Persuade: A Constructive Approach to Human Rights Treaty Interpretation' 23 Harv H R J (2010) 1, 7.

[202] 1155 UNTS 331, concluded at Vienna on 23 May 1969, in force since 27 January 1980; including as signatories Ireland (acceded 7 August 2006) and the Holy See (signed and ratified, 25 Feb. 1997); Arato (n 199) 289, 335.

into force of the non-retroactive VCLT, human rights fora have generally acknowledged the applicability of the VCLT rules of interpretation as customary international law.[203]

Thus, the Convention belongs to a category of human rights treaties which have distinctive features in common, such as their 'constitutional' nature and the non-reciprocal nature of the rights and obligations set forth therein.[204] Another characteristic shared among human rights treaties relates to the nature of human rights embodying a concept according to which the parties to a human rights treaty do not create the rights that the treaty protects; rather, they recognize rights that arise from the very nature of man, quite independently of the will or volition of the parties.[205] In that sense, States Parties through Article 28(1) CRC explicitly recognize the child's right to education thus emphasizing the very nature of the child's personality development which must not be interrupted by violent interference from outside.

In the following I will provide for a brief general exposition of VCLT principles and rules having relevance for the study as a whole including its latter chapters on the Holy See and Ireland.[206] At this stage, however, it is the topic of 'Interpretation of Treaties' as designated in Articles 31 through 33 VCLT which requires some elaboration for the purpose of framing my interpretive effort.[207] At this location one 'General Rule of Interpretation' is laid out in the four paragraphs of Article 31 VCLT. Here, the first three paragraphs of Article 31 VCLT state the interpretive rule in general terms and they begin:

---

[203] M Fitzmaurice, 'Interpretation of Human Rights Treaties' in D Shelton (ed), *The Oxford Handbook of International Human Rights Law* (OUP 2013) 739; see also M Fitzmaurice, 'The Practical Working of the Law of Treaties' in M Evans (ed), *International Law* (4th ed OUP 2014) 166.

[204] B Schlütter, 'Aspects of human rights interpretation by the UN treaty bodies' in H Keller et al (eds), *UN Human Rights Tretay Bodies, Law and Legitimacy* (CUP 2012) 261, 265.

[205] Fitzmaurice, 'Interpretation' (n 203) 742, 753 including Fn 62.

[206] Fn 202 above and third part below on 'Jurisdictions and Implementations'.

[207] Schlütter (n 204) 261, 311.

Article 31 – General Rule of Interpretation

1. *A treaty shall be interpreted in good faith in accordance with the ordinary meaning to be given to the terms of the treaty in their context and in the light of its object and purpose.*

Thus, reliance on the object and purpose of a treaty not only proves to be in accordance with Article 31(1) VCLT, but is particularly appropriate in the context of human rights obligations (requiring, in most jurisdictions, an act of domestic implementation). Being related to the doctrine of effectiveness the object and purpose test implies that treaties have a definitive force and effect; a treaty therefore may be interpreted expansively in order to ensure that all of its provisions have an independent non-superfluous meaning.[208]

Non-Violent Education as Object and Purpose of Articles 19 and 28, 29 CRC

As a living instrument the Convention enshrines the rights of every child without exception to a life of dignity and self-fulfilment to be progressively realized by educational means among others.[209] As indicated earlier an important aspect of the Convention's object and purpose consists in empowerment of children as independent holders of rights to be claimed and vindicated in practice.[210] With regard to freedom from violence this means that every child must everywhere be entitled to claim protection from all forms of violence, including sexual abuse, as a personal right. Consequently, children's rights to protection from violence must extend to all educational settings like schools and day-centres where children are regularly being separated from their primary caregivers for long hours of the day. As a venue for learning, development and socialisation, the school plays an important role in the life of young children and adolescents which implies that necessary measures to prevent and prohibit all forms of violence and abuse, including sexual abuse, will be taken. Reading Articles 19 and 28, 29 CRC from this object-and-purpose perspective leaves no doubt as to possible spheres of exemption where some form of violence against children might be admissible: no exceptions permitted. As the Committee succinctly phrased it, '[C]*hildren do not lose their human rights by virtue*

208 Fitzmaurice, 'Interpretation' (n 203) 751.

209 N Mandela, *Foreword* in *Implementation Handbook* (n 137) xi.

210 Fn 24 above and accompanying text.

of passing through the school-gates';[211] in other words, children are holders of the right to non-violent education as a matter of their own dignity and human rights.

This interpretive approach is supported by a CRC based understanding about the aims of education: Article 29(1) CRC underlines the individual and subjective right to a specific quality of education which must be aimed at ensuring that essential life skills, such as to resolve conflicts in a non-violent manner, are learnt by every child.[212] Correspondingly, it is important that teaching methods used in schools reflect the spirit and educational philosophy of the Convention and the aims of education as stated in Article 29(1) CRC.[213] Clearly, an educational institution where the inherent dignity of the child is not respected and which allows violent and exclusionary practices such as sexual abuse to occur is not one that meets the requirements of Article 29(1) CRC.[214]

Second Section: The Right to Non-Violent Education – A Model from Austria

In the following a quick side-look will be taken for acquiring a deeper conceptual understanding about non-violent education as a children's right including its constitutional law implications; therefore, an act of domestic legislation will be looked at without closer contextualization regarding the Republic of Austria as a jurisdiction. Essentially, this piece of legislation addresses non-violent education as a right of every child living in Austria and does so at a constitutional level hierarchically situating this right at a normative rank outstanding from the general level of Federal legislation. Accordingly, in Article 5 of the 2011 Federal Constitutional Law on the Rights of Children (*Bundesverfassungsgesetz Kinderrechte*), it was stated

Article 5

(1) *Every child has the right to non-violent education. Corporal punishment, inflicting mental suffering, sexual abuse and all other mistreat-*

---

[211] CRC/GC/2001/1 para 8; L Lundy, K Orr and H Shier, 'Children's Education Rights' in M D Ruck et al (eds), *Handbook of Children's Rights* (Routledge 2017) 364, 366.

[212] CRC/GC/2001/1 para 9.

[213] CRC/GC/2001/1 para 18.

[214] CRC/GC/2001/1 paras 8, 19.

ment are prohibited. Every child has the right to be protected against economic and sexual exploitation.
(2) (. . .).[215]

Remarkably, in this piece of legislation the right to non-violent education as explicitly stated through the very first sentence of Article 5 immediately unfolds into a generalized prohibition of several forms of grave mistreatment including sexual abuse. Next, an individualized right of protection regarding the risk of economic and sexual exploitation (para 1, 3rd sentence) is stated.

Seen from a perspective of Austrian constitutional law a selection of protective guarantees stipulated in Article 19 CRC were directly incorporated into internal laws by virtue of Artikel 5 *Bundesverfassungsgesetz Kinderrechte*;[216] and were even incorporated at the level of constitutional rights. In constitutional law terms, this statement of the right to non-violent education defines every child as a rights-holder, but leaves room for an identification of duty-bearers in accordance with the right thus stated. Additionally, the general prohibition following makes it obvious that no act of inflicting violence against a child, whoever the author, is permissible as a matter of law. Lastly, not merely an unspecified State duty was provided, but an individualized right to protection against economic and sexual exploitation is given into the hands of children themselves. Thus, in terms of constitutional law doctrine Artikel 5 *Bundesverfassungsgesetz Kinderrechte* makes for the classical case of a fundamental right (*Grundrecht*) being

---

215 My translation from *Bundesgesetzblatt für die Republik Österreich Teil I Ausgegeben am 15. Februar 2011: Bundesverfassungsgesetz über die Rechte von Kindern;* Article 5, authentic German version: ***Artikel 5** (1) Jedes Kind hat das Recht auf gewaltfreie Erziehung. Körperliche Bestrafungen, die Zufügung seelischen Leids, sexueller Mißbrauch und andere Mißhandlungen sind verboten. Jedes Kind hat das Recht auf Schutz vor wirtschaftlicher und sexueller Ausbeutung. (2) Jedes Kind als Opfer von Gewalt und Ausbeutung hat ein Recht auf angemessene Entschädigung und Rehabilitation. Das Nähere bestimmen die Gesetze;* see also CRC/C/AUT/CO/3–4, paras 3a, 10 (Committee reviewing this piece of internal legislation).

216 C Grabenwarter, 'Zur Frage der Integration der Kinderrechtskonvention in das österreichische Bundesverfassungsrecht' in Bundesministerium für Familien und Jugend (ed), *Studien zur Kinderrechtskonvention und ihrer Umsetzung in Österreich* (2014) 78.

guaranteed individually; situated at the highest normative level available within the State this legal guarantee is also enforceable.[217]

For the following, the three dimensions just outlined will help to define what may be seen as State duties or treaty obligations corresponding to the right to non-violent education as a children's right: first, to claim respect for the right comprehensively stated, through a high-ranking constitutional provision or similar; second, to accord legal protection to right-holders in their personal integrity, by virtue of a widely drafted prohibition covering all forms of ill-treatment; and third, to empower right-holders so as to claim their protective rights as a matter of procedures and entitlements available to them under their respective domestic laws.

Third Section: The Right to Non-violent Education, its Scope and Substance

As exemplified by this Austrian piece of constitutional legislation, the right to non-violent education regularly translates into an absolute prohibition of all acts of violent behaviour committed against children finding themselves in an educational situation involving a domineering presence of authority figures such as headmistresses, teachers, coaches, clerics or catechists. Others, such as school patrons, supervisors and school-inspectors might be co-responsible for inflicting or tolerating violence against schoolchildren. However, under no circumstance may educational authority be misused as a pretext for violations or infringements of the child's personal integrity, physically, mentally or psychologically. The educational environment may never be perceived as offering opportunities for a transgression of boundaries between individuals, to be respected as physically, mentally or morally demarcated spheres of dignity and development. Seen through the lens of the individual child as a holder of rights in education what flows from the right to protection from violence combined with educational rights as stipulated in the Convention, is the right to non-violent education as a treaty-based legal affirmation to be implemented accordingly.

From a perspective of receiving and interpreting the Convention as a human rights treaty, it remains crucial to accept that the right to non-violent education presents itself as a synthesis of existing rights, not as an invention of novel rights; as a newly invented right it might fall under the verdict

[217] Ibid 64.

of not being covered by the consent of the treaty-making Parties which features as the legal source of the treaty's binding effects.[218] Above it was demonstrated that an establishment of functional systems of education wich are free from all forms of violence including sexual abuse, is the object and purpose of Articles 19 and 28, 29 CRC in particular. Consequently, these specific provisions must be interpreted accordingly: education as detailed in the Convention presupposes educational institutions and processes free from violence and sexual abuse threatened or perpetrated against children. Likewise, protection from violence implies that protective measures are available from the State that help to keep education in schools permanently free from violence and abuse for every child.

In conclusion, as a CRC-based human right the right to non-violent education shows the following features. First, every individual child has the right of admission to an appropriate learning environment implying access to an acceptable educational institution and completion of core educational stages therein; such learning environment in both, its institutional and behavioural aspects, must be free from violence understood in a sense that includes sexual abuse as a violence-related risk for the wellbeing and development of children generally. Second, all means and processes used or instituted for educational purposes, be they directly related to public or private schooling in its operational aspects or indirectly related to the learning stage of childhood as a distinct developmental phase, must be of a general non-violent character, presupposing that same basic concept of violence. Third, education for all conceptualized on a basis of rights including the right to non-violent education, requires that comprehensive educational systems are instated and maintained in accordance with all other human rights encompassing children's rights as they were stipulated in the Convention; remedies accessible to children in case of an infringement of rights recognized by the Convention must equally be available.

The following part of the study will discuss State duties and obligations as they are flowing from legal guarantees stated in the Convention including the right to non-violent education as a children's right.

---

[218] Chinkin (n 31) 63, 67.

SECOND PART: Duties and Obligations

This second part of the dissertation will be informed by the following core research question: With respect to the right to non-violent education as a children's right, which are the general duties and obligations falling on State Parties that signed and ratified the UN Convention on the Rights of the Child?[219] While throughout the Convention text a legal language of obligations undertaken by State Parties is pervasive, important aspects of children's human rights remain unclear: which are the general duties and obligations in relation to non-state actors, and private providers of educational services in particular?

Fundamentally, behind this quest two simple truths lie hidden, the one being that human rights law does not implement itself; instead it requires social actors to mobilize around it and to demand changes on the ground.[220] Children themselves, including their agency understood as a general capacity to take meaningful action in any relevant social context, will thus become visible as one particular group of social actors whose participation is required for the purpose of human rights implementation.[221] Another foundational distinction is that ratification of human rights treaties is not *per se* the same as rights implementation but only the first step towards enjoyment of human rights by those for whom they were stipulated ('beneficiaries').[222]

In accordance with this basic outline, the materials discussed throughout this part of the thesis will mainly be documents issued by the Committee on the Rights of the Child (CRC-Committee or 'the Committee')

219 CRC/GC/2003/5 ("general measures of implementation").

220 Z Elkins, T Ginsburg & B Simmons, 'Getting to Rights: Treaty Ratification, Constitutional Convergence, and Human Rights Practice' 54 Harv Intern L J (2013) 61, 69.

221 Freeman (n 35) 21, 22; CRC/C/GC/7/Rev.1, para 2.

222 A Aust, *Handbook of International Law* (CUP 2005) 63, 79 (' ratification'); H Keller and L Grover, 'General Comments' (n 201) 116, 131 ('beneficiaries').

but by other specified treaty bodies also, such as the Committee on Economic, Social and Cultural Rights (ESC-Committee), or the Human Rights Committee holding an equally wide mandate. Regarding the categories of documents available from monitoring bodies, I will predominantly look into General Comments as they were topically arranged by those Committees. As Andrew Clapham fittingly observed with a view on publications issued by UN sponsored monitoring bodies '[T]*he texts produced by these bodies mostly concentrate on the treaty obligations of states to protect the beneficiaries of human rights from infringements of their rights by non-state actors.*'[223] Following this author's observation the right to non-violent education will be explored with an accent on corresponding obligations to protect children as beneficiaries of CRC rights from an infringement of their rights by non-state actors.[224]

More specifically, the following General Comments issued by the Committee will be consulted for this exploration of treaty obligations: 'General measures of implementation' (*GC 5* in the following), 'The right of the child to freedom from all forms of violence' (*GC 13*), 'The right of the child to have his or her best interest taken as a primary consideration' (*GC 14*), and 'State obligations regarding the impact of the business sector on children's rights' (*GC 16*).[225] My basic aim here is to explore and review critically what was formally stated about international obligations to protect children's rights in any domestic legal system, by the Committee but by other monitoring bodies also.

Chapter 1 – Terminology, Treaty Norms and Typologies

Introduction

Given that treaty language often is not very precise or well defined almost any study on international law topics needs to have an introductory

---

[223] A Clapham, *Human Rights Obligations of Non-State Actors* (OUP 2006) 318.

[224] A Clapham, 'Non-State Actors' in D Moeckli et al (eds), *International Human Rights Law* (3rd ed OUP 2018) 557.

[225] CRC/GC/2003/5 General Comment Nr 5 (2003); explicitly building on this document more details with regard to public budgeting were provided by CRC/C/GC/19 General Comment Nr 19 (2016); CRC/C/GC/13 General comment Nr 13 (2011); CRC/C/GC/14 General comment Nr 14 (2013); CRC/C/GC/16 General comment Nr 16 (2013).

section dealing with terminological issues;[226] notwithstanding the fact that the *1969 Vienna Convention* (VCLT) provides, in its Article 2, an itemized list of definitions such as 'treaty' (Nr 1 letter a), or 'reservation' (letter d) or 'party' (letter g). What renders the interpretative task even more demanding: in contrast to other human rights treaties the Convention displays no such list of agreed terms.[227] As a consequence, defining the right to protection from violence in terms of its corresponding obligations logically implies prior clarification about terms such as 'violence', 'sexual abuse' and 'reporting' or 'investigation' as mentioned in Article 19 CRC. Bridging the gap between fundamental rights and freedoms on the one hand and duties and obligations on the other, especially if on both sides many important details were not explicitly laid down in treaty terms, asks for an interpretive typology which helps to define what States must do under the treaty, and this is particularly true with regard to children's rights.[228] As stipulated in the Convention children's rights require an act of appropriation and transformation duly performed by each signatory, and the technical term used for such appropriation is 'implementation' as explicitly referred to in Article 4 CRC (Implementation of rights in the Convention).[229]

Clarification of Framework Terminology

As a multilateral treaty the *Vienna Convention* (VCLT) sets forth established rules of law respecting the operation of treaties thereby constituting the basic normative framework for development and reconstruction of detailed duties and obligations flowing from signature and ratification of human rights treaties such as the CRC.[230] Under CRC, more than 190

---

226 J Tobin (n 201) 1; M Hakimi, 'State Bystander Responsibility' 21 EJIL (2010) 341, 346 (ambiguous language); *Terminology Guidelines* (n 53) 1 (confusing terminology).

227 *Convention on the Rights of Persons with Disabilities* (CRPD), Article 2 Definitions; for the CRC system some definitions of terms were provided in Article 2 OPSC, see p 55 above.

228 Hakimi (n 226) 341, 347; N Cantwell, 'The human rights of children in the context of formal alternative care' in W Vandenhole et al (eds) *Routledge International Handbook of Children's Rights Studies* (Routledge 2015) 257, 260.

229 G Staberock, entry 'Human Rights, Domestic Implementation' in Max Planck Encyclopedia of Public International Law (MPEPIL) (2011).

230 Fn 202 and accompanying text; S Egan, *The United Nations Human Rights Treaty System: Law and Procedure* (Bloomsbury Professional 2011) para 1.03.

states have voluntarily assumed an international legal obligation to fulfil their duties in good faith and to abstain from misleadingly producing justifications for non-performance.[231] In Articles 26 and 27 VCLT captioned *'Pacta sunt Servanda'* and *'Internal Law and Observance of Treaties'* respectively,[232] through a truly principled language, it is stated: "*Every treaty in force is binding upon the parties to it and must be performed by them in good faith*" (Article 26 VCLT), and "*A party may not invoke the provisions of its internal law as justification for its failure to perform a treaty*" (Article 27 VCLT). Accordingly, it is for States Parties as primary duty-bearers to faithfully perform all treaties, including human rights treaties such as the Convention, which they effectively concluded under international law and to abstain from hiding behind their internal laws as an excuse for non-compliance.[233] In respect of human rights treaties analysed through the lens of VCLT provisions on observance of treaties, John Tobin further explains:

> [T]*he obligation to 'perform' anticipates that the ratification of a human rights treaty will carry practical consequences in terms of measures required by states to fulfil their obligations. Moreover, when this obligation is combined with the obligation of 'good faith' the result is that states may not adopt a passive response to the implementation of a treaty on the basis that the terms are unclear or ambiguous. On the contrary, it demands that states actively engage with such terms in order to produce an understanding of their content such that the treaty is capable of effective implementation.*[234]

Consequently, as a prerequisite for persuasive treaty interpretation leading to an effective implementation of rights recognized in the Convention,

---

[231] E Verhellen, 'The Convention on the Rights of the Child' in W Vandenhole et al (eds) *Routledge International Handbook of Children's Rights Studies* (Routledge 2015) 43, 55; J Tobin, 'Understanding a Human Rights Based Approach to Matters Involving Children' in: A Invernizzi et al (ed), *The Human Rights of Children* (Ashgate 2011) 61, 67.

[232] Verhellen (n 231 above) 43, 52; RCC canon law has a provision on "Agreements" (Canon 3 CIC) at the root of which lies the principle of *pacta sunt servanda*, see J M Huels in J P Beal et al (eds) *New Commentary on the Code of Canon Law* (Paulist Press New York 2000) 50.

[233] J Salmon in O Corten, P Klein (eds), *The Vienna Convention on the Law of Treaties, A Commentary* (2 vols, OUP 2011) 661.

[234] Tobin (n 201) 1, 16.

it is obligatory for States to engage with the exact terms of its provisions, even if some treaty terms may seem unclear or ambiguous at first.[235]

First Section: Terms for Implementing the Commitment Made

As the Committee sees it, clear operational legal definitions (to be established as a matter of internal legislation) are required of the different forms of violence outlined in Article 19 CRC in order to ban all forms of violence in all settings; included are situations – also termed as care settings – where simultaneously some form of care is provided by parents or otherwise.[236] Having analyzed 'violence' and 'abuse' as key terms,[237] the question arises: what does all this mean in respect of State duties and obligations, and in respect of implementation as an international obligation in particular?

With the view on an obligation to implement, this terminology has three main functions; first, by highlighting, through Article 19 CRC, its close relation to violence against children the criminal dimension of child sexual abuse is clarified further implying that nothing less than criminalization will be an appropriate response; second, for purposes of legislating on child abuse no arbitrary understanding about "*abuse*" as it may be defined in different societies or communities is acceptable;[238] and third, as substantive terms 'violence' and 'abuse' are closely related to a requirement stated in Article 3(3) CRC for consistent standards and supervision for all institutions, services and facilities operating within the jurisdiction.

Measures for an Implementation of Rights

Implementing measures to be taken by States Parties are practical consequences flowing from an obligation under international law for the purpose of fulfilment of that same legal obligation.[239] State Parties acting under an international human rights regime carry out their respective obligations through a combination of legislative, institutional, judicial, administrative, financial and other types of measures to be realized within their own

[235] *Terminology Guidelines* (n 53) 5 ('child' to include any person below 18 years of age).
[236] CRC/C/GC/13 para 18; CRC/C/GC/20 para 40 (legal age for sexual consent).
[237] See Fn 152 above and accompanying text.
[238] *Implementation Handbook* (n 137) 249.
[239] Fn 229 above and accompanying text.

constitutional framework.[240] As identified by the Committee, general measures of implementation are intended to promote the full enjoyment of all rights in the Convention by all children, through legislation, the establishment of coordinating and monitoring bodies – governmental and independent – comprehensive data collection, awareness-raising and training and the development and implementation of appropriate policies, services and programmes.[241]

In the words of Articles 4 and 19 CRC the range of implementing measures are sub-divided into functional categories, and it was furthermore stated as a general requirement that they need to be 'appropriate'; whereby it is implied that any such measure needs to be necessary, effective and proportionate in terms of means licitly used for reaching a legitimate end.[242] Scholarly writing rather tends towards drawing a distinction between substantive protections on the one hand and institutional ones on the other; whereas substantive aspects would be concerned about the nature, status and scope of rights protections under national law, institutional aspects are dealing with the types of institution which commonly play a role in the implementation, monitoring and protection of human rights. These are courts, the executive or the legislature, but also mechanisms such as ombudsmen or national human rights institutions.[243]

Sub-section (1) – Legislative and Administrative Measures

As the Committee sees them legislative measures refer to acts of internal legislation and to any regulation that legally defines frameworks, systems, and mechanisms for child protection, including a definition of the role and responsibility of any public agency involved; administrative measures, moreover, should reflect governmental obligations to establish policies, programmes, and also monitoring and oversight systems necessary for protection of the child from all forms of violence.[244] Detailing legislative and regulatory measures with particular attention paid to private service provi-

---

240 A Byrnes and C Renshaw, 'Within the State' in D Moeckli et al (eds) *International Human Rights Law* (3rd ed OUP 2018) 482.

241 CRC/GC/2003/5 para 9; U Kilkelly 'The Convention on the Rights of the Child after Twenty-five Years' in M D Ruck et al (eds) *Children's Rights Handbook* (Routledge 2017) 80, 87.

242 CRC/C/GC/13 para 39.

243 Byrnes and Renshaw (n 240) 482, 483.

244 CRC/C/GC/13 para 40 (legislative measures), para 42 (administrative measures).

ders *GC 16* found that States should enact legislation giving effect to the rights of the child on private third parties; legislative and regulatory measures must equally be adopted to ensure that business enterprises, such as independent educational institutions do not infringe on children's rights.[245]

Therefore, States Parties have an obligation to set standards in conformity with the Convention and closely monitor them; they must stay fully aware of a clear necessity for adequate oversight, inspection and monitoring of private service providers which, if lacking or deficient, can result in serious violations of children's rights such as violence, exploitation and neglect.[246]

Sub-section (2) – Social and Educational Measures

Social measures as seen by the Committee should reflect a commitment to fulfilling children's rights including the right to non-violent education, and to providing for basic and targeted services which may either be supplied by competent government agencies or by such non-state service providers as are acting under oversight from the government.[247] Educational measures may be defined by their addressees in that attitudes, traditions, customs and behavioural practices which condone or promote any form of violence against children should be targeted for elimination.[248] Thus, any government support in terms of funding attributed to an accredited school providing its educational services in a rights-compliant way, and to any other educational institution respecting children's rights may come under this rubric.[249]

---

245 CRC/C/GC/16 para 53 (legislative, regulatory and enforcement measures); Providing its own definition of the business sector *GC 16* refers to all business enterprises regardless of size, sector, location, ownership and structure; included in this definition are not for profit organizations playing an active role in the provision or management of services such as education, see CRC/C/GC/16 paras 3, 33; most Catholic schools in many different countries, therefore, qualify as a business enterprise for purposes of implementing children's rights.

246 CRC/C/GC/16 para 34.

247 CRC/C/GC/13 para 41.

248 CRC/C/GC/13 para 44.

249 Ibid para 44 (mentioning 'child-friendly schools' under letter d)

Sub-section (3) – Other Measures

By means of general comment, the Committee, through *GC 16* in particular, re-defined a whole range of measures which were freshly labelled as follows: 'Remedial measures', 'Policy measures', 'Coordination and monitoring measures', and 'Collaborative and awareness-raising measures'.[250] For an implementation of remedial measures States should focus their attention on removing social, economic and juridical barriers so that children can in practice have access to effective judicial measures without discrimination of any kind.[251] Policy measures for the encouragement of a business culture that understands and fully respects children's rights will have to include the adoption of zero-tolerance policies against violence in all business activities and operations including non-state educational services.[252] According to the Committee, States also have an obligation to monitor those violations or infringements of Convention rights which were committed or contributed to by educational enterprises, including in their global operations.[253] As a prerequisite, States must adopt and implement a comprehensive strategy to inform and educate all children, parents and caregivers that business has a responsibility to respect children's rights wherever they operate.[254]

Second Section: Treaty Norm Requirements

Having reviewed a range of measures for an implementation of children's rights time has come for an integration of the topic within a context of State duties and obligations specifically corresponding to the right to non-violent education. For a legal dissertation building on a technical term such as 'implementation' this is done by way of evaluating the term's legal-normative content: what precisely is the scope of the children's rights imperative requiring an implementation of legislative and other measures for the full realization of Convention rights including the right to non-violent education?

---

[250] CRC/C/GC/16 paras 66–72 (Remedial measures), paras 73–74 (Policy measures), paras 75–81 (Coordination and monitoring measures), 82–84 (Collaborative and awareness-raising measures).

[251] CRC/C/GC/16 para 68.

[252] Ibid para 73.

[253] Ibid para 76.

[254] CRC/C/GC/16 para 82; CRC/GC/2003/5 para 56 (Fn 259 below).

Sub-Section (1) – General Measures of Implementation (Article 4 CRC)

Articulating the nature and scope of State obligations, Article 4 CRC sets out an obligation to undertake all appropriate legislative, administrative and other measures for an implementation of all the rights recognized in the Convention, and devote the maximum amount of available resources to the realization of economic, social and cultural rights. In other words, several kinds of measures involving different branches of government will have to be adopted by States to bring domestic legislation, policy and practice into full conformity with principles and provisions of the Convention.[255] Importantly, States are not relieved of their obligations under the Convention if and when those government services that regularly impact on the realization of children's rights are delegated or outsourced to private business or to a non-profit organization.[256] Thus, the Committee in its *GC 5* explained and defined the concept of general measures for an implementation of children's rights:

> *While it is the State which takes on obligations under the Convention, its task of implementation – of making reality of the human rights of children – needs to engage all sectors of society, including children themselves. (…) … responsibilities to respect and ensure the rights of children extend in practice beyond the State and State-controlled services and institutions to include … non-State services and organisations.*[257]

As the Committee sees it, State Parties cannot avoid taking their implementing efforts beyond its own organs and agencies but must direct its legislative initiative to include private sector activities typically impacting on children and their lived experiences.

---

[255] CRC-Committee, *General Guidelines regarding the form and content of periodic reports to be submitted by States Parties under article 44, paragraph 1(b), of the Convention* (2005) para 11, reproduced in *Implementation Handbook* (n 137) 699.

[256] CRC/C/GC/16 para 25; CRC/C/GC/14 para 26; Committee expressing concern at the provision of services to child victims being to a large degree left to non-governmental organizations, Costa Rica CRC/C/15/Add.266 reproduced in *Implementation Handbook* (n 137) 256.

[257] CRC/GC/2003/5 paras 1, 56.

States Parties seen as Primary Duty-bearers

The exact wording in a great many articles from the Convention starts with a formulation like *"States Parties shall ... "*, whereby it becomes clear that any such obligation falls on States Parties which are perceived as primary duty-bearers accordingly.[258] By virtue of Article 4 CRC a relationship of rights-bearer and duty-holder is established referring to the concept of accountability which is said to be the key element of any rights based approach.[259] As addressed by the Committee, '*a comprehensive review of all domestic legislation and related administrative guidance to ensure full compliance with the Convention is an obligation*'.[260] Explaining in more detail its understanding about the review process here envisaged, the Committee adds three more elements to it, stating that the Convention needs to be considered not only article by article, but also holistically; moreover, that same review process needs to be continuous rather than one-off; and finally, while being built into the machinery of all government departments, it is also advantageous to have the whole process independently cross-reviewed by, *inter alia*, parliamentary committees, national human rights institutions, academics, affected children and young people also.[261]

Interdependence of Obligations

The CRC-Committee's *GC 5* declares itself open to a wider understanding about measures of implementation requiring the consideration of more general comments issued earlier by the Human Rights Committee or the Committee on Economic, Social and Cultural Rights (ESC-Committee), and they "should be seen as complementary".[262] At an early stage in its

---

[258] Through the Convention text treaty performance as required by States Parties is designated by verbs such as "*... respect and ensure ...* ", "*... to ensure ...* ", "*... to respect ...* ", "*... to assure ...* " at 25 instances, whereas the verbal construction "*... take measures ...* " or "*... undertake measures ...* " is used at 17 instances; D Fottrell, 'Children's Rights' in A Hegarty & S Leonard (eds), *Human Rights, An Agenda for the 21st Century* (Cavendish 1999) 167, 171.

[259] Tobin (n 231) 61, 69.

[260] CRC/GC/2003/5 para 18.

[261] Ibid.

[262] CRC/GC/2003/5 para 5 (explicitly referencing general comment No 3 issued by the Human Rights Committee in 1981, and general comments No 3 and No. 9 issued by ESC-Committee in 1990 and 1998 respectively; in the meantime the Human Rights

monitoring activity, the ESC-Committee elaborating on its concept of 'minimum core obligation' found that

> [A] *State party in which any significant number of individuals is deprived of ... , or of the most basic forms of education is, prima facie, failing to discharge its obligations under the Covenant* [on Economic, Social and Cultural Rights].[263]

In a similar vein, the Human Rights Committee, through its general comment dealing with the nature of general legal obligations, insists that the Covenant (on Civil and Political Rights) cannot be viewed as a substitute for domestic criminal or civil law; its core provisions (like an obligation to respect and ensure the rights recognized by the Covenant) do create obligations which are binding on States Parties and do not, as such, have direct horizontal effect (binding among private subjects) as a matter of international law.[264] Any such lack of direct horizontal effects, therefore, creates a need for comprehensive activity undertaken by national legislators who may find that their internal legislation requires supplementing in order to become CRC compliant.

Sub-Section (2) – Undertakings in Relation to Protection and Care (Article 3 CRC)

According to Article 3(2) CRC protection and care as necessary for the child's well-being entails an obligation to ensure child protection, and therefore to take legislative as well as administrative measures; simultaneously, account shall be taken of rights and duties of parents and others legally responsible.[265] Thus, an overarching obligation to take implementing measures that carry protective effects is set out by Article 3(2) CRC as becomes obvious from its close connection to neighbouring Articles 2(1) and 4 CRC treating implementation as an international obligation. As underlined by the Committee in its general comment the

Committee replaced its general comment from 1981 by its general comment No. 31).

263 UN document E/1991/23 para 10, Committee on economic, social and cultural rights, general comment No. 3 (1990): The nature of States parties' obligations (art. 2, para 1 of the Covenant).

264 CCPR/C/21/Rev.1/Add. 13, para 8; Schlütter (n 204) 264 ("horizontal" and "vertical effects").

265 *Implementation Handbook* (n 137) 40 (parents).

child's best interests encompass a threefold concept.[266] Thus, it contains a substantive right, a fundamental, interpretative legal principle and a rule of procedure requiring in particular that whenever a formal decision is to be made affecting children and their education, the decision making process must include an evaluation of possible impacts on children.[267] Finally, Article 3(3) CRC requires that safety standards be established by competent bodies for all institutions, services and facilities for children, and that it be equally ensured that all standards are complied with; expressly mentioned are the number and suitability of their staff as well as competent supervision.

Contexts of Privatization

For any context of 'Privatization' understood as an official (de facto) policy of handing over publicly controlled activities in the fields of health or care and education from government responsibility to non-state service providers, all three paragraphs in Article 3 CRC must be taken into account, as the Committee rightfully explained.[268] Addressing "public or private social welfare institutions" and also "institutions, services and facilities" the Convention text equally covers private sector organizations – operating either for-profit or non-profit – which, in their provision of services, may appear to be critically important to the enjoyment of children's rights.[269] Thus, the clear wording in Article 3 CRC indicates a scope of application wide enough to embrace all services acting on behalf or alongside government services as an alternative.

In that sense, duties and obligations flowing from a commitment to children's rights are extending to Catholic schools as a non-state provider of educational services. As a general observation dioceses, parishes, con-

---

266 CRC/C/GC/14, *General comment No. 14 (2013) on the right of the child to have his or her best interests taken as a primary consideration (art. 3, para. 1).*

267 CRC/C/GC/14, para 6 postulating that Article 3(1) CRC "creates an intrinsic obligation for States, is directly applicable (self-executing) and can be invoked before a court"; CRC/C/GC/20 para 22 (Committee referencing *GC 14* for its re-statement of the threefold concept).

268 CRC/GC/2003/5 paras 42–44; CRC/C/GC/7/Rev.1 para 32; the Committee even found that Article 3(1) CRC was directly applicable to business enterprises functioning as private or public social welfare providers, see CRC/C/GC/16 part III. section B; A Clapham, 'Non-state Actors' (n 224) 557, 560.

269 CRC/C/GC/14 para 26.

gregations or other religious bodies functioning as proprietors or managers of schools or educational facilities are thereby operating as non-state actors living essentially in the private sphere with no immediate government control over their day-to-day business.[270] Whenever secular governments decide to widely outsource their formerly owned educational responsibilities, be it to commercial providers of educational services or to faith-related groups like churches, synagogues or mosques, such policy-framed outsourcing creates challenges from a human rights point of view and from a perspective of CRC performance to be done faithfully in particular.[271]

Sub-Section (3) – Duties to Respect and Ensure Non-Discrimination (Article 2 CRC)

Using a strong language of "respect and ensure" the Convention, through its Article 2 CRC operative clause, shows equal regard for children's rights of a more Civil and Political character (to be respected), but also for Economic, Social and Cultural rights (to be ensured). Article 2 CRC leaves no doubt that the rights stipulated in the Convention must equally be respected and ensured to all children within the State's jurisdiction, regardless of the legal status of their actual place of learning in terms of private or public organisation.[272]

As an age-related aspect the right to non-discrimination (Article 2 CRC) regards children at the end of the age spectrum covered by the Convention, namely adolescents close to attaining 18 years of age: they are fully entitled to protection from all forms of violence, injury and abuse as stipulated in Article 19 CRC. In this respect the Committee emphasizes that the young person's right to exercise increasing levels of responsibili-

---

270 *O'Keeffe* v. *Ireland* (n 1) finding Ireland in violation of Article 3 ECHR because of the total absence of adequate reporting and complaints procedures; O'Mahony & Kilkelly (n 79) 320 (lack of effective state control).

271 A/HRC/29/30 Report of the UN Special Rapporteur on the right to education titled "Protecting Education from Commercialization", cited in A/HRC/29/L.14/Rev. 1 dated 1 July 2015 para 3, Resolution of the Human Rights Council on the right to education; Report of the UN Special Rapporteur on freedom of religion or belief (Heiner Bielefeldt), A/HRC/16/53 dated 15 December 2010 paras 54–56; A Mawhinney 'Freedom of religion in the Irish primary school system: a failure to protect human rights? (2007) 27 Leg Stud 379.

272 Article 2 P1 ECHR allows for a spectre of educational systems which come under an obligation to respect the right of parents in education.

ty does not obviate States' obligations to guarantee protection, including protection from violence.[273]

Third Section: Typological Details for an Implementation of the Right to Non-Violent Education

Having reviewed, in three previous sections, a set of treaty-based concepts, my analysis will proceed now to a discussion of more conceptual tools needed for re-defining, in a concrete yet comprehensive manner, obligations of implementation necessary for an achievement of realizing the right in practice. As a distinction to be relied on for any act of transposition whereby treaty-based children's rights are taken over into the specific context of one particular jurisdiction (including its laws, policies and practices) it proved helpful to distinguish between types of obligations, such as 'respect human rights', or 'protect human rights', or 'fulfil human rights'; any particular obligation may then be analysed as to its coherence and consistency from a typological viewpoint.

Sub-Section (1) – Typologies for Bridging the Gap between Rights and Obligations

For clarification of the normative foundations of international human rights several schemes for State duties and obligations have been identified or developed by recent academic writing. Fundamental rights and freedoms were positively defined in many different provisions of the nine core human rights treaties, including the CRC; their foundation is constituted by two central pillars, a 'Rights'-pillar and a 'Duties'-pillar, standing in a relation of correspondence.[274] As will be seen shortly, the recently developed tripartite typology of obligations (*'Respect', 'Protect', 'Fulfil',* or *'RPF'* for short) is one of the best elaborated conceptual tools available internationally for defining and delineating the full range of obligations undertaken under the Convention in particular.[275] Equally, for purposes of refinement

---

273 CRC/C/GC/20 para 19.

274 S Joseph and S Dipnell, 'Scope of Application' in D Moeckli et al (eds), *International Human Rights Law* (3rd ed OUP 2018) 110, 111; W Kälin and J Künzli, *The Law of International Human Rights Protection* (OUP 2009) 77.

275 F Mégret, 'Nature of Obligations' in D Moeckli et al, *International Human Rights Law* (3rd ed OUP 2018) 86, 97.

of the doctrine of international human rights, this tripartite typology has become the main reference for discussing the nature of obligations.[276]

For this analysis the materials used will mainly consist of general comments with a focus on comments drafted by either the ESC Committee or the CRC Committee both of which came to refer extensively to the RPF framework when defining, in detail, obligations of implementation. The legal-doctrinal task to be performed in any case of implementing treaty-based rights into internal legislation is to demonstrate a correspondence that can be established in a methodically reliable manner between express treaty norms on the one hand, and national laws and policies or programmes for civil governments, on the other.[277]

Sub-Section (2) – The Tripartite Typology ('Respect', 'Protect', 'Fulfil')

As indicated above, for my analysis focusing on the right to non-violent education I will widely rely on the tripartite – 'Respect', 'Protect', 'Fulfil' – typology of obligations. Serving as a normative basis to any such duty-scheme is the text of substantive treaty provisions, and of provisions taken from the Convention in this case; as an interpretive rule "ordinary meaning" as stipulated in Article 31 VCLT requires close obedience to the treaty text.

History and Background to the Tripartite Typology

In my introduction to this sub-section I referred to the tripartite typology for State duties and obligations as a recently developed one.[278] This characterization is in relation to the *International Bill of Human Rights* comprising of the 1948 Universal Declaration of Human Rights and both International Covenants (1966), on Civil and Political Rights and on Economic, Social and Cultural Rights respectively.

Other authors, Sarah Joseph and Sam Dipnall among them, refer to the tripartite typology as *'the classical tripartite description of a state's human rights duties, that is, to respect, protect, and fulfil human rights';* in the eyes of these authors that same typology can serve to reveal a more

---

276 Mégret (n 275 above) 86, 97; Kälin and Künzli (n 274) 96.

277 A R Mowbray, *The Development of Positive Obligations under the European Convention of Human Rights by the European Court of Human Rights* (Hart Publishing 2004) 2.

278 See p 90 above.

general duty with regard to private actors.[279] Exactly that seems to be one of this typology's specific merits: as part of a state's duty to protect a person's enjoyment of a human right, it must exercise due diligence by taking reasonable measures to prevent and punish actions by a private actor that prejudice the human rights of another.[280]

The notion of a multiple set of obligations engendered by any specific fundamental right was first articulated by Henry Shue in his work, *Basic Rights: Subsistence, Affluence and US Foreign Policy*.[281] Shue suggested 'a very simple tripartite typology of duties' based on the understanding that with every basic right, three types of duties correlate: duties to avoid depriving, duties to protect from deprivation and duties to aid the deprived.[282] Variations on this tripartite typology of duties were later offered by several commentators, with the terminology of obligations to respect, protect and fulfil human rights being first formulated by the 1987 UN Report on the Right to Adequate Food as a Human Right (Special Rapporteur Asbjorn Eide); in the meantime it is well established as a point of reference for manifold writing and research in the field of international human rights law.[283]

Scope and Content of the Tripartite Typology

In this typology, obligations to respect are negative obligations whereas obligations to protect and fulfil are positive obligations, requiring state protection from the acts of other persons and other positive action within the power of the State to fulfil a human right respectively.[284] As Shue himself later explained this 'very simple tripartite typology of duties' was not supposed to become a new frozen abstraction to occupy the same rigid

---

[279] Joseph and Dipnall (n 274) 110, 115.

[280] Ibid; CRC/C/GC/13 para 5.

[281] H Shue, *Basic Rights: Subsistence, Affluence, and US Foreign Policy,* (2nd ed Princeton University Press 1996); H J Steiner et al, *International Human Rights in Context* (3rd ed OUP 2007) 187.

[282] Mowbray (n 277) 223 (duty 'to avoid depriving' later reclassified as the duty to 'respect' rights).

[283] D J Harris, M O'Boyle et al (eds), *Law of the European Convention on Human Rights* (2nd ed OUP 2009) 19; *The Maastricht Guidelines on Violations of Economic, Social and Cultural Rights* 20 HRQ (1998) 691, 693; Mégret, 'Nature of Obligations' (Fn 275) 86, 97.

[284] Harris, O'Boyle et al (n 283 above) 19; Kälin and Künzli (n 274) 96.

conceptual space previously held by 'negative rights' and 'positive rights'; rather

> *The constructive point was: look at what it actually takes to enable people to be secure against the standard predictable threats to their rights – focus on the duties required to implement the right.*[285]

Regarding the genesis of this typology which was originally drafted and designed for a context of economic, social and cultural rights, it does not come as a surprise to find that the UN Committee on Economic, Social and Cultural Rights (ESC Committee) subsequently adopted and employed, from its General Comment No. 12 (1999) onwards[286], the tripartite typology.[287] Furthermore, with particular concern for economic, social and cultural rights being grossly violated the 1998 Maastricht Guidelines which are understood to reflect the recent evolution of international law from an international legal expert point of view explain:

> *The obligation to respect requires States to refrain from interfering with the enjoyment of economic, social and cultural rights. Thus, the right to housing is violated if the State engages in arbitrary forced evictions. The obligation to protect requires States to prevent violations of such right by third parties. Thus, the failure to ensure that private employers comply with basic labour standards may amount to a violation of the right to work or the right to just and favourable conditions of work. The obligation to fulfil requires States to take appropriate legislative, administrative, budgetary, judicial and other measures towards the full realization of such rights. Thus, the failure of States*

---

[285] Mowbray (n 277) 224 with reference to the second edition (1996) of Shue's original work.

[286] D McGrogan, 'The Problem of Causality in International Human Rights Law' 65 ICLQ (2016) 615, 619. U Khaliq and R Churchill (n 21) 199, 209.

[287] General comments issued by the ESC Committee with further reference to ICESCR articles: General Comment 12 (E/C.12/1999/5), *The right to adequate food (art. 11)*, para 15; General Comment 13 (E/C.12/1999/10), *The right to education (art. 13)*, paras 46–47, 50; General Comment 14 (E/CN.4/2000/4), *The right to the highest attainable standard of health (art. 12)*, paras 33–37; General Comment 15 (E/C.12/2002/11), *The right to water (articles 11, paragraph 1, and 12)*, paras. 20–29; General Comment 18 (E/C.12/GC/18), *The right to work (art. 6)*, paras. 22–28; General Comment 19 (E/C.12/GC/19), *The right to social security (art. 9)*, paras. 43–51; I E Koch, 'Dichotomies, Trichotomies or Waves of Duties' 5 H R L R (2005) 81, 87.

to provide essential primary health care to those in need may amount to a violation.[288]

Exemplifying the tripartite typology of obligations in this way, the expert authors of the Maastricht Guidelines contributed widely to the development of international law as envisaged by Art 38 ICJ-Statute where certain kinds of teachings were designated as a subsidiary source of international law.[289]

Four Specific General Comments

Through a twofold methodological approach the CRC Committee adopted that same tripartite typology, by referencing and thereby endorsing general comments issued by other monitoring bodies and by creating its own implementation categories, including the tripartite typology.[290] The aim of the exercise was to demonstrate that States Parties have an obligation under international law to respect, protect and fulfil children's rights as they were first stipulated in substantive provisions of the Convention. Thus, reference to general comments may serve to augment the Convention's potential by providing more detailed guidance on what State Parties must do to ensure compliance under various themes.[291] The four core documents to be reviewed here as evidence for use of the tripartite typology begin with General Comment No. 14 (best interests) and continuing through General Comment No. 17 (rest, leisure and play).[292] Here, I will look at this set of documents in combination.

---

288 'Guideline 6' *Maastricht Guidelines* (n 283) 691, 694 (underscores are italicized in the original); Koch (n 287 above) 81, 82.

289 See Fn 38 above ('sources').

290 General comments issued by the CRC Committee with express reference to CRC articles: No. 14 (CRC/C/GC/14) on the right of the child to have his or her best interests taken as a primary consideration (art. 3, para. 1) para 16 ; No. 15 (CRC/C/GC/15) on the right of the child to the enjoyment of the highest attainable standard of health (art 24) para 71; No. 16 (CRC/C/GC/16) on State obligations regarding the impact of the business sector on children's rights, para 26; No. 17 (CRC/C/GC/17) on the right of the child to rest, leisure, play, recreational activities, cultural life and the arts (art. 31) para 54; Referring to the tripartite typology in an unspecified manner, see CRC/C/GC/13 para 59.

291 Kilkelly (n 3) 179, 183.

292 *GC*'s 14 through 17 are more or less identically dated.

Evidence for the Tripartite Typology

The easiest case for description and analysis proves to be General Comment No. 14 on the right of the child to have his or her best interests taken as a primary consideration. Speaking about the nature and scope of obligations the Committee reminds all signatories to the Convention about a handful of "parameters" that should be borne in mind when giving full effect to the child's best interests, such as the universal, indivisible, interdependent and interrelated nature of children's rights.[293] Furthermore, '[T]*he obligation of State Parties to respect, protect and fulfil all the rights in the Convention*' is just another such parameter to be borne in mind. In General Comment No. 15 on the right of the child to the enjoyment of the highest attainable standard of health, *'State parties' obligations to respect, protect and fulfil'* are dealt with under *'Obligations and Responsibilities'*.[294] General Comment No. 16 concerned about the impact of the business sector on children's rights has a section titled *'The obligation to respect, protect and fulfil'* belonging to the comment's main part on the *'Nature and scope of State obligations'*.[295] Here, the Committee deals with three types of obligations in turn; another two paragraphs are added to that same section dealing with 'Remedies and Reparations' consecutively.[296] Finally, General Comment No. 17 on the right to rest and leisure has a whole part treating *'States parties' obligations'* where each of the particular obligations is detailed in turn.[297] Accordingly, where I can see consistency in the work of the Committee is in subsuming the tripartite typology under the scope and nature of State duties and obligations as displayed in these (and other) General Comments.

Special Rapporteur using the Tripartite Typology

Similarly, this tripartite typology was also employed and further developed through the work of the UN Special Rapporteur on the Right to Education (SREd).[298] Thus, the SREd finds that governments have specific

[293] CRC/C/GC/14 para 16.
[294] CRC/C/GC/15 paras 00 to 04.
[295] CRC/C/GC/16 paras 26–29.
[296] CRC/C/GC/16 paras 30,31.
[297] CRC/C/GC/17 paras 54–59.
[298] UN document A/HRC/23/35 dated 10 May 2013 (Report of the Special Rapporteur on the right to education, Kishore Singh, thematically focused on justiciability of the

obligations which must be fulfilled when implementing the right to education: an obligation to respect the right to education implies that States must avoid measures that hinder or prohibit the enjoyment of the right to education. Furthermore, an obligation to protect aims at State Parties to take measures that prevent third parties from interfering with the enjoyment of the right to education. And, finally, an obligation to fulfil (facilitate) the right to education implies that States must take positive measures that enable and assist individuals and communities to enjoy the right to education; additionally, the obligation to fulfil (provide) is stated here with reference to a more general rule requiring that States Parties must provide means for the fulfilment of Economic, Social and Cultural Rights when an individual or group is unable, for reasons beyond their control, to realize the right themselves by the means at their disposal.[299]

To sum up, the tripartite typology developed in consistency with ideas explained in general comments may help to build up the wider interpretive community, which by itself makes for an important contribution as a necessary feature of treaty interpretation.[300]

Sub-Section (3) – The Principle of Effectiveness

As a conceptual tool for elaborating on the right to non-violent education, I will mainly rely on the tripartite typology of obligations just described. Before turning to the demanding task of elaboration a final outlook is to be taken on another scheme of 'negative' or 'positive' obligations which is widely in use for an interpretation of ECHR provisions as demonstrated by the jurisdiction of the European Court in Strasbourg.[301] This scheme has been developed grounding on the treaty law principle of effectiveness implying that treaties are presumed to have a definite force and effect; thus, a treaty may be interpreted expansively in order to ensure that all of its provisions have an independent non-superfluous meaning.[302] Seen through the lens of the tripartite typology, obligations to respect are negative obligations by which the State is required to abstain from interference with human rights held by individuals. Obligations to protect and to fulfil are positive

right to education).

299 Special Rapporteur Kishore Singh (n 298 above).

300 Tobin (n 201) 1, 49.

301 Harris, O'Boyle et al (n 283) 18 (reference to Article 1 ECHR).

302 M Fitzmaurice, 'Interpretation' (n 203) 739, 751.

obligations, requiring respectively State protection from the acts of other (private) persons and other positive actions by which the State lawfully operates so as to fulfil a human right.[303] As will be seen later in more detail the ECtHR, in many instances, refers to the CRC and to materials issued by the Committee which helps to understand that in many respects the responsibilities *vis-à-vis* their children do overlap for many European States; all of them are also States Parties to the CRC.

Chapter 2 – The Right to Non-violent Education and the Tripartite Typology

Introduction

As indicated already[304] this second chapter will do the work of translation and application of a framework which was developed on the basis of a tripartite typology of treaty-based obligations. Generally defined in correlation to the right to non-violent education specific obligations will be elaborated through a detailed and itemised application of this RPF framework.Thus, inspired by a sequence of protective measures found in Article 19(2) CRC this research will gravitate around topics such as 'criminalization' or 'investigation', 'reporting' and 'inspection'. As the Committee sees it, States Parties under Article 19 CRC assumed special obligations which may be summarized:

> *These special obligations are due diligence and the obligation to prevent violence or violations of human rights, the obligation to protect child victims and witnesses from human rights violations, the obligation to investigate and to punish those responsible, and the obligation to provide access to redress human rights violations.*[305]

With regard to children and their right to be free from violence the Committee, furthermore, stated that "appropriate measures" (Article 19 CRC) require an integrated, cohesive, interdisciplinary and coordinated system of protection which incorporates the full range of measures identified in paragraph 1 (legislative, administrative, social and educational),

303 Harris, O'Boyle et al (n 283) 19; Mégret (n 275) 86, 97.
304 See p 89 above.
305 CRC/C/GC/13 para 5.

across the full range of interventions listed in paragraph 2 (identification, reporting, referral, investigation, treatment and follow-up of instances of child maltreatment).[306] For all purposes of building up this kind of integrated system of protection, therefore, the tripartite typology of obligations will have to come in as an interpretive device applied in relation to all relevant treaty provisions found in the Convention and other instruments pertinent to the topic.[307]

First Section: An Applied Framework of 'Respect', 'Protect' and 'Fulfil'

One of the earliest and also one of the most comprehensive explanations about the specific content of the tripartite typology stems from a General Comment, issued by the ESC- Committee and dealing with the right to education as a human right of "everyone", including children.[308] Clearly and straightforwardly, the key message from this foundational document (ICESCR) is stated as follows: '[L]*ike all human rights, the right to education imposes three types of obligations on States parties, namely the obligations to respect, to protect and to fulfil human rights.*'[309] Taken together with those special obligations under Article 19 CRC as they were re-stated above, a set of specific obligations which are flowing from the right non-violent education may be unpacked and unfolded.

Second Section: Duties and Obligations to Respect the Right to Non-violent Education

Following a brief re-statement of how this specific 'Respect'- type of obligation was defined it will be deducted in the following how, as a State Party to the Convention, any State comes under an obligation to

---

306 CRC/C/GC/13 paras 39, 45; On 'appropriateness' as a general requirement, see Fn 242 above.

307 Articles 3, 19 CRC (protection from violence) and Articles 28, 29 CRC (quality education); Other relevant instruments include the International Covenant on Civil and Political Rights (Articles 23, 24 ICCPR) and the International Covenant on Economic, Social and Cultural Rights (Article 10 ICESCR).

308 E/C.12/1999/10 (8 December 1999) paras 43–57; Committee referencing this ESCR general comment, see CRC/C/GC/16 (7 February 2013) para 25;

309 E/C.12/1999/10 para 46 *General Comment No. 13, The right to education (article 13 of the Covenant).*

abstain from inflicting violence on children in education, and also how the State is to refrain from funding third parties who inflict violence on children in education. As an obligation specified in correspondence to the right to non-violent education, an obligation to respect requires that the State – operating by means of its organs or agents – does not take any action that would result in preventing or limiting or otherwise interfering in the exercise by children, individually or as a group, of their right to non-violent education.[310] This particular type of obligation requires that whatever action is taken by the State in relation to educational or schooling systems operating under its jurisdiction, no element of interpersonal violence – physical, mental or emotional – must ever be included, directly or indirectly, to the detriment of schoolchildren or students affected. In this, no differentiation can be allowed as regards children being independently educated or in an outsourced institution partially or completely funded by the State, as opposed to children being educated in State schools fully instituted and directly managed by government authorities themselves; contrary to Article 2 CRC, this would clearly amount to a case of discrimination.[311] As stated by *GC 16* treating the nature and scope of State obligations in relation to the private (business) sector, States are not relieved of their obligations under the Convention when their functions, such as providing for institutionalised education in schools, are delegated or outsourced to a private business or non-profit organization.[312] By way of analogy one may also refer to a jurisprudence of the ECtHR holding that the State cannot absolve itself from its responsibility regarding the fundamental right of everyone to education by delegating its obligations to private bodies or individuals such as an independently managed educational institution.[313]

Principal Duty-Bearers: State Actors

As a baseline this obligation to respect implies that States should not

---

[310] K Hausler et al (eds), *Protecting Education in Insecurity and Armed Conflict: An International Law Handbook* (BIICL 2012) 17; E/C.12/1999/10 para 47.

[311] See Fn 272 above and accompanying text.

[312] CRC/C/GC/16 para 25; on *GC 16* see also Fn 256 above.

[313] *Costello-Roberts* v *UK* App no. 13134/87 (ECtHR, 25 March 1993) para 27 referenced also in *O'Keeffe* v *Ireland* (n 1) para 153 with a focus on the State's "positive obligation to protect".

directly or indirectly facilitate, aid and abet any violation or infringement of children's rights; furthermore, States have a general obligation to ensure that all relevant actors in the field including powerful non-state actors, equally respect children's human rights, in law and in fact.[314] Primarily seen as duty-bearers in this context of an obligation to respect are all official organs of the state, such as governmental or judicial bodies and, moreover, all other agents, individually or collectively, whose actions are directly attributable to that same State as a matter of law or, indeed, as a matter of fact. In this regard, several key situations were identified under international law when specific acts of an independent agent will be attributed to the State under whose (general) jurisdiction this agent is operating, such as when a State does not act to regain control where a certain group takes over an existing educational institution, or when a State encourages a corporate body to manage a school knowing that it had a record of abusing children;[315] whereas in the first scenario the State adopts or acknowledges the act as its own, its encouragement in the second scenario amounts to an issue of complicity in abusive practices.[316]

State to Refrain from Funding Third Parties who Inflict Violence in Education

In relation to its public budget an obligation to respect means that the State shall refrain from interfering with the enjoyment of children's rights, by, for example, discriminating against certain groups of children in budget decisions, or withdrawing funding or diverting resources away from existing programmes actually providing for children's enjoyment of educational rights.[317] Conversely, under an obligation to respect the right to non-violent education, the State must refrain from actively investing public resources in any privatized educational facilities which have no proven record of respecting children's rights.[318] As regards an obligation to ensure that rights-holders are equally respected by relevant non-state actors,

---

[314] CRC/C/GC/16 para 26; Joseph and Dipnall (n 274) 110, 115; Kälin and Künzli (n 274) 78, 81.

[315] *Scozzari and Giunta* v *Italy* Apps nos. 39221/98 and 41963/98 (ECtHR, 13 July 2000) paras 212, 216.

[316] Hausler et al (n 310) 27; Hakimi (n 226) 341, 357 (Delegates).

[317] CRC/C/GC/19 para 27.

[318] CRC/C/GBR/CO/5 para 18.

governments should take additional measures to make sure that public finances and other resources are exclusively invested in business activities, including commercially provided educational and alternative care services that are clearly committed to respect all human rights of children.[319] Equally, the State must desist, as an issue of complicity, from any permanent funding of schools as long as children's rights are not adequately realised by those responsible for the management and operation of the school or other educational institution concerned.

Especially with respect to private service providers in the field of care and education for schoolchildren, whether they operate for profit or as non-profit organisations, States Parties come under an obligation to adopt such legislative and administrative measures as were found to be indispensible for ensuring that children's rights are fully respected in practice.[320] Accordingly, with regard to the funding of educational institutions an obligation to respect predominantly implies a clear child-focused prioritisation of school-management found to be in compliance with CRC standards.

Third Section: Duties and Obligations to Protect the Right to Non-violent Education

Introduction

Generally, an obligation to protect children's rights envisages a State in action integrating its protective activities within a set of (legislative, administrative, social or educational) measures to be taken for prevention against any infringement or violation of rights originating in fact from third-party behaviour. Thus, it requires States to restrain third parties from interference with an enjoyment of their human rights by children.[321] Third-party behaviour as a technical term envisages other private individuals or groups in society, including business enterprises, charities or faith-based organisations independently operating within the jurisdiction. For finding itself under that same protective obligation, a duty-bearing State need not

[319] Principle 4 of the 2011 *UN Guiding Principles on Business and Human Rights* reads (extract): '*States should take additional steps to protect against human rights abuses by business enterprises … that receive substantial support and services from State agencies …* '; Grabenwarter (n 31) 394 (funding or co-funding of private schools).

[320] CRC/C/NZL/CO/5 para 13; Harris, O'Boyle et al (n 283) 704 (Article 2 P1 ECHR and the provision of state subsidy to private schools).

[321] See Fn 288 and accompanying text.

be participating in any action that by itself constitutes an infringement or violation of rights.[322]

Any treaty-based obligation "to respect and to ensure to all individuals" (Article 2 ICCPR) their human rights, or "to secure to everyone" (Article 1 ECHR) their human rights, will never be fully discharged if those rights are not equally protected against infringement originating from (privately controlled) third-party behaviour.[323] In an analogous manner it was stipulated in Article 2(1) CRC that all Convention rights must be respected and ensured to each child without discrimination which generally affirms that same level of an obligation to protect against third-party infringement. Above it was found, by way of treaty interpretation, that an obligation to protect generally implies a State that should act to prevent, prohibit and penalize foreseeable violations or infringements of human rights. As part of a state's duty to protect a person's enjoyment of his or her human rights, that same state must exercise due diligence[324] by taking reasonable measures to prevent and punish actions by a private actor that prejudice the human rights of another.[325] With particular concern for the right to non-violent education this type of 'protect'-obligation implies that children actively enjoying their educational rights in a schooling context must be kept safe from other private individuals engaging in violent or abusive behaviour that negatively impacts on rights-holding subjects.[326] Thus, protective obligations will be triggered independently from the source of threat with a focus on every individual child as a subject of educational rights that shall be enjoyed in any setting characterised as either 'private' or 'public'.

Sub-section (1) – Criminalization of violence

According to the Committee, States have an obligation to adopt all measures necessary to ensure that adults responsible for the care, guidance and upbringing of children will respect and protect children's rights; appropriate steps must be taken for prevention, criminal investigation and prosecu-

---

322 Hakimi (n 226) 341, 342.
323 Kälin and Künzli (n 274) 103.
324 Fn 305.
325 Hausler et al (n 310) 18; *Maastricht Guidelines* (n 283) para 18 "Acts by non-state actors".
326 E/C.12/1999/10 para 47 (education under Article 13 ICESCR); F Coomans (n 139) 232, 240.

tion of violent activities against children.[327] Article 19(1) CRC includes all forms of violence against children from which they must be protected by implementing measures, such as reporting, investigation or judicial involvement; more specifically, the duty to criminalize (or to penalise) certain forms of violent or abusive behaviour shall be discussed from a perspective of implementing children's rights to non-violent education.[328] Does the Convention require as an international obligation that States Parties have a general offence of child sexual abuse on their law-books, in order to comply fully with the terms of Article 19(1) CRC? Is the introduction of such an offence including a detailed list of clearly identified sexual activities in this child protection context, a must under the Convention?

For this context, a program of 'criminalization' generally refers to starting legislative procedures for an institutionalisation of legal-societal norms addressing human conduct that, if violated, might attract penal sanctions.[329] Making particular instances of child maltreatment (including preparatory activities) a crime thus contains an acknowledgement that, in principle, children and their rights are a matter of public concern involving the community as a whole. Thereby, as a policy measure criminalization articulates a particularly strong expression of disapproval made on behalf of the wider community which exactly corresponds to the spirit of the Convention as expressed through its preamble and Articles 19, 34 CRC (right to protection from all forms of violence and sexual abuse) in particular.[330]

In this way postulating a duty to criminalize violent behaviour perpetrated against children is fully consistent with the comment given by *GC 13* in connection with 'prevention' as a treaty term (Article 19 CRC): *'The Committee emphasizes in the strongest terms that child protection must begin with proactive prevention of all forms of violence as well as explicitly prohibit all forms of violence'*.[331] Another voice strongly arguing in the direction of criminalization may be found in the *World Report* (including

[327] CRC/C/GC/13 paras 9, 41, 46.

[328] Under CRC criminalization is seen as an obligation for the creation of statutory offences punishable within the State as a matter of its domestic law.

[329] P McGorrery, 'The Philosophy of Criminalisation' Crim L Philo (2018) 185, 187; R Wacks, *Law: A Very Short Introduction* (OUP 2008) 59 .

[330] CRC, Preamble 9th para ('... special safeguards and care, including appropriate legal protection, ... '); Lenzer (n 26) 276, 289.

[331] CRC/C/GC/13 para 46; also para 41 ('... ensuring absolute prohibition ... '), para 9 ('... to prohibit violence ... ').

the SRSG thematic report), where under the heading of *"Secure children's legal protection from violence"* it is recommended as a response:

> *Secure children's legal protection from violence by introducing effective legislation that explicitly prohibits all forms of violence against children in all settings, including in schools, setting out clear penalties for those who perpetrate violence against children, … .*[332]

Assuming that sexual violence against children appears to be a very grave assault on the rights and human dignity of the child, only criminal penalties will suffice for effective deterrence.

Although, as a legal system, the European system for the protection of human rights is not a core subject-matter of this study, a case may be made out for the two systems, CRC based on the one hand and ECHR based on the other, providing broadly equivalent levels of protection; thus, the European Court regularly makes reference to the Convention and to general comments issued by the Committee in cases concerning violence against children.[333] As such, ECHR law can add value to this study by introducing case law concerning specific sets of facts and instances of violence against children in a way that the CRC system has not generated up to now. Though it is to be acknowledged that the ECtHR is not claiming to interpret the CRC, a claim can be made that ECHR case law might provide a reasonable indication of how the Committee might view a specific situation were it to come before them, in a context of periodic reporting or an OP3 complaint.[334] It will therefore be interesting to see what under ECHR the implications of an obligation to protect are, since Baroness Hale in the House of Lords had observed: *'The* [ECtHR] *has taken particular note of the vulnerability of children in its judgments on the obligations of the state to protect people from inhuman or degrading*

---

[332] *Tackling Violence in Schools* (n 46) 40 (Conclusion Nr 2).

[333] Fn 349 below including the ECtHR case of *X and Y* v *the Netherlands* which appears to be the leading European case regarding an obligation to criminalize; European Agency for Fundamental Rights, *Handbook on European Law relating to the rights of the child* (Luxembourg 2015) 28, 114.

[334] Optional Protocol to the Convention on the Rights of the Child on a Complaints Procedure (2011); see also CRC/C/GC/13 para 47 where the case of *Olsson* v *Sweden (No.1)*, App no 10465/83 (ECtHR, 24 March 1988) is referenced for illustrative purposes.

treatment'.[335] To which extent this adjudicative practice from Europe overlaps with what may validly be assumed to be an obligation under the Convention as an instrument of universal applicability, will then become obvious from the following.[336]

ECHR Case law

Fundamentally, Article 1 ECHR obliges State parties to secure to everyone – including children – within their jurisdiction the rights and freedoms defined in the European Convention and its protocols. As explained by Mowbray with regard to the development of positive obligations under the European Convention on Human Rights:

> *One of the most prevalent types of positive obligation is the duty upon states to take reasonable measures to protect individuals from infringement of their Convention rights by other private persons. At its most basic level this positive obligation may be satisfied by the respondent state having adequate domestic legal provisions criminalizing the conduct which threatens another's Convention rights.*[337]

In that sense, under ECHR specific articles implying an obligation to protect in respect of children as holders of rights and freedoms include the freedom from inhuman and degrading treatment (Article 3 ECHR) and also the right to privacy and family life (Article 8 ECHR); regarding their scope of protection both provisions show a strong concern for the protection of an individual against interference with his or her integrity as a person, physically, mentally and emotionally.[338]

---

335 J Tobin, 'Judging the Judges: Are they Adopting the Rights Approach in Matters Involving Children?' Melbourne Univ L Rev (2009) 579, 610 referencing E *v* Chief Constable of the Royal Ulster Constabulary [2009] 1 AC 536, 543;

336 *Siliadin v France* App no 73316/01 (ECtHR, 26 July 2005) para 87 where the content of Articles 19, 32 CRC is explained with a view on the prohibition of slavery and forced labour under Article 4 ECHR.

337 Mowbray (n 277) 225; U Kilkelly, 'Protecting children's rights under the ECHR: the role of positive obligations' 61 NILQ (2010) 245.

338 Grabenwarter (n 31) para 2/Art 3; paras 7, 73/Art 8; *Siliadin v France* (n 336) paras 79, 89; *Söderman v Sweden* App no 5786/08 (ECtHR, 12 November 2013) para 80.

Freedom from Inhuman and Degrading Treatment (Article 3 ECHR)

Under Article 3 ECHR (Freedom from inhuman treatment), as the ECtHR holds, an obligation to protect may as well arise in circumstances where a private perpetrator was the cause of maltreatment which, by itself, must attain 'the minimum level of severity' as indicated by the wording in this article and further clarified in several judgements. As the Court found, children in particular are entitled to State protection, in the form of effective deterrence, against serious breaches of their personal and bodily integrity.[339] Along this line of reasoning States are seen to have an obligation to adopt criminal law provisions by virtue of which practices such as torture or similarly degrading treatment are penalised, and to apply them in practice.[340]

The leading ECHR case for this type of an obligation to criminalize was *A* v *United Kingdom* where the applicant was a 7 year old boy who was repeatedly and with considerable force caned by his stepfather.[341] When the boy was about 9 years old, his stepfather was charged with assault of which he was subsequently acquitted on the defence of reasonable chastisement.[342] The ECtHR was unanimous in its judgement that the beating of the applicant was sufficiently serious to fall within the scope of an Article 3 freedom from inhuman or degrading treatment. According to this judgment States were required to take measures designed to ensure that individuals within their jurisdiction are not subjected to inhuman or degrading treatment or punishment, including such ill-treatment administered by private individuals.[343] Similarly, the Court also held that the State is under an obligation to provide for criminal sanctions regarding the threat originating from third-party behaviour in the case of rape; crimes of this seriousness

[339] *Siliadin v France* (n 336) para 81 (referencing, at para 87, Articles 19, 32 CRC).

[340] Ibid para 89.

[341] *A v UK* App no 25599/94 (ECtHR, 23 September 1998); An obligation of preventing ill-treatment by a private person was first examined in *Costello-Roberts v UK* App no 13134/87 (ECtHR, 25 March 1993) where the Court held that a State must provide appropriate legal protection against disciplinary corporal punishment in private schools.

[342] Harris, O'Boyle et al (n 283) 106; O'Mahony (Fn 96) 315, 324; U Kilkelly,'The Best of Both Worlds for Children's Rights' 23 HRQ (2001) 308, 317.

[343] Harris, O'Boyle et al (n 283) 107; Mowbray (n 277) 158.

must be effectively investigated for the wider purpose of criminal prosecution.[344]

As the leading case for a finding of protective obligations regarding this particular kind of sexual violence (rape) perpetrated against minors the ECtHR decided *MC v Bulgaria* where the applicant was 14 years of age when she was raped by two men of her acquaintance.[345] Although intimate bodily interference was documented by medical examination, no criminal prosecution of the perpetrators identified followed since it could not be established that the minor victim had resisted or called for help in the course of the incident. The Court found a violation of Article 3 (prohibition of degrading treatment) and of Article 8 (right to respect for private life), noting in particular that there was an universal trend towards recognising lack of consent as the essential element in the definition of rape or sexual abuse as a crime. As a consequence, States came under an obligation to treat every non-consensual act of sexual interference as a matter for criminalization, regardless of any physical resistance shown by the victim of a particular case.[346] Moreover, the Court found that the principle of effective deterrence obliges States not just to enact laws criminalizing rape, but also to apply them in practice through effective investigation and prosecution.[347]

Right to private and family life (Article 8 ECHR)

In respect of the individual as a holder of protective rights and also regarding the seriousness of any interference into this private sphere of protection, under Article 8 ECHR the European Court holds that States have an obligation to establish and apply a criminal law system effectively punishing all forms of rape and sexual abuse.[348] Great significance is attached to the protection of minors and other vulnerable individuals; most pertinently, the seminal case of *X and Y v the Netherlands* found that an absence of legislation criminalizing sexual advances to a mentally handi-

---

[344] Grabenwarter (n 31) para 18/Art 3;

[345] *MC v Bulgaria* App no 39272/98 (ECtHR, 4 December 2003); A R Mowbray, *Cases, Materials and Commentary on the European Convention on Human Rights* (3rd ed OUP 2012) 157.

[346] *MC v Bulgaria* (n 345 above) para 166; *Lanzarote* Explanatory Report (Fn 155) para 121 on Article 18 (Sexual Abuse).

[347] *MC v Bulgaria* (n 345) para 153; C O'Mahony, 'Child Protection and the ECHR: Making Sense of Positive and Procedural Obligations' 27 IJCR (2019) 4.

[348] Grabenwarter (n 31) para 73/Art 8 ECHR; *Söderman v Sweden* (Fn 338) para 78.

capped adolescent meant that the State had failed to fulfil a positive obligation to protect the rights of the victim.[349] This judgement was given for a context of 'private life' (Article 8 ECHR) which also covered the physical and moral integrity of the person involved.[350] In *X and Y* a girl with a mental handicap was raped, in a home for children with mental disabilities where she lived, the day after her sixteenth birthday by a relative of the person in charge. She was traumatized by the experience but deemed unfit to sign an official complaint given her low mental age. Her father signed in her place, but proceedings were not brought against the perpetrator because, under national laws applicable to the case, the girl had to make the complaint herself.[351]

As fundamental values and essential aspects of private life were at stake, the Court reasoned that only criminal law provisions were found to be sufficient for effective deterrence from sexually abusive behaviour threatening the bodily integrity of a handicapped person of minority age. From this perspective which was equally inspired by Articles 19 and 37 CRC, children in particular, are entitled to State protection, in the form of effective deterrence against serious breaches of their personal integrity.[352] Similarly, in the case of *Söderman* v *Sweden* which concerned an isolated act of covert, non-consensual filming of a child for sexual purposes, the Court considered that, regarding serious acts such as rape and sexual abuse of children, it falls upon the State to ensure that efficient criminal law provisions are in place.[353] What becomes clear from this jurisprudence based on a right to respect for private life is that violent offences against children fall into a category of cases where the effective application of criminal law is required to ensure adequate protection from breaches of their physical integrity.[354]

---

[349] *X and Y v The Netherlands* App no 8978/80 (ECtHR, 26 March 1985); Grabenwarter (n 31) para 73/Art 8 ECHR.

[350] U Kilkelly, 'Article 8: The Right to Respect for Private and Family Life, Home and Correspondence' in D J Harris, M O'Boyle et al (eds) *Law of the European Convention* (2nd ed OUP 2007) 361, 382.

[351] Mowbray (n 277) 225; Kilkelly (n 350 above) 384.

[352] Mowbray (n 345) 145, 159; *Terminology Guidelines* (n 53) 15; Kälin and Künzli (n 274) 108.

[353] *Söderman* v *Sweden* (n 338) para 51 (referencing Articles 19, 34 CRC).

[354] Kilkelly (n 350) 361, 384.

Council of Europe Convention on the Protection of Children ('Lanzarote')

Although constitutionally rooted in the Council of Europe system for the protection of human rights this international law instrument stands out for its focus and determination regarding the protection of children against sexual exploitation and sexual abuse in Europe. Adopting its *Council of Europe Convention on the Protection of Children against Sexual Exploitation and Sexual Abuse* dated ('Lanzarote') 25 October 2007 the member States of the Council made a strong commitment to taking seriously the right of the child to such measures of protection as are required by his or her status as a minor, on the part of his or her family, society and the State.[355] Briefly referencing Article 34 CRC (Sexual Exploitation of Children) in particular, the *Lanzarote* drafters collectively demonstrated a willingness to prevent and combat sexual exploitation and sexual abuse of children wherever they happen to occur within the wide Council of Europe area and beyond; and also to protect the rights of child victims of abuse.[356]

At the core of this Convention its chapter VI (Articles 18–29) is all about criminalization (titled 'Substantive criminal law'), creating an obligation for member States to take all necessary legislative measures to ensure that certain ways of conduct deemed destructive to children's health and psycho-social development are effectively criminalized within their own jurisdiction.[357] Thus, an impressive list of special offences to be created at the internal level is set up for *Lanzarote*: 'sexual abuse', 'child prostitution', 'child pornography', 'corruption of children', and also 'solicitation of children for sexual purposes', to name but a few headings from the Convention's sixth chapter. Although a regional instrument many principles and rules stipulated through *Lanzarote* in some detail make sense for children everywhere in Europe and beyond.[358] As a result, no great tension would seem to be here since the Committee, through its *GC 13* in parti-

[355] Council of Europe Treaty Series (CETS) 201, 3rd preambular paragraph.

[356] *Lanzarote* (n 355 above) 10th preambular para and Article 1 Nr 1(a)(b) – Purposes of the Convention.

[357] Finally, in 2020 the Irish Minister for Justice announced Government approval for the ratification of the Lanzarote Convention (Press release originally published on 16 December 2020).

[358] *Lanzarote*, at 10th preambular para, references, *inter alia*, Article 34 CRC and also the 2000 OPSC as instruments belonging to the CRC system.

cular, emphasized in the strongest terms that all forms of violence against children must be prohibited implying that acts of child sexual abuse are criminalized in effect.[359]

Article 28 *Lanzarote* elaborates on a set of factual constellations to be criminalized as aggravating circumstances, and these situations defined *in abstracto* seem to be corresponding to typified situations as anticipated by Article 19 CRC (' ... *while in the care of parents, legal guardians or any other person who has the care of the child.*'); through that wording in Article 28(d) *Lanzarote* they were defined: ' ... *the offence was committed by a member of the family, a person cohabiting with the child or a person having abused his or her authority*'.[360] Not only were specified acts of sexual abuse clearly defined as a criminal offence, but these offences were also marked for harsher sanctions to be attributed to all perpetrators lawfully convicted, such as educators or teachers who are regularly understood to be 'a person in authority' in relation to the child entrusted to his or her care for educational purposes.[361]

Sub-section (2) – 'Mandatory Reporting' as an Obligation under the Convention

Within this wider framework of typified 'Protect'-obligations the question arises whether mandatory reporting as a government policy institutionalised for the protection of minors is equally covered by that same type of obligation. As listed in Article 19(2) CRC the range of interventions includes 'reporting of instances of child maltreatment' as a protective measure among others such as 'referral', 'investigation' and 'judicial involvement'.[362] Undertaken for the fulfilment of a State's duty to protect, a policy of 'mandatory reporting' might function as a measure that could

---

[359] Fn 331 and accompanying text.

[360] *Lanzarote* Article 28 (*Aggravating Circumstances*); *Lanzarote* Article 18 (Nr 1 b second indent) defines 'Sexual abuse' as intentional conduct engaging in sexual activities with a child where abuse is made of a recognised position of trust, authority or influence; or abuse is made of a situation of dependence (Nr 1 b third indent); as explained in *Lanzarote* Explanatory Report (n 155) para 199, a person having authority refers to anyone who is in a position of superiority over the child including a teacher.

[361] Article 15 *Criminal Law (Sexual Offences) Act* 2017 defines as a 'person in authority' any person who is or has been responsible for the education, supervision, training, care or welfare of the child.

[362] *Implementation Handbook* (n 137) 267.

help to prevent, prosecute and punish acts of violent behaviour originating from private actors. Since my main concern is about implementing the right to non-violent education, special regard must be had to all settings holding themselves out to be of an educational quality, like schools or other places of institutionalized care and education or training.[363] Respecting children and their rights *to*, *in* and *through* education, which are the features of a system for the reporting of child maltreatment that would be CRC compliant in practice?[364]

Mandatory Reporting and its Functions

Speaking in broad functional terms 'mandatory reporting' is a protective strategy for a swift transfer of factual information about abusive situations to an agency or institution which is duly authorized to receive such information and to act upon its receipt; any functioning mandatory reporting system would ensure referrals of child abuse to make their way into the hands of investigators, therefore leading to increases in detection and substantiation.[365] Accordingly, mandatory reporting laws were defined as creating a statutory obligation to report specific forms of child abuse to a government authority where the reporting person knows or reasonably suspects that abuse has occurred.[366] As a matter of fact, many liberal democratic jurisdictions have enacted legislation strictly requiring designated professionals such as doctors, nurses, police and teachers to report suspected cases of severe child abuse and neglect; in the ordinary course of things, many situations of ill-treatment will thus be brought to the attention of child protection agencies.[367]

The Convention's *Legislative History* reveals that one of the earlier proposals of Article 19(2) CRC regarding protective measures of implementation was far more detailed stipulating, *inter alia*, that States Parties must *'provide for the reporting of known and suspected cases of child abuse*

363 Fn 134 ('care setting').

364 Fn 189; L Lundy et al (Fn 211) 364, 369.

365 R Buckley, 'The Children First Bill 2014: A Step in the Right Direction?' 2 Ir Journ Fam L (2015) 34.

366 Ibid 34.

367 B Mathews, 'Exploring the Contested Role of Mandatory Reporting Laws in the Identification of Severe Child Abuse and Neglect' in M Freeman (ed), *Law and Childhood Studies: Current Legal Issues* vol 14 (OUP 2012) 302; *Implementation Handbook* (n 137) 267.

and neglect to the responsible authorities'.[368] Drawing on a general distinction between 'permissive' (for any adult who knows about or suspects child abuse) and 'mandatory' reporting (for certain professionals in relation to their work with children)[369] the policy's core constructive elements are built around the following set of questions: who must become a mandated person for purposes of reporting, what kind of information must be reported and to whom, and what, if any, sanctions for non-reporting must be provided?

My argument, then, is that an (international) obligation to create and initiate a system of mandatory reporting must be deduced from Article 19 CRC, albeit in a version that is clearly focused on the child concerned and also limited to a certain category of severe instances of child maltreatment; in particular, the reporting must be child-centred, not denouncing in character, and the mandate to report must cover all cases of sexual abuse, actually committed or reasonably suspected in good faith. My argument specifically builds on treaty law rules for textual and contextual interpretation, including an object and purpose rule, as laid out in Articles 31 and 32 VCLT.

Treaty Terms

For this study, the main challenge regarding an interpretation of terms lies in the wording of Article 19(2) CRC where 'reporting' as an intervention is actually seen with no mandatory element attached to it, and lies also in the fact distilled from the *travaux préparatoires* that the more detailed earlier proposals were subsequently eliminated and did not make it into the final version of the treaty. In the meantime (since the CRC's coming into force), however, fully reliable documentary reports became available about violence against children, such as the *World Report* but other reports also.[370]

---

368 *Legislative History* (n 131) 515, draft Article 8(a); equally relevant in this context: 'provide immunity for persons reporting cases of child abuse or neglect from prosecution arising out of such reporting, (b)' and 'provide that upon receipt of a report of known or suspected child abuse or neglect an investigation shall be initiated promptly to substantiate the accuracy of the report, (c)'; none of these proposals was taken over into the text of the treaty finally adopted; Detrick (n 164) 322.

369 C Wekerle, 'Resilience in the context of child maltreatment' 37 Child Abuse and Neglect (2013) 93, 95; *Lanzarote* Article 12(2) ('*... encourage any person who knows or suspects ...* '); *Implementation Handbook* (n 137) 267.

370 Fn 42, 43 above.

Learning lessons from these public inquiries one must come to the conclusion that a tailored version of mandatory reporting is generally required for implementing Article 19 CRC as a protection right, and for implementing the right to non-violent education in particular. Taking up 'reporting' as a protective measure listed in Article 19(2) CRC the Committee reads this term as requiring reporting mechanisms to be legislatively instituted for all professionals working directly with children to report instances, suspicion or a risk of violence.[371] As seen by the Committee, *'when reports are made in good faith, processes must be in place to ensure the protection of the professional making the report'*.[372] In effect, this is an interpretation following the ordinary-meaning rule in Article 31 VCLT for an interpretation of Article 19 CRC on the right to protection from all forms of violence.

As a treaty, the object and purpose of the Convention lies in its acceptance and empowerment of human beings below 18 years of age as legal subjects, not objects, and holders of specified human rights to be realised in effect; at a minimum, protective measures of reporting as envisaged by Article 19 CRC must therefore be made obligatory for professionals working directly with children, but should include legal guardians and primary or proxy caregivers as possible reporters.[373] Any mandate to report should be child-centred focusing on the integrity and well-being of the child as a rights-holding agent who is equally entitled to have a schooling life free from violence and abuse.[374] As a consequence, what must, under all circumstances, be reported are facts and dates about concrete situations involving children at risk insofar as those facts (if true) constitute knowledge or reasonable suspicion of sexual abuse perpetrated or threatened against children in education and care. The Committee, targeting domestic law systems in a context of periodic reporting, made it very clear that there must be a legal mechanism to ensure that any suspicion or knowledge about sexual abuse of children will be reported

371 CRC/C/GC/13 para 49; equally relevant are para 50 on 'Referral' and para 51 on 'Investigation'.

372 CRC/C/GC/13 para 49.

373 CRC/C/GC/13 paras 36, 49; K A Svevo-Cianci et al, 'The new UN CRC General Comment 13' 35 Child Abuse and Neglect (2011) 979, 982.

374 Fn 189 and accompanying text.

to, and received by competent authorities as a matter of urgency.[375] Considering adolescent health and development, in respect of institutionalized learning environments the Committee urges States Parties to take all necessary action to prevent and prohibit all forms of violence and abuse, including sexual abuse, and other inhuman, degrading or humiliating treatment or punishment in school, by school personnel as well as among students.[376] As a consequence, the contents of any reporting brought to the attention of competent authorities – 'what' must be reported – are facts and observations about the actual health and well-being of the child including behavioural aspects, such as extreme fears or disorders of a kind indicating adverse violence impacts. This is my argument based on the 'object and purpose'-element in the ordinary meaning rule mentioned above.

Sources

Beyond the Committee's *GC 13*, where I find elements of a children's rights compliant version of mandatory reporting is in Article 12 *Lanzarote;* here the necessary reporting measures were designed as follows.[377] All mandated persons, namely professionals called upon to work in contact with children, have to bring their reporting to the attention of services responsible for child protection; and the content of the reporting is about situations where reasonable grounds exist for believing that a child is the victim of sexual abuse.[378] Seen from a CRC perspective, as explained above, it makes a lot of sense to direct all reporting to the attention of government services responsible for child protection thereby focusing on effective protection of children, and less on prosecution of adult suspects.[379] As may be distilled from concluding observations recently issued, the Committee in effect progresses along the lines suggested here: an obligation to ensure mandatory reporting of cases of sexual abuse is deduced from Article

---

[375] CRC/C/COD/CO/2 para 50 (Democratic Republic of Congo); CRC/C/NZL/CO/5 para 24 (New Zealand); CRC/C/15/Add.85 para 16 (Ireland); see also Fn 380 below.

[376] CRC/GC/2003/4 para 17.

[377] *Lanzarote* Article 12 ('*Reporting suspicion of sexual exploitation or sexual abuse*').

[378] On 'Sexual Abuse' in *Lanzarote* Articles 18, 28 see Fn 360.

[379] CRC/C/GC/13 para 49.

19 CRC as a treaty norm addressing 'Violence against children' which is regularly brought up as a topic for state-reporting purposes.[380]

As regards ECHR jurisprudence, the ECtHR, in the majority opinion for the *O'Keeffe* case, details its assessment about the content of the positive obligation to protect, and this is in reference to an Article 3 ECHR freedom from inhuman or degrading treatment seen in conjunction with an Article 1 ECHR obligation to secure the rights and freedoms defined in the ECHR.[381] Importantly, as this court explains, the nature of child sexual abuse is such, particularly when the abuser is in a position of authority over the child, that the existence of useful detection and reporting mechanisms are fundamental to the effective implementation of the relevant criminal laws.[382] That same generalized assessment is again taken up in order to explain how the perceivable risk of sexual crime by adults against minors should have been addressed through the adoption of '*effective mechanisms for the detection and reporting*' of any ill-treatment by and to a State-controlled body.[383]

To sum up, a system of mandatory reporting to be administratively installed and maintained as an official policy for child protection is a requirement for CRC implementation and for implementing the right to non-violent education in particular; any knowledge or reasonable suspicion about abusive sexual activity involving a minor must become the subject-matter for reporting to competent authorities within the State. Every professional in the field of education, including teaching as well as non-teaching staff, who acquires any such knowledge or to whom a belief about a child being harmed has been disclosed, shall be mandated to report it to a competent authority. For this kind of reporting to become mandatory every act of unjustified non-compliance must be sanctioned but the child involved (as a victim or witness) shall have an option to make his or her opinion heard (Article 12 CRC) possibly leading, in rare cases, to no further action being taken.

---

[380] CRC/C/NZL/CO/5 (New Zealand 2016) para 24, CRC/C/GBR/CO/5 (Great Britain 2016) para 45(a); CRC/C/15/Add.85 para 16 (Ireland 1998); CRC/C/VAT/CO/2 para 44 (Holy See/2014); *Implementation Handbook* (Fn 138) 267 (Ghana, Belize).

[381] *O'Keeffe v Ireland* (n 1) para 148.

[382] ibid para 148 referencing *Juppala* v *Finland* App no 18620/03 (ECtHR, 2 December 2008).

[383] *O'Keeffe v Ireland* (n 1) para 162.

Sub-section (3) – Investigation of Complaints, Reports and Disclosures

In a manner comparable to earlier sub-sections of this chapter, what will be explored in the following is 'Investigation' as an obligation to be implemented domestically under the Convention. States Parties will be seen to come under an international obligation to develop and maintain structured investigative procedures for the protection of children from all forms of physical or mental violence including child sexual abuse. Article 19(2) CRC explicitly mentions 'investigation' as well as 'identification' itemised as protective measures belonging to an extended listing of measures generally required for protection from violence. Seen through the lens of the right to non-violent education what, in terms of treaty implementing measures, is meant by an obligation to investigate into allegations, complaints or reports and disclosures concerning child sexual abuse?

From a legal history point of view it might be worth mentioning that an earlier draft of what later became Article 19 CRC contained a more detailed provision of measures linking 'investigation' to a functional context of criminal law as a legal sub-system: '... *(c) provide that upon receipt of a report of known or suspected child abuse or neglect an investigation shall be initiated promptly to substantiate the accuracy of the report'*.[384] Finally adopted for Article 19(2) CRC an itemised list of protective measures includes 'investigation' as one among several 'effective procedures' installed for the protection from all forms of violence.

What may, nevertheless, be grasped from that step in the Convention's legislative history is the overall importance of implementing legislation to consider what the function of an individual complaint about child abuse shall be in relation to any formal procedure of investigation, administrative or criminal in nature.[385] What an official investigation into a case of suspected child abuse normally produces serves to prepare for an assessment about individual criminal liability falling on an offender, treated as a suspect in court. Also, administrative investigations into allegations of child sexual abuse initiated by the State's child welfare and protection services may lead to steps taken for safety planning with families and for

---

384 *Legislative History* (n 132) 512, 515 (Article 19 – Prevention of Abuse and Neglect); on the triple set of interventions in the draft, see Fn 368 above.

385 On the matter of 'prior complaint requirement' see *O'Keeffe* (n 1) para 170 ('1971 complaint'); *Annual Report* 2021 (n 112) 36.

keeping any potential source of abusive behaviour at a safe distance from children living in their homes and attending their local schools. Conversely, any lack in investigation will further contribute to a widespread practice and perception of de jure and de facto impunity as regards perpetrators of sexual offences against children.[386]

As the Committee generally commented, rigorous but child-sensitive investigation procedures help to ensure that violence against children is correctly identified, and will also help to provide evidence acceptable for court proceedings at state level.[387] As a consequence, what needs to be kept in mind here is a preventive as well as a sanction point of view implying that structured investigations *per se* into allegations of sexual violence against children will help to identify risk factors for individuals or groups of children. In any case, an obligation to conduct this kind of comprehensive investigations into child sexual abuse, statutorily implemented and administratively enforced, may act as a deterrent, to prevent ill-treatment by potential offenders, as perpetrators may fear discovery and punishment when an inquiry is held.[388] Moreover, effective investigations, especially of an administrative kind, will allow for action to be taken to prevent future instances of abuse by the same perpetrator(s). Thus, any obligation to investigate proves to present itself in two different dimensions: first, a procedural one to respond to the individual who made plausible allegations about sexual abuse and carry out an effective investigation; and second, as a substantive one to establish whether the complaint made indicates that further preventive action is needed to protect children at risk of abuse and to prevent ill-treatment from occurring.[389]

Investigation as an Effective Procedure

As a guarantor of human rights and to ensure effective investigative procedures, the State should have taken all necessary legislative or other measures in order to fulfil its international obligations under the Conventi-

386 CRC/C/GC/13 para 55; *Implementation Handbook* (n 137) 269.

387 CRC/C/GC/13 para 51.

388 A R Mowbray (n 345) 157 (implicit duty of investigation based on the *Assenov* judgment referenced at Fn 415 below).

389 *Annual Report of the Special Rapporteur on Child Protection* 2020 (Dr Conor O'Mahony) 37.

on and other relevant treaties.[390] Consequently, protective measures under Article 19 CRC have to be rigorous and effective, but child-sensitive at the same time.[391] Any instance of child maltreatment, especially those originating from the private sphere of a family home or from a similar private care setting, must be properly investigated by the State concerned, as becomes obvious from the wording in Article 19(1) CRC.[392] It is not only about the individual having allegedly acted as a criminal offender, and how his or her past behaviour is investigated and sanctioned that children's rights are primarily concerned; rather, what every single incidence of child maltreatment indicates in the direction of underlying and persisting risk factors or wider implications for the well-being of children is what matters most.[393]

Any treaty-based obligation to initiate official investigations regarding instances of child maltreatment will equally translate into administrative measures for an implementation of the right to be protected against all forms of violence and abuse (Article 4 CRC). Thus, seen through the lens of the right to non-violent education, an obligation to investigate instances of child maltreatment and make investigations effective is of an essentially protective character.[394] Building on evidence from past (abusive) behaviour an effective investigation into allegations of abuse mainly serves the purpose of keeping any potential source of abusive activities away from schoolchildren brought together for their healthy development and education.

Effectively integrating a strong procedural element Article 19 CRC creates international obligations for government authorities to receive every complaint about child abuse having occurred within the State's jurisdiction; thereupon a structured investigative relationship must be established between the complainant on the one hand, and an authorized government agency typically holding investigatory powers on the other.[395] Furthermore, all information received must be made the subject-matter of comprehensive legal and factual examinations consistent in thoroughness with the in-

---

390 Besides Articles 19, 39 CRC, *Lanzarote* and its Chapter VIII (Investigation, prosecution and procedural law) are of crucial importance here.

391 CRC/C/GC/13 paras 51, 57.

392 Fn 134 for 'care setting' (Article 19 CRC).

393 *Lanzarote* Explanatory Report (Fn 155) para 99.

394 A component of 'fulfil' is also involved, see Mégret (n 275) 86, 99.

395 As an international obligation, this duty to investigate encompasses complaints displaying minimal contacts to more than one jurisdiction, such as a perpetrator priest being removed to another country or continent in the meantime.

formation's legal significance indicating a serious human rights violation; as such, this procedural obligation to investigate is engaged as soon as a complaint or a report is made to the police or any authorised agent of the State.[396] Implying that *per se* an investigative procedure of this kind must be effective, it will have to lead to an establishment of all relevant facts of the case and also to an identification of individuals who appear to be responsible for child-related sexual activities of an abusive character. Practically, a large number of investigations into child sexual abuse will not disclose sufficient evidence to allow for a prosecution to criminal standards; in many cases of child sexual abuse an extended period of time elapsed before allegations were brought to the attention of authorities implying that robust evidence will never be easy to obtain.

Clearly, there is a risk of doing more harm than good if investigations are not performed in a way that respects acknowledged standards of child-sensitivity.[397] As a consequence, for the duration of an ongoing investigative procedure (and as part of it) comprehensive care and assistance must be available for the child victim as that same procedure obviously needs to be able to function without parental guidance for the child involved.[398]

ECHR Case law

Many practical examples of an 'investigative relationship' that was found to be deficient or non-existent altogether have been displayed by ECHR case law; reviewing these examples helps to shedding further light on the elements of an effective investigation into child abuse as required for implementing children's rights. A whole series of judgments dealt with cases involving rape or other forms of sexual violence perpetrated against minors where the ECtHR found that obligations to ensure effective official

[396] *O'Keeffe v Ireland* (n 1) paras 170–174.

[397] Thus, child victims of abuse must not repeatedly be interviewed, see *Implementation Handbook* (n 137) 268 with further reference to CRC/C/15/add.210 – Concluding Observations Czech Republic; case of *B v Russia* App no 36328/20 (ECtHR, 7 February 2023) finding a failure to protect the personal integrity of an extremely vulnerable child that lead to her secondary victimisation.

[398] Comprehensive 'witness protection' programmes are in existence, see International Criminal Court, The Office of the Prosecutor, *Draft policy on children* (June 2016) chapter V (paras 54–72); *Lanzarote* Article 31.

investigations were inadequately performed by organs of the State.[399] By way of analogy this jurisprudence lends support to an interpretation of Article 19 CRC and its protective obligation to undertake investigations into instances of child maltreatment: all minimally credible claims about severe ill-treatment made by, or on behalf of children deserve the highest level of attention and thoroughness as a consequence. Not surprisingly, source materials as referred to in the foregoing – Article 19 CRC and *GC 13* - have occasionally been recited in relevant ECHR case law whereby it becomes obvious that State obligations envisaged by either one or the other system (CRC/ECHR) are widely overlapping in effect.[400] Articles 3 and 8 ECHR in particular have been interpreted by the ECtHR in a manner that imposes demanding obligations on individual member States to protect children and their right to be free from violence and sexual abuse; especially since children are generally understood to be extremely vulnerable persons.[401]

In *CAS and CS* v *Romania* the ECtHR referenced Articles 19 and 39 CRC and also made reference to *GC 13*, stressing the importance of prevention and also the need for rigorous and child-sensitive investigation procedures.[402] In a series of cases involving children or adolescents seen as especially vulnerable persons the Court articulated an implicit (procedural) duty of investigation seen as an indispensible extension to substantive guarantees such as the prohibition of inhuman or degrading treatment under Article 3 ECHR.[403] As the Court sees it, even in the absence of any direct State responsibility for acts of violence, Article 3 ECHR must be read in

399 *PM* v *Bulgaria* App no 49669/07 (ECtHR, 24 January 2012); *CAS* and *CS* v *Romania* App no 26692/05 (ECtHR, 20 March 2012); *RIP* and *DLP* v *Romania* App no 27782/10 (ECtHR, 10 May 2012); *IG* v *Republic of Moldova* App no 53519/07 (ECtHR, 15 May 2012); *O'Keeffe* v *Ireland* (n 1); see also O'Mahony (n 347) 660.

400 *Juppala v Finland* (n 382) paras 23, 24 (citing Article 19 CRC verbatim, discussing Concluding Observations); *CAS and CS v Romania* (n 399 above) paras 51–53 (reproducing Articles 19, 34, 39 CRC in full, discussing *GC 13* in detail); *Söderman v Sweden* (n 338) para 51 (citing Articles 19, 34 CRC in full); All Council of Europe member States are simultaneously adhering to the CRC regime.

401 *CAS and CS v Romania* (n 399) paras 52–53; Kilkelly (n 342) 308, 326.

402 *CAS and CS v Romania* (n 399), para 53 with further reference to CRC/C/GC/13 paras 45–58 ("protective measures"); ECtHR explicitly noting, at para 76, that Romania had ratified both, CRC and *Lanzarote*.

403 Mowbray (n 345) 155, 157.

conjunction with Article 1 ECHR stipulating that rights and freedoms shall be secured to everyone within the State's jurisdiction.[404]

For my argument aiming at acknowledgement of an obligation under Article 19 CRC to look beyond routine investigations and establish a child-centred (or child-sensitive) investigative relationship the ECHR case of *CAS* and *CS* v *Romania* proves to be a highly illuminating one. As a leading case in respect of procedural obligations arising under Article 3 ECHR, it concerned an investigation into the allegation of repeated serious and violent sexual abuse of a seven year-old boy.[405] In its judgment the ECtHR found that Romanian authorities should have carried out effective investigations into acts of repeated rape perpetrated against the (applicant) child and should also have made sure that the victim boy had counselling or other forms of assistance such as support from a qualified psychologist for the duration of the investigations.[406] The key principles regarding effective investigation under the ECHR were set out by the Court:

> *Article 3 requires that the authorities conduct an effective official investigation into the alleged ill-treatment even if such treatment has been inflicted by private individuals ...*
>
> *For the investigation to be regarded as 'effective', it should in principle be capable of leading to the establishment of the facts of the case and to the identification and punishment of those responsible. (...).The authorities must have taken the reasonable steps available to them to secure the evidence concerning the incident, including ... eyewitness testimony, forensic evidence ... . Any deficiency in the investigation which undermines its ability to establish the cause of the injuries or the identity of the persons responsible will risk falling foul of this standard, and a requirement of promptness and reasonable expedition is implicit in this context.*[407]

The Court summarised its appreciation of general principles that, following the CRC regime *'a series of measures must be put in place so as to protect children from all forms of violence which includes prevention, redress and reparation'*.[408] Applying these principles to the case at hand

[404] *CAS and CS v Romania* (n 399) para 69.
[405] O'Mahony (Fn 347) 660.
[406] *CAS* and *CS* v *Romania* (n 399) para 82 (also referring to Article 39 CRC 'recovery and reintegration'); again referenced in *O'Keeffe v Ireland* (n 1) para 166.
[407] *CAS and CS v Romania* (n 399) paras 69,70; O'Mahony (Fn 347) 660.
[408] *CAS and CS v Romania* (n 399) para 72.

the Court found that investigations were ineffective because of delays in commencing it and in progressing key aspects such as ordering medical examinations of the victim or questioning the main suspect; authorities involved in the investigation did not try to weigh up the conflicting evidence and made no consistent effort to establish the facts by engaging in a context-sensitive assessment.[409]

As the Court, furthermore, considered

> [T]*he authorities were not mindful of the particular vulnerabilities of young people and the psychological factors involved in cases concerning violent sexual abuse of minors; particularities which could have explained the victim's hesitations both in reporting the abuse and in his description of the facts.*[410]

Thus, efficiency of investigations, in the eyes of the Court, regularly implies that during the investigative proceedings the child victim of sexual abuse must be accompanied by a qualified psychologist if that proves to be a necessary condition for having the facts comprehensively assorted and fully documented.

As regards administrative investigations to be undertaken by a local authority which was or ought to have been aware that the applicant minors were suffering or at risk of abuse, the case of *E* v *UK* is instructive as the Court found that a set of alarming circumstances in the children's life were observable to the authorities concerned.[411] From a perspective of Article 3 ECHR (Prohibition of inhuman or degrading treatment) the Court was satisfied that even if the social services were not actually aware that sexual abuse was inflicted on these children, they should have been aware that those children remained at potential risk; yet the social services failed to discover the exact extent of the problem and, potentially, to prevent further abuse from taking place.[412]

Risk Factors

Unsurprisingly, an analysis in terms of risk factors for the well-being of children lies at the heart of judicial considerations in this case of *E*

---

409 Ibid paras 74, 78.

410 Ibid para 81.

411 *E and others v the United Kingdom* App no 33218/96 (ECtHR, 26 November 2002); more detail on this case, see Fn 859 below.

412 *E and others v the United Kingdom* (n 411 above) paras 96, 97.

and others v UK, and counting among risk factors which, in a comparable situation, must necessarily trigger further investigations to be undertaken by social services are the following: a personal background to one of the adult caretakers of repetitive offending; a lack of acceptance regarding the serious nature of the charges laid against him as an offender; a series of disclosures made by children indicating an element of physical abuse present in their immediate environment; behavioural symptoms showing serious levels of distress and disturbance arising out of the situation of known abuse in their daily environment, among others.[413] Correspondingly, the steps that should have been taken by the services concerned include personalized work with children showing significant distress at their everyday situation which could have led to a further understanding of relationship or group dynamics; a close supervision over one or more of the children who had been living with a known and convicted offender; prompt communication to the social services of disclosures made by a hospitalised child (about violence perpetrated against her) and appropriate response thereupon.[414]

Another set of cases further illuminates on this topic of investigation as an obligation for situations involving a child victim of sexual abuse: the cases both, *Assenov* and *MC* v *Bulgaria* were brought by minors (featuring as applicants) who were essentially claiming violations of their rights under Article 3 ECHR prohibiting torture and inhuman or degrading treatment in absolute terms.[415] Whereas in *Assenov* the applicant was a 14 year old Bulgarian boy of Roma origin who claimed that he was, *inter alia,* beaten with truncheons by three police officers, in *MC* the applicant was a teenage girl who claimed that she was raped by two men none of whom acted in any sort of official capacity. In *Assenov* the ECtHR found a violation of Article 3 ECHR, as the local investigation into the adolescent's complaint of severe physical ill-treatment was not sufficiently thorough; qualified as procedural in character this kind of a violation of rights could arise even in

---

413 Ibid para 95; although this particular case was about abuse within the family home, its considerations are mostly apt for applicability in a school context (schoolhouse or classroom) which seems to be just another care setting.

414 Ibid paras 97, 98.

415 *Assenov and others* v *Bulgaria* App no 24760/94 (ECtHR 28 October 1998); *MC v Bulgaria* (n 345); Mowbray (n 345) 156, 157; European Union Agency, *Handbook* (Fn 333) 115, 116, 121.

circumstances where it has not been established that ill-treatment (beating with truncheons) actually occurred. The Court reasoned that where an individual raises an arguable claim that he or she has been seriously ill-treated by the police or other such agents of the State unlawfully and in breach of Article 3 ECHR, that provision read in conjunction with the State's general duty under Article 1 of the Convention, requires by implication that an effective official investigation must follow; this investigation should be capable of leading to the identification and punishment of those responsible for the mistreatment.[416] Comparably, in *MC* the Court found a violation of Article 3 (and also of Article 8) ECHR based on an assessment that local authorities had not effectively investigated the events that had led to the rape committed by private individuals against the applicant minor. As the Court reasoned, 'investigation' as an obligation under the procedural limb of Article 3 ECHR cannot be considered to be limited solely to cases of ill-treatment by State agents.[417] In effect, what these judgments with express reference to Article 3 ECHR created was a distinct procedural obligation to conduct an official investigation into all claims of ill-treatment which, as an investigative procedure, requires a high degree of thoroughness corresponding to the seriousness of the complaint made on behalf of the child victim; the perpetrators of serious ill-treatment should be sought via effective investigations whether they be State agents or private individuals.[418]

Sub-section (4) – Rigorous School Inspections as an Obligation under CRC

Pursuant to Article 3(3) CRC, States Parties assume an obligation to ensure that institutions, services and facilities responsible for the care or protection of children do conform with the standards established by competent authorities; four distinct areas were specified in this Article to which conformity with established standards relates, namely 'safety', 'health', the 'number and suitability of staff' as well as 'competent supervision'. Consequently, a comprehensive review of the legislative framework applying to child-related institutions and services, whether run directly by the State, or by voluntary and private bodies, is required for implementing Article 3

[416] *Assenov v Bulgaria* (n 415) para 102; Mowbray (n 345) 156; Harris, O'Boyle et al (n 283) 110.
[417] *MC v Bulgaria* (n 345) para 151; Mowbray (n 345) 157; O'Mahony (n 347) 660.
[418] Harris, O'Boyle et al (n 283) 110.

CRC; this review needs to cover the full range of services existent, such as care, including foster care and day care, health and education.[419]

Logically deductible from the wording in Article 3(3) CRC, for any such supervision to be competent standards must be established for institutions, services and facilities, and the State must ensure compliance through appropriate inspection and monitoring.[420] Bearing in mind those areas specifically addressed, namely 'number and suitability of staff' and 'competent supervision', States Parties must ensure that staff possess the appropriate psychosocial qualities and are suitable, sufficiently numerous and well-trained; and that they have access to specialist professional resources and support, including a supervisory and monitoring system for public and private programmes, institutions and services.[421]

Corresponding to the right to non-violent education, an obligation aiming at a system of rigorous school inspections to be instituted and maintained by organs of the State might impose itself on States Parties. Clearly belonging to the range of interventions as stipulated in Article 19(2) CRC are forms of prevention and identification found to be comparable, on an analytic level, to 'reporting', 'referral' and 'investigation' the main function of which is a timely transfer of risk-related information to an agency capable of response; lawfully performed school inspections might well have just this kind of preventive effect with regard to the protection of schoolchildren from violence, injury or abuse.

An Adequate Regime for School Inspections

As illustrated by the ECHR case of *O'Keeffe v Ireland* just having something denoting as a system of School Inspectors existing on paper cannot suffice for adequate protection of schoolchildren as long as their statutory mandate does not cover for inspectors to inquire into or to monitor a teacher's treatment of children.[422] Obviously, what happened within the Irish school system in the absence of adequate inspection regimes underlines the case for school inspections to be regarded as a means of effective

---

[419] *Implementation Handbook* (n 137) 41.

[420] UN Resolution A/HRC/29/L.14/Rev.1 para 2 (Human Rights Council).

[421] CRC/C/GC/7/Rev.1 para 23.

[422] *O'Keeffe v Ireland* (n 1) paras 164, 173; *'Ryan'* vol 1 chapter 14 ("the Brander Chapter") referenced by *O'Keeffe* para 79.

prevention against violence and abuse anywhere.[423] Looking a bit deeper into *O'Keeffe* shows that the ECtHR scrutinized two different quasi-statutory mechanisms on which the Irish Government relied in its argument before the Court, namely 'Reporting' and 'Inspections'.[424] Described as a 'system of School Inspectors' the national Rules pertinent to the system envisaged that regular visits to and examinations of all 'National Schools' had to take place; in particular the manner in which incidental and general inspections were to be carried out and how the work of teachers had to be assessed was detailed through an administrative Circular historically dating from the 1960s, and seemingly never updated.[425] Regarding the foundational task of inspectors to supervise and report upon the quality of teaching and academic performance, the ECtHR found the (historic) mechanism thus outlined to be totally inadequate. As the Court in respect of the (historic) guidelines explained,

> [T]*here was no specific reference* (...) *to an obligation on Inspectors to inquire into or to monitor a teacher's treatment of children, to any opportunity for children or parents to complain directly to an Inspector, to a requirement to give notice to parents in advance of an Inspector's visit or, indeed, to any direct interaction between an Inspector and pupils and/or their parents. The rate of visits by Inspectors* (...) *did not attest to any local presence of relevance.*[426]

Re-reading this judgment through the lens of an enquiry into implementing obligations, it becomes obvious that the absence of an effective inspection regime was one of the key stated reasons for the Court's finding of a violation of ECHR rights in that case.[427] Maybe as yet another approach towards this obligation-focused research it helps to remember what was stated in reaction to the findings of *'Ryan'* which as a Commission of Inquiry report uttered a clear recommendation pointing to the need for independent regular inspections of all services for children.[428] Consistently, this particular recommendation was developed as a response to a

---

[423] *O'Keeffe v Ireland* (n 1) para 165.
[424] Ibid paras 164, 61; O'Mahony and Kilkelly (n 79) 320, 325.
[425] *O'Keeffe v Ireland* (n 1) para 61.
[426] Ibid para 164.
[427] Fn 437 below and accompanying text.
[428] *'Ryan'* vol IV para 7.12.

specific finding that '*[t]he system of inspection by the Department of Education was fundamentally flawed and incapable of being effective*'.[429] In her wide-sweeping analysis of legal issues arising from Ireland's child abuse reports Ursula Kilkelly, moreover, stated that as a precise legal issue the establishment of robust and effective mechanisms to ensure the protection of children became obvious.[430]

As a point of normative reference for this analytic focus Article 19 CRC and *GC 13* as the leading CRC-based interpretative instrument for the protection from violence were clearly identified.[431] Again, what '*Ryan*' found remarkable was a deferential and submissive attitude of the Department of Education towards the (religious) Congregations which compromised the ability to carry out its statutory duty of inspection and monitoring.

Text-based Interpretation

Neither the list of measures from the first, nor the range of interventions as spelled out in the second paragraph of Article 19 CRC literally refers to "inspection" as an itemized obligation to be fulfilled by means of internal legislation that is being drafted as a matter of treaty implementation. By the same token, either "identification" or "prevention" both of which belong to the listing in Article 19(2) CRC might support a case for school inspections to come under an implementing obligation rooted in the right to non-violent education in particular.

Suggesting that, as a human rights treaty the Convention and the range of protective measures to be taken in accordance with Articles 3, 19 CRC in particular, may envisage a system of rigorous school inspections, is certainly not too far from the Convention's object and purpose which is empowerment and legal subjectivity for children as right-holders enjoying their educational rights (Articles 28, 29 CRC) in practice. And, as the Committee rightly observed in regard of adolescent health and development, the school as an educational setting plays an important role in the life of many adolescents, as the venue for learning, development and socialisation.[432] No State Party to the Convention may, therefore, isolate itself from taking

[429] '*Ryan*' vol IV para 6.06.
[430] Kilkelly (n 67) 8, 15; O'Mahony and Kilkelly (n 79) 320, 321.
[431] Kilkelly (n 67) 16.
[432] CRC/GC/2003/4 para 17.

note of real life situations observable at such an important place but must make sure it receives firsthand information about the wellbeing of children kept under the authority of teachers, coaches or educators for long hours of the day.

As a monitoring body the Committee looked at it from a slightly different angle starting from an analysis of general measures of implementation (Article 4 CRC) which must comprehend all appropriate legislative, administrative and other measures for an implementation of the rights recognized in the Convention.[433] As a consequence, *GC 5* on measures of implementation discusses a variety of administrative measures which include *"rigorous inspection"* to ensure compliance with the Convention; this is in a context of 'Privatization' which by itself is seen as a process in relation to services (widely conceived as of an inherently public character) such as health or education. Since that process can have a serious impact on the recognition and realization of children's rights, inspections to ensure compliance with the Convention must come in as a measure of implementation.[434] According to the Committee, monitoring disciplinary systems (in schools) and the treatment of children must be part of a sustained supervision of all institutions which is required by the Convention; thus, educational administrators and supervisors do clearly have a role to play for an assessment about the quality of the learning environment.[435] In respect of the right to freedom from violence, governmental obligations as understood by the Committee should be reflected by administrative measures to establish monitoring and oversight systems required to protect the child from all forms of violence.[436]

Thus, as a protective mechanism statutorily mandated rigorous on-site inspections will function as a simple device to ensure that complaints about ill-treatment of children do in fact reach those empowered to respond. In sum, what proved to be a core issue from the viewpoint of children's rights is not if anything like an institutionalized Inspectorate under the roof of a national Government department is up and running in practice; what matters most is the precise mandate of such an inspectorate, including its general authority and specified powers needed for discharging

---

433 CRC/GC/2003/5 – '*General measures of Implementation*'.
434 CRC/GC/2003/5 para 44; Fn 269 for 'privatization' and 'marketisation'.
435 CRC/C/GC/8 para 43; CRC/GC/2001/1 para 22.
436 CRC/C/GC/13 para 42.

that mandate effectively.[437]

Sources of Legal Obligations

As indicated already, education rights as spelled out through Articles 28, 29 CRC provide for a treaty basis upon which a set of obligations pertaining to a duty to install and maintain a system of rigorous inspection may be elaborated. Thus, Article 28 CRC includes provisions requiring school discipline to be administered in a dignity-consistent manner and for States to take measures to promote regular school attendance. Article 29 CRC defines the aims of education to include quality education as well as tolerance, equality and respect for human rights.[438] With particular concern for State obligations and government responsibilities corresponding to Article 29 CRC, it may be argued that inspection and regulation systems must be in place for ensuring compliance with established standards assuming that non-violent approaches to school discipline and behaviour control are fully covered by those standards.[439]

ECHR Case Law

Although the human rights framework from which the ECtHR developed, in a a case such as *O'Keeffe,* its own assessment was not predominantly inspired by reference to children's rights, the Convention and Article 19 CRC in particular were briefly cited as a source of international law and practice relevant to that case.[440] In contrast to the historic situation in Ireland, to observe children in their school or classroom and to monitor how they are being treated by their teachers is absolutely paramount for any mandate of inspection to become CRC compliant. More specifically, any inspection regime in accordance with Article 19 CRC must generally anticipate the risk of ill-treatment as envisaged by this Convention article, such as '*all forms of physical or mental violence, injury or abuse, neglect or negligent treatment, maltreatment or exploitation, including sexual abuse*'. In this, the case of *O'Keeffe* provides general instruction to States about their duty to protect children from harm; but, as O'Mahony and Kil-

---

437 Fn 422 above and accompanying text.

438 Fn 140 and accompanying text.

439 E/C.12/1999/10 para 49 (ESC Committee).

440 *O'Keeffe v Ireland* (Fn 1) para 96.

kelly explain, '[i]*t is especially relevant to child protection in settings like schools where children are especially vulnerable'*.[441]

What, finally, may be drawn as a conclusion from ECHR case law is that human rights-based obligations originally attributed to the State, especially those pertaining to protection from violence, must not be delegated to private bodies or individuals; indeed, as a matter of human rights law no such delegation is ever valid or acceptable in any circumstance.[442] More specifically, with respect to its protective obligation towards minors in primary schools the State cannot absolve itself from any such obligation, regardless of the organisational model of public or private education generally practised within the jurisdiction.[443] Consequently, from this legal aspect a strong argument may be built for making the installation and maintenance of a system of comprehensive government-led school inspections obligatory, as the State must not insulate itself from liability for what occurs in (state-funded) primary schools.

Participation Rights and Rigorous Inspection

Additionally, another fundamental rights provision from the CRC bears on the matter of rigorous inspection, including details of the mandate to be given to inspectors, and that is Article 12 CRC containing the right of the child to be heard, widened by the Committee into a general principle of having children participate in all matters affecting them.[444] Article 12(1) CRC requires states to assure to children capable of forming their own views the right to express those views freely in all matters affecting them; it requires those views to be given due weight in accordance with the child's age and maturity. Article 12(2) CRC links this requirement with the child's right ("opportunity") to be heard in any judicial and administrative proceedings affecting the child in a manner consistent with the procedural rules of national law.[445] Envisaging school inspections to be an administrative proceeding affecting the child, Article 12(2) CRC stipulates for the benefit of the child to be provided with an opportunity to be heard in

441 O'Mahony and Kilkelly (n 79) 320, 328.

442 *O'Keeffe v Ireland* (Fn 1) para 150.

443 Ibid; see also Fnn 256, 320 and accompanying text.

444 CRC/C/GC/2003/5 para 12; CRC/C/GC/12 para 67.

445 U Kilkelly, *Foreword* in A Parkes, *Children and International Human Rights Law* (Routledge 2013) xix.

any such proceeding. In her research on monitoring CRC implementation across Europe Laura Lundy found that an obligation on inspectors to have regard to children's views in the inspection process clearly belongs to a recent educational policy imperative driven to a significant degree by Article 12 CRC.[446]

To sum up, as a legislative and also as an administrative measure for the protection of schoolchildren from all forms of physical and mental violence, a statutory regime of rigorous school inspections is required by the Convention, and by Articles 3, 4, 12, 19 and 28, 29 CRC in particular. As grounding on, among others, Articles 3(2), 19 CRC, the right to non-violent education requires that educational institutions be rigorously inspected by way of government-led on-site inspections when the mandate statutorily entrusted to inspectors entails a duty to interact efficiently with children involved as a matter of their own human rights. As a violence-related risk of significance child sexual abuse must equally be covered by the statutory mandate handed out to inspectors for their professional discharge under the auspices of the Minister responsible for education and schools.

Fourth Section – Duties and Obligations to Fulfil the Right to Non-violent Education

Regarding the right to non-violent education as a children's right the following analysis is turning to a 'Fulfil'-type of implementing obligation under the Convention, after a 'Respect'-type and also a 'Protect'-type obligation were discussed previously.

Sub-Section (1) – Definition Restated

As an element belonging to the tripartite typology of obligations, an obligation to fulfil requires the taking of appropriate legislative, budgetary, administrative, judicial and other measures towards an achievement of the full realization of Convention rights many of which, education rights among them, have a strong component of individual entitlement in terms of assistance to be provided by the State. Thus, a more specific obligation to facilitate an enjoyment of non-violent education is included as well as, in certain conditions, an obligation to provide for the means necessary for

[446] Lundy (n 182) 393, 404.

realizing education rights in practice.[447] Accordingly, to fulfil comes in two different sub-types of State action, namely facilitation in practice regarding an individual right-holder's capacity to fully enjoy his or her right to non-violent education, or direct provision of means for an individual's entitlement to be fully realised in practice; critically, the point is that any proven violation or infringement of rights (whoever the author of such violation or infringement) is not stated as a legal prerequisite for triggering that same obligation as a matter of international human rights law.[448]

Regarding the sequence of RPF-obligations any specific obligation that comes under this particular heading of 'Fulfil' must systematically have the force to complete or to bring together comprehensively what is needed for an overall achievement of the realisation of the right to non-violent education. Thus, in this 'Fulfil'-section a few topics will be discussed, such as 'Incorporation' or 'Inter-agency cooperation', which cut across the whole range of specified rights of the child as stipulated in the text of the Convention. As a matter of providing a school curriculum adapted to the needs and interests of learners and students in schools it will be shown that comprehensive sexuality education should be made mandatory for children during all stages of their compulsory education. Lastly, an obligation to fulfil the right to non-violent education encompasses a school-based provision of human rights education and of disseminating the principles and provisions of the CRC as a stimulus for general awareness and vindication of children's rights.[449]

Sub-Section (2) – Incorporation not an Obligation under CRC

Generally regarded as a fundamental requirement of international human rights law, all treaty norms must be recognised in appropriate ways within the domestic legal order.[450] Accordingly, this sub-section takes a brief look into the text of the treaty in order to explore whether, under the Convention, States Parties find themselves under an international obligation to incorporate some or all of the CRC's substantive provisions

---

[447] Fn 299 above and accompanying text.

[448] Hakimi (n 226) 341, 347.

[449] Fn 492 below and accompanying text.

[450] E/C.12/1998/24 para 2, reproduced in: International Commission of Jurists, *Courts and the Legal Enforcement of Economic, Social and Cultural Rights* (Geneva 2008) 7.

into their domestic legal order.

A Terminology of Incorporation for Treaty Law Purposes

Although not fully settled as a technical term in the field of international law, denoting as 'incorporation' is an operation of locally (or internally) co-ordinated governance measures whereby a human rights treaty, such as the Convention, becomes internally effective.[451] In that sense and from a perspective of functionality, incorporation whereby substantive treaty provisions are intentionally given internal legal effect must be seen as one specified means of implementing the rights recognized in the Convention. Accordingly, used as a legal technical term "incorporation" for this context translates into "the act of legislative implementation of a treaty".[452]

For the CRC measures of implementation were spelled out in Article 4 CRC according to which States shall take all appropriate legislative, administrative and other measures for the implementation of the rights recognized in the Convention. Additionally, an express obligation as stipulated in Article 2(1) CRC provides that the rights set forth in the Convention must be respected and ensured to each child without discrimination; from the text of this article, however, no more detail as to the precise method of respecting fundamental rights and ensuring non-discrimination within the jurisdiction is extractable.[453] Equally, no explicit obligation flowing from any of the substantive CRC articles pertinent to the right to non-violent education, such as Articles 3(2), 19 and 28, 29 CRC, specifically covers 'incorporation' as a means for facilitating the realization of this children's right in practice.[454]

When traditionally, the method of national implementation of international obligations has been regarded as an internal affair and supervisory bodies have concerned themselves only with the result in a specific case when there has been a complaint of breach, signs of a more intrusive

---

[451] Aust (n 222) 81; CRC/GC/2003/5 para 20; CCPR/C/21/Rev.1/Add13 para 13 (Human Rights Committee).

[452] M Waters, 'Creeping Monism: The Judicial Trend toward Interpretative Incorporation of Human Rights Treaties' (2007) 107 Columb L Rev 628, 698.

[453] European Commission for Democracy through Law (Venice Commission), *Report on the Protection of Children's Rights* (3 April 2014) para 28.

[454] Especially the list of protective measures in Art 19(2) CRC does not refer to incorporation.

approach are perceivable in the meantime.[455] Although recent comparative research is providing some evidence pointing to the factual correlation between a legal status accorded to children's rights under several national laws, and substantive entitlements for children being enforced in practice, no general duty to incorporate with regard to the Convention as a whole may as yet be established under international law.[456]

Sub-Section (3) – Inter-Agency Cooperation for the Fulfilment of CRC Obligations

For all purposes of realising children's rights in practice a multitude of organs and agents of the State including social workers, police, lawyers, judges and courts staff, a wide range of healthcare professionals as well as teachers and school staff, will have to come into play; hence, the general need for inter-agency cooperation. A range of administrative measures are needed for effective implementation, such as the development of particular governance structures, training and awareness raising and other activities to be detailed in the following. As explicitly recommended through *'Ferns'* in particular, an Inter Agency Review Committee should exist at the level of each (Irish) diocese bringing together representatives of the Church, the police and social or health services involved in child protection locally; the mandate of such a meeting should be to exchange relevant information about allegations of abuse and to ensure that authorities concerned have a full appreciation of all of the allegations made.[457] From this functional perspective, enjoyment of their rights by children will necessarily be affected by many different Government departments and other governance bodies or services controlled by the Government, but non-State services and organizations also.[458] As the Committee explained in its general comment on general measures of implementation:

---

455 E Denza, 'The Relationship between International and National Law' in M Evans (ed) *International Law* (4th ed OUP 2014) 412, 416.

456 L Lundy, U Kilkelly, B Byrne, 'Incorporation of the United Nations Convention on the Rights of the Child in Law: A Comparative Review' 21 IJCR (2013) 442, 452; Kilkelly (Fn 241) 80, 87.

457 *'Ferns'* 23 (Management of the Diocese), 35 (The Inter Agency Review Committee), 196 (Recommendations).

458 CRC/C/GC/16 para 33.

> *The Committee believes that effective implementation of the Convention requires visible cross-sectoral coordination to recognize and realize children's rights across Government, between different levels of government and between Government and civil society – including in particular children and young people themselves.*[459]

Furthermore, in their *GC 13* on freedom from violence the Committee repeatedly stressed the importance of inter-agency collaboration.[460] As a string of strategies for an effective implementation of the Convention the Committee had provided, by means of their *GC 5,* closer detail on the points described below; at the same time it found that, being a treaty body, it is not advisable for it to attempt to prescribe detailed arrangements appropriate for very different systems of government across States.[461]

First Strategy, Developing a comprehensive national strategy rooted in the Convention:[462] As the Committee commends the development of a comprehensive national strategy or national plan of action for children built on the framework of the Convention, a strategy relating to educational situations of both public and private organization and how the right to non-violent education can be brought to bear on each of these situations is required. For this strategy to be given authority it needs to be endorsed at the highest level of Government and it will have to include the description of a sustainable process for realizing children's education rights throughout the State; in order to function comprehensively, it will go beyond statements of policy and principle, to set real and achievable targets regarding the elimination of violence from the educational process or mitigating its impact.

Second Strategy, Coordination of implementation:[463] Children's human rights being interrelated as a matter of principle it must be ensured that obligations inherent in ratification of the Convention are recognized right across Government, including departments concerned with Finance, Planning or Employment. As a way of formally achieving coordinated governance practices inter-ministerial and interdepartmental committees might be put into operation.

---

459 CRC/GC/2003/5 para 27; Kilkelly (Fn 241) 80, 88.

460 CRC/C/GC/13 paras 42, 50.

461 CRC/GC/2003/5 para 38.

462 CRC/GC/2003/5 paras 28–36; L Lundy et al (Fn 456) 442, 459.

463 CRC/GC/2003/5 paras 37–39.

Third Strategy, Data collection and analysis:[464] As an essential aspect of children's rights implementation a set of reliable data on real life situations involving children in formal education and children as victims of sexual offences, should be collected at the national level and should also be disaggregated to allow for discrimination to be identified. Research found that the collection of good quality data on children's lives is particularly important in facilitating an examination of the disparity between 'the de jure protection and the de facto realization of human rights' when this kind of disparity is specifically relevant for the realisation of children's education rights.[465] For Convention obligations to be fulfilled it must be ensured that reliable and disaggregated data are publicly available in order to assess and monitor the extent to which children are able to vindicate their educational rights in practice.[466]

Fourth Strategy, Making children visible in budgets:[467] As a typified obligation 'Fulfil' in particular requires that measures are taken which enable and assist children to enjoy their right to non-violent education; that provision be made for children who are unable, for reasons beyond their control, to realize their educational rights themselves by means at their disposal; and that children's rights are promoted for raising public awareness about budget-making procedures and their long-term impacts on issues of access to, and quality of education.[468]

Fifth Strategy, Training and capacity building:[469] Since the purpose of this kind of training is to emphasize the status of the child as a subject of rights, to increase knowledge and understanding of the Convention and to encourage respect in practice for its provisions, a wide spectrum of professionals regularly working with and for children, including community and religious leaders, teachers, lawyers, the judiciary, health professionals and social workers, need to receive systematic children's rights training and capacity building. Especially for teachers playing a vital role for detecting and reporting child sexual abuse, this training should be systematic, ongoing and integrated into educational curricula.

---

464 CRC/GC/2003/5 paras 48–50; L Lundy et al (Fn 456) 442, 460.
465 L Lundy et al (Fn 456) 442, 460.
466 CRC/C/GC /19 para 27.
467 CRC/GC/2003/5 paras 51, 52.
468 CRC/C/GC/19 para 27.
469 CRC/GC/2003/5 para 53–55.

Sixth Strategy, Independent human rights institutions:[470] Complementary to effective Government structures installed for the benefit of children as right-holders, independent human rights institutions monitor and evaluate the State's progress towards implementation and realization of children's rights on the ground; their role and function, therefore, implies that departments of the Government cooperate efficiently with and respond to initiatives launched by such human rights institutions as were authorised within the jurisdiction.

Sub-Section (4) – Comprehensive Sexuality Education

Already, for their very first general comment on the aims of education the Committee with reference to Article 29(1) CRC succinctly stated that the child's right to education is not only a matter of access (Article 28 CRC) but also of content; in accordance with this approach, Article 29(1) CRC must be read as underlining an individual and subjective right to a specific quality of education.[471] Therewith in accordance, what was termed comprehensive sexuality education (UNESCO) is nowadays seen as an essential component of a broader quality education;[472] its school-based provision may be firmly grounded in obligations emanating from the Convention such as an obligation to have a system of non-violent education available that is accessible, acceptable and adaptable for children and adolescents within the jurisdiction.[473] Thus, comprehensive sexuality education denotes as a curriculum-based process of teaching and learning about the cognitive, emotional, physical and social aspects of (human) sexuality.[474]

As an important aspect of life-skills this kind of programme for curricular education in schools plays a critical role for the safety and well-being of participants, and for the prevention of sexualized violence in particular. Research has shown that comprehensive sexuality education, to be integrated into the general curriculum for schools, has a potential for empowerment and resilience against violent aggression and assault, espe-

---

470 Ibid para 65; L Lundy et al (Fn 456) 442, 457.

471 CRC/GC/2001/1 paras 3, 9; Fn 179 above and accompanying text.

472 UNESCO, *International technical guidance on sexuality education* (rev ed, 2018) 12.

473 UN document A/65/162 para 24, 40; on the '*4-A-scheme*' for education rights, see Fn 184 and accompanying text.

474 UNESCO, *International technical guidance* (n 472 above) 16.

cially as far as the risk of child sexual abuse is concerned.[475] Consequently, as a measure of an essentially educational character (Article 19 CRC), comprehensive sexuality education needs to be analysed here from a vantage point of an obligation to fulfil children's rights to non-violent education.

Sexuality Education Policies

As was observed with particular regard for public programmes of comprehensive sexuality education, these programmes should be delivered by well-trained and supported teachers in school settings, as they provide an important opportunity to reach large numbers of young people with sexuality education before they become sexually active.[476] Being educational in character this kind of measures for protection from violence are generally appreciated because of their preventive effects regarding the risk of child sexual abuse; seen in closer detail, however, there may be uncertainties in the measurement of their efficiency in terms of risk prevention.[477] Along these lines the Committee also found that an effective implementation of rights under Article 29(1) CRC requires a fundamental reworking of curricula to include the various aims of education such as the development of the child's personality, human rights, tolerance and equality of sexes; and the systematic revision of textbooks and other teaching materials, as well as school policies.[478] What is true of the child's right to education in general, specifically applies to the right to non-violent education including the right to comprehensive sexuality education.[479]

Not surprisingly, educators and educated alike express their views that any school curriculum claiming to be of relevance to contemporary education in schools should go beyond biological fact knowledge about puberty and physical maturity to cover the topics of 'respect' and 'consent' when it comes to interpersonal and inter-sex communication more broadly.[480] As

---

475 A Daly, C O'Sullivan, 'Sexuality Education and International Standards: Insisting Upon Children's Rights' 42 HRQ (2020), 835, 837.

476 UNESCO, *International technical guidance* (n 472) 12.

477 A/65/162 para 40; A Pellai, M Caranzano-Maitre, 'Primary prevention of child sexual abuse: Child focused interventions' (2015) 15 Ir Journ Appl Soc Sc 29 .

478 CRC/GC/2001/1 para 18.

479 On this interconnection, see Fn 200 above and accompanying text.

480 Daly, O'Sullivan (Fn 475) 835, 840; National Council for Curriculum and Assessment (Ireland), *Background paper and brief for the redevelopment of Senior Cycle SPHE* (September 2022) 6.

the Committee also made clear in their commenting, *'basic skills include ... life skills such as the ability to make well-balanced decisions; to resolve conflicts in a non-violent manner; and to develop a healthy lifestyle, good social relationships and responsibility ...* '.[481] Especially at the stage of compulsory education in schools comprehensive sexuality education therefore appears to be an indispensible means of prevention against violence and abuse, contributing substantially to fulfil the right to non-violent education in practice. Any failure to consider wider societal contexts in which sexual encounter takes place, including its social and emotional elements, risks leaving children liable to being either victims or perpetrators (or both) of sexual abuse.[482]

As an integral aspect of quality education, and of the right to non-violent education in particular, programmes for comprehensive sexuality education were developed and tested for adaptation to, and implementation in school settings all over the world.[483] Generally speaking, a provision of school-based programmes appears to be a widely used strategy for the prevention of child sexual abuse.[484] As a consequence, schools have emerged as an important prevention setting providing access to large populations of children and adolescents, without stigmatising those who may be at particular risk of abuse.[485] Ideally, school-based sexual abuse prevention programmes focus on children and adolescents as beneficiaries of prevention; they seek to prevent child sexual abuse by providing students with knowledge and skills to recognise and avoid potentially abusive situations, and with strategies to physically and verbally repel uninvited sexual approaches. Also, these programmes endeavour to minimise harm to children and adolescents by disseminating messages about appropriate help-seeking in the event of abuse or attempted abuse.[486]

Apart from Article 19 CRC, a strong normative argument favouring an

481 CRC/GC/2001/1 para 9.

482 Daly, O'Sullivan (n 475) 835, 841; A/65/162 para 74.

483 N Stanley et al, 'Preventing domestic abuse for children and young people: A review of school-based interventions' 59 Children and Youth Service Review (2015) 120; K Walsh et al, 'School-based education programmes for the prevention of child sexual abuse' Cochrane Database of Systematic Reviews (2015) Issue 4 Art. No CD004380; A Pellai, M Caranzano-Maitre (n 477) 27.

484 K Walsh et al, 'School-based education programmes' (n 483 above) 7.

485 Ibid 8.

486 Ibid 8.

instigation of development for this kind of educational programme may be gained from Article 6 *Lanzarote*; by virtue of which (European) States are obligated to ensure that all children, during all stages of their compulsory education, receive information on the risk of sexual exploitation and abuse, as well as on the means to protect themselves.[487] In a similar vein, *GC 13* defines educational measures for children by reference to the provision of accurate, accessible and age-appropriate information on life skills, self-protection and specific risks such as sexual abuse; as implementing measures they should have an empowering effect regarding child rights in general and may be provided through the school curriculum in particular.[488]

As another leading document, holding out to be a framework based on international best practices in this regard, the 'International technical guidance on sexuality education' produced under the auspices of UNESCO explicitly references the CRC as a human rights convention which it takes up as a template for its own elaborations.[489] Taking for itself a rights-based approach, not a narrower defined health-based one, the guidance provided through this UNESCO document emphasizes values, such as inclusion, respect, equality, empathy, responsibility and reciprocity as inextricably linked to universal human rights.[490] This concept of education, as understood by the guidance document,

> [a]*ims to equip children and young people with knowledge, skills, attitudes and values that will empower them to: realize their health, well-being and dignity; develop respectful social and sexual relationships;* [...] *and understand and ensure the protection of their rights throughout their lives.*[491]

As here conceptualised comprehensive sexuality education makes a valuable contribution to fulfil the right to non-violent education in effect.

Even if its effectiveness as a measure for prevention against the risk of child sexual abuse should not be conclusively proven, I would argue for sexuality education to be fully accredited as an educational measure to come under the rubric of implementing measures as understood by Articles 4

[487] *Lanzarote* (n 355) Article 6.
[488] CRC/C/GC/13 para 44.
[489] UNESCO, *International technical guidance* (n 472) 13.
[490] Ibid 34.
[491] Ibid 16.

and 19 CRC; Articles 28, 29 CRC on children's education rights lend further support to this argument, because of the requirement for all education to be responsive to students' identified needs, and age and developmentally appropriate, inclusive and holistic in its approach. In conclusion, under an obligation to fulfil the right to non-violent education an important educational measure to be taken by the State will consist of a provision of school-based programmes for comprehensive sexuality education as designed along the lines drawn by UNESCO document 'Technical guidance'.

Equally belonging to this section on 'Fulfil'-obligations elaborated by way of reference to the tripartite typology another set of educational measures for the protection from violence needs to be mentioned here. As an implementation strategy aiming at education and training for rights-holders and others involved Article 42 CRC clearly requires States to ensure that the provisions of the Convention are made widely known to adults and children alike.[492] Ensuring that children know about their rights and how these might be claimed and vindicated in practice therefore appears to be an essential element to any rights-based strategy for implementation.

Fifth Section – Conclusions

Reviewing the right to non-violent education through the lens of a typology of obligations brought to light an astonishing wealth of duties and obligations which States Parties must fulfil as a matter of CRC compliance. Primarily, for States to respect children and their right to non-violent education means that no organ or agency of the State including government employed school personnel may ever get involved with violent behaviour, including sexual child abuse, directed at the personal integrity of the learning child. Furthermore, as an important aspect of an obligation to respect it became evident that States must not provide regular state funding to educational institutions which have no clear record of taking children's rights seriously; this should happen by *inter alia,* instigating and maintaining practical procedures for children to protect themselves against sexual abuse, or to call for help in case of need. Not surprisingly, what comes under the heading of 'protect' makes for the bulk of detailed obligations found to be in correspondence to the right to non-violent education under-

[492] Article 42 CRC reads (extract): *'States Parties undertake to make the principles and provisions of the Convention known, ... , to adults and children alike'.*

lining its basic character as a protection right defined for an educational context.[493] Having a set of statutes on the law books effectively criminalizing child abuse is an obligation in itself; however, this will not suffice for protecting schoolchildren against violence and sexual abuse, as long as an unhindered transfer of abuse-related information is not encouraged, even mandated by means of an effective reporting system statutorily established to cover as mandated persons those who work with and for children in schools. Every plausible complaint about, or allegation and disclosure of, child sexual abuse will have to be officially investigated by qualified personnel in a timely, efficient and child-sensitive manner. As a matter of prevention a strong statutory mandate for comprehensive school inspections, involving an active participation of students and pupils concerned, must be handed out to trained experts acting under authority from the ministerial level. As an important subject-matter to be taught from a perspective of autonomous personality development, comprehensive sexuality education proves to be an education-related obligation under the Convention, to be fulfilled for purposes of immunizing children and adolescents againt sexualized violence in schools; this topic's potential to contribute to a build up of self-protective strategies for children in education must not remain unrealised. Likewise, human rights education provided for children, parents and professionals working within the education system is obligatory under the Convention which through an express provision to disseminate and make widely known the principles and provisions therein contained presents a strong case for building the capacity of rights-holders to claim their rights effectively.

The following part of the study will, in an embedded manner, discuss details about legislative, administrative, social and educational measures taken for an implementation of the right to non-violent education into internal legal orders such as the one maintained by the Holy See or Ireland.

---

493 See p 102 above.

THIRD PART: Jurisdictions and Implementations

Introduction

For this part of the study specified subjects of international law, each captured as a 'jurisdiction' in terms of international human rights law, will come to the fore, and their legal status as well as their implementing practice insofar as they became States Parties to the Convention will be described and analysed in more detail. This part of the dissertation will zone in on two different jurisdictions and explore the extent to which the right to non-violent education has been unpacked as a matter of internal legislation, administrative practice and policy; in particular, international obligations as undertaken in this respect, and how they are being fulfilled internally – or remaining unfulfilled – may now be validly assessed and comparatively analysed. For the following, my comparator jurisdictions will be the Holy See on the one hand and Ireland on the other.

With this analytic focus in mind the only way ahead is from a perspective of 'implementation' which is the transposing procedure necessarily employed when turning abstract treaty guarantees into individualised entitlements for children to be successfully claimed as a matter of law, in fora of either national courts or administrative authorities.[494] Thus, implementation features as an overall process to ensure the realization of all rights in the Convention for children living within their jurisdiction; thereby the task of implementation needs to engage all sectors of society and also children themselves.[495]

In its basic outline, this part of the study shall have two main chapters, one dealing with the Holy See (*chapter 1 – The Holy See*), and a second one

[494] Fn 255 and accompanying text ('implementation' under Article 4 CRC).

[495] CRC/GC/2003/5 para 1; CRC/C/GC/20 para 37.

dealing with Ireland (*chapter 2 –Ireland*) both of which in their respective capacity as a State Party have gone through several cycles of state reporting in accordance with procedural articles in the Convention (Articles 43, 44 CRC). Opening each chapter, some foundational aspects will be discussed pertaining to each signatory's legal status in terms of public international law, and also in terms of international human rights law.[496]

As a further consequence, this discussion will widely make use of legal terminology extracted from the human rights lexicon including its treaty law fundamentals essentially codified through the *Vienna Convention*, introduced already as an international law document.[497] In parallel, some terminology will be borrowed from the wide body of canon law for the Roman Catholic Church (RCC) recently consolidated in its Code of Canon Law (*Codex Iuris Canonici*) which was promulgated in 1983 for the so-called *sui juris* Catholic Church of the Latin West.[498] Fundamentally, in relation to this context of children's human rights the Catholic Church understands itself as a non-territorial entity which may be defined as a spiritual community of faith, hope and charity constituted as a visible society founded on the communion of faith, sacraments, discipline, and governance by its internal legal system, namely canon law.[499]

Actual figures and global data in respect of the RCC as a provider of child-related services worldwide may add to the picture here; key statistical data were provided by the Holy See for purposes of state reporting to the CRC-Committee as follows.[500] As of 31 December 2008 there were about 195.000 Catholic schools in the world attended by almost 55 million students when types of schools counted for the purpose were

---

496 T Buergenthal, 'Human Rights: From San Francisco to The Hague' 77 ZaöRV (2017) 289, 300.

497 Fn 202 above and accompanying text.

498 This 1983 Code of Canon Law universally looks at Catholic churches of the so-called Latin West targeting all churches which come under the jurisdiction of the Roman Pontiff regardless of their location in geographical terms; it is made up of 1752 single *Canones*/Canons assembled in seven books each dealing with specified (internal) functions, such as 'teaching', 'sanctifying' and 'penalizing'; see *'Ferns'* (Fn 75) for a recognition of *"Canon Law as a scientific legal system"*; McAleese (Fn 7) 69.

499 CRC/C/VAT/Q/2/Add.1 para 8.

500 CRC/C/VAT/2 paras 33–35; CRC/C/SR.1852 (30 April 2014); No detail available as to 'National Schools' in Ireland, and if they were equally counted as 'Catholic Schools' for the purpose of state reporting by the Holy See.

encompassing kindergartens as well as primary and secondary schools (junior and senior).[501] Recently, in September 2017, the following data were provided by Professor Mary McAleese: as a religion-based institution the RCC globally governs the faith lives of over 300 million children under 18 years of age; 200.000 Catholic schools across five continents are catering for the needs of some 60 million students, a majority of whom, according to the Holy See, do not profess the Catholic faith.[502] As such, again according to Professor McAleese, the RCC appears to be "the biggest non-governmental provider of educational and welfare services to children in the world"; with over three hundred million child members it is therefore one of the most significant global non-governmental contributors to the lives of children.[503] These figures will not be disputed in detail here, but may appear as an indicator of relevance for the topic in general, and as a matter of plausibility for the selection of jurisdictions made for this comparative study.

Justification of Choice

For any research into this field of implementing children's rights, the core question remains: why Canon Law; and why the Holy See? A chapter from *'Murphy'* (*'The Role of Canon Law'*) stands out which is the 2009 Commission of Inquiry Report into the Archdiocese of Dublin recording the manner in which complaints about clerical child sexual abuse were dealt with by Church and State authorities.[504] The commissioners found that an understanding of aspects of canon law and internal Church procedural rules was essential to understanding how allegations and suspicions of clerical child sexual abuse were handled by Church authorities.[505] In parti-

---

501 Figures for 2011 from *Annuarium Statisticum Ecclesiae* (Statistical Yearbook for the Church): 209.670 schools in total providing for 57.612.936 students, see http://press.vatican.va/content/salastampa/it/bolletino/pubblico/2013/12/19/0853/01918.html . Also available from CRC/C/VAT/Q/2/Add.1, p 20.

502 The Royal Irish Academy, *Mary McAleese Presents Research into the Catholic Church, Child Protection, Canon Law and the United Nations,* YOUTUBE (September 7, 2018), https://www.youtube.com/watch?v=RbOicUyHfHE ; P McGarry, 'Vatican's stance on children is not acceptable, says McAleese' *Irish Times* (12 Sept 2017), exclusively retrievable from wwwirishtimes.com; printed 12 September 2017;

503 McAleese (Fn 7) 3.

504 Fn 65 for details.

505 *'Murphy'* para 4.1 (Introduction).

cular, it had become obvious to the Commission that offending priests used their status as clerics and their privileged access in order to groom and abuse children;[506] also, it had been factually established that Catholic Church authorities, in dealing with complaints against its clerics, gave primacy to its own ecclesiastical laws. Therefore, as the report states,

> *Since, no matter what penalties are imposed on a clerical abuser by the State, only a canon law process can affect his status as a cleric or a priest, an understanding of the role of canon law is necessary in order to fully understand the response of the Church authorities to complaints of child sexual abuse.*[507]

Along these lines, the Commission also considered that clear and precise rules are required to ensure that priests suspected of abusing children are not allowed to use their status to give them privileged access to children.[508] Since the power to remove priests from ministry is available only from canon law which provides the key infrastructure for removing abusive clergy from pastoral ministries, the penal process rooted within this body of law must become effective as a means of controlling clerical child sexual abuse. However, as the Commission became aware of, this kind of effectiveness had been lacking for decades in practice.[509] Furthermore, the Commission understood that canon law provides the Church authorities with a means of doing justice to victims of all ages, including paying compensation to them. In practice, however, canon law was used selectively when dealing with offending clergy, to the benefit of the cleric and the consequent disadvantage of the child victim; not a single case had the Commission encountered where canon law was invoked as a means of doing justice to victims.[510] Similarly, other Commission of Inquiry reports from Ireland, but legal commentators also, documented their efforts to understand the role and function of canon law as a legal system because this was perceived to be essential for an understanding about the manner in which allegations and suspicions of clerical child sexual abuse were managed by Church authorities.[511]

[506] Ibid para 4.2 (Introduction).

[507] Ibid para 4.1 (Introduction).

[508] Ibid para 4.90.

[509] Ibid.

[510] Ibid para 4.3 (introducing its chapter on the role of canon law).

[511] Treating 'Canon Law', as in *'Ferns'* (p 20–38), *'Murphy'* (chapter 4 'The Role of

As indicated earlier, both of my comparator jurisdictions, Ireland and the Holy See also have a well-documented history of a multitude of abusive incidents, including child sexual abuse perpetrated by clerics or, indeed, happening in an education-related situation involving lay teachers or other school personnel operating under clerical management. As a complex observation in itself this involves issues of sheer prevalence in statistical terms on the one hand, and published documentation in terms of State-sponsored Commissions of Inquiry reports, such as *'Ferns'*, *'Ryan'*, *'Murphy' and 'Cloyne'*, on the other.[512] Whatever the methodological approach taken the scale and extent of the problem of Church-related child sexual abuse is enormous both in terms of incidents of maltreatment and in terms of typified situations putting children at risk.

Chapter 1 – The Holy See

Throughout this chapter the right to non-violent education, its corresponding duties and obligations will be discussed with particular concern for the Holy See as a subject of public international law and as a State Party to the Convention.[513] As an introductory notion the term 'Holy See' (or 'Apostolic See') here denotes the central organ for government of the Roman Catholic Church (RCC), consisting in itself of the Pope and a number of congregations or dicasteries (central administrative offices) each respectively deemed competent for dealing with defined aspects of global church life; it is headquartered in the Vatican territory located in the city of Rome/Italy.[514]

Canon Law') and *'Cloyne'* (chapter 4 'Church child protection procedures and guidelines 1996–2009'); G Robertson, *The Case of the Pope* (Penguin Books 2010) 53–86; CRIN, *A Preliminary Report* (no date) 7 ('penalties'); Keenan (Fn 61) 209.

512 McAlinden (Fn 69) 189, 191; CRC/C/SR.1852 (30 April 2014) para 2 (WHO estimates).

513 Holy See ratification status for CRC: signature date and ratification date are both on 20 April 1990; for both CRC-OPAC and for CRC-OPSC signature date is 10 October 2000 and ratification date is 24 October 2001; OPCP not ratified by the Holy See; see UNTS Database chapter IV no 11 (CRC), no 11a (CRC-OPAC), no 11b (OPSC); the text of Holy See reservations and declarations is attached to CRC status report (UNTS Database ch IV no 11); see also Fn 592 below.

514 CRC/C/SR.255 para 19; T G Hailu, 'The Holy See: The Government of the Catholic Church' (2017) 25 IJCR 779; By way of legal reform, in 2022, the Roman Curia was

This general purpose of analysis requires a presentation in two main sections: one section dealing with international obligations as effectively undertaken by the Holy See in respect of children's rights (*First Section: Obligations Undertaken)*, and another section aiming at an assessment about the actual state of achievement in the realization of obligations previously undertaken (*Second Section: Obligations Unfulfilled*). As a consequence, materials considered will be taken from treaty law sources, such as the Convention (CRC) or the *Vienna Convention* (VCLT) for the first section, and will also be taken from a range of UN documents produced for the purpose of state reporting to the Committee or other treaty bodies (ICERD, CAT), such as periodic reports or concluding observations, for the second one.[515] Since binding effects of an international obligation generally incurred by signature and ratification of the Convention may be modified, limited or excluded by means of reservations, understandings and declarations, the Holy See's terms of ratification will be tested in detail against VCLT provisions pertinent to the case.[516]

First Section: Obligations Undertaken

Clearly, by signature and ratification of the Convention the Holy See has undertaken manifold legal obligations as substantiated in Articles 3(2) and 19 CRC in particular; those same undertakings relate, in the case of Article 19 CRC, to appropriate measures of protection against all forms of physical or mental violence; and further relate, in the case of Article 3(2) CRC, to ensuring the child such protection and care as is necessary for his or her well-being.[517] Linguistically, taking off from a slightly different point of departure, Articles 28, 29 CRC have as their core subject-matter

---

reorganized so as to reduce its offices and functions to a set of 16 dicasteries, see Apostolic Constitution *"Praedicate Evangelium"* (19.03.2022).

515 Alternative reports to the Committee are available from a range of NGO's such as CRIN or 'Survivors Network' with many submissions from civil society organizations retrievable from the Committee website, http://tbinternet.ohchr.org ; McAleese (Fn 7) 401.

516 W Schabas, 'Reservations to the Convention on the Rights of the Child' (1996) 18 HRQ 472; LeBlanc (n 18); Hailu (n 514), 779, 789.

517 The Holy See may be subsumed as a State Party in terms of substantive CRC provisions; referring to itself as 'a State Party to the Convention', see *Comments of the Holy See on the Concluding Observations of the Committee on the Rights of the Child* published (without date) 26 September 2014, para 1.

a recognition of the child's right to education (Article 28(1) CRC), and an international agreement (Article 29(1) CRC) about the aims of education as previously guaranteed, respectively. As a synthesis of rights the right to non-violent education encompasses a bundle of protection rights specified with respect to educational settings like schools, and also combined with a set of corresponding obligations, such as 'criminalization' or 'mandatory reporting' and 'investigation', which were shown to be international obligations inherently implied within a notion of treaty implementation.[518] Furthermore, implementation as an international treaty-based obligation pertains to legislative, administrative, social and educational measures for the realization of children's rights in practice. Articles 2 and 4 CRC read in conjunction as they indeed must be, contain an overall undertaking by CRC State Parties according to which all Convention obligations must be implemented within their jurisdiction in a way that practically ensures rights and freedoms to children as beneficiaries of the Convention.[519]

Regrettably, from this basic concept of implementation the Holy See unilaterally turned away without reason, and started creating its own particular understanding about terminological distinctions to be drawn when bringing the Convention to bear on its own internal legal order. Through a verbose declaration, the Holy See, in the middle of presenting state reporting documents to the Committee (during its second reporting cycle), found that the term "implementation" was hitherto used incorrectly; as a consequence, it declared, this word shall be exclusively employed with regard to applying the Convention as a legal instrument within the specific territory of Vatican City State only. Alternatively, to describe what it does internationally the Holy See as a State Party to the Convention intended to use (as a substitute, not a supplement) a much weaker language instead, such as "to encourage" or "to promote" children's rights.[520] Apparently, this change in terminology serves as a marker for distinctions unilaterally drawn so as to imply that a legal obligation undertaken on behalf of the Holy See to implement Convention rights shall strictly be limited to Vatican City State territory. Regarding the fact that on a global scale this territory appears to be minuscule and as a place of residence only serves to a small number of children, this limitation does not make any practical sense.

[518] For specified obligations, see p 101.

[519] Fn 272 above (Article 2 CRC), Fn 255 above (Article 4 CRC).

[520] CRC/C/VAT/Q/2/Add.1 paras 7, 11, 20; McAleese (Fn 7) 33, 424.

Against this background eventually leading to a denial of responsibilities, it is remarkable to observe how the Holy See changed its legal position between reporting cycles (CRC related) roughly stretching over a period of ten years; and also in regard to other human rights treaties signed and ratified by the Holy See, the 1966 International Convention on the Elimination of All Forms of Racial Discrimination (ICERD) and the 1984 Convention against Torture and Other Cruel, Inhuman or Degrading Treatment or Punishment (ICAT) among them.[521] UN documents stemming from the Initial Reporting Cycle (1994/5) to the Committee comparatively reviewed against materials from the Second Reporting Cycle (2011–2014) clearly evidence this change of legal positions. Having reviewed, in detail, all information given by the Holy See to the Committee over the course of its Initial Reporting Cycle (1994/5), Prof McAleese states:

> *What is* [. . .] *of interest here is that the Holy See delegation took no exception to being asked to explain how canon law had adapted to the* [Convention] *and engaged without qualification in discussing the matter in terms designed to reassure the* [Committee] *that canon law was compliant with the* [Convention].[522]

The big difference between both reporting cycles was that clerical child sexual abuse had hardly been present as an issue for the first and had become the dominant topic for the second. Whereas an understanding about children's rights to be implemented *via* performing revisions of, or making amendments to existing legislation was accepted at an earlier stage, that same understanding was found to be problematic, or even impossible to follow, with regard to implementing CRC standards as explicitly marked for amendment by the Committee in its 2014 Concluding Observations.[523] Thus, in the behaviour of the Holy See as a State Party to

---

[521] McAleese (Fn 7) 398 (ICERD Committee); In the bundling of documents, I follow Prof McAleese (p 407) who designated the 1994/95 reporting cycle as 'Initial Reporting Cycle' (Initial reports, CRC/C/3/Add.27), while a 'Second Reporting Cycle' (Second Reports, CRC/C/VAT/2) only followed in 2011/14 which included the second, third and fourth report submitted, in 2011, by the Holy See as a consolidated document; final documents concluding this second cycle were the Committee's Concluding Observations (CRC/C/VAT/CO/2, Jan 2014) and the Holy See *Comments* (n 517) dated Sept 2014.

[522] Ibid 416.

[523] CRC/C/VAT/CO/2 para 39, 44; Holy See *Comments* (n 517) para 3; K McManus,

the Convention and as a treaty-making subject of international law more generally, a certain lack of consistency is demonstrable which, in relation to this State Party in particular, gives a false impression of robbing the Convention of its legal force.

Clarifying Legal Identities

As another peculiarity in the case of the Holy See two closely related aspects need to be clarified first before the picture about international obligations undertaken will become complete; one aspect looks at the Convention's scope of application on the duty-bearing side, and another one looks at the subject-matter of obligations incurred by State Parties under this instrument. First, clarifying the identity of duty-bearers under the Convention leads on to this research question: upon signature and ratification of the CRC on behalf of the Holy See, who exactly in terms of a functioning legal entity may be identified as having undertaken its legal obligations under international law?[524]

In the case of the Holy See an intricate terminological problem needs to be resolved beforehand as the term *Holy See* carries three different meanings altogether:[525] the Pope together with central Vatican offices, the Pope in primacy over other bishops as successor of St Peter, and the centralized governance body for the Catholic Church (RCC) as a corporate whole. Which of these is the correct one, applicable to the Holy See as a State Party to the Convention?

Once clarified, the subject-matter of obligations thus undertaken may be further defined and detailed: what exactly is the scope of obligations falling on the Holy See as a duty-bearer under the Convention when the validity of reservations and a declaration attached to its international act of ratification is questionable? In the following, my first sub-section will

---

'The Holy See's Compliance with the United Nations Convention on the Rights of the Child' (2019) 12 DePaul J Soc Just, Iss 1, Art 4.

524 CRC/C/VAT/Q/2/Add.1 para 2; addressed in CRC/C/VAT/CO/2 para 8 as *'The dual nature of the Holy See's ratification of the Convention … '*; H E Cardinale, *The Holy See and the International Order* (Colin Smythe Gerards Cross 1976) 82, 256.

525 Can 361 CIC reads: *'In this Code, the term Apostolic See or Holy See not only refers to the Roman Pontiff but also to the Secretariat of State, the Council for the Public Affairs of the Church, and other institutions of the Roman Curia, … '*; M Barbato, 'A State, a Diplomat, and a Transnational Church: The Multi-Layered Actorness of the Holy See' 21 Perspectives (2013) 27, 36.

elaborate on the legal identity of the Holy See as a subject of public international law, and as a State Party to the Convention (*Sub-section 1 – Duty-Bearer Identification*). Building thereupon another sub-section will refer to the scope and content of obligations incurred by the Holy See (*Sub-section 2 – Implementation of Obligations*). My final sub-section, then, will analyse the validity of reservations and declarations as they were attached to its international act by the Holy See (*Sub-section 3 – Validity of Reservations*).

It will be demonstrated that a fully functional governance entity, globally centralized and with the Holy See as its immediate embodiment, continuously exercises a kind of legal-constitutional sovereignty over the Roman Catholic Church of the Latin West (RCC); it, thereby, comes under an international treaty-based obligation to implement children's rights into its own internal legal order (essentially constituted by its body of canon law), reservations and declarations made by the Holy See notwithstanding.

Sub- Section (1) – Duty-Bearer Identification

Historically, when the Convention was signed and ratified on behalf of the Holy See, the functioning legal entity thereby undertaking international obligations was a centralized governing body exercising its supreme legal authority accorded to it as a matter of canon law.[526] Consequently, for the purpose of treaty implementation what thereby came under the Holy See's governance was the Catholic Church (RCC) seen as a corporate whole ("moral person"), including its particular churches as understood and defined in terms of canon law.[527] Certainly, by signature and ratification of the Convention (including deposit of its international act), not merely did the Holy See engage its authority for ruling over the administration of Vatican City State (VCS) as another established subject of international law, but clearly went far beyond that.[528] However, official documents cir-

---

[526] As a corporate whole the RCC operates under coordinate or collegiate leadership of a selected group of clerics acting as persons in authority; defined by the *Codex* (canon 204 §2 CIC): *'This Church, constituted and organized in this world as a society, subsists in the Catholic Church governed by the successor of Peter and the bishops in communion with him'*, see also R J Kaslyn in *New Commentary on the Code of Canon Law* (Paulist Press New York 2000) 247; M McAleese, *Quo Vadis* (The Columba Press 2012) 103.

[527] CRC/C/VAT/Q/2/Add.1 para 8; CRC/C/VAT/2 para 2.

[528] J Troy, 'The Pope's own hand outstretched': Holy See diplomacy as a hybrid mode of diplomatic agency' 20 Brit Journ Polit Intern Rel (2018) 521, 526.

culated on behalf of the Holy See make unfounded claims to the effect that, as a governing body, its legal reach beyond the territory of Vatican City State is severly restricted; as a consequence, it is argued, international obligations falling on the Holy See as a State Party to the Convention are limited, because no corresponding territory other than that of VCS exits.[529] The following analysis will show that a reductionist understanding about the identity of the Holy See as a State Party to the Convention has become untenable as an argumentative position under both international law and canon law.

Somewhat in contrast, the *Pontifical Commission for the Protection of Minors* sitting as a consultative institution formally instituted as part of the Roman Curia (located within the Dicastery for the Doctrine of the Faith[530]) visibly accepts their responsibility for implementing children's rights as found in the Convention; as clearly realized by this Commission those rights must be implemented into existing canon law instruments to be amended accordingly, or freshly drafted in the near future.[531] Thus, when creating a template for canon law-based (national) guidelines on protection from abuse this Pontifical Commission included an explicit reference to Articles 3, 19 CRC in order to strengthen the argument for children's rights to be fully appropriated by collegial bodies canonically legislating for their respective territory wherever this may be situated on the globe; addressees for this guidelines template include Episcopal Conferences (bringing together bishops regularly operating under the same civil jurisdiction) worldwide.[532]

In the following I will demonstrate that in acceding to agreements and treaties the Holy See regularly engages the Catholic Church as a global community for which, at the international level, it acts as a representative by providing missions for plenipotentiaries attending international con-

529 Holy See *Comments* (n 517) para 3.

530 Adress of His Holiness Pope Francis to the Members of the Pontifical Commission for the Protection of Minors (29 April 2022); this Commission was, in 2014, first set up by Pope Francis, see chirograph *Institution of the Pontifical Commission for the Protection of Minors,* 24 Feb. 2014 in AAS 107 (2014) 562–563.

531 Pontifical Commission on the Protection of Minors issuing *Guidelines Template* (27 May 2016) with reference to Articles 3, 19 CRC, for child protection guidelines to be drafted, as a matter of canon law, by Bishops' Conferences worldwide, available at wwwprotectionofminors.va (last accessed 06 Febr 2017).

532 Ibid.

ferences and by functioning as the central organ of governance for the global community thus represented.

A very short History

Possibly the single most important aspect of a legally crafted relationship between the Holy See operating as a religious institution centralized trans-nationally, and civil governments of all times and places is the long-standing practice of concluding "Concordats", by which trans-boundary agreements between the Holy See, and state actors located all over the world, were designated.[533] Strictly speaking, a concordat is defined as a bilateral treaty under international law concluded between the Holy See regularly acting on behalf of the Catholic Church (RCC) and an established government acting on behalf of a nation-State, the subject matter of which pertains to a range of religious, educational or social activities performed by authorised agents of the Church within the borders of that state.[534]

Historically, the Lateran Treaties (1929 AD) concluded between pope and king, are one of the most widely known examples of bilateral treaty-making in the field of general relations between State and Church, each understood as a corporate entity for its respective legal sphere.[535] Closer in time and in relation to the topic is an *Agreement between the Holy See and the Republic of Malta on Church Schools* dating from 1991 which was signed on behalf of the Holy See by an Apostolic Nuncio and by the Minister of Education and the Interior on behalf of the Republic of Malta; this internationally rooted agreement regulates Maltese "Church Schools", their organisation and funding in terms of means provided for the running and upkeep of educational institutions within the State. Interestingly, by referencing canon law as a binding legal instrument, this agreement exemplifies the implementing function canon law may have for an administration

---

[533] J Grant and J Barker, 'Holy See', *Encyclopaedic Dictionary of International Law* (3rd ed OUP 2009); Aust (n 222) 55; J Listl, 'Konkordat' in W Kasper et al (eds) *LThK* (2009); S Ferrari, 'Concordats' *MPEPIL* (2006); C McCrudden, 'Legal and Roman Catholic Conceptions of Human Rights' (2012) 1 Oxf Journ L Rel 185, 187.

[534] Listl (n 533 above) 263; Ferrari (n 533 above) para 1;

[535] Listl (n 533) 265; Ferrari (n 533) para 2.

of justice regarding educational institutions situated on a national territory specified for the purpose.[536]

By virtue of that 1929 Treaty between the Holy See and Italy, the State of the Vatican City or Vatican City State (VCS) was legally created encompassing a territory of approximately 108 acres situated in the city of Rome/Italy with a present-day population of about 500 inhabitants, mostly clerics and other religious personnel.[537] Featuring full State-like sovereignty as explicitly enunciated in this particular instrument, however, is not a necessary prerequisite for becoming a duty-bearing subject under international human rights law, or attaining observer status with the United Nations ('Non-member permanent observer state'), for that matter.[538]

As was clarified by the ICJ in its 1949 *'Reparations for Injuries'* Opinion, there can be subjects of the international legal system that are not States; as the Court explains, the subjects of law in any legal system are not necessarily identical in their nature or in the extent of their rights, and their nature depends on the needs of the (international) community. The progressive increase in the collective activities of States, as the Court furthermore observed, had already given rise to instances of action upon the international plane by certain entities which are not States; obviously, these subjects do not all possess the same rights and duties.[539] While Robert McCorquodale found the court's opinion to be articulating an important statement of international law principles that could be applied to any non-state actor, Heribert Franz Köck, based on this opinion of the court, made a connection between the Holy See (as a non-state actor) and international legal personality as a practice-related concept.[540] Others in the field of canon law scholarship followed suit and thereby this ICJ opinion came to be

---

536 *Agreement between the Holy See and the Republic of Malta on Church Schools* dated 28 November 1991 (updated 1993); McAleese (n 7) 345.

537 J Grant and J Barker, 'Lateran Treaty' (Fn 533); G Westdickenberg, 'Holy See' *MPEPIL* (2006) paras 18–21; Actual figures (31 children registered) in CRC/C/VAT/Q/2/Add.1, p 20.

538 An observer status was formally accorded to the Holy See by U. N. General Assembly Resolution A/58/314 dated 16 July 2004; McAleese (n 7) 370; H F Köck, 'Holy See' *EPIL* (1992) 866; J D van der Vyver, 'Sovereignty' in D Shelton, *Oxford Handbook of International Human Rights Law* (OUP 2013) 379, 383.

539 ICJ Reports 1949, 174, at p 178;

540 R McCorquodale, 'The Individual and the International Legal System' in M Evans *International Law* (4th ed OUP 2014) 280, 282; Köck (n 538) 866;

accepted as a principal grounding for the claim of a legal personality to be accorded to the Holy See under international law.[541]

As a novel approach, this 1949 ICJ Opinion allows for an understanding about the Holy See's international personality being established on social need, rather than on an application of conventional personality concepts supplying a kind of legal fiction as it is being accorded to a plurality of nation-States established as such.[542] Based on this understanding, an organized entity such as the Holy See derives its international personality by executing functions recognized as significant for the international community as a whole; safeguarding the exercise of freedom of religion rights for a global multitude of individual right-holders (including their local communities) being just one such function.[543]

A View from within the Church

Equally, the *Codex* itself looks at the Catholic Church in terms of a corporate personality when declaring that '[T]*he Catholic Church and the Apostolic See have the character of a moral person by divine ordinance itself*' (can 113 §1 *CIC*). As understood in the wording of this particular canon, a moral person is a group or succession of natural persons who are united by a common purpose and, hence, have a particular relationship to each other and, because of that relationship, may be considered as a single entity; a moral person precedes, logically and usually chronologically, the establishment of a corresponding juridic person.[544] Against this

---

[541] R A Melnyk, 'Pontifical Legation to the United Nations' (2009) 98 Periodica 365, 372; R J Araujo and J A Lucal, 'A Forerunner for International Organizations: The Holy See and the Community of Christendom with special emphasis on the Medieval Papacy' (2006) 20 Journ L Rel 305, 323.

[542] Köck (n 538); Araujo and Lucal (n 541 above) 323; E de Brabandere, 'Non-state Actors, State-Centrism and Human Rights Obligations' Leiden Journ Intern L (2009) 191, 197.

[543] Köck (n 538); Araujo and Lucal (n 541) 323; OSCE Office for Democratic Institutions and Human Rights (ODIHR), 'Guidelines on the Legal Personality of Religious or Belief Communities' (Warsaw 2014); Declaration on the Elimination of All Forms of Intolerance and of Discrimination Based on Religion or Belief, adopted 25 Nov. 1981 (G.A. Res. 36/55).

[544] R T Kennedy in J P Beal et al (eds) *New Commentary on the Code of Canon Law* (Paulist New York 2000) 154 (can 113 CIC); 'Apostolic See' for a canon law context is co-terminous with 'Holy See' in use for a wider diplomatic and international law context.

background the Holy See, by reason of its moral personality, may well be perceived to be standing in isolation for purposes of purely internal church governance; at the international level, however, its legal subjectivity is not different from that realized by the Catholic Church as a whole.[545] As canonically recognised the Catholic Church, therefore, does not come in as a distinct legal subject in contrast to the Holy See; rather, dialoguing with States both entities have ever been presenting themselves as one partner.[546] As H E Cardinale explained in his influential textbook for Vatican diplomats,

> [A]*ccording to Canon Law the universal Church is a society in its own right – an entity* sui juris *– which pursues specific social aims by its own means, quite independently of any State or any other international body. It is obvious that no national, local or any particular church is in question, but the Catholic Church, who is universal by her very nature, that is, she is not restricted by the territorial boundaries of the States; she exists and works in the international field by virtue of her juridical and autonomous status, which she could not do if she were not endowed with sovereign attributes like all other members sui juris of the international community.* [...]. *As a subject of international law, the Catholic Church is an atypical organism. That is to say, considering her particular purpose and her peculiar nature and social structure, the Church cannot be put on exactly the same level as a State, or any other subject of international law. Hence her position is analogous to, but not identical with, that of a national State.*[547]

Obviously, this legal terminology based on key concepts such as 'society/subject', 'body/organism' or 'moral person' and used in order to define and delineate a corporate entity as such, is not just in use as shorthand for legislative or administrative purposes purely internal to the Church; rather, it clearly evidences an underlying conceptual understanding of great relevance, historically and equally for present-day contexts.[548] In sum, what most international lawyers would refer to for all practical purposes is the Holy See effectively representing the Catholic

545 J M T Okolo, *The Holy See: A Moral Person, The Juridical Nature of the Holy See in the Light of the Present Code of Canon Law* (Pontificia Universitas Urbaniana Facultas Iuris Canonici, Romae 1990) 266.

546 Ibid 267.

547 Cardinale (n 524) 80, underscores italizised in the original.

548 J Greenberg and M J Sechler, 'Constitutionalism Ancient and Modern: the Contributi-

Church (RCC) at the international level; thus, as a globally organised community of believers it is perceived as having an international legal personality but it is not a State.[549]

Arguing for Binding Effects

Along this line of reasoning, I would argue based on its international legal personality that the Holy See and its commitment made in relation to implementing children's rights gains its significance from the network of concordats drafted, established and maintained under international law as applied in conjunction with the Church's (RCC) own ecclesiastic laws.[550] With particular concern for 'concordat'-like agreements, Canon 3 *Codex Iuris Canonici*, in a super-monist way of incorporation, clearly articulates a wide-ranging principle of supremacy effectively accorded to certain kinds of treaties.[551]

Clearly, the CRC is just one such convention multilaterally agreed upon by the Holy See with a multitude of nations, including sponsorship provided by the United Nations.[552] In full, canon 3 CIC reads (in translation/authentic text):

> *The canons of the Code neither abrogate nor derogate from the agreements/*conventiones *entered into by the Apostolic See with nations or other political societies/*cum nationibus aliisve societatibus politicis. *These agreements therefore continue in force exactly as at present, notwithstanding contrary principles of the Code.*

Taken literally this canon refers to international agreements already in force at the time of the (new) 1983 *Codex Iuris Canonici* entering into force on 27 November 1983 which, as a consequence, would exclude the CRC

---

ons of Roman Law, Canon Law and English Common Law' (2013) 34 Cardoz L Rev 1021, 1037; Okolo (n 545) 209.

549 Schabas (n 516) 472, 479; McAleese (n 7) 373.

550 CRC/C/VAT/2 para 4; on concordats regarding Catholic schools in Malta and Croatia, see Fn 536 and accompanying text.

551 S Ferrari (n 533) para 12; Araujo and Lucal (n 541) 327; N Doe in J Witte and F S Alexander (eds), *Christianity and Law* (CUP 2014) 271, 287; J M Huels in *New Commentary on the Code of Canon Law* (Paulist New York 2000) 50; Klaus Lüdicke (Hrsg), *Münsterischer Kommentar zum Codex Iuris Canonici* (Ludgerus 1987) Can 3 (Verhältnis zum internationalen Vertragsrecht).

552 Araujo and Lucal (n 541) 305, 325.

(which came into force on 02 September 1990) from its scope of application; most canonists however read this fundamental norm from a perspective of *mens legislatoris* (mind of the legislator) which gives it a wider meaning. The practical reason for this is that for the RCC a legitimate interest continually persists to conclude and enter into international agreements with states.[553] As a core argument based on which a wider reading must prevail in effect one may also refer to this particular Codex rule (can 3 CIC) merely translating into canonical language a principle of *pacta sunt servanda* which, by itself, has ever been accepted as providing the normative basis for all (international) treaty-making, be it of a purely civil or partly canonical character.[554] As the leading commentary (for the English-speaking world) on canon law explains in regard to Canon 3 CIC,

> [T]*he Roman Catholic Church is unique among world religions for its highly developed diplomatic relations with civil governments and its participation in world affairs and representation in world organizations. This uniqueness is due not to the fact that the pope is a temporal ruler of the Vatican City State, but to the influence of the Church itself with a billion members throughout the world, a unified governance at the universal level, national hierarchies organized into conferences of bishops, and a global corps of papal legates.*[555]

As a consequence, two distinct legal principles drawn together from Canons 113 and 3 CIC read in conjunction, imply that the CRC as signed and ratified by the Holy See exercises its binding effect on the Catholic Church (RCC) as a corporate whole which accordingly comes under an international treaty-based obligation to implement the Convention's substantive provisions into its internal legal order. Embodying this legal order the 1983 Code of Canon Law (*Codex Iuris Canonici*) is the primary location for an implementation of individualized children's rights as received from the Convention.

---

[553] U Rhode, *Relazione giuridiche tra la Chiesa e la società civile,* Typoscript produced for a Canon Law course at Pontificia Università Gregoriana (2022/23) 145, accessible via wwwulrichrhode.de ; Huels in *New Commentary* (n 551) 50; Lüdicke (n 551) Can 3.

[554] Huels in *New Commentary* (Fn 551) 50; For the text of Art 26 VCLT, see Fn 232; Pontifical Council for Justice and Peace (ed) *Compendium of the Social Doctrine of the Church,* para 437.

[555] Huels in *New Commentary* (n 551) 51.

Recent Specification

Not surprisingly, given widespread diplomatic recognition of the Holy See's international legal personality, the United Nations, in 2004, formally acknowledged the Holy See's observer status as a participant to this international organization.[556] This was realised through a General Assembly resolution which must be read as a strong affirmation of the 'social need' (ICJ) for establishing the personality of the Holy See as a matter of international law. Accordingly, the formal decision to generally accept it as a participant into the work of the United Nations came with a resolution by which the UN General Assembly decided that the Holy See should be accorded the rights and privileges of participation in selected UN fora, conferences and organisations as a non-member permanent observer state.[557] In a preamble to this GA resolution several human rights treaties which were ratified by, or to which the Holy See acceded as a party is referenced, including the CRC among others. Formally according an elaborated status to the Holy See as a participant in the work of the United Nations was thereby set in close context to an observance of international obligations in the field of human rights, including children's rights as stipulated in the Convention.

Unfortunately, a bitter strife followed after conclusion, in 2014, of the second reporting cycle in regard of international obligations under the Convention, documenting itself most unusually through an adversarial exchange of written opinions between the Holy See and the Committee.[558] A long list of issues dealing with a well documented history of incidents of child abuse, as well as handling officially a multitude of cases of child abuse by clerics came up in the course of the second reporting cycle, and was brought to the centre of attention.[559] As a consequence, the Committee, in its 2014 concluding observations, set up an extended list of recommendations touching on a wide range of issues which must be solved either by way of an overhaul, or by way of amendments made to canon law provisions and canonical procedures as hitherto practised.[560]

---

556 McAleese (n 7) 370 with Fn 101.

557 UN GA Res A/58/314 dated 16 July 2004 (n 538); Melnyk (n 541) 365, 386.

558 Fn 521 above for details.

559 'List of Issues' (CRC/C/VAT/Q/2, 1 July 2013) and 'Replies' (CRC/C/VAT/Q/2/Add.1, 6 December 2013).

560 CRC/C/VAT/CO/2 para 14 ('Legislation'); McAleese (n 7) 442; McManus (n 523) 18.

Sub-Section (2) – Implementation of Obligations

As a duty-bearer under the Convention the Holy See was reminded of its implementing obligations in every conceivable detail when the Committee, in January 2014, published their concluding observations on the second periodic report of the Holy See. Concerns and recommendations as formulated by the Committee and most relevant to the topic at hand read as follows:

1. The Holy See was found by the Committee to have failed to address most of the recommendations made in earlier observations, in particular the failure to withdraw the reservations which the Committee considers undermine the full recognition of children as subjects of rights; steps must be taken to ensure the Convention's precedence over internal laws and regulations;[561]
2. The Committee recommended that a comprehensive review of its normative framework be undertaken by the Holy See; canon law in particular must be brought into full compliance with the Convention;[562]
3. There was criticism of the Holy See's failure to establish a high-level mechanism, properly financed and resourced, for coordination of all Convention related implementing activities throughout the Church and its institutions;[563]
4. The Committee complained about the failure by the Holy See to establish an independent mechanism to monitor respect for and compliance with children's rights by individuals, institutions and schools operating under the authority and supervision of the Holy See;[564]
5. The Holy See was believed to have failed to take adequate measures to disseminate the Convention globally; accordingly, it was recommended that knowledge about and awareness of the provisions of the Convention be included in school curricula at all levels of the Catholic education system;[565]
6. The Committee was critical of a lack of systematic training on the provisions of the Convention not made available to members of the clergy

[561] CRC/C/VAT/CO/2 paras 10–12.
[562] Ibid para 14.
[563] Ibid paras 15,16.
[564] Ibid paras 19,20.
[565] Ibid paras 21,22.

as well as religious orders and institutions working with children; accordingly, for teachers' training programmes and for seminaries mandatory modules on children's rights must be included;[566]

7. On the subject of child sexual abuse the Committee noted its particular concern that "the Holy See has consistently placed the preservation of the reputation of the Church and the protection of the perpetrators above children's best interests", as observed and documented by several public commissions of inquiry; in this regard, the Holy See is encouraged to provide guidance to all persons in authority for making the best interests of the child a primary consideration in every area, including when dealing with cases of child sexual abuse;[567] the Committee was gravely concerned that the Holy See has not acknowledged the extent of the crimes committed, has not taken the necessary measures to address cases of child sexual abuse and to protect children, and has adopted policies and practices which have led to a continuation of abusive practices by, and an impunity of perpetrators;[568] the Committee urged that the Pontifical Commission for the Protection of Minors should be an independent body capable of investigating allegations of clerical child sexual abuse and administrative mishandling of such complaints; Church reporting of all such allegations to the civil authorities should be mandatory; Church personnel should be instructed that in cases of conflict the obligation to report prevails over canon law provisions; alleged and convicted abusers should be removed from ministry; Church archives should be made accessible in the pursuit of clerical and hierarchical accountability; crime prevention policies and victim reintegration programmes should be developed as should educational initiatives designed to make children better aware of sex abuse and how to protect themselves; the Holy See should ratify the Council of Europe Convention on the Protection of Children against Sexual Abuse and Sexual Exploitation;[569]
8. Reminding the Holy See of its obligations under Article 19 CRC to take all appropriate measures for the protection of children from all forms of violence, canon law must be amended to explicitly prohibit all corporal punishment of children, including within the family; also, seen as a

[566] Ibid paras 23, 24.
[567] Ibid para 30.
[568] Ibid para 43.
[569] Ibid para 44.

failure of the Holy See it has not enacted guidelines and rules clearly banning corporal punishment of children in Catholic schools;[570]

9. The Holy See was accused of weakening international preventive efforts to reduce parental abuse and neglect of children by its insistence that in deference to parental rights, State intervention was only justified in cases of proven abuse; prerogatives of the parents should in no way undermine children's rights to be protected from abuse and neglect;[571]
10. The right of adolescents must be ensured to have access to adequate information essential for their health and development and for their ability to participate meaningfully in society; in this respect the Holy See should ensure that sexual and reproductive health education be part of the mandatory curriculum for Catholic schools;[572]
11. The Committee reproached the Holy See's continued addressing of "abuse cases through canon law proceedings, which do not provide for the protection, rehabilitation and compensation of child victims"; child victims and their families have often been blamed by religious authorities, discredited and discouraged from pursuing their complaints and in some instances humiliated, as noted *inter alia* by the Ryan Commission in Ireland;[573] comprehensive procedures for an early identification of child victims of sexual and other forms of abuse must be developed, and accessible, confidential, child-friendly and effective reporting channels for children who are victims or witnesses of sexual abuse must be installed;[574]

Somewhat in contrast to this enormously detailed catalogue of failures, the underlying topic of 'implementation' in the direction of which the Holy See widely failed to activate its legal machinery for the protection of children, was treated in just a short introductory paragraph by the Committee;[575] nevertheless, for its subsequent comments on the Committee's observations the Holy See found in this the thrust of its disagreement.[576] Usually, legal commentators refer to this short paragraph taken from

570 Ibid para 40.
571 Ibid para 41, 42.
572 Ibid para 57.
573 Ibid para 60.
574 Ibid para 61.
575 CRC/C/VAT/CO/2 para 8 ("Specificities").
576 *Holy See Comments* (Fn 517) paras 9, 10; Rhode (n 553) 129.

those 2014 Concluding Observations ('paragraph 8') for a postulation of widespread obligations incurred by the Holy See as a State Party to the Convention, without realizing that this particular paragraph cannot mean to be more than just a short introductory re-statement of specificities partly claimed by the State Party itself.[577]

Obligations Categorically Denied

What became apparent, over the course of this second reporting cycle, must be described as a fundamental disagreement between the Committee and the Holy See about the general scope of obligations which seem to be straightforwardly flowing from the text of the Convention as the Committee sees it; in contrast, the Holy See denies any such obligation ever extending to legislative activities targeting specific matters as they are presently regulated in the *Codex*. As proferred by the Holy See, its legal defense is building on an intrinsic link between 'implementation' as an obligation and 'territory' as a socio-legal reality.[578]

Here, the underlying concept still is about implementation as an overall obligation of particular significance to the Convention as evidenced by Article 4 CRC.[579] Accordingly, in the following I will concentrate on the validity of reservations and declarations under international law, as this seems to be a legal subject-matter at the core of an institutionalized human rights dialogue which will go on as long as the Holy See, having authored three reservations and one interpretative declaration, keeps holding itself out as a State Party to the Convention.[580] Unfortunately, nowhere in its recent state reporting documents the Holy See explains exactly which part of its declaration or reservations it wishes to rely on for a modification or an exclusion of legal effects originally created by virtue of specific provisions, such as Article 4 CRC (duty to implement) or Article 19 CRC (duty

---

577 Hailu (n 514) 779, 784; McManus (n 523) 18; I Cismas, 'The Child's Best Interests and Religion: A Case Study of the Holy See's Best Interests Obligation and Clerical Child Sexual Abuse' in E E Sutherland et al (eds), *Implementing Article 3 of the Convention on the Rights of the Child: Best Interests, Welfare and Well-being* (CUP 2016) 6.

578 Fn 529 and accompanying text.

579 Fn 519 and accompanying text.

580 CRC/C/OPSC/VAT/1 para 7; LeBlanc (n 18) 357; the follow-up state report of the Holy See (CRC) was due on September 2017, but no document was produced as by the time of writing (spring 2023).

to protect against violence).[581] What is apparent from the documents, however, is a certain tendency of the Holy See to partly evade legally binding effects created under international law as an autonomous and independent legal system to which it had linked itself in terms of treaty law *via* State consent.[582] Apparently, any treaty-based duty to fully implement Convention rights into its internal legal order is accepted by the Holy See only in respect of Vatican City State which is a territory under its exclusive control but only has a tiny minority of citizens and inhabitants aged 18 years or less.

Sub-Section (3) – Validity of Reservations and Declaration

In the following, what seemingly is an easy exercise needs to be performed in two steps: state the international law of reservations and then run a test in regard of reservations and declarations attached to its international act by the Holy See when ratifying the Convention, including deposition of that same international act with the General Secretary of the United Nations.

Re-statement of the Law on Reservations

As indicated by Article 19 VCLT, the validity of reservations will generally be determined on the basis of an 'object and purpose' test; meaning that where a reservation is not prohibited by the treaty or falls within the specified permitted categories, a State may make a reservation provided it is not incompatible with the object and purpose of the treaty.[583] In consistency with this general treaty law rule, Article 51 CRC states that a reservation incompatible with the object and purpose of the Convention shall not be permitted.

Furthermore, the Committee, in its *GC 5,* just indicates that any kind of reservation poses problems for ensuring full and unqualified respect for the human rights of children, but no guidance is offered as to concrete standards against which the validity of reservations might be measured and determined in practice.[584] For their 2014 Concluding Observations the Committee express their concern that the Holy See's reservations to the

581 CRC/C/VAT/Q/2/Add.1 para 7.
582 Cismas (n 577) 3; McManus (n 523) 3.
583 CCPR/C/21/Rev.1/Add.6, para 6 referencing Article 19 VCLT.
584 CRC/GC/2003/5 paras 13–16.

Convention undermine the full recognition of children as subjects of rights; moreover, the applicability of the Convention looks (to the Committee) like being conditioned by its compatibility with the sources of Vatican City State law. What is presupposed here is that, as a standard, the Convention's precedence over internal laws and regulations must not be hampered by way of making reservations.[585]

What, furthermore, the Human Rights Committee commented on the object and purpose of ICCPR as a human rights treaty, may well serve as guidance for testing reservations made in regard to other human rights treaties including the CRC. What must be seen as the object and purpose of this Convention is the following: to create legally binding standards for children's rights (1); and placing them in a framework of legal obligations (2); and to provide an efficacious supervisory machinery for treaty obligations undertaken (3).[586] At the outset, therefore, it may be stated that any reservations or declaration unilaterally declared by the Holy See in regard to obligations under the Convention and not found to be in compliance with these aims yet unspecified, cannot validly be upheld as a matter of law.[587] Incompatibility of a reservation with the object and purpose of a treaty, as explained by ILC scholars for their *Guide to Practice*, is given if it affects an essential element of the treaty that is necessary to its general tenor in such a way that the reservation impairs the raison d'etre of the treaty.[588]

As a consequence, if the Holy See having signed and ratified the Convention wishes to stay away (as a legislator *ad internum*) from its *Codex* and keep its *Canones* as previously un-amended, there seems to be one escape route only: claim the legal effects of a reservation which is the accepted treaty law instrument generally serving "to exclude or to modify the legal effect of certain provisions of the treaty in the application to that State" (Article 2(1) d VCLT). In the following, however, it will be demonstrated that none of the reservations or declaration actually entered upon by the Holy See can have these particular excluding or modifying effects. As

---

585 CRC/C/VAT/CO/2 para 11.

586 CCPR/C/21/Rev.1/Add.6 para 7 (Human Rights Committee); see also Fn 24 above.

587 Article 21 VCLT treating legal effects of reservations; UN document A/66/10/Add.1 *Report of the International Law Commission* General Assembly, Official Records, Sixty-sixth Session Supplement No. 10 *Guide to Practice* section 4.5 and Commentary 391.

588 A/66/10/Add.1 *Guide to Practice* (n 587 above) 351; Hailu (n 514) 779, 789.

a State Party the Holy See remains legally bound, under international law (Article 4 CRC), to fully implement all rights in the Convention within its own internal legal order accordingly.[589]

Two different legal documents stand out for considering the validity of this kind of treaty reservations, one is a General Comment issued in November 1994 by the Human Rights Committee and specifically aiming at reservations made upon ratification of human rights treaties, and the other is a *Guide to Practice on Reservations to Treaties* published as a UN document in 2011 by the International Law Commission.[590]

Testing Holy See Reservations against Treaty Standards

As briefly mentioned a 'reservation' was legally defined (Article 2 VCLT) as encompassing any unilateral statement made by a State, when signing, ratifying or acceding to a treaty, whereby it purports to exclude or to modify the legal effect of certain provisions of the treaty in their application to that State. Furthermore, *GC 24* details that a reservation

> *must be specific and transparent, so that the Committee, those under the jurisdiction of the reserving state and other States parties may be clear as to what obligations of human rights compliance have or have not been undertaken. Reservations may thus not be general, but must refer to a particular provision of the Covenant and indicate in precise terms its scope in relation thereto.*[591]

Since these requirements were specifically stated by the Human Rights Committee *'to address the problem of reservations to human rights treaties'*, they may equally be applied to the Convention as a human rights treaty, regardless of the fact that their immediate relation is to ICCPR-based obligations. Respecting the Convention, six brief statements, under the heading of 'Reservations and Declarations', were entered upon by the Holy See having signed and ratified the instrument, in connection with its international act deposited with the UN Secretary General.[592]

---

[589] LeBlanc (n 18) 381; VDPA (1993) Part II paras 5, 46.

[590] CCPR/C/21/Rev.1/Add.6 (11 November 1994), *GC 24* in the following; A/66/10 Add.1 *Guide to Practice* (n 587).

[591] *GC 24* (n 590 above) para 19; Similar requirements in Article 57 ECHR.

[592] The Holy See 'Reservations' and 'Declarations' read (extract): ***Reservations:*** a) [The Holy See] interprets the phrase 'Family planning education and services' in article 24.2, to mean … ; b) [The Holy See] interprets the articles of the Convention in

Two Reservations and an Extended Declaration

Grounding on what it designates as a 'Reservation', the Holy See interprets the Articles of the Convention in a way which safeguards the primary and inalienable rights of parents, in particular insofar as these rights concern education (Articles 13 and 28 CRC) and further topics;[593] equally, by way of a 'Reservation', the Holy See declares that the application of the Convention be compatible in practice with the particular nature of the Vatican City State (VCS) and the sources of its objective law.[594] Moreover, featuring as a 'Declaration' an intention is made known that, in consideration of its singular nature and position, the Holy See, in acceding to the Convention, does not intend to derogate from its specific mission which is of a religious and moral character.[595]

What is problematic about these particular statements as here rephrased in summary form mainly touches on their content, not their format. Thus, respecting the content of the Convention, no primary and inalienable rights of parents are stipulated which might need safeguarding against encroachments possibly implicated by vindicating children's rights. Generally seen as a primary point of reference for parents' rights Article 26(3) UDHR states that parents have a prior right to choose the kind of education that shall be given to their children. As a consequence, this particular Holy See reservation seems to be incompatible with the object and purpose of the Convention primarily proclaiming children's rights (to quality education, among others); whereas the child's parents, their rights and responsibilities, were recognised in the text itself, through specific provisions inserted into Articles 3, 5, 14, 18, 29 CRC in particular.[596] This reservation's incompatibility with the object and purpose of the Convention rests

---

a way which safeguards the primary and inalienable rights of parents, in particular insofar as these rights concern education (articles 13 and 28), … ; c) [The Holy See declares] that the application of the Convention be compatible in practice with the particular nature of the Vatican City State and the sources of its objective law (art. 1, Law of 7 June 1929, n. 11) … ; ***Declarations:*** … In consideration of its singular nature and position, The Holy See, in acceding to this Convention, does not intend to prescind in any way from its specific mission which is of a religious and moral character.

593 Fn 592 above, letter b.

594 Fn 592, letter c.

595 Fn 592, last sentence.

596 Tobin (n 136) 53; L Lundy et al (n 211) 364, 366.

on its disregard for a core requirement of systematic interpretation, namely observing levels of specificity: since the rights of parents were treated exhaustively at the level of specific rights (such as educational rights) there is no room for a further balancing of rights if not done for weakening the compromise reached already.

Furthermore, as a matter of treaty law the Convention's normative weight as a human rights treaty must not be conditioned by reference to its compatibility with any particular State Party's internal laws; any such qualification seems to be in contravention of the general rule about observance of treaties, Articles 26 (*Pacta sunt servanda*) and 27 VCLT (*Internal law and observance of treaties*). Finally, again as a matter of treaty law, no legal significance can be attributed to a signatory's motives lying behind its decision to become a State party to the Convention; this contravenes the basic interpretation rule of Article 31 (1) VCLT which states that the principle of textuality must be followed as a primordial rule for interpretative efforts.

Accordingly, my focus here will be on the legal effects of Articles 2, 4 CRC which, by way of generalising treaty provisions, stipulate far-reaching obligations aimed at ensuring implementation of the right to non-violent education. Therefore, the question arises whether, by virtue of a statement unilaterally made, those same legal effects may validly be modified or excluded.[597] Possibly the statement made in the set of "Reservations" (letter c) dealing with the particular nature of VCS, or the final (un-itemized) statement concluding the set of 'Declarations' and dealing with the singular nature and position of the Holy See, may qualify as a valid reservation with regard to international obligations flowing from the Convention.[598] Because of their generality and vagueness, however, both these unilateral statements measured against treaty law requirements and *GC 24* in particular, seem highly problematic.

Validity of VCS Reservation

According to this reservation the application of the Convention must be compatible in practice with the particular nature of the Vatican City State

[597] Fn 520 and accompanying text ("encourage and support"); McAleese (n 7) 438.

[598] In the following 'VCS Reservation' for the earlier statement, 'Holy See Declaration' for the latter one.

and the sources of its objective law.[599] No explanation was given in this statement as to what the particular nature of VCS was, or what concept of 'compatibility in practice' between the legal sources of VCS law and the Convention as applied in practice, should be underlying.[600]

As mentioned above the Vienna Convention sets out the basic rule (formulated in Articles 26, 27 VCLT) according to which no State Party may rely on its internal laws as a justification for its failure to perform, in a manner faithful to the terms of the treaty, that same treaty. Since, essentially, the sources of VCS State law are found in its canonical legal order (*Codex* and a few more instruments[601]) that same canon law based legal order appears to be an embodiment of this State Party's internal laws on which, accordingly, the Holy See may not rely as a justification for its failure to implement treaty-based children's rights.[602] However, with respect to VCS as a territory under its exclusive administration the Holy See actually made a significant effort to implement children's rights by drafting, in 2013, fresh criminal legislation for the protection of minors; those freshly drafted VCS laws were then presented to the Committee for insertion into its state reporting documentation.[603] What was documented by this particular legislative activity expressly designated as an act of implementing an instrument belonging to the CRC-system (namely OPSC) amounts to a declaration of compatibility between its own VCS reservation and an implementation of children's rights into the Holy See's internal legal order: clearly, that reservation, its requirement of compatibility in particular, did not pose a problem for the Holy See as a legislator when freshly making internal laws for the protection of children.[604]

William Schabas found this unilateral statement made by the Holy See to be irritating in that '*it would appear from such a reservation that the Holy See does not really expect the Convention to apply to the Vatican City*

---

599 Hailu (n 514) 779, 800.

600 Fn 588 and accompanying text.

601 McAleese (n 7) 386, 388; Hailu (n 514) 779, 801.

602 Art. 1 (*Fonti principali del diritto*) N. LXXI – Legge sulle fonti del diritto (1 ottobre 2008) attached to and referenced in CRC/C/VAT/Q/2/Add.1 (Replies, December 2013) paras 17, 18.

603 CRC/C/VAT/Q/2/Add.1 (Replies, December 2013) paras 17, 18.

604 Legge N. VIII (as attached to Holy See Replies, n 603 above) refers to international agreements necessitating an insertion of new crimes into VCS legislation.

territory'.[605] This author identifies this one as a reservation remarkably similar in scope to 'Islamic' reservations typically declaring that 'principles of Islamic laws and values' must prevail under all circumstances.[606] With express reference to Schabas' paper ILC experts in their *Guide to Practice* found this text of the VCS reservation to be concerning in a way similar to so-called 'sharia reservations' assuming that because of its vagueness or generality it cannot be upheld.[607]

In conclusion, this VCS reservation declared with respect to the Convention is not valid as an instrument for excluding or modifying the legal effects of Articles 2, 4 CRC as far as it touches on an obligation to fully implement children's rights, and the right to non-violent education in particular.

Validity of Holy See Declaration

According to this declaration the Holy See, in acceding to the Convention, "*does not intend to prescind* [sic!] *in any way from its specific mission which is of a religious and moral character*".[608] From an international law perspective this unilateral statement made by the Holy See can have no legal effect and this is for reasons of a more linguistic character; but also for reasons especially relating to the substance of children's rights as spelled out in a number of CRC provisions.

Again, Article 31 (1) VCLT sets out the principle of textual interpretation for treaties in three elements: the text of the treaty, the context to its terms and also its object and purpose. Thus, in any case of treaty interpretation it is in the text of specific treaty provisions that the basis for interpretative activity must be laid, and no undocumented intention of the parties to the treaty (such as *to prescind* or *not to prescind*) can come in as a substitute for that. As a consequence, no particular obligation emanating

---

605 Schabas (n 516) 472, 479.

606 Schabas (n 516) 478; this kind of 'Islamic' reservations are generally seen as highly problematic: S Harris-Short, 'International Human Rights Law: Imperialist, Inept and Ineffective? Cultural Relativism and the CRC' 25 HRQ (2003) 130, 135.

607 *Guide to Practice* (n 587) section 3.1.5.2 para (7);

608 Linguistically, an expression such as '*to prescind from* (a mission or similar) … ' has no very determinate meaning in modern English; as a negation ('*not to prescind from*'), moreover phrased as an intent ('*does not intend to prescind from*') it is sheer vagueness; CRC/C/VAT/2 para 12 ('to derogate … from'); Holy See *Comments* (n 517) para 14 ('… not contradict … ').

from the Convention as a core human rights treaty is being modified or excluded by means of this declaration and the Holy See as a State Party to thc Convention fully remains duty-bound to implement all children's rights emerging from the Convention.

As in the case of the VCS reservation above no explanation was given in this declarative statement as to the Holy See and its international personality although the text of the declaration starts with a reference to the Holy See's '*singular nature and position*'. Adding to its linguistic indeterminacy this vagueness in legal-constitutional terms renders the whole statement completely ineffective; certainly no such fundamental obligation as the one contained in Articles 2, 4 CRC calling for a full implementation of Convention obligations will thus be modified or excluded as a consequence.[609] Thus, the following section shall explore, whether international obligations flowing from the CRC have been fulfilled by the Holy See as a State Party to the Convention.

Second Section: Obligations Unfulfilled

Introduction

As a matter of coherence I should briefly refer back to what came out of my re-lecture of several *Abuse Reports* from Ireland, in terms of itemized conclusions: canon law as the Church's internal body of laws, totally un-amended as it was at the time covered by the reports, proved to be absolutely not fit for purpose when it comes to protecting children and their basic human rights.[610] Accordingly, there is plenty of room for improvement regarding canon law provisions that must be reviewed and amended towards an ever more faithful performance of the Convention as a human rights treaty. In particular, protection rights including the right to non-violent education as rooted in the Convention must be fully implemented into the body of canon law which the 1983 Code of Canon Law documents. Since it is for canon law – and for canon law only – to remove offending clergy from their positions of ecclesiastical status and authority in regard of minors and other vulnerable persons, this is the prime location for effective amendments.[611]

[609] *GC 24* (n 590) para 9 (Human Rights Committee).

[610] See p 43 above addressing 'Canon Law' under (4).

[611] See Fn 507 above and accompanying text (*'Murphy'*).

Thus, the question arises whether legislative activities recently taken by the Holy See for amendment of its internal legal order do, in fact, implement human rights for the benefit and in the interest of children including millions of students in Catholic schools worldwide? In other words, did the Holy See undertake a comprehensive review of its normative framework, in particular canon law, with a view to ensuring its full compliance with the Convention, as suggested by the Committee?[612] Again, Mary McAleese offers an observation in respect of one of the core Holy See offices involved, namely the Congregation for Catholic Education which *'has not dealt to any significant extent with the broad realm of the rights of children in Catholic schools under canon law and in the light of the Convention'*.[613] To a certain degree this observation is symptomatic for the Holy See's general attitude in respect of the Convention: a laudable instrument for the world, but not a legally binding instrument for the Church as a whole.

In the following I will re-build my structure earlier developed for an analysis of the obligation to protect the right to non-violent education. From a more general typology-based perspective the four main obligation aspects were unfolded which will now be followed through to the level of legislative and administrative practice as attributable to the Holy See: 'Criminalization', 'Mandatory Reporting', 'Investigation' and 'Inspection' as they may be captured here for short.[614] Insofar as they are rights-based in a similar way, other obligations will also be discussed in the following, such as 'Inter-agency cooperation'.

Sub-section (1) – Is Child Sexual Abuse a Crime under Canon Law?

My introduction here is with reference to an earlier piece of analysis when 'criminalization' was discussed as an obligation under the Convention, and to *GC 13* in particular which, on the basis of Article 19 CRC made a strong case for criminalizing child sexual abuse and exploitation in terms of express legislation to be drafted internally.[615] From a viewpoint of children's rights what must be protected *via* criminalization as a legislating techni-

[612] CRC/C/VAT/CO/2 para 14; see also Fn 574 above.

[613] McAleese (n 7) 30.

[614] See p 97 above; for purely practical reasons, 'Comprehensive sexuality education' will not be covererd in detail due to the fact that the Holy See does not own and manage its own institutions of primary and post-primary education.

[615] Fn 331 and accompanying text.

que, is the child's right to his or her personal integrity, bodily, mentally and morally.

As mentioned earlier, what poses a main problem for legislation presently in force as a matter of canon law penalizing sexually abusive behaviour in the Church, is the general lack of precision and discernment.[616] Also, from within the Church a clear insight was developed according to which existing internal procedures ('Canonical Penal Processes' as they were addressed collectively) dealing with sexual abuse are deficient as a legal sub-system, in that the role of the victim of sexual abuse in canonical proceedings is limited inappropriately; as recently declared by one of the most senior Holy See representatives these shortcomings were clearly identified as a *lacuna* in the law.[617]

To illustrate my first point, for this particular context the core canonical definition of delinquency regarding sexual offences is encompassed by offending '... *against the sixth commandment of the Decalogue*' (can 1395 §2 CIC); indeed, the particular offence created by virtue of canon 1398 §1 CIC addresses '... *an offence against the sixth commandment of the Decalogue with a minor,* ... '.[618] Taken literally, since the sixth commandment of the Decalogue (*'You shall not commit adultery'*) presupposes at least one married person among those offending, no offence will ever be committed if an unmarried minor is involved as a victim of sexual abuse perpetrated by an equally unmarried cleric against that same minor.[619]

---

616 Fn 123 and accompanying text.

617 C J Scicluna, 'Taking Responsibility for Processing Cases of Sexual Abuse Crisis and for Prevention of Abuse', Presentation at the Vatican Meeting *"The Protection of Minors in the Church"* (21–24 February 2019) 2.

618 Can 1395 CIC reads (extract): '*§2. A cleric who has offended in other ways against the sixth commandment of the Decalogue, ... , is to be punished ... ; §3. A cleric who by force, threats or abuse of his authority commits an offence against the sixth commandment of the Decalogue or forces someone to perform or submit to sexual acts is to be punished ... ;* Canon 1398 reads (extract): *§1. A cleric is to be punished ... , if he: 1°commits an offence against the sixth commandment of the Decalogue with a minor ... ; 2°grooms or induces a minor ... to expose himself or herself pornographically or to take part in pornographic exhibitions, whether real or simulated... ; 3°immorally acquires, retains, exhibits or distributes, ... , pornographic images of minors ... . §2. A member of an institute ... or of a society ... , or any one of the faithful who enjoys a dignity or performs an office or function in the Church, who commits an offence mentioned in §1 or in can 1395 §3 is to be punished ...* '.

619 In practice, this version of *delictum contra sextum* has been taken by canonists to

From this point of view, as a means of prevention against, and prohibition of sexual abuse committed by clerics and other church personnel, this offence as circumscribed at this location in the *Codex* seems to be dysfunctional. However, for stating its case about the universal law of the Church treating sexual abuse of a minor by a cleric or religious as one of the most serious offences in the Church, the Holy See referred the Committee to this particular canon in the *Codex* as a piece of evidence.[620]

The ecclesiastical legislator, through this simple circumscription, usually captured '*delictum contra sextum*', aims at a definition of the scope of sexual offences punishable in the Church; according to recent canonical legislation this delict against the sixth commandment of the Decalogue shall consist of: first, '*forcing someone, by violence or threat or through abuse of authority, to perform or submit to sexual acts;* second, *performing sexual acts with a minor*; and third, *the production, exhibition, possession or distribution of child pornography*'.[621] As explained by a Vatican handbook for bishops the typology of the delict is quite broad; it includes sexual relations (consensual or non-consensual), physical contact for sexual gratification, exhibitionism, masturbation, the production of pornography, inducement to prostitution and conversations or propositions of a sexual nature.[622]

Clearly, this official understanding within the Church about offences that must be framed and defined for application by bishops and other adjudicators is lacking in many respects, such as a definition of differentiating factors to protect individuals and individual freedoms; is also lacking in a

---

forbid any activity of a sexual character realized by a cleric who is under an obligation of celibacy, see Aymans-Mörsdorf-Müller, *Kanonisches Recht* (Band IV, Ferdinand Schöningh 2013) 243.

620 CRC/C/VAT/2 para 98 letter (f); at the time, can 1395(2) CIC read (extract): '*A cleric who … has committed an offence against the sixth commandment of the Decalogue, if the delict was committed … with a minor … is to be punished …* '.

621 Apostolic Letter in the form of Motu Proprio of the Supreme Pontiff Francis '*Vos estis lux mundi*' (9 May 2019, updated with minor changes on 25 March 2023), Article 1 – Scope of application; this instrument builds on what has been in existence as an offence (*delictum contra sextum*) with no intention to define new crimes.

622 Dicastery of the Doctrine of the Faith, *Vademecum* on Certain Points of Procedure in Treating Cases of Sexual Abuse of Minors Committed by Clerics (Version 2.0, 5 June 2022) para 2; most of the constituting details are spelled out in the law itself only in a rudimentary fashion, see Fn 618 above.

plain definition of punishable acts, is lacking in a definition of perpetrators to be punished or victims to be rehabilitated, and is also lacking in a plain provision of adequate sanctions normatively attached to an offence proven. None of the details constituting an offence of child sexual abuse is clearly and coherently spelled out in the law-book treating penal sanctions, namely *Book VI* of the 1983 Code of Canon Law; most of it must be collated from several instruments drawing together offences against special obligations and other offences such as breaking the seal of the confessional.

Similarly, a leading commentary for the English-speaking world explains in regard of canon 1395 CIC (as reproduced above) which generally speaks of an external sin "against the sixth commandment of the Decalogue"

> *Regrettably, the exact meaning of this phrase is not entirely clear. It may mean technically adultery or sexual delicts involving clerics and married women. However, it is also used as a circumlocution for other types of sexual misconduct, heterosexual or homosexual, e. g., rape, fornication or incest.*[623]

The contrast is striking indeed: as applicable to VCS, canonical legislation fully worked out penal laws containing a whole title in nine articles where, among others, sexual violence against minors and sexual activities with minors are properly addressed in plain (Italian) language.[624] Even supposing that penal laws in the Church may have a function different from offences statutorily defined in a secular State legal order, this formulaic description – "delicts against the sixth commandment of the Decalogue" – is by far too wide and imprecise for effective deterrence from committing acts of sexual violence against children in education.[625] Unsurprisingly, the Committee, in its 2014 Concluding Observations, strongly recommended for the Holy See to make an amendment to its canon law provisions in order to identify child sexual abuse as a serious crime that must be punished in all proven cases, including those where the perpetrator was a cleric.[626]

At long last, the Holy See has become active as a legislator in respect of VCS legislation which, in 2013, was amended so as to include statuto-

---

623 T J Green in *New Commentary on the Code of Canon Law* (Paulist New York 2000) 1599 with Fn 288 (can 1395 CIC as unamended).

624 Fn 604, Legge N.VIII: *Norme complementari in materia penale*.

625 H Hallermann, *"Präzisierung und Erleichterung?"* Kirche und Recht 2013, 178, 190.

626 CRC/C/VAT/CO/2 para 44 letter (d).

ry crimes captured as *'Sexual Violence against Minors'* or as *'Sexual Acts including Minors'* stated in a piece of legislation modelled after corresponding crimes in the Italian Penal Code.[627] Interestingly, as a preamble to this particular VCS statute (*Legge N. VIII, 11 luglio 2013)* a short explanatory justification for drafting an amendment was given referring to the fact that the Holy See ratified several *'international conventions'* requiring that respective statutory crimes be defined in order to suppress criminal behaviour thereby determined.[628] Thus, the Holy See seems to be fully aware of its international obligations to undertake legislative and administrative measures for a criminalization of child sexual abuse as a matter of crime prevention in the Church; however, as understood by the Holy See, an international obligation thus specified must be limited in effect to VCS territory as a jurisdiction defined in terms of its (narrow) territorial boundaries. The truth of the matter is that no such limitation is acceptable, either as a matter of treaty interpretation concerning the Convention or as a matter of canon law concerning the *Codex*.

To answer my research question initially posed, as regards the criminalization of child sexual abuse the Holy See as a legislator only partially honoured its commitment made under Articles 4 and 19 CRC in particular; what was recently drafted by the Holy See as a matter of VCS legislation instituted on the basis of canon law as its legal-constitutional foundation, should be further developed into the realm of canons in the penal law section of the *Codex* which must now be reviewed and amended accordingly.[629]

---

627 CRC/C/VAT/Q/2/Add.1 para 17 with reference to an attachment including *Legge N. VIII: Norme complementaria in materia penale* (Fn 604); the Committee welcomes this initiative and also another piece of VCS legislation (same date) containing amendments to the Criminal Code and the Criminal Procedure Code (*Legge N. IX*), see CRC/C/VAT/CO/2 para 5.

628 *Legge N. VIII* (n 604) preamble, my translation: '... *la Santa Sede ... ha ratificato diverse convenzioni internationali che richiedono la definizione di corrispondenti fattispecie penali al fine della repressione di determinate condotte criminose'*.

629 Reforming Book VI of the *Codex* by Apostolic Constitution '*Pascite gregem dei'* (June 2021) did not substantially change *'delictum contra sextum'* as the main offence of sexual abuse, see cann 1395, 1398 CIC (n 618).

Sub-section (2) – Is Reporting of Child Abuse Mandatory under Canon Law?

Another topic discussed already as an implementing measure for the fulfilment of obligations under the Convention will here be re-visited with particular attention paid to the Holy See as a State Party to the Convention.[630] For realising children's rights and the right to non-violent education in particular, mandatory reporting was identified as a prime measure, legislative and administrative in nature, for the protection of children against all forms of inter-personal violence perpetrated or threatened against them.[631]

Holy See Position on Mandatory Reporting

As a point of departure it should initially be recalled that the Committee, in their 2014 concluding observations recommended in no uncertain terms that the Holy See *'establish clear rules, mechanisms and procedures for the mandatory reporting of all suspected cases of child sexual abuse and exploitation to law enforcement authorities'*.[632] As a consequence, the key question for this section in the study will be the following: how did the Holy See as a State Party to the Convention read this particular recommendation, and did it begin to undertake steps for the realisation of its obligations under the Convention in this regard; and, if it did, which steps were taken?

Due to its irregular nature as a non-state actor on the one hand, simultaneously behaving as a widely accepted subject of international law on the other, the Holy See takes a special stance on the topic of mandatory reporting; as a child protection policy it might, in principle, become an institution of canon law *via* an amendment to the *Codex* while simultaneously being implemented (under the Convention) into many different State legal orders. Seen from a perspective of the individual child as a holder of rights, this overall constellation was identified as a complicating factor: many Catholic children live in jurisdictions which are themselves States Parties to

630 Fn 362 and accompanying text.
631 Fn 374 and accompanying text.
632 CRC/C/VAT/CO/2 para 44 letter (e); see also p 164 (item nr 7) above.

the Convention coming under an obligation to implement protective measures such as mandatory reporting.[633] As Prof McAleese further explains:

> *Canon Law has no legal status in most other* [than VCS] ... *State Party jurisdictions but if its effects are to limit or compromise the Convention based rights of a child within the territory of another State Party the latter may well be answerable before the* [Committee].[634]

As a consequence, whatever the immediate relationship between the Holy See and the Convention, the Holy See's teaching or laws affecting children everywhere are potentially open to indirect challenge under the Convention, *via* State Parties hosting Catholic institutions, and how they are reporting to the Committee.[635] Additionally and quite independently from this kind of indirect challenge, reporting of "sexual misconduct", in the meantime, became an issue for canon law as an autonomous legal order.[636] As such canon law must, therefore, be made compatible with Convention standards even if, as a legal order it is applicable to Catholics only, in most cases.

The Possibility of Conflicting Demands

As practice has shown conflicting demands on the individual concerned as a possible reporter are to be envisaged:[637] a cleric, for instance, finding himself under a legal obligation to report his suspicion or knowledge about child sexual abuse emanating from the State legal order of his place of professional service, may think this demand to be in contravention of his canonical rights and duties as rooted in the seal of confession or in the requirement of secrecy.[638] Obviously, the sheer existence of this kind of conflicting demand poses a serious problem for canon law in general, and for the Holy See as a legislator, since its own legislative and administrative

---

633 McAleese (n 7) 33.

634 ibid 34.

635 CRC/C/IRL/CO/3–4, paras 33, 34 (Ireland, 2016); CAT/C/IRL/CO/1 paras 20/1 (Ireland, 2011).

636 Scicluna (Fn 617).

637 Fn 121 above; On the blockage caused by Holy See intervention, see Fn 646 below and accompanying text.

638 *'Murphy'* reporting, at para 1.33, about an archbishop from Dublin remaining deeply troubled when allowing access to archdiocesan files for the Police.

activities must not, directly or indirectly, contravene Convention standards as they are applicable almost everywhere in the world.[639] Consequently, as a legislator of widespread reach (in geographical terms) the Holy See must try to keep any risk of legal conflict and confusion as low as possible; otherwise, as demonstrated historically, children and their rights and freedoms risk to be severely undermined.[640]

As a legal research document the 2011 Response of the Holy See to the Government of Ireland (responding to *'Cloyne'*) may be appreciated for its discussion of secular and canonical (Irish) legislative efforts treating mandatory reporting as a child protection policy; and the 2019 *MP Vos estis lux mundi* is a highly relevant canon law document authored by the Holy See which, for the first time, inaugurates something like a reporting system universally applicable as a matter of canon law.[641]

Holy See Response to the Government of Ireland regarding 'Cloyne'

Through this *Response* document the Holy See retrospectively tries to explain and justify how it had positioned itself in regard to a local initiative undertaken by bishops in Ireland for strengthening their grip on the problem of having to deal effectively with allegations of child sexual abuse against priests and religious. As a policy option mandatory reporting appears to be relatively close to the mind of the drafters of *Framework Document* (authored by a study group of the Irish Bishop's Conference) which unambiguously provided for the reporting of complaints. In contrast, the voice from the Holy See makes itself heard by articulating grave concerns against mandatory reporting as a cause for violations of canonical procedures to the detriment of priests or religious accused of sexual abuse.[642] Reading this 2011 *Response* in connection with *'Cloyne'* and also in connection with the *Framework Document* provides for a deep insight into the actual position of the Holy See when confronted with locally rooted initiative for legislation, including mandatory reporting as a legislative or administrative measure for the protection of children.

---

639 L Lundy et al (n 211) 364, 366.

640 *'Cloyne'* para 4.21 (Nuncio Storero's letter); *'Murphy'* paras 7.13/4 (*Framework Document*); Holy See *Response* (n 93) 3; Keenan (n 61) 194.

641 Holy See *Response* (n 93); MP *'Vos estis lux mundi'* (n 621).

642 *The Framework Document* in *'Ferns'* 32 (brief description), *'Murphy'* paras 7.1–7.57; *'Cloyne'* paras 4.10–4.16.

As early as 1994 a *Framework Document* was designed as a policy document later elaborated under the aegis of the Irish Bishop's Conference as a code of recommended practice for handling complaints about clerical child sexual abuse which were brought to the attention of bishops in Ireland or otherwise they became aware of; through a passage in that *Framework Document* the bishops in Ireland recommended the following as a reporting policy guideline for their dioceses:

> *In all instances where it is known or suspected that a child has been, or is being, sexually abused by a priest or religious the matter should be reported to the civil authorities. Where the suspicion or knowledge results from the complaint of an adult of abuse during his or her childhood this should also be reported to the civil authorities.*
>
> *The report should be made without delay to the senior ranking police officer for the area in which the abuse is alleged to have occurred. Where the suspected victim is a child, or where a complaint by an adult gives rise to child protection questions the designated person within the appropriate health board* [...] *should also be informed. A child protection question arises in the case of a complaint by an adult where an accused priest or religious holds or has hold a position which has afforded him or her unsupervised access to children.*[643]

While, as a policy outline this document does not provide for a sanction in the case of non-reporting, at least it sets a clear standard in that any suspicion or knowledge about child sexual abuse shall regularly be reported to law enforcement authorities in the State. Although children to be protected from violence on a basis of individual rights, do not feature prominently as an overall concern in this policy draft, unsupervised access by clerics to children is mentioned as a problem for child protection in cases of complaints by adults.[644]

As a result, this approach taken by bishops in Ireland for an installation of reporting mechanisms proved to be not too far from what would be required for the fulfilment of obligations under the Convention.[645] However, any further development of child protection policies for the Catholic

[643] *'Murphy'* para 7.7, *'Cloyne'* para 4.11, Holy See *Response* (n 93) 6–14.

[644] *'Cloyne'* para 4.13.

[645] It also seems to be in compliance with the letter and spirit of the Vatican presentation "*Taking Responsibility*" (n 617) 3.

church in Ireland was interrupted by an intervention from the Holy See who had qualms about mandatory reporting as a child protection policy to be fully established and practically followed by bishops in Ireland, and sent a written note of concern (generally labelled as *'Storero'*-letter) to the Irish bishops accordingly.[646] Seemingly, the basis of this Holy See concern was that the reputation and good name of a priest is being put at risk by a reporting of abuse to the authorities.[647] In no case, however, may this be accepted *per se* as a valid argument against mandatory reporting conceptualised as a child protection measure under the Convention, since reputations of alleged abusers can be validly protected by means of confidentiality; any residual risk must be weighed against the risk of allowing suspected abusers to remain at large. Seen from an abstract legal-functional point of view the main question arising would be to find out if mandatory reporting as a policy option regularly increases the likelihood of false or derogatory accusations against priests or other 'persons in authority', but no evidence for this kind of conclusion is currently available.[648]

MP Vos estis lux mundi

Just recently, the Holy See introduced a new kind of reporting system which was globally set into force for the Catholic church (RCC) worldwide by an act of canonical legislation denoting as *Motu Proprio* (Lat. 'out of my own initiative') dated 9 May 2019, the initial wording of which starts by citing a biblical text *'Vos estis lux mundi'*.[649]

Although not marked as an act of implementing Convention obligations, this piece of internal Holy See legislation (decreed on behalf of the Roman Pontiff, Pope Francis) sets out procedures to be universally adopted for the prevention and combat against crimes of sexual abuse in the Church. By virtue of its Article 3 this law mandates that clerics and members religious report to ecclesiastical authority whenever they have 'notice of or well-founded motives to believe' that some sexual abuse or cover-up has been committed; moreover all laypersons are encouraged to report clerical sexual abuse or its cover-up to the competent ecclesiastical autho-

646 Holy See *Response* (n 93) 4; CRC/C/VAT/CO/2 para 43.
647 *'Murphy'* para 7.13.
648 See Fnn 365, 367, 369 above and accompanying text.
649 MP *"Vos estis lux mundi"* (n 621).

rities.[650] Expressly articulated in this piece of legislation, '*An obligation to keep silent may not be imposed on the person claiming to have suffered as a result of a delict or on the witnesses with regard to the contents of their report* ... '. [651] Additionally, a person who neglects to report an offence, when required to do so by canonical law, may be punished by force of a penal law provision in the *Codex*, can 1371 §6 CIC.

Certainly, there is no requirement stated in this law for clerics to report to civil authorities; what is underlined, however, is that a canon law obligation to report to an ecclesiastical authority does not interfere with, nor change, any reporting obligation that may exist in any particular State's internal legislation. As a matter of compliance with State laws Article 20 of the Motu Proprio clarifies that '[T]*hese norms apply without prejudice to the rights and obligations established in each place by state laws, particularly those concerning any reporting obligations to the competent civil authorities*'.[652] Obviously, this general reference to an undefined multitude of national civil laws on mandatory reporting is not the same as an immediate normative prescription ordered by virtue of canon law itself mandating the reporting of all cases of clerical sexual abuse to law enforcement authorities. Seen from a Convention obligations point of view, this particular act of internal Holy See legislation, although a step in the right direction, counts for little in terms of faithful treaty performance regarding obligations correlative to the right to non-violent education. What should be made obligatory as a basic rule clearly set out in canon law provisions targeting bishops and other Church personnel in authority, is the reporting of all incidents of child sexual abuse to law enforcement authorities in the State concerned; regardless of the fact that either a cleric or a lay person will be treated as a suspect in the following.[653]

---

[650] Article 3 – Reporting, MP '*Vos estis lux mundi*' (n 621) reads (excerpt): '*§1 ... whenever a cleric ... has notice of, or well-founded motives to believe that one of the facts* [delicts against the sixth commandment of the Decalogue, as spelled out in Art 1] *has been committed, that person is obliged to report promptly the fact to the local Ordinary ... . §2 Any person can submit a report concerning the conduct* [delicts as spelled out in Article 1] ... '.

[651] Article 4 §3 MP '*Vos estis lux mundi*' (n 621); in effect this amounts to an abolishment of 'Pontifical Secrecy' (n 120).

[652] Article 19 MP '*Vos estis lux mundi*' (n 621) – Compliance with state laws.

[653] Speaking globally, there may be situations in some countries of a differing legal culture where due process rights are just not available for (Christian) suspects, or unduly

As a basic rule this requirement follows from an appreciation of child sexual abuse as a serious crime which canon law does not have the means to deal with appropriately. Pointing in that same direction is an instruction given to bishops according to which all relevant agreements entered into by the Holy See with national governments must always and in any event be observed;[654] assuming the CRC to be one such agreement and further assuming that mandatory reporting is an obligation under the Convention, any mandate to report as enforced by State Parties to the Convention must equally be followed by every bishop involved.

Sub-section (3) – Investigative Mechanisms under Canon Law

Above, it was shown that according to Article 19 CRC State Parties come under an international obligation making it obligatory for government agencies to immediately receive every single complaint containing minimally plausible information about child abuse; what must be established thereupon is a structured investigative relationship between the supposed child victim on the one hand, and an authorized government authority typically holding investigative powers on the other.[655] Any such complaint brought to the attention of either the police or child protection agencies in the State must lead to an instigation of investigative procedures that have to be effective, but child-sensitive at the same time.[656] What can all this mean for the Holy See as a State Party to the Convention representing the Catholic church as its governing body?

As a legal topic 'Canon Law on investigating complaints' was explored already by *'Murphy'* from a Commission of Inquiry perspective focusing on an institutional response to complaints, suspicions and knowledge of child sexual abuse as given by the Archdiocese of Dublin.[657] According to a legal overview (including a discussion of the content of specified canon law norms) provided by that report, the responsibility for dealing with complaints about clerical sexual abuse rests with the diocesan bishop or

harsh punishment is to be expected for any convicted perpetrator; this cannot fundamentally change the nature of Holy See obligations under the Convention.

[654] Dicastery of the Doctrine of the Faith (DDF), *Vademecum* (n 622) para 48.

[655] Fn 394 and accompanying text.

[656] Fn 396 and accompanying text.

[657] *'Murphy'* paras 4.30–4.44.

with Religious Superiors in the case of religious orders.[658] What is highly problematic about this approach as a normative concept is that bishops who were shown to be instrumental in covering-up incidents of child abuse had no interest in commencing formal investigations which, if diligently and thoroughly performed, might lead to questions being asked about their own governing abilities or their own individual competence as a leader in the diocese.

As explained in my conclusions, this 'cover-up' dimension integrally belonging to the whole issue of clerical child sexual abuse needs to be addressed as a real life phenomenon; *'Ferns'*, *'Murphy'* and *'Cloyne'* in particular do speak loudly about this.[659] Not surprisingly, the Holy See as a legislator re-considered this dimension of Church-related abuse and clarified that a grave lack of diligence on behalf of a bishop in handling clerical child sexual abuse cases could found a penal action against that offending bishop, and result in his removal from office.[660] As a whole, does the Holy See's own internal legal order, essentially documented in Book VI and Book VII of its *Codex Iuris Canonici* provide for a system of properly functioning investigative instruments and procedures as required by the Convention in the interest and for the benefit of children? Also, are existing investigative instruments fit for purpose, especially in regard of children who were raped or sexually assaulted by clerics fully and formally attached to the Catholic Church and officiating by an authority lent from that church?

Practical Investigations

The Committee, interestingly, seems to have no interest in canon law based investigative institutions regularly operating ('in-house') under the authority of the Holy See and dealing with individual cases of abuse; instead, it urges the Holy See to make sure that all suspected cases of child sexual abuse and exploitation are immediately reported to law enforcement

658 *'Murphy'* para 4.33; DDF, *Vademecum* (n 622) Introduction.
659 See p 42 ('Dimensions of Abuse').
660 Apostolic Letter in the form of Motu Proprio *'As a loving mother'* (4 June 2016); this piece of legislation clarifies about 'grave reasons' which, under existing canon law (can 193 §1 CIC), may lead to removal from ecclesiastical office in the case of a bishop neglecting his duties; DDF, *Vademecum* (n 622) para 21.

authorities in the State concerned.[661] This particular recommendation, however, cannot solve the problem of priests who came under (a well founded) suspicion of abusing children; they must immediately be removed from ministry and only a canon law process can affect their status as a cleric or a priest since the power to remove priests from ministry is available only from canon law.[662]

Historically, canon law has ever been providing for a set of disciplinary mechanisms serving the purpose of investigating individual cases of "sexual misconduct" when the presumed perpetrator was a cleric.[663] As mentioned above, the role of a child victim in canon law-based investigative proceedings is clearly understood, nowadays, to be un-necessarily restricted; mainly because children as holders of rights just do not appear anywhere in the canon law instruments pertinent to the issue, a *lacuna* seems to open in the law.[664] Therefore, the 2016 *Guidelines Template* provides *de lege ferenda* for means of support for those who are making reports about child abuse within the Church; at least a qualified support person should be available to those who report abuse, if they so wish.[665]

Rules and Procedures

In terms of canon law-based authority the fundamental rule in Book VII ('Processes') of the *Codex* dealing with preliminary investigations (can 1717 CIC) empowers and obligates the local bishop to make careful investigations into the behaviour of clerics that indicates an ecclesiastical delict being committed (can 1717 §1 CIC).[666]

Functioning as a triggering event the so-called *notitia de delicto* which translates into a piece of information received (by the bishop) about a possible delict need not be a formal complaint, and indeed, may come from a

---

661 CRC/C/VAT/CO/2 para 44.

662 See Fn 508 and accompanying text.

663 Scicluna (n 617) 2.

664 See Fn 617 and accompanying text.

665 Pontifical Commission for the Protection of Minors (n 531), *Guidelines Template* No 9 'Responding to Complaints of Abuse'.

666 Can 1717 §1 CIC reads (translation from Latin according to *New Commentary on the Code of Canon Law*): '*Whenever an ordinary has knowledge, which at least seems true, of a delict, he is carefully to inquire personally or through another suitable person about the facts, circumstances and imputability, …* '.

variety of sources.[667] Once the allegation has been found to have at least a '*semblance of truth*' the bishop, either personally or through some suitable person, is obliged to start a formal investigation known as the preliminary investigation (*investigatio praevia*). This, as outlined in can 1717 §1 CIC, requires the bishop to inquire about the facts and circumstances and about the imputability (guilt) of the offender. As explained by the Vatican handbook for bishops the preliminary investigation serves as a means for gathering information needed for a more detailed inquisition into the complaint (*notitia de delicto*); equally, the plausibility of the initial report must be ascertained implying that based on an assumption of truth regarding the facts reported a canonical offence might have been committed.[668]

Not many details regarding rules of evidence or in respect of the status of an accused person during this kind of preliminary investigation, are explicitly regulated in this particular canon law context; as a failure in legal guidance this may lead to passivity and secretiveness. Another special piece of canonical legislation requires that the result of an investigation about sexual misconduct of clergy with minors under the age of 18 years should be directly referred to the Holy See Dicastery for the Doctrine of Faith (formerly known as the Congregation for the Doctrine of the Faith), or DDF for short.[669] Regularly, the local bishop transmits all necessary information to the DDF and expresses his opinion on the procedures to be followed and the measures to be adopted in the short and long term; that same Holy See office (DDF) would then indicate how to proceed to the bishop concerned. In most cases referred to the DDF a canonical penal process is authorised by the Holy See and a majority of canonical penal processes are of the extra-judicial or administrative type, as described in can 1720 CIC.[670]

---

[667] DDF, *Vademecum* (n 622) para 9, 10.

[668] Ibid para 33.

[669] Motu Proprio '*Sacramentorum Sanctitatis Tutela*' (30 April 2001) Article 16 as amended by Apostolic Letter *Delicta Graviora* (18 May 2001); confirming that bishops are to refer all credible allegations of sexual abuse of minors by clerics to the Congregation for the Doctrine of the Faith (CDF), see CDF *Circular Letter* of 3 May 2011.

[670] Can 1720 CIC reads (translation from Latin according to *New Commentary on the Code of Canon Law*) (extract): '*If the ordinary thinks … : 1°he is to inform the accused of the accusation and the proofs, giving an opportunity for self-defense, … : 2°he is to weigh carefully all the proofs and arguments with two assessors; 3°if the delict is certainly established and a criminal action is not extinguished, he is to issue a decree … , setting forth the reasons in law and in fact at least briefly*'; DDF,

Regularly, during the investigative process the priest accused is called to the accusations and gets a chance to review the evidence;[671] he has a right to present recourse to the DDF against a decree condemning him to a canonical penalty. In its handbook for bishops the DDF also explains how to proceed, should the necessity arise to hear minors: the laws of the jurisdiction concerned must be followed, as well as methods suited to their age or condition.[672] Likewise, the bishop responsible for the investigation is authorised to apply precautionary measures (can 1722 CIC[673]) limiting or prohibiting the exercise of ministry. As *Murphy* again reports, administrative leave is a well accepted and standard procedure for lay people accused of child sexual abuse in the Church.[674] Such leave involves the temporary removal of individuals from their duties, with pay, during the course of an investigation of their behaviour. Similarly, in certain circumstances, a priest may be subject to various forms of censure (sanction) as a matter of canon law: one such censure is removal of faculties which can prevent the priest from carrying out some or all of his priestly functions, thereby helping to prevent an ongoing abuse of his status in the Church to the detriment of innocent children.[675]

Two aspects of the whole investigative procedure as hitherto described are crucially important here: first, to bring in a senior level Curial office, namely DDF, for authorisation and close supervision of judicial processes practically executed at the local (diocesan) level, clearly demonstrates that the Holy See is in fact highly active, in terms of canon law application and enforcement, beyond territorial borders enclosing VCS as an entity under

Vademecum (n 622) para 77.

671 DDF *Vademecum* (n 622) para 52.

672 ibid para 51.

673 Can 1722 CIC reads (translation from Latin according to *New Commentary on the Code of Canon Law*) (extract): '… , *the ordinary, … , at any stage of the process can exclude the accused from the sacred ministry or from some office and ecclesiastical function, can impose or forbid residence in some place or territory* … ' ; DDF, *Vademecum* (n 622) paras 61–65.

674 *'Murphy'* para 4.45.

675 Can 1331 §1 CIC reads (translation from Latin according to *New Commentary on the Code of Canon Law*) (extract): "*Suspension … prohibits: 1°either all or some acts of the power of orders; 2°either all or some acts of the power of governance; 3°the exercise of either all or some of the rights or functions attached to an office* … ."; T J Green in *New Commentary on the Code of Canon Law* (Paulist New York 2000) 1551.

its exclusive governance;[676] which makes the Holy See equally liable to fulfil its obligations under the Convention. And, second, canon law-based penal processes (including investigative procedures) cannot possibly function as a substitute for regular prosecutions initiated as a matter of Criminal laws applicable in those jurisdiction(s) where the abuse(s) happened; therefore, all reporting to the law enforcement authorities in the State(s) concerned of knowledge or reasonable suspicion about child sexual abuse must be made mandatory as a matter of canon law universally applicable.

Sub-section (4) – School Inspections under Canon Law

As earlier explained, under CRC an obligation arises requiring that States Parties establish and maintain a system of rigorous school inspections providing for a wealth of relevant information flowing from the grassroot level of school practice to the governance level of ministerial office from where administrative regulation and protective policies are regularly drafted and implemented.[677]

Seen from a canon law perspective, Catholic schools play a dominant role for the child's education and upbringing leading to proper formation in the faith: a whole *Codex* chapter in ten separate canons (cann 796 to 806 CIC) sets up principles and rules for bishops, for Catholic parents, headmasters, teachers, and also for those civil socicties into which a child was born locally to Catholic parents. No provision in this part of the *Codex* explicitly addresses the child to be educated as a rights-bearing individual holding a right to non-violent education as a matter of his or her human rights.

Principally, it all starts with a branding rule according to which a *Catholic School* is understood to be an institution, either directed by the competent ecclesiastic authority or by a canonically approved congregation or which has been acknowledged as such in writing by an ecclesiastical authority, can 803 §1 CIC. As a consequence, no school, even if it is in fact Catholic, may name and designate itself a '*Catholic School*' unless a competent ecclesiastical authority has given its prior consent, can 803 §3 CIC. As stated in can 803 §2 CIC, all learning and teaching practised in a Catho-

676 The Dicastery's (DDF) legal activities regularly and intentionally become effective wherever the addressee of its instructions (a diocesan bishop in most cases) resides on the globe.

677 p 132 above.

lic school must be grounded in Catholic doctrine; all teachers must excel in doctrinal correctness as well as probity of life practices. Consequently, another canon specifies the authority of the local ordinary (bishop) and extends it to the right of appointing or removing teachers of religion, *'if a reason of religion or morals requires it'* (can 805 CIC); although no further detail is given in the law as to what might constitute a valid reason for removing teachers from their post, and if a minimally plausible allegation of child sexual abuse counts for such a reason in this context. Moreover, every Catholic school is subject to the authority of the Church expressed in general norms established by the Episcopal conference (can 804 CIC), and is also subject to regulation, oversight and visitation rights by the diocesan bishop (can 806 CIC).

By virtue of another Apostolic Constitution *'Praedicate Evangelium'* (2022) the whole Curia organisation was again reformed and the role and function of the *Dicastero per la Cultura e l'Educazione* (Office for Culture and Education) are spelt out in the document's fifth chapter (Articles 153–162). At this location the competence of the Curial *Dicastero* is regulated and, in no uncertain terms, Article 153 *Praedicate Evangelium* clearly enunciates that this Curial office develops the principles by which Catholic schools are governed.[678] Here, again, another senior level Holy See institution is constitutionally defined as having a governing role to play for child-related services available on the ground. As a matter of fact, this particular Holy See institution has been highly active in producing documents of advice for Catholic schools worldwide covering topics such as the universal human right to education and schooling, or the right of individuals to choose their own schools and type of education.[679] Regrettably, this Congregation (now: Dicastery) has not occupied itself with the wider realm of children's rights *in* education, in Catholic schools that is, under canon law and in the light of the Convention.[680] Similarly, one searches in vain for Holy See guidelines regarding procedures to be followed or standards to be kept when inspecting Catholic schools as a matter of good governance through oversight and visitation in the Church.

---

678 Article 153 *Praedicate Evangelium* reads, my translation (extract): '*§2. The Dicastery is constituted by … and by the section for Education where foundational principles in relation to Education in schools are developed, …* '.

679 McAleese (n 7) 30.

680 Ibid 30.

In canon law terms what has otherwise been designated as 'inspection', especially in relation to schools or similar educational institutions, comes through a terminology of vigilance and visitation; as mentioned above canon 806 CIC gives a right to watch over and visit the Catholic schools in his territory, to the diocesan bishop.[681] Apart from focusing on the bishop's right, not on a duty, to visit Catholic schools located on the territory of his diocese, no guidance for the scope and extent of the bishop's supervision is provided by this particular canon; whether measures of child protection from sexual abuse are covered by the bishop's vigilance remains doubtful as a consequence.[682]

To sum up, from a perspective of children's rights to be implemented into canon law those pieces of regulation already existing in the *Codex* prove to be incomplete and gravely deficient, in that an important topic is missing from the legal mandate given for school inspections internally performed by church authorities as a matter of oversight and supervision. Within the *Codex,* none of those education related canons (taken from the chapter "On schools") is treating the subject of protection from violence and abuse in any particular detail; as if, for Catholic schools, the problem did not exist which cannot be true as a matter of fact.

Sub-section (5)- Inter-agency Cooperation

With respect to a 'Fulfil' type of obligation the topic of inter-agency cooperation was discussed earlier to demonstrate that rights-based child protection which is an inherently multi-disciplinary space urgently requires close cooperation between competent agencies responsible for children's health and safety, as well as education, care and crime prevention.[683] Especially with respect to protection from violence and abuse it became evident that child protection services as set up and administered by the Government must closely cooperate with law enforcement agencies such as the police and prosecution services in order to facilitate effective crime prevention, and minimise the risk of re-traumatization for children victimized already.

Since the Holy See is not a State there is no easy answer to this quest for inter-agency collaboration as a matter of children's rights, and for

[681] Canon 806 CIC addresses the bishop's right to watch over Catholic schools.

[682] S A Euart in *New Commentary on the Code of Canon Law* (Paulist New York 2000) 960.

[683] Fn 457 above and accompanying text.

an obligation to fulfil the right to non-violent education in particular. As a compartmentalized governance institution the Holy See, and its dicasteries, must make every effort to find practical ways of collaboration which help to secure their rights for all children, Catholics and non-Catholics alike, attending Catholic schools. Centrally managed and controlled procedures for removing offending clerics from office and, indeed, from access to children in education must not be complicated or time-consuming but swift and straightforward in practice. In response to revelations about child abuse by clerics and Catholic run institutions, Pope Francis, in 2014 set up the Pontifical Commission for the Protection of Minors which had a mandate to advise the Pope, supreme legislator, supreme adjudicator and supreme administrator, on internal Church initiatives to promote local responsibility for the protection of children and vulnerable adults.[684] As such, this Pontifical Commission which was first created as a coordinating body of advisors in matters relating to child protection, seemingly lost its independent status and was, just recently, subsumed into the disciplinary section of the Dicastery for the Doctrine of the Faith;[685] there it has no remit with regard to receiving or adjudicating on individual complaints. Since it was earlier presented as a first step towards setting up an independent body to receive complaints from minors directly, this latest measure of reorganization proves to be a step backwards, not forwards to a coordinated implementation of CRC rights into canon law.[686]

Conclusions

Seen from a perspective of faithful treaty performance the Holy See clearly lacks behind, and this is not so much with regard to a set of specific legislative or administrative measures required for an implementation of the right to non-violent education. Refusing to accept its most fundamental obligation to implement and also to respect and ensure children's rights with legal effect for the global Catholic Church, the Holy See keeps

---

684 See Fn 530 above and accompanying text.

685 Apostolic Constitution *Praedicate Evangelium* (n 678) Article 78.

686 McAleese (n 7) 441; *Address of His Holiness Pope Francis to the Members of the Pontifical Commission for the Protection of Minors* (n 530).

violating in effect the most widely respected customary international law principle, namely *pacta sunt servanda*.[687]

The Holy See, by categorically denying its fundamental obligation to implement Convention rights into its own *Codex*-based legal order, which *per se* appears to be fully operational as a legal instrument for effective church governance globally enforced, keeps millions of children attending Catholic schools, in a state of quasi-rightlessness. As a consequence, seen from a vantage point of children and their guaranteed rights to protection from violence, an imminent risk of sexual abuse, either perpetrated by clerics or by laymen operating under authority of ecclesiastic managers, is not efficiently minimized as a result.

In more detail, the following may be stated as an itemized list of conclusions:

1. By signature and ratification of the Convention the Holy See committed itself on behalf of VCS and also on behalf of the Catholic Church (RCC) aggregated as a unified body of particular churches dispersed all over the globe and hierarchically organised, to implement children's rights into its own internal legal order. Embodied in its *Codex Iuris Canonici* (CIC) the multitude of ecclesiastic laws must accordingly be reviewed and amended so as to become CRC compliant in practice. None of the reservations or declarations entered into by the Holy See can fundamentally alter or limit its implementing obligation under the Convention.
2. As an obligation flowing from Article 19 CRC, and aiming at an implementation of legislative measures for an effective deterrence of violent and abusive behaviour against children, 'criminalization' is only partly fulfilled; with regard to the small territory of VCS as a nearly childless subject of international law. In contrast, those fundamental canon law provisions which are usually referenced (*delictum contra sextum*) when dealing, from within the Church's juridical system, with cases of child sexual abuse, prove to be by far too lax and imprecise; this amounts to a violation of an obligation to protect children's rights.
3. 'Mandatory Reporting' as a child protection policy was partly implemented into canon law by means of a special piece of legislation recently decreed on behalf of the Roman Pontiff (Motu Proprio *"Vos estis lux mundi"*). As an implementing measure this particular canon law instru-

[687] Fn 232 and accompanying text.

ment has weaknesses in that reporting to law enforcement authorities in the State concerned was not made obligatory.

4. Existing mechanisms for an investigation of cases of suspected child sexual abuse in the Church are not addressing children as victims of violence and sexual abuse, although as a group they have ever been the likeliest to be abused by clerics and other persons in authority. Oscillating between Vatican-generated instructions and local juridical activities most investigators in the Church are lacking proper guidelines for rights-based procedures and standards. Victim rights are totally absent from the body of laws dealing with canonical investigations making them gravely deficient and unfit for purpose in terms of its compliance with a protect type of CRC obligation;
5. 'Inspection' traditionally understood and practised as a means of canonical oversight with regard to Catholic schools in particular (visitation by the local bishop), is lacking a legally defined mandate to inquire into protection for schoolchildren against v+iolence and abuse; means for self-protection must equally be made available and accessible for children in this context.
6. As a designated location for establishing means and ways of inter-agency collaboration the Pontifical Commission for the Protection of Minors is lacking in independence from hierarchical influence or manipulation which means that an important fulfil-type of obligations under the Convention remains under-performing.

The following chapter will look deeper into the law, policy and practice of children's rights in Ireland, and explore the extent to which the right to non-violent education has been successfully implemented into this jurisdiction's internal order.

Chapter 2 – Ireland

Introduction

At the forum of HRC sponsored Universal Periodic Review,[688] Ireland in early 2012 provided a brief response to the long list of recommendations presented to it by individual members of the UN Human Rights Council; then, it was cursorily stated:

> *While the CRC has not been formally incorporated into Irish law, both the spirit and aims of the Convention are significantly reflected in Irish public policy and Irish law is in conformity with the Convention. The Convention is reflected in key legislative and policy developments in recent years relating to the protection of children.*[689]

Although a similar approach was recently taken by the Irish Government, in its periodic reporting documents,[690] it remains to be seen if, upon close scrutiny, such a wide sweeping self-exoneration may stand its test.[691] As a signatory to the Convention which came into effect as a treaty for Ireland on 28 September 1992 the Irish Government has become highly active in taking measures for the implementation of children's rights in some areas, and has remained shamefully passive in others.[692] In general, the executive power of the State will, subject to the provisions of the Constitution, be exercised by or on authority of the Government as Article 28 of the Constitution proclaims, but Irish Courts have consistently emphasised their unique role in the enforcement of personal rights, and this role is constitutionally acknowledged by a provision in Article 34(1) of the Constitution according to which justice in the State shall be administered by judges. As Article 34.3.2 of the Constitution, furthermore, enunciates the role of judges consists of, but is not limited to judicial review of legislation; in fact,

---

[688] Universal Periodic Review (UPR) is an UN institutional element at the Human Rights Council (HRC).

[689] A/HRC/19/9/Add.1 para 17.

[690] CRC/C/IRL/5–6 para 27.

[691] K Lynch, 'The Status of Children' in K Lynch (ed) *Equality in Education* (Gill&Macmillan 1999) 162, 164.

[692] Following the judgment in the case of *O'Keeffe v Ireland* (n 1) the Irish Government chose to offer no more than minimum payments to a small proportion of survivors; see *Annual Report* 2021 (Fn 112) 36.

contemporary Irish doctrine now describes all intervention in the work of either the legislature or the executive as "judicial review".[693]

This chapter will demonstrate the precise extent to which Ireland as a State Party to the Convention made provision for protecting the substance of rights and the right to non-violent education in particular; as this should be observable in terms of the State's compliance with its international obligations elaborated with the help of the tripartite scheme of obligations.

Dualism and Monism in Ireland

The Irish State, in terms of international law, clearly positions itself within the dualist tradition explicitly proclaiming that for a human rights treaty like the Convention to become an integral part of its internal legal order an act of national legislation is required;[694] unless the treaty has been incorporated into domestic law by way of some constitutional or legislative Act, it necessarily remains unenforceable. In no uncertain terms the Constitution, through its Article 29(6) in particular, states: '[N]*o international agreement shall be part of the domestic law of the State save as may be determined by the Oireachtas'*.[695]

As was ruled by Murray C.J. in regard to the ECHR, it may equally be stated in respect of the Convention as a human rights treaty that it *'may only be made part of domestic law through the portal of Article 29.6 and then only to the extent determined by the Oireachtas and subject to the Constitution'*.[696] Moreover, under the Constitution, only the Oireachtas (Irish parliament) has the power to give effect in *'the domestic law of the State'* to the terms of an international agreement; whereby any possible direct effect created by virtue of national adjudication is similarly excluded.[697] In contrast to Ireland's 2003 *European Convention on Human Rights Act* no such piece of incorporating legislation exists (as yet) for the

693 *P.O'T v Child and Family Agency* [2016] IEHC 101 para 17; M de Blacam, *Judicial Review* (Bloomsbury Professional 2017) 385.

694 Fn 722 below and accompanying text.

695 M Cahill, 'McD v L and the Incorporation of the European Convention on Human Rights' 45 Irish Jurist (N.S.) 221, 223 quoting Murray CJ ("very clear terms"); *Dos Santos & Ors v The Minister for Justice & Ors* [2013] IEHC 237 para 36 ("... constitutional rigour ... ").

696 Cahill (n 695 above) 223.

697 *McD v L* [2009] IESC 81, para 86 in fine;

CRC as a human rights treaty.[698]

State Obligations Focused

In the following, two different sections will focus their attention on international obligations created, detailed and documented by way of treaty-making in which Ireland actively participated. Against this wider background this study will explore the right to non-violent education as a children's right, including its corresponding international obligations and how they were partly fulfilled or remain unfulfilled for children in Ireland. Furthermore, as Article 44 CRC stipulates, regular state reporting to the UN Committee indicating factors and difficulties which affect the degree of fulfilment of those obligations,[699] is part and parcel of the commitment made by virtue of becoming a State Party to the Convention (*First Section: Obligations Undertaken*). As a consequence, fully accepting those CRC-based obligations into Ireland's domestic legal order, centrally building around its written Constitution already embodying an elaborated set of 'Fundamental Rights' (Articles 40–44), proves to be a primary task of enormous complexity.[700] Demonstrations will be made in the following that those obligations were only partially fulfilled, and more needs to be done especially in the fields of 'investigation' and 'Inter-agency collaboration'.[701] (*Second Section: Obligations Fulfilled*).

First Section: Obligations Undertaken

As explained at the outset of this part of the dissertation, 'implementation' as an international obligation grounding in the Convention and its Article 4 in particular, provides for a fine point of departure when analyzing the legal status of children including the actual state of children's rights, within a specific jurisdiction such as Ireland.[702] Read in conjunction as they indeed must be, Articles 2 and 4 CRC contain an overall undertaking by States Parties according to which all Convention obligations must be implemented in a way that ensures rights and freedoms to children, either

---

698 Byrnes and Renshaw (n 240) 482, 488.

699 Lundy et al (n 456) 442, 463.

700 Articles contextualizing an integration of CRC rights are Article 40 on 'Personal Rights', and Article 41 on 'The Family', and Article 42 on 'Education'.

701 See p 244 below ('Investigation') and p 274 below ('Inter-agency Collaboration').

702 Fn 494 above.

individually or collectively, as beneficiaries of the Convention.[703] Indeed, what is normatively implied by implementation in terms of legislative, administrative, social and educational measures to be taken by governments is fully contingent upon local conditions impinging on 'effectiveness' and 'enjoyment' in respect of children's rights;[704] generally, monitoring bodies such as the Committee are primarily concerned about results in terms of human rights being accorded in practice to those who are seen as beneficiaries of the treaty. As a focal point for measures to be taken by any jurisdiction aiming at an implementation of children's protection rights, my set of measures (itself developed on the basis of the tripartite typology of obligations) to be captioned here as 'Criminalization', 'Reporting', 'Investigation', 'Inspection', 'Inter-agency collaboration', 'Comprehensive Sex Education' and 'Human Rights Education' respectively, will serve as some sort of a 'to do' list for the State to bring its law, policy and practice in line with international standards (*seven Sub-Sections further below*).

It will be seen that, from a perspective of children's rights, the legal landscape in Ireland shows some sort of ruggedness in character presenting itself in need of better coordination and collaboration among many different agents of the State. Fully established by virtue of its written Constitution as a democratic and independent one, that same State must be ready to show some better resolve as a mediator between competing interests when confronting (or collaborating with) authorities that have been traditionally claimed from an ecclesiastic background.[705] Talking from an experience based on a *concordat* type of agreement, the Irish State will therefore need to enter into negotiations of this sort with the Holy See in order to clarify about spheres of responsibility.

Recommended Measures for Implementation

Chief among the recommendations made by the Committee, in its re-

---

[703] On Article 2 CRC see p 89; on Article 4 CRC see p 84.

[704] C O'Mahony, 'The Challenge of Constitutionalising Children's Rights in Ireland' (2009) 11.

[705] McAlinden (n 69) 189.

cent observations on the latest periodic reports from Ireland,[706] were that the State should take the following necessary measures:

1. To fully incorporate the Convention into domestic law and also to ratify the second Optional Protocol (OPSC);[707]
2. To implement specific legislation to ensure that the Convention, its general principles in particular, is respected, including in administrative proceedings and decision-making processes;[708]
3. To provide the national Department of Children and Youth Affairs (now: Department of Children, Equality, Disability, Integration and Youth/DCEDIY) with a clear mandate and sufficient authority as well as adequate resources to coordinate all activities related to the implementation of the Convention; to incorporate a child rights-based approach into the State budgeting process;[709]
4. To strengthen its efforts to provide adequate and systematic training of professionals working with and for children on children's rights and on a child rights-based approach to actions and decisions affecting children; to ensure that all such professionals in the education, health and justice sectors receive specialized training on identifying and responding to cases of violence;[710]
5. To develop procedures and criteria to provide guidance to all relevant persons in authority for determining the best interests of the child and for giving it due weight as a primary consideration;[711]
6. To ensure an effective implementation of legislation recognizing the right of the child to be heard in relevant legal proceedings, particularly in all forms of family law proceedings; to strengthen measures to promote the meaningful and empowered participation of children within the family, the community and schools; to consider carrying out a national referendum on lowering the voting age to 16 years;[712]

---

706 CRC/C/IRL/CO/3–4 *Concluding observations on the combined third and fourth periodic reports of Ireland* (29 January 2016); CRC/C/IRL/CO/5–6 *Concluding observations on the combined fifth and sixth periodic reports of Ireland* (7 February 2023).

707 CRC/C/IRL/CO/3–4 paras 9,77; CRC/C/IRL/CO/5–6 paras 6, 47.

708 CRC/C/IRL/CO/3–4 para 11; CRC/C/IRL/CO/5–6 paras 15(a), 16(a), 18(a)(b).

709 CRC/C/IRL/CO/3–4 para 14; CRC/C/IRL/CO/5–6 para 9.

710 CRC/C/IRL/CO/3–4 para 22; CRC/C/IRL/CO/5–6 paras 12(b), 18(c), 24(i), 38.

711 CRC/C/IRL/CO/3–4 para 30; CRC/C/IRL/CO/5–6 para 16(b).

712 CRC/C/IRL/CO/3–4 para 32; CRC/C/IRL/CO/5–6 para 18.

7. To ensure the allocation of adequate resources to its Child and Family Agency to enable it to respond to child protection referrals and address the needs of children in a timely manner; to ensure sufficient 24-hour refuge accommodation for persons affected by domestic violence and their children; to encourage community-based and other programmes aimed at preventing domestic violence, child abuse and neglect with an emphasis on children in alternative care;[713]
8. To adopt a comprehensive sexual and reproductive health policy for adolescents and ensure that sexual and reproductive health education is part of the mandatory school curriculum;[714]
9. To enable children to apply for protection and safety orders, and ensure that children have access to legal support and confidential and child-friendly complaints mechanisms in schools;[715]
10. To ensure the prompt and effective investigation of all cases of violence against children; to take vigorous measures for preventing, investigating and prosecuting the exploitation of children online; to ensure that all children who are victims or witnesses of violence have prompt access to child-friendly and multisectoral remedies and comprehensive support; to consider as a standard procedure the acceptance of audio-visual recordings of the child victim's testimony as evidence;[716]
11. To ensure the systematic collection and analysis of data on violence against children and on cases that have been reported, investigated and prosecuted;[717]
12. To ensure that child victims of past abuse have access to justice and effective remedies, and in particular examine situations of persons whose complaints have not received adequate attention.[718]

As taken by both concluding observations (2016, 2023) this comprehensive review from outside documents, especially in regard of protection from violence and abuse, a legal status for children in Ireland that needs further development and elaboration. By means of taking the Convention and its articles on violence against children as its compass, legislative, administra-

[713] CRC/C/IRL/CO/3–4 para 38; CRC/C/IRL/CO/5–6 para 24(a)(d).
[714] CRC/C/IRL/CO/3–4 para 58; CRC/C/IRL/CO/5–6 para 33(b)
[715] CRC/C/IRL/CO/3–4 para 63; CRC/C/IRL/CO/5–6 para 24(b)
[716] CRC/C/IRL/CO/5–6 para 24 (c)(e)(f)(g).
[717] CRC/C/IRL/CO/5–6 paras 10, 24 (k).
[718] CRC/C/IRL/CO/5–6 para 24 (l).

tive, social and educational measures are to be implemented accordingly.[719]

Is Ireland under a Duty to Incorporate the Convention?

Since the Committee has been fairly consistent in recommending the Convention to be fully incorporated into Irish law (point nr 1 above)[720], the following question arises: is this indeed an international obligation to which the Irish State, having unreservedly ratified the treaty, must submit as a matter of implementing the Convention?

Above, in a context of spelling out Convention obligations to respect, protect and fulfil the right to non-violent education, it was found that no State Party to the Convention is under a general duty to incorporate the Convention into its own internal legal order as long as children's rights are protected and vindicated in practice.[721] Since an extensive body of Irish case-law treating constitutional rights has been developed over decades, what is following is a review of the amount of weight Irish courts have given to the Convention, notwithstanding the fact that, as an international document, it does not form part of the domestic law of the State.

Convention-based Obligations: Un-Incorporated, yet to be Considered

Addressing the formal position of the CRC within the Irish legal system, one may observe that the text of this UN Convention has never in its entirety been incorporated into Ireland's internal legal order. More specifically, considering section 3 of Ireland's 2003 *European Convention on Human Rights Act* which requires every organ of the State to act in compliance with ECHR norms, there is no provision giving equivalent effect to any provision of the CRC; this was confirmed in the context of Article 3 CRC (Best interests of the child) in the High Court case of *Dos Santos* concerning an application for leave to seek judicial review of deportation orders made by the Executive.[722] Clearly, this is not to say that the best interest principle cannot, for the benefit of children living in Ireland, enjoy a certain degree of protection in defined circumstances, at both statutory and

---

[719] CRC/C/IRL/CO/3–4 para 37; CRC/C/IRL/CO/5–6 para 24.

[720] CRC/C/15/Add.85 para 4; CRC/C/IRL/CO/2 para 9; CRC/C/IRL/CO/3–4 para 9; CRC/C/IRL/CO/5–6 para 6.

[721] Fn 456 and accompanying text.

[722] *Dos Santos* (n 698) para 34.

constitutional level.[723] Though Ireland has enshrined the best interest principle in legislation and Art 42A of the Constitution also makes reference to it, this principle, as Geoffrey Shannon observes, has *'yet to be fully integrated in decision-making as regards policy akin to that envisaged'* by the Committee's *GC 14* on the 'Right of the Child to have his or her Best Interests taken as a Primary Consideration'.[724]

As an unincorporated human rights treaty the Convention does not have to entirely remain devoid of any legal effect benefitting those for whom it was drafted in the first place; rather, as Melissa Waters found, a judicial trend toward interpretive incorporation of human rights treaties (labelled 'creeping monism' by her) lately became perceivable even among common law jurisdictions traditionally subscribing to 'dualism' as a public international law doctrine.[725] As was observed by Kearns J. in the High Court of Ireland upon re-examination of judicial principles decades earlier stated in Irish authorities and concerning the role of the courts in adjudicating upon international obligations based on human rights treaties, *'Irish courts are not inhibited or precluded from identifying principles of international law and considering if and how those principles apply domestically'*.[726] Accordingly, in the following two general aspects of applying CRC principles domestically will be looked at before turning to protection from harm and education to be explored as Personal Rights under the Constitution.

Dualism in the Text of the Constitution of Ireland

So, remaining in terms of a legal-constitutional body of law to be re-contextualized by an international human rights treaty such as the Convention, is a combination of Articles 15 and 29 of the Constitution of Ireland by virtue of which a strong type of dualist approach has ever been adhered to. Therefore, while a certain constitutional rigour seems to be embo-

---

723 Art 42A Constitution of Ireland, Section 3 Guardianship of Infants Act 1964; Sections 3 (2), 24 Child Care Act 1991; Adoption Act 2010; Child and Family Agency Act 2013; Section 7 Children First Act 2015; Section 27 Domestic Violence Act 2018; Shannon (n 75) para 14–07.

724 G Shannon, *Children and Family Relationships Law in Ireland* (Clarus Press 2016) para 3–17.

725 Waters (n 452) 628, 633.

726 *Dos Santos* (n 698) para 69.

died in Article 29.6 of the Constitution clearly proscribing any court-led direct enforcement of unincorporated treaty obligations, Irish courts, over the years, have developed practical solutions simply based on an assumption straightforwardly phrased '... , *the fact that it* [scil. the Convention] *has been ratified cannot be ignored'*.[727] With particular concern for the best interest principle as enshrined in Article 3 CRC, McEochaidh J. found that some principled observations were possible in this regard:[728]

i) *No provision of the UN Convention on the Rights of the Child could enter Irish law where a contrary rule exists, whether in the Constitution, in a statute or in judge-made law;*

ii) *Laws adopted after the ratification by Ireland of the Convention are to be interpreted and applied in consonance with the Convention unless a contrary intention is apparent from the legislation.*

As an example of systemic integration bringing together the jurisdiction's dualist approach with a positive fact of having established, by virtue of the treaty's ratification, the State's consent to be bound by the Convention, these judge-made conclusions stated above will serve here as a foundation for my argument in the following.[729] In essence, my argument is that a dynamism of implementing children's rights is clearly observable in the State regardless of the fact that the Convention text has never been fully incorporated.

Values Reflected by Article 3 CRC

One field where practical solutions as mentioned before came into operation is the relevance of the CRC to a ministerial discretion exercisable in

---

[727] Ibid; As another illustration of judicial pragmatism in this regard, one might refer to an obiter made by Humphreys J. in a 2016 judgment concerning care orders where it was stated that no leave can be granted on the ground that places direct reliance on the UN Convention since it was not part of Irish law, ' ... *although the applicant can rely on it as persuasive authority if and to the extent that it is indirectly incorporated through the ECHR'*, see F.G. v The Child and Family Agency & Ors [2016] IEHC 156 para 25.

[728] *Dos Santos* (n 698) para 69 in fine;

[729] Byrnes and Renshaw (n 240) 482, 488; On 'systemic integration' as an international law topic, see C McLachlan, 'Legal Theory, The Principle of Systemic Integration in International Law' (UN Audiovisual Library 2012).

the immigration context; therefore, the best interests of the child-principle as stipulated in Article 3 CRC was identified as a provision which, though not directly applicable, reflected values that might inform the contextual approach to statutory interpretation and judicial review.[730] Since the right to non-violent education is strongly linked to Article 3(2) CRC detailing the child's protective interest, an obligation to determine and balance the best interests of the child as a primary consideration, may help to inform the contextual approach to statutory interpretation and judicial review whenever required under Irish law; any such interpretation actually reflecting those CRC-based values and principles is to be preferred accordingly. However, there remains a big difference in practice between making it obligatory for a judge in court to take the CRC into account when interpreting a statute which is part of a daily routine in this profession, versus asking a registered school-teacher, for instance, to take it into account when deciding whether an abuse report must be formally launched to the authorities or not. As will be seen shortly, especially in relation to the issue of 'Mandatory Reporting', any such way of arguing indirectly obligations based on the Convention may nevertheless acquire some weight.[731]

Sub-section (1) – Constitutional Rights Established for Protection from Harm

Addressing the natural and imprescriptible rights of the child at a very abstract level, one may ask whether the children's right to be protected against all forms (or sources) of violence and sexual abuse is just one of those natural rights of the child on which Article 42A ("Children") of the Constitution seems to be building.[732] Above and beyond this newly inserted constitutional provision, children as citizens enjoy personal rights under Article 40.3.1 ("Personal Rights") of the Constitution whereby the State pledges to guarantee in its laws to respect, and by its laws to defend and vindicate the personal rights of its (child) citizens.

Traditionally, the natural rights of the child were found to be a right to be fed and to live, to be reared and educated, to have the opportunity of working and of realising his or her full personality and dignity as a human

---

730 *A.S.M.A & anor v Minister for Justice and Equality & ors* [2013] IEHC 381 para 13.

731 Fn 836 below and accompanying text.

732 Article 42A of the Constitution refers to ' … *the natural and imprescriptble rights of all children …* '.

being;[733] it was held that the child has a right to bodily integrity and has an unenumerated right to an opportunity to be reared with due regard to her religious, moral, intellectual, physical and social welfare.[734] In the case of Ireland as a jurisdiction the true challenge proved to be what may be described as "constitutionalising children's rights", meaning that children, at a constitutional level, were to be directly accepted as independent holders of fundamental rights and freedoms, and not just indirectly as members of the family unit group addressed in Article 41 of the Constitution.[735] At the level of personal rights implicitly protected by the Constitution, the right to bodily integrity affords some protection against sexual violence and abuse; in *Ryan* v *Attorney General* it was defined by Kenny J.:

> *In my opinion, one of the personal rights of the citizen protected by the general guarantee is the right to bodily integrity. I understand the right to bodily integrity to mean that no mutilation of the body or any of its members may be carried out on any citizen under authority of the law except for the good of the whole body and that no process which is or may, as a matter of probability, be dangerous or harmful to the life or health of the citizen or any of them may be imposed (in the sense of being made compulsory) by an Act of the Oireachtas.*[736]

So far, this protective right has been defined as a right to be free from violations caused or inflicted by State action, it shows no dimension of protection against private non-state actors behaving in a threatening or bodily aggressive manner against other people including children. However, there is case law establishing the point that private actors may not violate their co-citizen's constitutional rights with impunity.[737] Likewise, no dimension of child-specific vulnerabilities has been addressed under the

[733] *G v An Bord Uchtála* [1980] IR 23

[734] Shannon (n 75) para 1–14 further referencing Irish case law; O Doyle, *Constitutional Law: Text, Cases and Materials* (Clarus 2008) para 4–03.

[735] O'Mahony (n 704).

[736] *Ryan* v *Attorney General* [1965] IR 294, 314.

[737] *Educational Co of Ireland Ltd* v *Fitzpatrick (No 2)* [1961] IR 345, in which Budd J stated at pp 368–369: '*Obedience of the law is required of every citizen, and it follows that if one citizen has a right under the Constitution there exists a correlative duty on the part of other citizens to respect that right and not to interfere with it*'; note, that this general statement is subject to the principle in *McDonnell* explained below (Fn 738).

right to bodily integrity as established under the Constitution. That sort of (peer on peer) protection is covered by the relevant criminal and civil laws and is not considered to be within the scope of the constitutional right *per se.*[738] Indeed, the State protects this right by enacting laws proscribing acts of violence and other abusive behaviour, and by putting in place effective procedures for an investigation, prosecution and punishment of acts contravening those laws.[739] Thus, it may be assumed that every victim of sexual violence and abuse has suffered an infringement of his or her right to bodily integrity implicitly guaranteed by the Constitution; this assumption must be fully valid for every single child victim also, since, under the Constitution of Ireland, the right to bodily integrity is equally accorded to the individual child as a person.[740] Along these lines, Article 42A was drafted and approved by referendum in the year 2012, leaving the exact content of children's rights under this provision including all corresponding obligations of the State, to be defined by the courts on a case-by-case basis. To date there has not been a court decision specifically holding that this provision (Art 42A of the Constitution) makes it obligatory for the State to take measures for the protection of children against sexual abuse perpetrated against them by members of their family and household, or from any other person in authority, such as a school-teacher or an ordained cleric operating from within a relatively closed care context. A few recent judgements, however, are hinting at a conclusion according to which the basic provision in Article 42A of the Constitution obliges the State to take steps to protect children against sexual abuse: in *GS* v *Commissioner of An Garda Siochána* McDermott J stated that '[T]*he State and its agencies are obliged to protect and vindicate the personal rights of children and vulnerable persons by ensuring that unsuitable persons are not given access to them or cause them harm …* '.[741] Here, in a quite formulaic way the personal

---

738 In *McDonnell* v *Ireland* [1998] 1 IR 134, Barrington J. commented at p 148 that *'constitutional rights should not be regarded as wildcards which can be played at any time to defeat all existing rules. If the general law provides an adequate cause of action to vindicate a constitutional right it appears to me that the injured party cannot ask the court to devise a new and different cause of action'.*

739 T O'Malley, *Sexual Offences: Law Policy and Punishment* (Roundhall Dublin 1996) 28; for more detail on investigations, see Fn 843 below.

740 O'Malley (n 739 above) 26, further referencing Irish case law.

741 *GS* v *Commissioner of An Garda Siochána* [2017] IEHC 190 para 29; In *P.O'T v CFA* (n 696), the High Court appeared to implicitly accept that Article 42A gives children

rights of children were being balanced against another person's rights to earn a livelihood and fair procedures which were engaged on behalf of the adult applicant by an operation of the administrative Code of Practice.

Again, this is not to say that children in Ireland cannot claim their rights to be protected from torture or ill-treatment or punishment or to have their private and family life protected; these, however, are rights which, as documented by *O'Keeffe* must successfully be claimed, under Articles 3 and 8 ECHR respectively, at the European Court in Strasbourg.[742] In fact, there has never been a case in which someone has fully argued that a failure by the State to protect a child from sexual abuse by a private actor, was a violation of constitutional rights; strictly speaking, this legal issue therefore remains open. Thus, a corresponding constitutional right to protection from violence is not regularly available for children claiming their constitutional rights in Ireland. Finally, it must be noted that the Irish Constitution does not know a doctrine of positive obligations like that operated through its ECHR jurisdiction by the ECtHR;[743] from an Irish perspective it would be considered to be a breach of the separation of powers to dictate to the Oireachtas what legislation should be enacted.

Sub-section (2) – Educational Arrangements as Provided by the Constitution of Ireland

Another field on which practical solutions, by way of implementing CRC based obligations, come into operation in terms of obligations undertaken constitutionally is "Education" as distinctively addressed by Article 42 of the Constitution of Ireland and spelled out at this location through a personal right of parents to choose and direct the child's education; whereas the right of the child is to receive an education appropriate to his or her needs.[744] In contrast, Articles 28, 29 of the Convention comprehensively proclaim educational rights as children's rights, but these articles have not been incorporated into Irish law, either directly or indirectly.[745] Although the constitutional provision is worded in such a way that the obligation on

---

a right to be protected against sexual abuse.

[742] case of *O'Keeffe v Ireland* (n 1).

[743] Grabenwarter (n 31) para 18/Article 3, para 72/Article 8; Kilkelly (n 337) 245.

[744] Article 42 of the Constitution '... *guarantees to respect the inalienable right and duty of parents ...* '.

[745] For the text of Articles 28, 29 CRC see Fn 137 and accompanying text.

the State is to fund rather than provide education, the one and only explicit pledge by the State to underwrite socio-economic rights is to be taken from Article 42.4 which reads (extract):

> *4. The State shall provide for free primary education and shall endeavour to supplement and give reasonable aid to private and corporate educational initiative, ... with due regard, however, for the rights of parents, especially in the matter of religious and moral formation.*

As it actually stands, this article's meaning seems to be one of securing an institutional arrangement, historically accumulated and continually practised, between the State, the Church and the parents. Thus, in *O'Keeffe v Hickey*[746] Hardiman J. explained how, through the wording in the Constitution, a certain normative value was attributed to the managerial structure which had been practised traditionally in regard of 'National Schools': '[T]*he obligation in Article 42 (4) on the State to 'provide for' free primary education reflected a largely state-funded, but entirely clerically administered, system of education'*.[747] Practically, education in Ireland will widely be delivered by autonomous quasi-private scholastic institutions (having their autonomy secured as a matter of their freedom of thought, conscience and religion), whose teachers' salaries are paid by the State and who deliver a curriculum set by the State (patronage model). Thus, constitutionally speaking, it is being emphasised that the State's obligation is not to educate but to provide for it.

Seen from a perspective of children's rights, what matters most is the absence of a clear line of legal accountability between the State (as a primary duty-bearer under the Convention) and the actual treatment of children attending Ireland's 'National Schools' as a matter of compulsory education. As a consequence, teaching staff and other school personnel employed and managed by non-state corporate or ecclesiastic providers of educational services can regularly have unsupervised access to vulnerable children of minority age.[748] From a normative point of view, what is required under an obligation to protect children's rights is not that *per se* the Irish Government must be in an exclusive role of being a first-hand provider of services

---

746 *O'Keeffe v Hickey* [2008] IESC 72.

747 *O'Keeffe v Ireland* (n 1) para 33 reproducing the decision of the Supreme Court of Ireland (n 746 above).

748 Fn 746 above.

to all children of school-age; correspondingly, it is not the government's almost complete reliance on non-state actors for discharging its own educational obligations that mainly causes concern.[749]

What seems to be highly problematic, however, is any sort of legal vacuum created between a State practice of children being taken into 'National Schools' in great numbers on the one hand, and an overly distanced position of responsible organs or agents of the State with an ability to receive complaints or to respond adequately to any incident of maltreatment; at the time of *O'Keeffe* at least this kind of vacuum existed in practice. Further below, when analyzing school inspections as a topic for CRC implementation it will be seen whether this is still the case today.[750]

Responsible Funding of Education

As was demonstrated above, an obligation to respect children's rights furthermore requires that no public resources may be provided to any privately managed (including ecclesiastically controlled) child care or educational enterprise which lacks in commitment as regards safeguarding children's rights in the operation of its business.[751] As a consequence, Ireland must be concerned about a change of system in order to secure that no more public funds may go to any private organization, including religiously affiliated providers of educational services, unless a clear record of respect for and protection of children's rights is proven.[752] Accordingly, an effective provision for children and their education rights as envisaged by Article 42.4 of the Constitution requires that all education thus provided must be of a violence-free character, rights-based in theory and in practice. This understanding builds on the right to non-violent education as captured by Articles 3, 19 CRC in particular which, though not being directly applicable as such, must function as a persuasive source for legal interpretation at least.

---

749 Similarly, ECHR Article 2 P1 allows for a variety of functions assumed by the State in relation to education, see Grabenwarter (n 31) 389, 394.

750 p 264 below (Sub-section 4).

751 Fn 318 and accompanying text;

752 *Education Act* 1998 s 12 provides for annual funding of schools in accordance with criteria set by the Minister; Lynch (n 694) 162, 163.

To sum up, obligations undertaken by the State in respect of the right to non-violent education are pointing in two different directions from here, one of which aims at the protection of children from violent and abusive behaviour perpetrated against them by private third parties operating from within a relatively closed care context; and the other is pointing towards every individual child made visible as an independent holder of fundamental rights and freedoms to be claimed directly against the State as a guarantor of children's rights. Speaking into an Irish legal-constitutional context, it would be welcome for the right to non-violent education to be substantially guaranteed at the level of "Personal Rights" mentioned in the Constitution. As it stands, the text of the 1937 Constitution of Ireland does not provide as clear a basis for a right to non violent education as the Convention does. At the same time it is not plainly inconsistent with the protection of such a right, since it protects a right to education, and some judgments have suggested that it also gives children a right to be protected from sexual abuse.

Second Section: Obligations Fulfilled

Introduction

Although, over the years, a relatively complex architecture of child protection measures has been erected at the hands of a sequence of Governments and Minsters in Ireland,[753] the general approach to child protection in Irish schools has not been drawing inspiration from a consideration of children's human rights. Children were never accorded rights *in* education so as to include a right to protection from violence and abuse fully adapted to children as independent holders of rights who regularly find themselves in an educational situation such as the one prevailing typically in schools or parishes.[754]

Like every other human right the right to non-violent education as a children's right must be respected, and must be protected and must also be fulfilled for every child living in Ireland (RPF-obligations). As was demonstrated above, this essentially implies that the State and its organs must abstain from acting out or actively supporting violent behaviour directly or

[753] CRC/C/IRL/CO/3–4 para 13.

[754] U Kilkelly, *Children's Rights in Ireland, Law, Policy and Practice* (Tottel Publishing 2008) 252 (compliance with EU legislation).

indirectly impacting on the learning child, and must also make sure that private third parties do not behave in such a violent manner. Likewise the State must refrain from funding private educational providers who do not respect the right to non-violent education. Thus, violence-free education must be made available and accessible for every child in Ireland, free from discrimination of any kind.[755] In closer detail the following sub-sections will explore what has been achieved in terms of realisation of the right to non-violent education, mainly on a sub-constitutional level, for children in Ireland; again, the seven bundles of measures bound together topically as 'Criminalization', 'Mandatory reporting', 'Investigation', 'Inspection', 'Incorporation', 'Inter-Agency Collaboration' and 'Comprehensive Sex-Education' respectively will present themselves in this order.

Sub-Section (1) – Criminalization as an Implementing Measure under Irish Law

Having generally dealt with 'criminalization' as an international obligation for the protection of the child's right to freedom from violence, abuse and neglect (Article 19 CRC) in particular,[756] that same topic needs to be re-considered here for the purpose of making an assessment about the extent of Ireland's compliance with such CRC standards as they were accepted unreservedly. From the tripartite typology of obligations (RPF), it is an obligation to protect the human rights of children which is particularly relevant here: States Parties to the CRC are under an obligation to protect children against infringement of their rights guaranteed under the Convention, by private third parties, and any such third party behaviour potentially leading to an infringement of rights must be proscribed and criminalized accordingly.[757] Consequently, the following needs to be asked as a research question here: are the range of criminal offences that are currently in place, along with the penalties flowing from them, sufficient to function as a deterrent against the sexual abuse of children in Ireland?

Historically, the sexual abuse of a minor has ever been a criminal offence under Irish law and under the *Offences Against the Person Act* 1861 in particular; by force of this statutory enactment the crime of rape

[755] Fn 272 and accompanying text.

[756] Fn 327 and accompanying text.

[757] Fn 331 and accompanying text; 'third party' meaning any private individual in relation to any individual child.

was sanctioned with penal servitude for life (Section 48) and similarly, an indecent assault upon a female carried a time of imprisonment as its sentence (Section 51).[758] Furthermore, the *Criminal Law (Amendment) Act* 1935 was designed to make further provision for the protection of under-age girls and to amend the law concerning sexual offences; thus, any girl under fifteen years of age could not and cannot consent to any form of sexual contact and any such contact was and still is a crime. In addition to these statutory offences any act of sexually contacting a minor, in most cases, amounted to ordinary assault under Irish law.[759]

Legislative Developments

A wave of legislation started from the early 2000s in response to reports about widespread child sexual abuse, including sexual abuse committed by clerics (covered-up in many instances) and other persons in authority such as teachers, childcare workers and professionals whose work regularly brings them into close contact with children.[760] An accent will, therefore, be laid on criminal offences and penalties the (Irish) law of which will be reviewed here as it currently stands.

Sexual Assault and Rape

Historically, as a legal term 'sexual assault' has often been used in a generic manner to describe the entire range of offences involving sexual aggression by one person on another, irrespective of the victim's age; the common law offences of indecent assault covered virtually any form of sexual activity that did not constitute rape.[761] Since, under Irish law, the offence has never been defined by statute, the elements of the offence must be outlined from the relevant common law principles developed by the courts over the years; essentially, the offence consists of touching another person in a sexual way without that person's consent.[762] The penalty for

---

[758] *Offences Against the Person Act*, 1861 (as amended); for more detail, see p 221 below.

[759] *O'Keeffe v Ireland* (n 1) para 63; Judge Charleton, at para 20 of his dissenting opinion, referencing the 1935 Act.

[760] Y Murphy, 'Clerical Child Abuse-The Irish Experience' 3 Vict Univ L Just Journ (2013) 19, 20.

[761] *'Murphy'* para A2.1; C Hanly, *An Introduction to Irish Criminal Law* (3rd ed Gill Education 2006) 328.

[762] *'Murphy'* para A2.2; Hanly (n 761 above) 328; *Criminal Law (Rape) (Amendment) Act* 1990, section 2 reads (extract): *'The offence of indecent assault upon any male*

sexual assault is imprisonment of up to ten years unless the (child) victim was aged below seventeen years of age at the time of the assault, in which case the maximum penalty is fourteen years' imprisonment.[763]

In general, where there is consent to sexual activity, no assault may be established at law because the act is not committed against the (approached) person's wishes. From a children's rights point of view it is imperative that States Parties do take into account the need to balance the protection needs of adolescents against their evolving capacities, and define an acceptable minimum age when determining the legal age for sexual consent.[764] Under Irish law, an adolescent under the age of 15 years is never deemed capable of consenting to sexual activity as a matter of strict principle; which means that a person who perpetrates a sexual act upon a child under the age of 15 years would be unable to avail himself of a defence that this child was consenting to the activity performed. Therefore, section 2 *Criminal Law (Sexual Offences) Act* 2006 as amended by section 16 *Criminal Law (Sexual Offences) Act* 2017 establishes an offence of sexual act with child under the age of 15 years which is committed if a person engages or attempts to engage in a sexual act (as defined in the 2006 Act) with such child; a maximum penalty of life imprisonment being stipulated in that same section. According to section 16(6) of the 2017 Act absolutely no defence of consent is admissible for this particular age group.

With no particular concern for adolescents (who are included), a statutory definition of consent in relation to sexual offences is provided in section 9 of the *Criminal Law (Rape) (Amendment) Act* 2009 as amended by section 48 of the *Criminal Law (Sexual Offences) Act* 2017 according to which a person consents to a sexual act if he or she freely and voluntarily agrees to engage in that act; however, situations in which a person is deemed not to consent are equally circumscribed in this statute. Thus, under the (threatened or feared) application of force, under an influence of alcohol or drugs or while being asleep or unconscious, there is no room for

---

person and the offence of indecent assault upon any female person shall be known as sexual assault'.

763 While still seen as a common law offence, section 37 of the *Sex Offenders Act* 2001 provides for more stringent penalties for the sexual assault of a minor, see Hanly (n 761) 328; *'Murphy'* para A2.8.

764 CRC/C/GC/20 para 40.

consent.[765] Furthermore, it is statutorily prescribed that consent to a sexual act is not of itself constituted by any failure or omission on the part of the person assaulted to offer resistance to an act.[766]

The law in relation to the issue of a guilty mind of the perpetrator as to the age of the victim possibly invalidating his or her consent given underwent amendments in several stages. This is documented by a type of statutory rape offence (formerly designated as unlawful carnal knowledge) in the *Criminal Law (Amendment) Act* 1935, section 1(1) which was declared unconstitutional by the Supreme Court in the case *of CC v Ireland,* due to the absence of any possibility of arguing reasonable mistake as to the age of the child involved.[767] Following that judgment fresh legislation came into force through section 3 of the *Criminal Law (Sexual Offences Act)* 2006 establishing the offence of 'defilement of a child', which was later substituted by an entirely new section 17 of the *Criminal Law (Sexual Offences) Act* 2017 captioned 'Sexual act with child under 17 years of age'. This new version still makes it an offence, punishable with a maximum of 7 years imprisonment, for a person to engage or attempt to engage in a sexual act (as defined in the 2006 Act) with a child under the age of 17 years. As a modification detailed in this new Section 17, consent on the part of the child provides no defence; except where the child involved had attained the age of 15 years but was under 17 years of age, and the defendant is younger or less than 2 years older than the child, and was not in an exploitive relationship with the child.[768] Section 17(3) of the 2017 Act provides a defence for the defendant to prove that he or she was reasonably mistaken that, at the time of the alleged commission of the offence, the child involved had attained 17 years of age. Thus, section 17 places the onus of proving a reasonable mistake as to the age of the child on the defendant, while section 17(5) provides that the standard of proof required

[765] Section 48(2) of the *Criminal Law (Sexual Offences) Act* 2017.

[766] Section 48(5) *Criminal Law (Sexual Offences) Act* 2017.

[767] *CC v Ireland* [2006] 4 IR 1; Hanly (n 761) 332 (context of exploitative sexual offences); L McGowan, 'Sexual Offence, Constitutionality' (2006) 70 J Crim L 406, 411.

[768] Section 3 *Criminal Law (Sexual Offences) Act* 2006 as amended by section 17 *Criminal Law (Sexual Offences) Act* 2017 where conditions for a defence of consent are detailed in subsections (6) and (8), so-called 'young person's defence'.

was that applicable to civil proceedings, regularly implying the balance of probabilities.

Presently, in this area the law is uncertain, since in *CW v Minister for Justice* the High Court declared that section 3 of the 2006 Act as substituted by section 17 of the 2017 Act, is invalid as contrary to Article 38.1 of the Constitution; key among this court's reasoning being that it is constitutionally impermissible to impose more than an evidential burden on an accused who wishes to invoke the 'reasonable mistake' defence available from section 3 of the 2006 Act.[769] As stipulated at this location in the *Criminal Law (Sexual Offences) Act* 2017 a standard of proof to the civil standard is contrary to the constitutionally guaranteed presumption of innocence, the High Court found.[770] The issue was partly to do with the standard of proof, but partly also with the onus of proving the reasonable mistake as placed on the defendant. According to the 2017 amendment, section 17(3), it is for the defendant to prove that he had made a reasonable mistake as to the age of the child, rather than placing the burden on the prosecution to prove that he had not. In combination, shifting the burden of proof on the defendant and setting the standard of proof at the level applicable to civil proceedings undermined the presumption of innocence.

Seen in comparison, Irish Criminal Law generously allows for the 'reasonable mistake' defence proffered on behalf of the person who is being held suspect of having committed an age-dependent sexual offence, and his or her *mens rea* (guilty mind or criminal intent).[771] Indeed, if an age limit (below the age of adulthood) for sexual consent to be given by an adolescent can be tolerated as such for rendering laws CRC compliant (as the Committee seems to suggest), an honest mistake on behalf of the adult-perpetrator (as argued in cases like *CC* or *CW*) must be allowed for, as long as strict liability is not seen as the only way of protecting children's rights under the Convention. Any form of

[769] *CW v Minister for Justice* [2022] IEHC 336; 'evidential burden' relates to the burden borne by a party who contends that a particular issue should be put before the decision-maker; see *Annual Report of the Special Rapporteur on Child Protection* 2022 (Prof Conor O'Mahony) 124 for detailed analysis.

[770] *CW v Minister for Justice* (n 769 above) para 38.

[771] T O'Malley, 'Criminal Law (Sexual Offences) Act 2017 – The Offence Provisions', *Presentation to the 18th Annual National Prosecutors' Conference* (25 November 2017) 9.

non-consensual sexual activity, it remains important to stress, would be covered by the provisions on rape as stipulated in the 1990 Act (see below).

Forms of Rape

As regards rape which is a common law offence that was made punishable, in Ireland, by the *Offences Against the Person Act* 1861, section 48; this offence is statutorily defined as to the *actus reus* of rape and also in relation to its *mens rea* by the *Criminal Law (Rape) Act* 1981, section 2(1). As to its nature as a crime, it is now seen as one of the most serious offences known to Irish law, causing long-term emotional damage as well as physical harm to the victim. Accordingly, a penalty of up to life imprisonment for those convicted of rape has ever been allowed dating back to the 1861 Act mentioned above.

Since the enactment of the *Criminal Law (Rape) (Amendment) Act* 1990 there are two forms of rape known to Irish law: there is rape as upheld by the common law and now properly defined in section 2 of the *Criminal Law (Rape) Act* 1981, and there is also an offence of rape under section 4 of the *Criminal Law (Rape) (Amendment) Act* 1990 too. Both offences carry a maximum sentence of life imprisonment and in relation to the prosecution of child sexual abuse allegations they could both be used as reported in some instances.[772] In the following terms the crime has been ascribed a definition in section 2 of the *Criminal Law (Rape) Act* 1981:

(1) A man commits rape if:

a) *he has sexual intercourse with a woman who at the time of the intercourse does not consent to it; and*
b) *at the time he knows that she does not consent to the intercourse or he is reckless as to whether she does or does not consent to it,* … .

As it stands, this section of the 1981 Act maintains an explicitly gender-biased formulation of the crime: rape can be committed only by a man against a woman. In order to remedy a legal situation perceived to be problematic because of gender-biased language in the rape laws, the *Criminal Law (Rape)(Amendment) Act* 1990 was enacted which created

[772] *'Murphy'* para A2.11.

a parallel rape offence also labelled as 'Rape under section 4'.[773] This offence allows for a prosecution as rape of penetrative acts that were not included in section 2 of the 1981 Act: anal and oral penetration and penetration by an object; accordingly, it equally carries a maximum sentence of life imprisonment.[774]

Offence by Person in Authority

Since this study centrally explores children's protection rights to be implemented into educational or care contexts, some attention is required for the legislative concept of 'person in authority', capturing teachers, trainers or carers, who may possibly be seen as authors of threatening behaviour or criminal acts perpetrated against children of school-age and beyond.[775] Thus, under Irish laws, an offence is committed by a person in authority who engages or attempts to engage in a sexual act with a child who has attained the age of 17 years but is under the age of 18 years; a maximum penalty of up to 10 years imprisonment is stated in the law for this offence.[776] In relation to a child against whom an offence (of a sexual nature) is alleged to have been committed, the term "person in authority" is defined as encompassing, *inter alia*, any person (other than family or household members) who is or has been responsible for the education, supervision, training, care or welfare of the child.[777] This statutory definition covering the majority of teaching or training staff employed for service in schools or educational establishments is very wide indeed; however, a statutory defence was introduced for the belief of the defendant that he or she was not a person in authority (see below).

Section 3A(3) of he *Criminal Law (Sexual Offences) Act* 2006 (as inserted by section 18 of the *Criminal Law (Sexual Offences) Act* 2017) allows for a defence of reasonable mistake that at the time of the alleged commission of the offence, the child involved had attained the age of

[773] O'Malley (n 739) 12.

[774] *'Murphy'* para A2.14; Hanly (n 761) 318.

[775] This concept's significance is equally perceivable from section 3(1) and 3(2) *Criminal Law (Sexual Offences) Act* 2006 as amended by section 17 of the *Criminal Law (Sexual Offences) Act* 2017 (penalties).

[776] Section 3A of the *Criminal Law (Sexual Offences) Act* 2006, as inserted by section 18 of the *Criminal Law (Sexual Offences) Act* 2017.

[777] Section 15 *Criminal Law (Sexual Offences) Act* 2017.

18 years; a 'reasonable person' test being added to this defence, section 3A(4). According to section 3A(5) the standard of proof required for the 'resonable mistake' defence as to the age of the child is set at the level applicable in civil proceedings which throws up similar questions as the ones posed in the case of *CW*.[778] Another defence relates to the reasonable belief of the defendant that he or she was not, in relation to the child concerned, a person in authority, section 3A(6). As inserted by the *Criminal Law (Sexual Offences) Act* 2017, section 3A(7) makes clear that consent of the adolescent involved is not a defence available for this offence.

Protection from Sexual Exploitation

Within the wider field of 'Sexual Offences' one of a threefold set of categories was found to consist of (sexual) acts which are essentially exploitative in nature and are deemed criminal even if the victim has, at least on a superficial level, consented to sexual activity.[779] Thus, Irish law makes special provision for the protection from sexual exploitation of certain categories of people who are deemed to be especially vulnerable, children being the primary such group to come under an umbrella of protective criminalization. As a novelty, an exploitative momentum (enabling the 'use' of one person by another) was made clearly visible in many offences involving any kind of power imbalance resulting from a material difference in age, gender, capacity or maturity. Besides the more general sexual offences such as sexual assault or rape, the whole set of exploitative sexual offences including 'Sexual Exploitation of Children' came under revision recently.[780] Legislating in terms of 'sexual exploitation' with the aim in mind to criminalize different aspects of abusive behaviour perpetrated against children well reflects the terminology of the Convention, as protection from sexual exploitation and sexual abuse is *per se* an obligation under the Convention (Article 34 CRC).[781]

---

778 See Fn 769 above.

779 O'Malley (n 739) 1.

780 *'Murphy'* Appendix 2 paras A2.1 through A2.47 (overview); Hanly (n 761) 332; *Criminal Law (Sexual Offences) Act* 2017, in 17 sections, displays a whole part 'Sexual Exploitation of Children' (Part 2).

781 *Terminology Guidelines* (n 53) 24, entry 'Child sexual exploitation'.

As defined in section 2 of the *Criminal Law (Sexual Offences) Act* 2017, in relation to a child 'sexual exploitation' means:

a) inviting, inducing or coercing the child to engage in prostitution or the production of child pornography;
b) the prostitution of the child or the use of the child for the production of child pornography;
c) the commission of an offence specified in the Schedule [to the Sex Offenders Act 2001[782]] against the child, causing another person to commit such an offence against the child, or inviting, inducing or coercing the child to commit such an offence against another person;
d) inducing or coercing the child to engage or participate in any sexual, indecent or obscene act;
e) inviting the child to engage or participate in any sexual, indecent or obscene act which, if done, would involve the commission of an offence against the child, or
f) inviting, inducing or coercing the child to observe any sexual, indecent or obscene act, for the purpose of corrupting or depraving the child.

From the perspective of Article 19 CRC it seems to be necessary and sufficient that no commercial intention or exchange in remuneration needs to be proven (by thc Prosecution) for establishing it as a crime what has been listed as exploitative activities in this definition. Article 19 CRC sets up the child's protection rights to cover all forms of violence, neglect and abuse irrespective of any commercial implications or monetary compensation offers as otherwise suggested by a terminology of 'sale' (of children).

Furthermore, at the level of statutory provision the *Criminal Law (Sexual Offences) Act* 2017 has been creating offences relating to the obtaining and providing of children for the purposes of sexual exploitation;[783] it defines a range of violent or coercive acts against children as criminal offences, such as online grooming and other acts related to inducing child prostitution.[784] Not only a possession of child sexual abuse materials was criminalized, but also the access (or streaming) of such material on the

782 This Schedule includes most general sexual offences, such as rape, statutory rape, sexual assault and incest, see Hanly (n 761) 335.

783 *Criminal Law (Sexual Offences) Act* 2017, section 3.

784 *Criminal Law (Sexual Offences) Act* 2017, section 8 (Use of information and communication technology), section 11 (Organising etc. child prostitution).

Internet;[785] in addition to materials in which real children were depicted, the organization, production and distribution of such materials depicting simulated children was equally outlawed.[786] Furthermore, by virtue of the *Criminal Law (Sexual Offences) Act* 2017 several new child abuse offences have been created, including an offence of inviting, inducing or coercing a child to engage in sexual touching (s 4); engaging in sexual activity in the presence of a child (s 5); causing a child to watch sexual activity (s 6) and meeting a child for the purpose of sexual exploitation (s 7).[787] Regrettably from a CRC perspective, the definition varies from one of these offences to another, although for most of them a child is a person under the age of 17 years. In consistency with the recent legislation's general aim of criminalizing a range of exploitative behaviours, in its interpretive section (s 2) the 2017 *Criminal Law Act* provides for a twofold definition of 'sexual activity' applicable for this context, and for offences established under sections 5 (Sexual activity in presence of child) and 6 (Causing child to watch sexual activity) in particular. This definition envisages an activity perceived as sexual 'because of its nature' (letter a) but also addresses an activity which because of prevailing circumstances or purposes involved independently acquires a connotation of being sexual (letter b).[788] Thus, no awareness of the victim child as to the sexual character of the activity in which he or she was involved needs to be proven by the Prosecution, and regarding the protective object and purpose of CRC based obligations to criminalize this is to be welcomed.

Reckless Endangerment

As a lesson to be learned from Commission of Inquiry reports (*'Ferns'* in particular), a new criminal offence of reckless endangerment was introduced by Section 176 of the *Criminal Justice Act 2006* into Irish law.[789] This offence may be committed by a person who has authority or control

---

785 *Criminal Law (Sexual Offences) Act* 2017, section 14 (Possession of child pornography).

786 *Criminal Law (Sexual Offences) Act* 2017, section 9 (b) ('child pornography').

787 O'Malley (n 771) 1.

788 *Criminal Law (Sexual Offences) Act* 2017, section 2 entry 'sexual activity'.

789 Listed in Schedule 3 *Children First Act* 2015 as an offence to come under the definition of 'sexual abuse'; *'Ferns'* 197 (recommendation Nr 14); Kilkelly (n 67) 12.

over a child or over an abuser, and who intentionally or recklessly endangers a child by:

a) *causing or permitting any child to be placed or left in a situation which creates a substantial risk to the child of being a victim of serious harm or sexual abuse, or*
b) *failing to take reasonable steps to protect a child from such a risk while knowing that the child is in such a situation;*

when simultaneously a statutory definition of the term 'abuser' is given according to which an abuser means an individual believed by a person who has authority or control over that individual to have seriously harmed or sexually abused a child. What is being targeted here is the passivity of bishops, headmasters and other figures holding supervisory powers over teachers, childcare workers and professionals whose work brings them into contact with children; having acquired knowledge about incidents of child abuse these authority figures remain passive in the face of an at-risk-situation when they should and could have stepped in to protect the children concerned.[790]

As a statutory offence it applies to activities or omissions of those in authority which causes or permits a child to be left in a situation of substantial risk of serious harm or sexual abuse, and criminalizes such actions or omissions accordingly (letter a). In addition, this section also stipulates that it is an offence to fail to take reasonable steps in that regard to ensure that children (below 18 years of age) under their care or authority are free from sexual abuse or serious harm (letter b). Extensively in its terms, this offence criminalizes any behaviour of authority figures that causes, permits or otherwise fails to act in the face of a situation where they know that there is a substantial risk to a child of such harm or sexual abuse ensuing from a failure to act.[791] As a penalty for such an offence a maximum term of ten years imprisonment was statutorily stipulated which is a heavy burden for someone who is not an abuser himself.

Remarkable in relation to this particular piece of legislation is its indirect appeal to be responsible and act accordingly without waiting for official intervention to come in and clear a situation rife with risk for children. In analogy to Article 19 CRC envisaging all forms of physical

[790] *'Ferns'* 197, Kilkelly (n 67) 12.
[791] *'Murphy'* para A2.45 – A2.47;

or mental violence, abuse or neglect including the range of protective measures to be taken in response, this legislative approach at least has the great advantage of providing for a strong incentive to act, and not remain passive in the sight of children at risk of violence or abuse. However, since some of the key terms used for creating this offence are drafted in a way that seems to be lacking in precision ('substantial risk', 'reasonable steps') its functional value for effective prosecution and timely conviction appears to be limited.

Conclusion

To conclude, the 2017 *Criminal Law (Sexual Offences) Act* in particular comprehensively addresses the sexual exploitation of children and targets those who engage in this criminal activity which in itself was extensively re-defined to include a vast array of activities exploitative in character or substance.[792] Thus, it starts off by creating offences relating to the obtaining and providing of children for the purposes of sexual exploitation, but the offence of sexual act with child was equally re-drafted and widely elaborated including rules apportioning evidential burden or burden of proof that were found to be not fully compatible with constitutional standards. Also, offences of the types of activity which may occur during the early stages of the predatory process prior to the actual exploitation of a child are clearly laid out through this piece of statutory legislation. In its main part many aspects indispensible for protection from sexual violence and abuse were conclusively dealt with, but its 'honest-mistake'-rules seem to be over-generous unduly favouring due process aspects to the benefit of the structurally stronger part in what, in almost every case, boils down to an intimate confrontation between an adult perpetrator and a child victim.[793] Protective rights of children who cannot guard themselves by correcting mistakes made by the perpetrator (and, in many cases, knowledgeable to him only) were not adequately weighed in for this balance, it seems.

The *Lanzarote* Explanatory Report found Europe to be not sufficiently consistent in relation to the protection of children against sexual abuse and exploitation, and strongly recommended that States should develop

[792] O'Malley (n 771) 1.
[793] O'Malley (n 739) 26.

an effective system of reporting and investigation, within a child-sensitive system of criminal proceedings.[794] To these topics I will now turn.

Sub-Section (2) – Mandatory Reporting as an Implementing Measure under Irish Law

Introduction

As was explained earlier, mandatory reporting functions as a protective strategy for an unimpeded transfer of factual information on child-related violence to an agency or institution in the State which is duly authorized to receive such information and to act upon its receipt.[795] Generally, cases of child abuse may be detectable in either the community or in educational settings of a more private character. In this respect a government-led policy of mandatory reporting may equally serve as a remedy against what was described as an issue of 'cover-up': '*... the meticulous concealment of abuse and abusers ...* '.[796]

As retrospectively observed and documented, sexually aggressive acts against children in care or education regularly manifest themselves as a hidden crime falsely suggesting a high degree of personal intimacy between the child and his or her caregiver-abuser;[797] many child victims, therefore, will have a problem of not being listened to, or not being taken seriously when making a complaint about sexual abuse, especially when complaining to people involved in perpetrating it. Additionally, it has widely been observed that children abused or threatened with abuse rarely disclose in full what is happening to them against their will; thus, as a response mechanism mandatory reporting laws have to capture a wide range of circumstances going beyond disclosures actually made by children themselves.[798]

---

794 *Lanzarote* Explanatory Report (n 155) para 7.

795 Fn 375 and accompanying text.

796 Y Murphy (n 760) 19.

797 B Mathews et al, 'Impact of a new mandatory reporting law on reporting and identification of child sexual abuse: A seven year time trend analysis' 56 Child Abuse and Neglect (2016) 62.

798 A M Pietrantonio et al, 'Mandatory reporting of child abuse and neglect, Crafting a positive process for health professionals and caregivers' (2013) 37 Child Abuse and Neglect 102, 103 (discussing empirical research about who is reporting maltreatment); Wekerle (n 369) 93, 94.

Again, in order to make an assessment about Irish Law on mandatory reporting as to its compatibility with CRC standards one may ask: is a reporting of serious concerns to a competent authority made mandatory for all forms of child abuse (1); are there sanctions in place for a breach of disclosure and reporting duties (2); and are there legal protections available, necessary and sufficient for encouraging reports made in good faith, by either qualified observers[799] or made as disclosures, by children themselves (3)? With these questions in mind, in the following a range of legislative or administrative measures will be reviewed and tested against standards derived from the right to non-violent education.[800]

Withholding Information as an Offence

Under the *Criminal Justice (Withholding Information on Offences against Children and Vulnerable Persons) Act* 2012 a criminal offence is constituted if a person withholds information relating to a serious offence, including a sexual offence, perpetrated against a person below 18 years of age. An offence arises where that same person knows or believes that an arrestable offence was committed against a child, and he or she has information which would help arrest, prosecute or convict another person for that offence; but fails to disclose that information to a member of the Gardaí (Irish police). Statutorily defined in Section 2 of the 2012 *Criminal Justice Act* the *actus reus* of the offence consists of a failure to disclose qualified information relating to a serious offence which has been committed against a child, without reasonable excuse.

As regards the (prior) offence probably committed against a child, this 2012 Act sets out a prolonged list of legally captured criminal offences, such as 'murder', 'rape' or 'sexual assault', but also 'trafficking of children' or 'reckless endangerment' among others.[801] As a consequence, no ambiguities remain in the law as to the seriousness of the preceding offence committed against children, which must not be covered up. The information that needs to be disclosed must be of a very stringent quality

799 CRC/C/GC/13 para 49.

800 See p 115 above for details.

801 *Criminal Justice (Withholding of Information on Offences Against Children and Vulnerable Persons) Act* 2012, section 2 in conjunction with Schedule 1 (Offences against children for purposes of offence under section 2); Schedule 1 to the 2012 Act has been adapted twice in the meantime.

or else, withholding this information will not become an offence; the Act only applies to a non-disclosure of knowledge or belief about a serious criminal offence already committed or of information relating to it.[802] As identically set out in Sections 2 and 3 of the 2012 Act, the *mens rea* of this offence contains two separate elements: knowledge or belief that a serious offence has been committed against a child (letter a), and knowledge or belief that his or her information about the offence committed might be of material assistance for purposes of criminal investigation (letter b).[803] Admittedly, a purely subjective standard applies as to the serious offence committed, and also as to the quality of information held or withheld by the person accused of an offence under this Act and its relevance to criminal investigations (twice, this defendant 'knows or believes'). Nevertheless, the quality and density of the information unduly withheld from the police remains of an extremely exclusive character in the wording of this offence, and every subjective standard in the law usually makes the work of the prosecution even more difficult when it comes to proving, or producing relevant evidence for the mental state of the person accused.

Exceptions

As an important exception, fully in compliance with an approach promoting the child victim's physical and psychological recovery (Article 39 CRC), the child against whom a serious offence such as rape or sexual assault was committed in the first place, shall not be guilty of an offence of withholding information, as explicitly stated in Section 2(3) of the 2012 *Criminal Justice Act*.[804] Conversely, the right of the child to disclose in person the commission of an arrestable offence perpetrated against him- or herself, to the Gardaí remains unprejudiced, as Section 4 of the 2012 Act clearly presupposes.[805] To be welcomed from a point of view taking se-

[802] This stringency is understandable against the background of cases when bishops fully knew about clerical perpetrators of child abuse, and opted for covering-up.

[803] *Criminal Justice Act* 2012, section 2(1) reads (extract): '*. . . , a person shall be guilty of an offence if-(a) he or she knows or believes that an offence, . . . , has been committed . . . , and (b) he or she has information which he or she knows or believes might be of material assistance . . .* '; O'Malley (n 771) 8.

[804] *Criminal Justice Act* 2012, section 2(3) reads (extract): '*The child against whom the . . . offence concerned was committed . . . shall not be guilty of an offence . . .* '.

[805] *Criminal Justice Act* 2012, section 4(2) reads (extract): '*. . . the right of the child . . . against whom the . . . offence . . . concerned was committed to disclose the commis-*

riously the individual child's right to be heard (Article 12 CRC), this legal statement from the defence section of the Act provides for clarification.

Although not an exception *stricto sensu,* in its Section 2(4) the 2012 *Criminal Justice Act* provides for another statutory clarification treating "any right or privilege" by virtue of which a person may normally be entitled to refuse to disclose information. Since this study is centrally concerned about clerical child sexual abuse, a side-look will be taken here on the so-called sacerdotal privilege which, as a matter of law, implies that any information obtained under the seal of confession by a Roman Catholic priest must never be disclosed by that same priest under any circumstance.[806] As further clarified in Subsection (4) *'any right or privilege that may arise in any criminal proceedings ... entitling a person to refuse to disclose information'* remains un-prejudiced by the offence of withholding information as newly created by Section 2 of the 2012 *Criminal Justice Act*. In plain English: any priest (or bishop) who committed an offence of withholding information on certain offences against children is therefore criminally liable under Section 2 of the 2012 Act, regardless of the fact that he may otherwise be entitled to refuse disclosure of information by virtue of his sacerdotal privilege.[807]

Finally, the 2012 *Criminal Justice Act* addresses an issue of overlapping duties and declares, for the avoidance of doubt, that its newly created obligation to disclose information is in addition to any other information-sharing obligations.[808] Thus, the provisions of this legislation must be construed so as to be in addition to any reporting requirements to which mandated persons may become subject under the *Children First Act* 2015 (to which I will turn in a moment).

---

sion of that offence, ... '.

[806] The 1983 *Codex* provides for legislation confirming the inviolability of the sacramental seal; so far Irish common law has afforded the seal some protection; for details, see M Mullaney, 'Mandatory Reporting and the Seal of Confession' 62 The Furrow (2011) 523, 524 (reference to *Cook v. Carrol* 1945); McAleese (n 7) 188.

[807] On the reverse question, whether any piece of information exclusively obtained by a priest under the seal of confession remains untouched by an obligation to disclose as created by Section 2 of the 2012 Act, see Fn 839 below.

[808] *Criminal Justice Act* 2012, section 2(5) reads (extract): '... *the obligation imposed on a person ... to disclose information ..., is in addition to, and not in substitution for, any other obligation that the person has ...* '.

Defences to the Offence of Withholding Information

Equally helpful for an understanding about the criminal momentum at the core of a section 2 offence are the four defences provided for in Section 4 of the 2012 *Criminal Justice Act* which allow for a release from criminal liability for non-disclosure based on reasonably grounded views pertaining to the best interests of the child; as long as the reporter-to-be knew of and relied upon those views.[809] If any such sensibly elaborated view about non-disclosure was formed either by the matured child victim him- or herself (subsections 1, 2), or in a responsible manner by the child's parents (subsections 4, 5), or in an equally responsible manner by a qualified professional close to the child (subsections 8, 10), then a statutory defence to the offence of withholding information will be available for the accused person, as the case may be. Interestingly, the age limit for the capacity of the child to form an acceptable view about non-disclosure is set, in Section 4(2) of the *Criminal Justice Act* 2012, at 14 years below which it is presumed that any such view formed by the child victim will not be taken into consideration. Here is an irritating discrepancy relating to the legal age of consent fixated at 15 years for purposes of criminalising rape and sexual assault where the victim is an adolescent. Why an adolescent should be seen to be sufficiently mature so as to make an essential contribution to halting the prosecution of a case of withholding information at the age of 14 years when he or she needs to be at least 15 years of age for consenting to sexual activity involving an adult, is not obvious. Insofar as the age-limit provided for in this particular piece of legislation is stipulated as a rebuttable presumption, I see no conflict regarding the Convention principle of evolving capacities (Article 5 CRC).

Actually, the bar for a section 4 defence, in terms of grounds for forming a view in support of non-disclosure, is raising quite high: as substantiated in Section 4(6), only if the defendant had reasonable grounds for forming their view about non-disclosure, and, in so doing, acted and are continuing to act *bona fide* in the best interests of the child, a defence

---

[809] *Criminal Justice Act* 2012, section 4(1) reads (extract): '... *it shall be a defence for the accused person to show-(a) that the child ... against whom the ... offence concerned was committed made known his or her view ... that the commission of that offence, ..., should not be disclosed ..., and (b) that he or she (the accused person) knew of and relied upon that view*'.

shall be available for them.[810] Since the grounds based on which the view promoting non-disclosure was formed, have to be "reasonable grounds", an objective element is successfully injected into this test here; even if this particular parent-defendant's private view still lies at the heart of the statutory defence. Obviously, the best interests of the child come to bear on this legislation making a statutory defence available for certain grave cases of non-disclosure.[811] Seen from a children's rights point of view implying that children and their best interests must become a matter for widespread public concern, what I find problematic in respect of these statutory defences as provided for in Section 4 of the 2012 *Criminal Justice Act*, is the following. It seems that a view about the child's best interests formed and communicated in an exclusively private context, should *per se* be sufficient for steering the case of a serious criminal offence (committed against a child) away from organs officially responsible for public prosecution within the State.

Penalties for Withholding Information

According to the 2012 *Criminal Justice Act,* penalties for withholding information are stipulated in a way that makes this Act not easy to apply in practice for anyone: judges, juries, defence-lawyers or parents and children themselves questioning about their respective duties. Section 7 provides for a maximum term of imprisonment of 12 months (or a class A fine), on summary conviction (subsection a); the years of imprisonment provided, on conviction on indictment, are of a varying duration according to the gravity of the preceding offence against children in relation to which the accused person failed, in a timely manner, to disclose relevant information (subsection b).[812] Starting with a term not exceeding 10 years, in

[810] *Criminal Justice Act* 2012, section 4(6) reads (extract): '... *the parent or guardian concerned had reasonable grounds for forming the view concerned ... and, in so doing, he or she acted and is continuing to act bona fide in the best interests of the child ...* '.

[811] Acording to Article 3(1) CRC courts of law, including courts judging on criminal matters, have to primarily consider the best interests of the child in all actions concerning children.

[812] *Criminal Justice Act* 2012, section 7 reads (extract): *'A person guilty of an offence under section 2 or 3 shall be liable-(a) on summary conviction, to a class A fine or imprisonment for a term not exceeding 12 months or both, or (b) on conviction on indictment, to a fine or imprisonment or both according to the gravity of the ...*

case the preceding offence against children is one for which a maximum sentence of imprisonment for life applies (subsection b (i)), the respective terms of imprisonment as a penalty for withholding information are half the duration of the terms applying to the underlying offence against children (subsection b (ii) and (iii)), and go down to a term not exceeding 3 years (subsection b (iv)).

To sum up, this 2012 *Criminal Justice Act* criminalizing the withholding of information on offences against children provides for a craftily engineered legislative response to public inquiries that had produced a plethora of documentation concerning cases when powerful authority figures in certain families, in the State or in the Church had set themselves above the Law.

More Protections against Cover-Up

The *Protections for Persons Reporting Child Abuse Act* 1998 protects anyone reporting a case of suspected child abuse to designated officers of CFA/Tusla, to the Health Service Executive (HSE) or to members of the Gardaí as long as the report is made in good faith and is not malicious. As a legal protection it implies that even if a case of suspected child abuse is reported and it proves unfounded, a plaintiff who took legal action against the informer would have to demonstrate that the informer had not acted reasonably and in good faith when making the report.[813] A similar kind of reporting laws planned for enactment by Costa Rica was explicitly applauded by the Committee in a context of Article 19 (2) CRC detailing protective measures such as 'reporting'.[814]

Reporting by Professionals in their Role as Mandated Persons

As regards the overall topic of mandatory reporting the main piece of internal legislation for Ireland was provided by the *Children First Act* 2015 which, through its Part 3 (sections 14 through 18) in particular, makes it mandatory for key professionals to report serious child welfare and protection concerns to the Government's Child and Family Agency (CFA/Tusla);

---

offence ... concerned ... '.

813 Under the common law defence of 'qualified privilege' anyone making a report in good faith and in the child's best interests may also be protected from civil liability.

814 *Implementation Handbook* (n 137) 266.

thus, an individualised obligation relating to concerns that must be reported was placed on a statutory footing by virtue of this Act.

Accordingly, in its section 14 the *Children First Act* 2015 sets out the objective scope of this reporting mandate (extract):

> *... where a mandated person knows, believes or has reasonable grounds to suspect, on the basis of information that he or she has received, acquired or becomes aware of in the course of his or her employment or profession ..., that a child – (a) has been harmed, (b) is being harmed, or (c) is at risk of being harmed, he or she shall, as soon as practicable, report that knowledge, belief or suspicion, as the case may be, to the Agency* [CFA/Tusla].

As fully elaborated in Section 2 (Definitions) of the 2015 Act the definition of harm, in relation to a child meanwhile extends to assault, ill-treatment or neglect of the child in a manner that seriously affects or is likely to seriously affect the child's health, development or welfare; or, alternatively, to sexual abuse of the child which, in turn, is defined by reference to a scheduled list of offences such as rape, sexual assault, sexual act with child or reckless endangerment, among others.[815] Thus, any reasonable suspicion specifically concerned about sexual abuse of a child immediately becomes the subject-matter of a mandated report to CFA/Tusla. As understood for this statutory definition of harm in relation to a child, 'ill-treatment' means to abandon or cruelly treat the child, or to cause or procure or allow the child to be abandoned or cruelly treated;[816] similarly, 'neglect' means to deprive the child of adequate food, warmth, clothing, hygiene, supervision, safety or medical care;[817] and, lastly, 'welfare' includes the moral, intellectual, physical, emotional and social welfare of the child.[818]

Turning to the personal scope of the reporting mandate, included as mandated persons are psychologists, social care workers, social workers, paramedics, registered teachers, Gardaí, guardian *ad litem*, child care staff, youth workers, clergy and foster carers among others.[819] Every individual belonging to one of these classes of professionals is legally specified

---

815 *Children First Act* 2015, section 2 (Definitions), entries 'harm' and 'sexual abuse' referencing Schedule 3 of the Act which, in turn, features a list of 14 itemized offences.

816 *Children First Act* 2015, section 2 (Definitions), entry 'ill-treatment'.

817 Ibid, entry 'neglect'.

818 Ibid, entry 'welfare'.

819 *Children First Act* 2015, section 2 (Definitions), entry 'mandated person' in conjunc-

as a mandated person *per se* for purposes of the 2015 Act. Clearly, the combined scopes of this statutorily ordained reporting mandate cover an enormously wide ground of child-related well-being concerns, and also involve a significant number of professionals working with children, on a regular basis or just incidentally.

No guidance for the balancing of interests is given in this legislation regarding established professional standards and duties which may or may not be easily compatible with an extended obligation to report such as this one. As a consequence, some questions as to possible conflicts or even blockages possibly hindering an unimpeded transfer of relevant information to child protection services remain unanswered in the law. Accordingly, I will have to attempt at an answer to some of these questions further below, especially with respect for teachers registered with the Teaching Council and in respect of schools and their patronage and management operating under the general oversight of the Department of Education and Skills, and its Inspectorate in particular.[820] Moreover, serious concerns over gaps in child protection were articulated in respect of non-teaching staff employed as school staff for institutions which have boarding facilities on offer.[821]

Extensions and Exemptions

The scope of the reporting mandate under the 2015 Act is even further extended by virtue of Section 14(2), and requires mandated persons to report any harm-related disclosure by a child to CFA/Tusla. As an exemption, stipulated in Section 14(3), a mandated person shall not be obliged to make a report where his or her knowledge or belief is about non-exploitative sexual activity with a 15 to 17 year old child;[822] similarly, no reporting re-

---

tion with Schedule 2 'Mandated Persons' which features a list of 18 classes of professional activities.

820 Fn 832 and accompanying text.

821 C O'Brien, 'Boarding schools to be inspected for first time amid concerns over gaps in child protection' in *Irish Times* (16 December 2022).

822 Four main conditions are itemized in section 14(3) of the 2015 Act for this exemption: no material difference in age or maturity (letters a and b), the relationship being of a non-exploitative character (letter b), no transfer of information initiated by the child as a harm-related disclosure to the mandated person (letter c), and an option for non-reporting clearly communicated by the adolescent to the mandated person concerned (letter d).

quirement arises where a mandated person's concerns are the result of information received from another mandated person, as clarified in Section 14(4) of that same Act.

In correspondence to earlier legislation,[823] the core section on reporting by a mandated person – Section 14 of the 2015 Act – provides that reporting obligations under this section are in addition to, and not in substitution for, any other obligations that the mandated person has to disclose information to the Child and Family Agency (subsection 11); similarly, that same section propounds as a distinction that nothing shall affect any other obligation a person has to disclose information to An Garda Síochána under the *Criminal Justice (Withholding of Information on Offences against Children and Vulnerable Persons) Act* 2012.[824] In respect of school-based educational practice, this means that in any situation where a teacher or staff member receives a disclosure of abuse, or has information in relation to serious offences committed against children, it remains their personal responsibility to ensure that they comply with all requirements of that 2012 Act, regardless of any communication that may simultaneously be running between CFA/Tusla, and the school, its patrons or management.

Safeguarding as a Statutory Obligation

Moreover, Part 2 of the *Children First Act* 2015 provides for comprehensive risk assessment and planning for a strong organisational culture of safeguarding in all services made available to children;[825] because of an overlap of duties falling on schools, its owners and management under the 2015 Act, and registered teachers featuring as mandated persons, these safeguarding duties specified in the Act will be considered here in conjunction with reporting duties as described above. Additionally, through the 2015 Act provision is made for a register of non-compliance,[826] and also for a statutory underpinning of the existing Children First Inter-Departmental

[823] Fn 808 and accompanying text concerning *Criminal Justice Act* 2012 section 2.

[824] Ibid.

[825] *Children First Act* 2015, Part 2 (Child Safeguarding Statements), in particular section 10 (Child safeguarding) and section 11 (Risk assessment and child safeguarding statements etc).

[826] *Children First Act* 2015, section 12 (Non-compliance with request to furnish child safeguarding statement) and section 13 (Register of non-compliance).

Implementation Group which promotes and oversees cross-sectoral implementation and compliance with *Children First* guidance documents.[827]

To be clearly distinguished from 'harm' as a technical term comprehensively defined in Section 2, the 2015 Act, in its Section 11, refers to 'risk' which is designated as any potential for harm to a child while availing of the service provided as a "relevant service" by the operator of that same service; the school's owners or a school board of management being a primary example of an operator of this kind. As spelled out in Section 11(1) of the Act, that same provider of educational service must undertake an assessment of any risk thus defined (letter a); as a provider of services he must prepare and make known a comprehensive Child Safeguarding Statement (letter b) in relation to his organisation;[828] and he must appoint a relevant person, also known as a 'Designated Liaison Person' (or DLP, for short) for purposes of this Act.

In order to secure compliance with statutory obligations imposed on providers of child-related services under the *Children First Act* 2015, a complicated procedure has been established concerning a case of non-compliance with the request to furnish a Child Safeguarding Statement (Section 12); however, for cases of non-reporting this piece of legislation provides for no specific sanction, but rather interlinks with that earlier *Criminal Justice (Withholding of Information on Offences against Children and Vulnerable Persons) Act* 2012 as indicated above and clearly spelled out in Section 14 of the *Children First Act* 2015.[829]

Mandatory Reporting from within a School Context

As another key child protection measure being particularly relevant to primary and post-primary schools the requirement on mandated persons (including registered teachers and teaching clergy) to report child protec-

[827] *Children First Act* 2015, Part 4 (Children First Inter-Departmental Implementation Group etc); more on this mechanism for administrative cooperation, see Fn 963 below and accompanying text.

[828] As part of their respective school's Child Safeguarding Statement all boards of management are required to formally adopt and implement DES *Child Protection Procedures for Primary and Post-Primary Schools* (n 936 below) para 1.1.14.

[829] *Children First Act* 2015, section 14(12) reads (extract): '*Nothing in this section shall operate to affect any other obligation that a person has to disclose information … under the Criminal Justice (Withholding of Information on Offences Against Children and Vulnerable Persons) Act 2012 …* '.

tion concerns over a certain threshold to CFA/Tusla is being highlighted here.[830] Categorically, all sexual abuse is seen to seriously affect the child's well-being and must therefore be reported immediately under all circumstances.[831] The reporting procedure to be followed by registered teachers in respect of their role as mandated persons, includes a requirement to liaise with the Designated Liaison Person (DLP) and, where applicable, to submit mandated reports jointly with the DLP to CFA/Tusla; but this kind of procedural detail was not fully elaborated in the 2015 Act itself.[832]

As indicated above, an overlap of duties and obligations rooted in either the 2012 Act, which creates an obligation for everyone to disclose specified information on serious offences to the Gardai, or the 2015 Act by virtue of which registered teachers are mandated *qua* professional status to report child protection concerns to Tusla, may potentially cause confusion for teachers and DLP's.[833] There are competing priorities in respect of obligations under the 2012 *Withholding* legislation, and the Act of 2015 which touches on several kinds of harm to a child, including sexual abuse reports that must be furnished to CFA/Tusla immediately. Since, as a matter of law, the provisions of the 2012 *Withholding* legislation are in addition to the reporting obligations under the *Children First Act* 2015,[834] the 2017 DES *Procedures* clearly outline the fact that a member of school personnel has dealt with a child protection concern under the Procedures does not absolve that person of their legal obligation to disclose relevant information to the Gardaí under the 2012 Act.[835] Likewise, if one or both teachers concerned (including a DLP) have dealt with the matter by reporting their information to the Gardaí as required by the 2012 Act, and if the information equally relates to a matter that comes under the *Procedures* they must also act in compliance with all requirements of those same procedures.[836]

---

830 The threshold mentioned is given in the Act itself, see Fn 815 ('harm').

831 DES *Child Protection Procedures* 2017 (n 835 below) para 4.3.5.

832 M Nohilly, 'Child Protection Training for Teachers' (2019) 19 Ir J Appl Soc Stud 76.

833 M Nohilly, 'Becoming and being DLP: Designated Liaison Person's experience of the role in the Irish primary school' (2018) 37 Irish Educational Studies 19, 22.

834 *Education First Act* 2015, section 14, subsection (12) read in conjunction with *Criminal Justice Act* 2012, section 2, subsection (5) .

835 Department of Education and Skills (DES) *Child Protection Procedures for Primary and Post-Primary Schools* 2017 para 1.3.6; see Fn 936 below for details on *Procedures* 2017.

836 Ibid para 1.3.6.

Depending on the particular situation, the *Procedures* (elaborating on the requirements of the 2015 Act) and the 2012 *Criminal Justice Act* may require that a teacher or school staff member reports to both their DLP and to An Garda Siochána.

As Nohilly resumes:

> *Given that both Acts* [scil. the 2012 Criminal Justice Act and the 2015 Children First Act] *have different reporting procedures to different organisations, there is potential for confusion and lack of clarity for teachers and DLPs.*[837]

Although it may be more or less clearly spelled out in the text of the *Procedures*, the role of the DLP in the school context appears to be a challenged and isolated position and, for DLPs to fully comply with their obligations more training is needed. When the reality of supporting a hurt child and liaising with staff, families and outside agencies such as CFA/Tusla are taken on board, the isolation and sole responsibility of the role become more apparent.

Thus, seen from a children's rights perspective better training and support should be made available by the State to those education professionals who are working as frontline guarantors of the right to non-violent education helping schoolchildren to make the best possible use of their respective capabilities in practice.

The Problem of 'Cover-up' in the Church

As earlier mentioned, *'Murphy'* and *'Cloyne'* in particular were inquiring into administrative activities ('ecclesiastical governance') that, over decades, had been performed from within Catholic dioceses in Ireland such as Dublin or Cloyne where most of what was later analysed, through officially published inquiry reports, as 'cover-up' had occurred.[838] In effect, this kind of governance activity amounted to helping perpetrators of child sexual abuse to evade regular justice. In response to these findings it was made a criminal offence, under the *Criminal Justice (Withholding of Information on Offences against Children and Vulnerable Persons) Act* 2012, to withhold information about a serious offence against children.

---

[837] Nohilly 'Becoming and being DLP' (n 833) 22.

[838] Fn 65 above (*'Murphy'*), Fn 66 above (*'Cloyne'*).

One further aspect of this *Withholding* legislation is particularly relevant to all cases of clerical child abuse when the canonical seal of confession regularly comes into play, which legally protects the confidentiality of communication between an ordained priest and parishioners seeking help, advice or absolution from that priest in the sacramental sphere.[839] Under Irish law, this seal of confession, also known as 'sacerdotal or priest-penitent privilege', was afforded some protection in terms of common law as developed following the case of *Cook* v *Carroll* which, to this day, is the leading Irish authority on the topic.[840]

When, under the Act of 2012, an ordained priest may *per se* be entitled to refuse disclosure of information specifically obtained under the seal of confession, might he not otherwise come under an obligation to report, as a person mandated under the *Children First Act* 2015, child-related concerns about ill-treatment? Unlike the 2012 Act there is no 'reasonable excuse' or 'rule of law' exception in section 14 of the 2015 Act. Rather, priests to be subsumed as members of the clergy (Schedule 2, 15 (g)) are mandated persons and there is nothing in the Act of 2015 that could be construed as a legal protection of the seal of confession as such. Additionally, as scheduled in the Act of 2015 (Schedule 1, 7) any work or activity as a minister or priest which would bring that minister or priest into contact with a child, is deemed to be a relevant service covered by the scope of the Act, including its statutory obligations of reporting (section 14).[841] No individual cleric performing his ecclesiastic services as a professional in the field of school-based education and care can, therefore, be exempted from reporting obligations under the law. As a consequence, section 14 of the 2015 Act requires that any 'knowledge, belief or suspicion' (subsection 1) or 'disclosure' (subsection 2), developed on the basis of information received as a professionally operating educator must be reported by a mandated person, irrespective of the fact that he may be an ordained cleric.

---

839 Fn 826 above; McAleese (n 7) 187; Holy See *Response* (n 93) 14; S Kirchner, 'Das Beichtgeheimnis zwischen staatlichem und kirchlichem Recht' Jurisprudencija/Jurisprudence (2012) 1317, 1326.

840 *Cook v. Carroll* [1945] I.R. 515; McAleese (n 7) 188.

841 Fn 819 above; McAleese (n 7) 189.

Conclusion

Resuming this subsection on 'Mandatory Reporting' it may be attested that Ireland, by enacting legislation for establishment and maintenance of a comprehensive system of information transfer about child abuse to responsible organs of the State, acts in compliance with basic CRC requirements. Thus, most classes of professionals working with children are subject to mandatory reporting laws covering all forms of violence against children.

What seems problematic is a split in the law between crime-related information on the one hand which is being fed into a crime prevention and enforcement system, and child abuse concerns on the other which, if found serious enough to do so, are being directed to the attention of specialised care and support agencies in the State; from a personalised child rights perspective this makes no sense. Every individual child victim is – and remains – an independent holder of freedoms and rights whose bodily or mental integrity has already come under severe distress as a matter of fact.

As given in section 2 of the *Children First Act* 2015 the statutory definition of a threshold of harm above which a mandated persons must report her concerns, is over-complex involving different levels of terminological abstraction. Thus, harm may come as assault, ill-treatment or neglect seriously affecting the child's well-being when each of the key terms used in practice requires more steps of terminological analysis in detail. Alternatively, as another form of harm, sexual abuse requires an analysis of a dozen of statutory provisions to be taken from a wide range of statutory enactments.[842] Although, in accordance with the wording in section 14 of the *Children First Act* 2015 child abuse concerns do not in every single case have to be reported as knowledge, but may also be reported as (information based) belief or suspicion, an over-complex definition of harm – in three different temporal relations – applies. Thus, the law may easily prove to have an effect of causing a blockage against the necessary flow of information.

[842] Fn 815 and accompanying text.

Sub-Section (3) – Investigation as an Implementing Measure under Irish Law

Introduction

Another topic that requires closer analysis from an implementation point of view is 'investigation' of complaints made about violence or sexual abuse against minors.[843] As a protective measure 'investigation' functionally builds on 'reporting' (whether initiated by a child, by a representative or by an external party), and may lead on to 'judicial involvement' meaning apprehension and prosecution or conviction of the person accused of a criminal offence as a result of investigations completed.[844] In parallel, investigations of an administrative character may help to facilitate preventive measures for protecting children from (further) violence or abuse. Also, a sharing of information gathered, *via* administrative investigations, about abuse suspected against or committed by an identified individual proved to be another necessary preventive measure for safeguarding children; especially for children congregated for purposes of care and education.[845]

Moreover, criminal investigations into sexual violence against children have an enormous functional value for raising, within government circles, the level of alertness bearing on the incidence, prevalence and types or extent of child sexual abuse at a given time in any society, and the Irish situation offers some interesting insights in this regard.[846] In order to shape the Government's response to revelations of historical sexual abuse in schools run by religious orders the Department of Education, in March 2023, announced details of a scoping inquiry which will be informed by

---

[843] Fn 392 and accompanying text.

[844] CRC/C/IRL/CO/2 para 37 (all reported cases of abuse and neglect to be adequately investigated).

[845] Irish High Court case of *MQ v Gleeson* [1998] 4 IR 85 concerned a man suspected of child abuse who was (later) accepted at a child care qualification course; having concluded their investigations the local health board furnished a report to the organisers of the course who took steps to remove him from the list of participants; the High Court held that the health board's duties obliged it to take the steps which it had taken; building on and confirming this jurisdiction: *CD v CFA* [2020] IEHC 452 (Fn 866 below).

[846] *'Ryan'* vol. V 383 (Ferriter Report).

reports and experts from a range of areas.[847]

Unlawfully Protected from Investigation

Since this study is also concerned about clerical child abuse, a short side-look on a practice and perception of impunity observable in the past may be helpful, especially as the (historic) situation in Ireland is well documented and researched in the meantime.[848] There are lessons to be learned from an Irish past when official organs of the State were not willing or unable to investigate allegations of child sexual abuse brought against clerics, teachers or school-personnel, and other authority figures in society. From a social science point of view Marie Keenan resumed her re-lecture of many different (official) inquiry reports from early 21st century Ireland but from other jurisdictions also:

> *The dioceses were seen as having orchestrated efforts to protect abusing clergy from investigation, arrest and prosecution by civil authorities, and by so doing to protect the religious institutions from adverse publicity that might have affected their economic welfare.*[849]

What becomes obvious from this observation is that abusing clergy were protected from proper investigations with the help of senior figures in the Church undertaking orchestrated efforts to provide a strange form of shielding to the benefit of known offenders.[850] As explained above,[851] most forms of withholding information on serious offences against children have been statutorily criminalized as a response. Any information obtained by the Gardaí (Irish police) as an outcome of a statutory duty to disclose under the *Withholding* legislation will now be used for investigative purposes possibly leading to arrest and detention, prosecution or conviction of (clerical) offenders accordingly. Unfortunately, most victims of clerical sexual abuse choose not to make statements to the police and

---

847 Department of Education, '*Minister Foley announces details of Scoping Inquiry to shape Government's reponse to revelations of historical sexual abuse in schools run by religious orders*' (7 March 2023).

848 Keenan (n 61) chapter 1; '*Ryan*' vol V 383 'Ferriter Report'; McAlinden (n 69) 189.

849 Keenan (n 61) 202; a *diocese* is an ecclesiastic entity regularly headed by a bishop as its leader.

850 CRC/C/VAT/CO/2 para 38.

851 Fn 802 and accompanying text.

this could easily lead to clerical abuses remaining under-investigated as a result.[852] What would seem to be highly problematic, in this context, is a Garda policy according to which incidents of abuse will not be recorded (with investigations not proceeded) in cases of victims who are initially unwilling to make a complaint to the Gardaí but are referred to them by a third party, such as a Church.[853] As a policy this practice is not in accordance with CRC obligations to investigate every plausible complaint or disclosure of abuse.

Requirements of Effectiveness and Child-Sensitivity

The European Court of Human Rights in particular has made it abundantly clear that every plausible complaint made concerning an act of violence or sexual abuse, especially if perpetrated against a minor, must be effectively investigated in a manner that respects the requirements of child-sensitivity, and that this kind of thorough investigation is a positive obligation under the ECHR falling on the member State concerned.[854] Accordingly, what needs to be explored here are the human rights parameters of child protection activities undertaken by CFA/Tusla ('the Agency') acting as an executive organ of the State: trained social workers initiate formal inquiries into allegations of child abuse which may lead to a finding officially asserting that an individual has committed an act, or acts of abuse. Depending on the circumstances of the case this kind of social work investigations by CFA/Tusla can operate simultaneously with criminal investigations by the Gardaí; since both agencies have independent statutory obligations, they will therefore be examined in turn.[855]

As further detailed below, it is CFA/Tusla's statutory obligation and responsibility to promote the welfare of children under the *Child Care Act* 1991 and under the *Child and Family Agency Act* 2013.[856] In practical terms the Irish system of administrative or social work investigations

---

852 A/HRC/40/51/Add.2 para 74 (UN Special Rapporteur).

853 A/HRC/40/51/Add.2 paras 74, 80 (UN Special Rapporteur); Garda Síochána *Policy on the Investigation of Sexual Crime, Crimes Against Children, Child Welfare* (2nd ed 2013) para 5.6.

854 Fn 401 above.

855 CFA/Tusla operates on the basis of the *Child and Family Agency Act* 2013.

856 For the text of section 3 *Child Care Act* 1991 and of the *Child and Family Agency Act* 2013, see Fn 866 below and accompanying text.

presently functions as a three-step procedure, entailing investigations into an allegation of sexual abuse of a child (1), making a formal finding as to the truth of that complaint (2), and a notification of third parties (beyond public entities immediately involved) about the findings made by the Agency (3). While each of these steps is worthy of analysis in its own right, the main accent here will be laid on 'investigation' (1) which regularly functions as the gateway into the whole procedure demarcating the extent of child maltreatment that has come under scrutiny from the authorities. In order to promote the welfare of children who are not receiving adequate care and protection, CFA/Tusla inquiries are built on for the design of general measures of risk identification but also for more detailed measures of risk mitigation applicable in every single case investigated.[857]

ECHR Case Law

Here, the reason for looking deeper into ECHR case-law lies in the following: as a matter of international law, the ECHR is binding on the Irish State by virtue of its being a Council of Europe member State. Furthermore, this binding effect translates into obligations imposed on CFA/Tusla, on the Gardaí and on Irish courts *via* the *European Convention on Human Rights Act* 2003 which obliges every organ of the State to perform its statutory function in a manner compatible with the State's obligations under the European Convention.[858]

As a consequence, in search of specific human rights obligations, the 2002 ECHR case of *E and others v the United Kingdom* needs to be kept in mind for supporting a comprehensive understanding about 'investigation' as an administrative measure for the protection of children against sexual abuse.[859] As explained earlier, the Court found a violation of Article 3 ECHR, since the pattern of a lack of investigation, communication and co-operation by the relevant authorities disclosed in this case must be regarded as having had a significant influence on the actual course of events causing a multiplicity of harm to children.[860] It is worth emphasising, that

---

857 *Child Care Act* 1991 section 3(1), Fn 866 below.

858 *European Convention on Human Rights Act,* 2003 sections 2, 4 (courts), section 3 (organs of the State performing administrative functions).

859 *E and others v UK* (n 411); *Annual Report* 2020 (n 389) 38.

860 *E and others v UK* (n 411) para 100.

a procedural obligation to conduct an effective investigation arises in all cases when a complaint is made, even if that complaint is ultimately not substantiated in the investigation.[861]

In the ECHR case of *CAS and CS v Romania* investigations were undertaken which the ECtHR found to be ineffective on the basis of a combination of failures, including delays in commencing it and in progressing key aspects such as questioning the alleged perpetrator; all of which made the authorities appear as displaying a 'lax attitude' on their part.[862] Again, alluding to formulations firstly coined by the Committee, the European Court reiterated its emphasis on a requirement that investigations have to be rigorous and child-sensitive; their particular concern was that the authorities did not weigh up all conflicting evidence and made no consistent efforts to establish the facts by engaging in a context-sensitive assessment.[863] Moreover, no proper counselling services were provided to the child during investigative proceedings or afterwards, which was not consistent with the need to provide adequate measures for recovery and reintegration (Article 39 CRC).[864] As the UN Special Rapporteur found upon her 2019 visit to Ireland, there are a number of issues impeding the successful prosecution of child sexual abuse, including challenges that the police face with the gathering of evidence, unclear testimony about incidents and difficulty proving the specific legal elements of the crimes; in particular she found that delays in investigations and court proceedings may mean victims are obliged to testify well after the incident which can lead to difficulties in obtaining corroborating evidence.[865]

Statutory Instruments and High Court Judges

In Ireland a statutory jurisdiction for CFA/Tusla to make inquiries into targeted allegations of sexual abuse derives from the *Child Care Act* 1991, section 3, which covers a wide range of situations for which the welfare of children requires official promotion; thus, CFA/Tusla has responsibility for providing care and protection to children in circumstances where their parents are not able to do so. Section 3(1) of the *Child Care Act* 1991 as

---

[861] Fn 396 above and accompanying text.

[862] *CAS and CS v Romania* (n 399), paras 69, 70.

[863] Ibid para 78 repeating CRC/C/GC/13 para 51 verbatim.

[864] *CAS and CS v Romania* (n 399) para 82.

[865] A/HRC/40/51/Add.2 para 24 (UN Special Rapporteur).

originally enacted provided that '[i]*t shall be a function of every health board to promote the welfare of children* [. . .] *who are not receiving adequate care and protection*'. The functions of the HSE were then transferred to the CFA by the *Child and Family Agency Act* 2013.[866]

In regard of administrative inquiries into allegations of sexual abuse the powers under this subsection of the 1991 Act were construed in very broad terms by the High Court (Mr Justice Barr) as follows:

> *I have no doubt that in the exercise of their statutory function to promote the welfare of children, health boards are not confined to acting in the interest of specific identified or identifiable children who are already at risk of abuse and require immediate care and protection, but that their duty extends also to children not yet identifiable who may be at risk in the future by reason of a specific potential hazard to them which a board reasonably suspects may come about in the future.*[867]

It is to be noted that in *Gleeson* not only the matter of making targeted inquiries into allegations of child sexual abuse was at issue but that, furthermore, the health board concerned was found to be entitled to form an opinion that the person under investigation was permanently unfit for child care work in general; and to communicate its opinion to others beyond the investigative procedure in hand.[868] As observed by O'Mahony, this High Court judgment '... *has subsequently come to be recognised as establishing the foundational principles governing the investigation of complaints of abuse including notification about complaints to third parties*';[869] when potential employers (intending to employ the person against whom allegations were made) are typically seen as a third party in that sense.

Clearly, there is a parallel between ECHR case law as referred to above and this High Court judgment in that a certain range of future (or hidden) risks to children must equally be anticipated and dealt with by way of preventive measures. Included as such are investigations into allegations of child sexual abuse, the making of conclusive findings and a notification of third parties. For Ireland, a significant volume of case law based on the

---

866 *CD v The Child and Family Agency* [2020] IEHC 452 para 15 (legislative history of the 1991 *Child Care Act*).

867 *MQ v Gleeson* (n 845) at para 94.

868 Fn 845 above.

869 *Annual Report* 2020 (n 389) 39.

interpretation of the existing provisions of the *Child Care Act* 1991 has been produced in the meantime which does not come as a surprise given the stakes involved. Individuals against whom allegations of child sexual abuse were made (and officially investigated as a consequence) went to court challenging many aspects of the procedure in order to have all investigations against them halted or notifications disrupted. The key points established in the case law are the following:

1. Tusla's duty to investigate complaints and to communicate information regarding risks that are identified arises independently of the criminal justice process;
2. Investigations are to be conducted according to the civil (not a criminal) standard of proof, meaning the balance of probabilities;
3. Tusla may, in reaching its conclusions for a finding, rely on different types of evidence, but a more cogent evidence may be required depending on the seriousness of the allegations;
4. The individual under investigation from Tusla inquiries has the right to fair procedures – similar to those guaranteed as a matter of due process – in the conduct of the investigations;
5. If the triggering complaint is deemed to be founded after appropriate investigation, it is then a matter for Tusla to select the appropriate means to protect any children it finds to be at risk from the abuser in question;
6. Any dissemination of information (about the veracity of allegations) should be minimal and only to the extent necessary to protect children who may be at risk;
7. While challenges to investigations by way of judicial review should normally occur after the conclusion of the investigation, it may be permissible to bring such a challenge prior to the conclusion if the challenge concerns a new point of principle concerning a shortcoming in the procedures applied by Tusla.[870]

Undoubtedly, these principles established to be part of Irish case law in the field are open to legislative modification as a matter of constitutional powers accorded to the State's main legislative organ, the Houses of Oireachtas. As a consequence, one must ask if administrative procedures essentially controlled by CFA/Tusla which include a finding officially asserting that an individual has been guilty of abusive acts, is consistent with the

[870] In providing this oversight, I essentially follow *Annual Report* 2020 (Fn 389) 41.

right of the child to have his or her allegations investigated and protective measures initiated as a consequence; and if any such jurisdiction to make a finding is necessary and sufficient for a fulfilment of the State's obligations under the Convention.

Incidentally, certain aspects of the matter were recently brought before the High Court, in the case of *CD v The Child and Family Agency* where they were phrased as an open question:

> *Does the Child and Family Agency have jurisdiction to make a finding that an allegation of child sexual abuse is founded or unfounded, as opposed to simply finding that a future risk of child abuse exists in a particular case?* [871]

For his judgment Humphreys J. concluded that a finding of whether a complaint of child abuse and neglect is founded or unfounded is not *ultra vires* the Child and Family Agency and that section 3 of the *Child Care Act* 1991 does provide a sufficient statutory basis for such findings.[872] As its point of departure, this judgment explains that on the logic of *MQ v Gleeson,*[873] the duty to promote the welfare of children in need of protection is a foundation for a wide-ranging power to investigate and make findings of child abuse against potentially anybody against whom an allegation is made, because any child abuser could in future abuse children in need of protection. That logic, however, as aptly characterised by Humphreys J., *'is a very slender and wobbly basis for an entire statutory jurisdiction to conduct child sexual abuse inquiries and findings'*.[874] A similar conclusion was reached by O'Mahony in his analysis of the current legal framework regarding (retrospective) allegations when he found that the general terms of section 3 *Child Care Act* 1991 are arguably unfit for purpose as a legal basis for this specialised and technical area of child protection work.[875]

In practice, however, administrative investigations initiated by CFA/Tusla will never occur in a vacuum; rather, they are based on an allegation or complaint received by the Agency and they regularly function as a bridge between this complaint and such preventive action as was designed to mitigate the risk identified by way of investigations. Moreover,

871 *CD v CFA* (n 866).
872 Ibid para 30.
873 Fn 845.
874 *CD v CFA* (Fn 866) at para 17.
875 *Annual Report* 2020 (n 389) 44.

in *Gleeson* an anchoring moment was inserted into the case law by making reference to a 'specific potential hazard' (for children not yet identifiable) which the authorities reasonably expect to come about in the future.

Children's Rights in Context

A particular gap in the legal framework that arises from reliance on the general terms of section 3 *Child Care Act* 1991 as a basis for investigating and responding to complaints of abuse is that there is no proper statutory guidance on how competing rights of children and the person who became subject to allegations of abuse should be weighed against each other. Arguably, in this the system for investigating complaints (including so-called retrospective allegations) is lacking in core victim-centred or trauma informed elements, meaning that the interests and voices of child victims are structurally neglected or not listened to in most instances.[876] Weighing even heavier, there is a probability of ineffective investigations being triggered (but not concluded) that fail to lead to steps being taken for the mitigation and elimination of detectable risks of abuse, thus leading to continued abuse in the future. Hitherto, children's rights in Ireland were only seen as having a very weak impact on the matter of official investigations into allegations of sexual abuse to be undertaken for the protection from violence. In *Gleeson* Mr Justice Barr seemingly looked at specific identified or identifiable children and, furthermore, widened his view to include children not yet identifiable who may be at risk in the future; the main thrust of his opinion, however, was about statutory duties accorded to (as it was then) health boards all over the country and their function to promote the welfare of children. Whatever the reason for this lack of consideration, children and their right to be protected from violence did not visibly form part of his opinion. In *CD* v *The Child and Family Agency* Humphreys J even declared that the matter of investigative powers exercised by the CFA must be viewed in the context of the rights of the child as recognised in Article 42A.1 of the Constitution; but, as he concluded, any such review cannot help to answer the question at issue before him.[877]

Putting the matter into a children's rights context, however, it may be stated that from this perspective a thorough and child-focused investigation

---

[876] *Annual Report* 2020 (n 389) 48 with further reference to J Mooney referenced at Fn 56.

[877] *CD v CFA* (Fn 866) para 18.

into plausible complaints of sexual abuse has become imperative, since the right to be protected under Article 19 CRC covers all forms of physical or mental violence, injury or abuse, neglect or negligent treatment, maltreatment or exploitation, including sexual abuse; and the right to be protected extends to all children including situations where their parents cannot or do not properly care for them. Likewise included are children situated in non-familial care-settings like schools and parishes where they may be at risk of being neglected or abused.[878] Accordingly, the focus of any such investigation into allegations of sexual abuse must be on every identifiable situation of children at risk, extending to risk factors such as individual perpetrators suspect of having abused children in the past, among others.

Based on a parliamentary Act, what should be accorded to a competent administrative body is a clear jurisdiction to initiate and conclude this kind of (administrative) investigations, including the legal authority to share any relevant information with third parties involved. As such, this is a requirement flowing from the children's right to be protected from harm and its corresponding obligation to protect and vindicate that same right in effect.

Retrospective Allegations

Focusing the situation in Ireland, as an additional aspect one must ask: how far back stretches an obligation to investigate complaints about sexual abuse concerning a person who may or may not have been sexually assaulted as a child, and who brought his or her plausible allegations to the attention of the authorities as an adult many years or even decades later?[879] What if the suspected offender whose behaviour has never before been investigated is still alive and living as a citizen within his or her particular community which may be the same as the (former) child victim's or a different one? Does this constellation constitute a due process problem only in regard of past crimes perpetrated against this particular complainant who, finally, brought his or her historical complaint of a sexual crime; or is there also an issue as regards a risk of future offences against (more) children which will be perpetrated by that same offender because of the psychologically impulsive nature of sexually abusive behaviour? Characteristically,

---

878 Fn 134 (care-settings).

879 *'Ryan'* Executive Summary, 12 for the demographic profile of witnesses.

this complainant is no longer at risk of being abused, but the alleged abuser may continue to pose a risk to other children many years after the instances of abuse complained of.

For this context of retrospective allegations of abuse, the case law shows that the ECHR obliges Ireland to take steps for the protection of children – whether unidentified or identified as a possible victim – against a risk of sexual abuse in circumstances where State authorities are or ought to be aware of the existence of that risk. Again, from an ECHR perspective an Article 3 prohibition of inhuman or degrading treatment and an Article 8 right to family life provide for the treaty law foundations based on which protective obligations of the State to investigate allegations of sexual violence against children were construed.[880] Accordingly, if an investigation into a retrospective allegation deems that allegation well founded, then State authorities are aware that a risk of sexual abuse emerged, and an obligation to mitigate that risk is engaged.[881] As a matter of substantive obligations, the duty to protect against foreseeable risks was extended beyond specific risks to identified individuals to include general risks to unidentified children by the ECtHR judgement in the case of *O'Keeffe* v *Ireland*.[882] Thus, child protection concerns come to the foreground when CFA/Tusla takes up allegations of child sexual abuse, because the abuser against whom allegations were made may be posing a current risk to children identifiable by the Agency. Here, the aim is to protect children presently threatened by violence or abuse from being victimized in the immediate future. The issue usually articulates itself by reference to a terminology of 'retrospective allegations' as used for policy documents such as 'Child Abuse Substantiation Procedure (CASP)' re-issued by CFA/Tusla in June 2022.[883]

Not surprisingly, in many such cases challenges to investigations by way of judicial review proceedings are brought by the individual under in-

---

[880] Fn 418 and accompanying text.

[881] Department of Children and Youth Affairs (ed), EAG Discussion Paper (10 April 2019) Appendix 9: *Retrospective Allegations of Child Sexual Abuse: The Legal Framework* prepared by Dr C O'Mahony, p 7.

[882] *O'Keefe v Ireland* (n 1) para 168; O'Mahony (n 347) 667.

[883] Tusla Child and Family Agency *Child Abuse Substantiation Procedure* (CASP) Version 1.2: June 2022 available at wwwtusla.ie ; *EAG Discussion Paper* (n 884) 11; Garda Síochána *Policy* (n 853) para 7 (Historical/Delayed Complaints of Sexual Crime); DES *Child Protection Procedures* 2017 (n 936) para 4.6.

vestigation because of retrospective allegations, and the procedural request aims at halting any such investigation from proceeding to the final stage on the ground that they are being prejudiced in effect.[884] As submitted by the applicant to the court for judicial review, due to a great distance in time former events possibly constituting child sexual abuse may not be retrievable in an unbiased manner. Again, the relevant law as regards retrospective allegations is stated in Section 3 of the 1991 *Child Care Act,* as referred to above.[885] At present, since it generally allows for child welfare promotion, this is the only provision of statutory legislation distantly relating to the issue of retrospective allegations. There is, however, no mentioning of targeted investigative procedures such as recorded interviews or forensic examinations or cross-examinations and the like to be initiated by CFA; Section 3 was just not drafted with retrospective allegations in mind. The High Court in *MQ v Gleeson*, nevertheless, confirmed the application of this provision to the issue.[886] According to this judgment a section 3 duty of identification applies both to children under immediate risk and also to children who, although not immediately identifiable, may become subject to a risk which the Agency reasonably suspects to come about in the future.[887] As further elaborated by this judgment, section 3 of the *Child Care Act* 1991 not only authorizes but obliges CFA/Tusla to take steps for the protection of children in circumstances where it is reasonably suspected that a specific potential hazard will come about in the future: an individual judged by his or her former behaviour, might constitute a risk that children will be abused again by that same person.[888]

Arising as a question here is the matter of effectiveness meaning that this particular approach to retrospective allegations *via* administrative investigations (including third-party notifications) conducted by social care professionals may be effective as a means of preventing future abuse and to protect children from harm; or alternatively, this approach may be lacking in effectiveness due to its weak and underdeveloped legal framework. No statutory guidance is given on the balance to be struck between due process rights of the person under investigation and the right

---

884 Garda Síochána *Policy* (Fn 853) para 7.1.

885 Fn 866 and accompanying text.

886 Fn 845 and accompanying text.

887 Ibid at para 94.

888 Ibid.

of children to be protected from harm.[889] Clearly hampered by frequent referral to judicial review procedures in court the efficiency of this kind of administrative investigations is presently seen to be unsatisfactory. As critically reviewed by the Special Rapporteur on Child Protection, *'a defensive practice (on behalf of CFA/Tusla) has the potential to translate into ineffective investigations that fail to uncover crucial information, or overly cautious safety planning or information sharing that fails to effectively protect children from future abuse'*.[890]

Statutory Enactment Underpinning Investigative Proceedings

In accordance with the reasoning articulated by Mr Justice Humphreys I can only suggest that perhaps the Oireachtas (Irish parliament) might consider that this particular area warrants a more explicit statutory underpinning for the procedures of investigation of child harm.[891] As a fundamental human right the children's right to protection from all forms of violence and abuse (Article 19 CRC) is of such an importance that clear and unambiguous rules must be laid down, by force of parliamentary legislation, providing for a clear and specific mandate covering an investigation of complaints, as well as a decision if the allegation is founded or unfounded, and a sharing of information with third parties.

Meanwhile, this crucial work of investigating child abuse concerns runs on the basis of a policy document issued by Tusla under the name of Child Abuse Substantiation Procedure (CASP) which is for use by social workers who carry out what is called a 'substantiation assessment', to conclude if child abuse has happened or not.[892]

Criminal investigations

Fairly obvious from a children's rights perspective, every sexual offence perpetrated against a minor, must be fully and formally investigated from a criminal law perspective, and any such investigation must be conducted by qualified professionals following a rights based and child sensitive approach.[893] Following through with this approach implies that victim

[889] *Annual Report* 2020 (Fn 389) 46 (risk of ineffective investigations).
[890] Ibid 47 (potential lack of sensitivity).
[891] *CD v CFA* (n 866) para 30.
[892] Tusla *CASP* (n 883) 18.
[893] Fn 395 and case-law referenced at Fn 400.

rights are primarily accorded to the child individually meaning that any individual child may have the full status of a victim of crime; not his or her parents, or guardians, or other caretakers involved.[894] For this context, the core piece of statutory legislation, namely the 2017 *Criminal Justice (Victims of Crime) Act* has a whole section on complaints (section 12) which builds on an assumption that a victim, including a child victim, may have a legal representative who must be admitted to accompany the victim when making a complaint.[895] Thus, the formal complaint triggering investigations and criminal proceedings remains the (child) victim's one and certain obligations and policy provisions relate to what has been designated as 'child complainants of sexual crime' in Garda terminology.[896]

Beyond substantive criminal law provisions, for child victims or witnesses of sexual offences a range of procedural protections had been in force which were recently strengthened by means of two complex pieces of criminal legislation, enacted as the *Criminal Law (Sexual Offences) Act* 2017, and the *Criminal Justice (Victims of Crime) Act* 2017.[897] Just from a preliminary provision in this 2017 *Criminal Justice Act* it becomes obvious that children's victim rights are at the core of this piece of legislation, since the law itself requires to make sure that children's rights are safeguarded, even if that means someone reasonably believed to be a child but whose minority age cannot be (positively) proven unduly benefits from protective provisions in the Act.[898]

Securing the Child's Testimony

In terms of criminal investigations into child sexual abuse it has become urgently important that procedural rules were adopted which help to safeguard the child victim's testimony in effect. Any such testimony must be taken and recorded for further reference in a way that helps to ensure it will stand the test of cross-examination by the person who has come

---

894 *Terminology Guidelines* (n 53) 77; G Shannon, *Child Law* (n 75) para 14–124; O'Malley, *Sexual Offences* (n 739) 24.

895 *Criminal Justice (Victims of Crime) Act* 2017 section 12(1).

896 Garda Síochána *Policy* (n 853) para 21.1.

897 Whereas the *Criminal Law (Sexual Offences) Act* 2017 predominantly deals with 'criminalization', the *Criminal Justice (Victims of Crime) Act* 2017 seems to be mainly concerned about 'special measures'.

898 *Criminal Justice (Victims of Crime) Act* 2017, section 2(3): '... *shall be presumed to be a child* ... '.

under suspicion of sexual abuse and must stand trial accordingly. As a consequence, the issue arises whether the provisions governing pre-recorded or live video-link testimony (given by a child victim or witness) meets all necessary standards of constitutionality, especially as regards the accused person's rights; otherwise that same testimony given and recorded would not be admissible in a criminal trial against the perpetrator.[899] Again, Ireland as a jurisdiction has been reasonably active in the field of statutory legislation installing and refining criminal investigative procedures that were tailored for application in cases where persons under the age of 18 years have become victims of sexual offences.

As regards the conduct of interviews and medical (forensic) examinations the 2017 *Criminal Justice Act* generally stipulates that any interview of a victim be carried out as soon as possible after the complaint was made, and also that any such interview be carried out only where necessary for the purpose of investigating the offence complained of; equally, the official in charge of the investigation must make sure that any medical examinations of the victim are limited to those which are strictly necessary for the purpose of the investigation concerned.[900] Another issue that should be mentioned here is the development of the Barnahus/Onehouse model, which will make the investigation of child sexual abuse cases significantly more child-friendly once it is fully rolled out and implemented. In September 2019, two different ministerial offices launched Barnahus/Onehouse as a multi-agency integrated service developed to accomodate the needs of children who have experienced sexual abuse. A set of services necessary to address the investigation and treatment of child sexual abuse are combined in a single location where specialist police and social services would be co-located including forensic examination, interviewing and counselling or therapeutic services for children.[901] Thus, the need for child survivors of abuse to travel to multiple locations and repeat their own account on multiple occasions is being avoided which helps to mitigate an inherent

899 Doyle (n 734) para 2–09; Shannon (n 75) para 14–120; Rape Crisis Network Ireland *Hearing Every Voice* (March 2018) 8.

900 *Criminal Justice (Victims of Crime) Act* 2017, s 14 (Conduct of interviews and medical examinations), s 14(1) letters b and c (interviews); s 14(6)(medical examinations).

901 *Annual Report* 2021 (Fn 112) 34; *Annual Report* 2020 (n 389) 23; A/HRC/40/51/Add.2 (UN Special Rapporteur); CRC/C/IRL/5–6 para 153; CRC/C/IRL/CO/5–6 para 24.

risk of secondary traumatisation associated with urging children to engage with therapeutic services and the criminal justice system separately.

A System of Special Measures

Just like many other jurisdictions with prosecution services and courts operating on the basis of a common-law tradition, Ireland has a developed system of 'special measures', to combat secondary victimization and to assist witnesses to give their best evidence.[902] As a set of special measures to be taken during investigations, for the purpose of interviewing the (child) victim the following has been explicitly provided for by means of statutory legislation: that any such interview be carried out in specially adapted premises; and be carried out by persons who have been specially trained for the purpose; and that each interview belonging to a series of interviews be conducted by the same officer.[903] Also, where the alleged offence involves specific forms of inter-personal violence, the victim to be interviewed may make a request that the interview be carried out by a person of the same sex.[904] Based on the formal assessment of a victim's protection needs, as provided for in section 15 of the 2017 *Criminal Justice Act,* these special measures are not obligatory *per se* but may be implemented in accordance with the preceding assessment of the victim; of which, in turn, the law says that it shall be carried out in respect of every victim of an alleged offence.[905] Thus, it had been legally provided already prior to both 2017 *Criminal Law* and *Criminal Justice* Acts that children could give testimony by video link[906] or behind screens shielding them from seeing the accused person in court proceedings related to sexual offences. These measures, by force of recent legislation, were enabled to be taken in any other case in which a failure to do so could lead to a re-victimization or intimidation of or retaliation against any child victim

---

902 RCNI 'Hearing Every Voice' (n 899) 8.

903 *Criminal Justice (Victims of Crime) Act* 2017, s 17 (1)(a): (modalities of interviews with the victim).

904 *Criminal Justice (Victims of Crime) Act* 2017, s 17(1)(b): (alleged offence involving sexual violence, gender-based violence or violence in a close relationship).

905 *Criminal Justice (Victims of Crime) Act* 2017, s 15 (Assessment of victim); more on this, see Fn 912 below and accompanying text.

906 *Criminal Evidence Act* 1992 s 13 (Evidence through television link), s 16 (complainants statement or video recorded interview taken for evidentiary purposes).

or child witness.[907]

Procedural Protections Strengthened

Regarding the ECHR case of *CAS and CS v Romania* it is impressive to find such thing as an elaborated assessment procedure laid out in section 15 of the *Criminal Justice Act* 2017 which enables an early identification of protection needs of the victim, including where the victim is a child.[908] Even before the initiation of court proceedings and outside of the court setting, in all cases covered by this legislation an assessment shall be carried out for the purpose of ascertaining whether the victim might benefit from protection measures available during the course of an investigation and also during the course of any criminal proceedings following thereupon.[909]

Moreover, one further section from this 2017 *Criminal Justice* Act specifically deals with special measures during investigations (section 17), and another section incorporates rules relating to special measures during criminal proceedings which are listed here as 'the exclusion of the public' (section 19 (2)(a)) and 'enabling the victim to give evidence through a live television link' (section 19 (2)(c))[910] As defined by that same Act, all protection measures are intended to secure the safety and welfare of the (child) victim by limiting or preventing contact with, or repeat victimization, retaliation or intimidation of, the victim by an alleged offender or any other person on his or her behalf.[911] In addition, the 2017 Acts both, *Criminal Law Act* and *Criminal Justice Act* expand the types of crime for which child witnesses may submit pre-recorded interviews as evidence in lieu of in-person testimony to include all offences that entail a risk of re-victimization or intimidation of or retaliation against the child.[912] They put measures in place to prevent children from being

---

907 *Criminal Justice (Victims of Crime) Act* 2017, ss 15, 19 (Special measures during criminal proceedings).

908 *CAS and CS v Romania* (n 399) para 82.

909 *Criminal Justice (Victims of Crime) Act* 2017, s 15 (Assessment of victim) which refers to 'protection measures' as defined in s 2 of that same Act and also to 'special measures' as detailed in ss 17, 19 of the same Act.

910 *Criminal Justice (Victims of Crime) Act* 2017 s 19 contains further rules mainly relevant for adult victims of sexual offences.

911 *Criminal Justice (Victims of Crime) Act* 2017 s 2, entry 'protection measure'.

912 *Criminal Law (Sexual Offences) Act* 2017, s 36 (Evidence from behind a screen etc., Wigs and gowns, Protection against cross-examination by accused), s 37 (Video re-

personally cross-examined by the accused in sexual offences cases and enable children to be accompanied in court by a close friend, a family member or support professional.[913] Although curtailing to a certain extent the accused person's fundamental right to cross-examine any witness against him, a witness statement made and recorded in accordance with these sections from the 2017 *Criminal Justice Act* will not be obtained unlawfully; in the absence of other concerns it must be fully admitted to the trial against the accused accordingly.

Exemptions

Regarding special measures to be applied during criminal investigations (Section 17 of the 2017 *Criminal Justice Act*) there is a problem of extending legal exemptions that might easily be claimed for undermining the whole architecture of protection measures as provided for in Section 15 of that same Act. As itemized in Section 17(2) a special measure deemed beneficial in regard of the victim's protection needs shall be made available to the victim (who may easily be a child) unless legal, operational or practical constraints render it impossible (letter a); an urgent need to interview the victim arises (letter b); the application of a special measure would be prejudicial to a criminal procedure (letter c); or the application of the special measure would be contrary to the administration of justice.[914]

Since one of these very widely drafted exemptions ('unless') will easily be shown to be applicable at almost any stage of the investigative procedure, it is, in effect, at the investigator's discretion to opt for an application of such special measures as were already found to be beneficial regarding the individual victim's protection needs. This is contrary to a basic requirement for any parliamentary legislation to be determinative in regard of rights and duties that should have been comprehensibly balanced against each other.

Conclusion

As it currently runs, the system of administrative investigations into al-

---

cording of any statement made during an interview with competent person), s 38 (live television link or similar device).

913 *Criminal Justice (Victims of Crime) Act* 2017, s 18 (Appropriate Person).

914 *Criminal Justice (Victims of Crime) Act* 2017 s 17(2) Special measures during investigations.

legations of child sexual abuse operating on a very general statutory basis in connection with policy documents elaborated by an administrative body (CFA/Tusla) is lacking in efficiency as regards the need to identify serious risk of sexual abuse for children, and to mitigate or eliminate that same risk in effect. Children and their right to be protected against all forms of violence are not fully vindicated by the State, contrary to Articles 3, 19 of the Convention requiring the State to implement investigative measures functioning effectively and efficiently; they may be of an administrative nature, but child-sensitive procedures for criminal investigations must equally be available. Accordingly, since quite a few sources of abusive behaviour against persons who have been children at the time will remain undetected, due to inefficient investigations into retrospective allegations, this is problematic especially for educational and care contexts.

Whereas criminal investigations into allegations of child sexual abuse do happen in Ireland in considerable numbers, as evidenced by a 2017 study conducted by the Garda Inspectorate,[915] the UN Special Rapporteur found that a lack of regular reporting on sexual offences (investigated or prosecuted) against children is not helpful for an identification of underlying factors of child sexual abuse.[916] What is missing, from a children's rights perspective, is a set of regularly gathered data collated at the level of central government and providing for an estimate on the scope and different forms of sexual abuse and exploitation of children in Ireland.

Based on an implicit understanding about its obligation to protect but also to respect children's rights as a jurisdiction, Ireland enacted legislation – the *Criminal Justice (Victims of Crime) Act* 2017 in particular – which can help to avoid the dangers of children being re-victimized as a result of regular criminal procedures to which they might be subjected as either victims or witnesses of crime. Obviously, the final test for this legislation, and whether procedures legally enshrined will prove to be rigorous and child sensitive at the same time, will come with years of application in the courts of Ireland, but the existing legal framework seems to be in furtherance of that object and purpose.

---

[915] A/HRC/40/51/Add.2 para 22 (UN Special Rapporteur).

[916] Ibid, para 22.

Sub-Section (4)- School Inspections as an Implementing Measure under Irish Law

Introduction

Again, taking the tripartite typology of obligations as a point of departure, an element of 'respect' but mainly 'protect' comes into my focus of attention now, as school inspections will be evaluated as a measure for the implementation of the right to non-violent education. An obligation to respect children's rights implies that agents of the Minister such as officials belonging to the Inspectorate do not actively violate the rights of children; clearly, inspectors shall not attempt to, or sexually abuse children, nor shall they willingly support or cover-up the crimes of others. The real value, however, of school inspections for purposes of this analysis lies in preventing and detecting child sexual abuse, its sources and enabling factors. Mounting and maintaining a nationwide system of school inspections, and how this fits into the tripartite typology of obligations, presents itself as an issue here. Since, in this particular area of school oversight, the State undoubtedly is under an obligation to protect children's rights, it is inevitable that a functioning line of responsibility and accountability exists between the Government representing the State and what happens to its schoolchildren on the ground.[917]

Some sort of a governance structure for prescribing and enforcing standards through provision of a curriculum and school supervision has ever been a main feature of the Irish system of primary and post-primary education.[918] However, it was no earlier than the 21st century's third decade that amid concerns over gaps in child protection boarding schools were to be inspected for the first time; as the Department of Education's Inspectorate has been carrying out compliance checks in day schools inspections for boarding schools are likely to involve similar matters in the future.[919]

Functioning under the *Education Act* 1998, section 13, the Inspectorate as an administrative division of the Department of Education and Skills has ever been carrying out inspections in primary and post-primary schools and centres for education; also, the Inspectorate publishes inspection re-

[917] *Education Act* 1998, see Fn 920 below.

[918] *O'Sheil v. Minister for Education* [1999] 2 IR 321, at 346–348 (history of education).

[919] C O'Brien, *'Boarding schools to be inspected for first time amid concerns over abuse in Spititan-run schools'* in *Irish Times* (16 December 2022).

ports on individual schools and centres for education, through its website to be accessible to everyone. From a children's rights perspective, what needs to be explored here is the scope and content of those inspections in terms of issues, topics and concerns regularly addressed by inspectors and, if protection from sexual violence and abuse is covered by the mandate legally handed out to the Inspectorate for fulfilment. Fundamentally, for every person concerned in the implementation of the *Education Act* 1998 this Act, which also provides for an Inspectorate of schools, states as a primary object that the constitutional rights of children must be given practical effect.[920]

In terms of a systemic failure to prevent and detect sexual abuse in the Irish education system, O'Mahony and Kilkelly take from *Ryan* (2009):

> *The Ryan report found that sexual abuse was endemic ... and also occurred ... ; that the system of inspection carried out by the Department of Education was flawed and incapable of being effective, and that the Department's deferential and submissive attitude towards the congregations compromised its ability to carry out inspection and monitoring of schools.*[921]

Similarly, in its *O'Keeffe* judgment the European Court in respect of two different oversight mechanisms treating a reporting process on the one hand and the system of school inspectors on the other, clearly stated, '... *that the mechanisms ... did not provide any effective connection between the State authorities and primary school children ...* '.[922] Obviously, for any system of public education to be compliant with learners' rights and children's rights in particular, school inspections need to be practically effective as a means for the identification and prevention of child abuse in schools. Even fifty years after the factual scenario on which the case of *O'Keeffe* relied which took issue with Ireland's primary school system of the 1970s there is more concern over gaps in child protection as the Department of Education is to begin inspecting boarding schools for the first time in 2023.[923] Concerns have been articulated that existing child protection rules do not explicitly cover boarding schools; new child protection measures for schools with boarding facilities will include

920 *Education Act 1998*, s 6(a).
921 O'Mahony and Kilkelly (n 78) 320, 321.
922 *O'Keeffe v Ireland* (n 1) para 165.
923 C O'Brien, *'Boarding schools to be inspected for first time'* (n 919 above).

non-teaching staff such as members of the clergy and others.[924] Moreover, as in all human interaction there may be problems of attitude which carry the risk of contaminating the wider power relationship between school inspectors authorised by the Minister on the one hand, and institutional providers of educational services on the other.

An Oversight Framework for School Inspections

Since the law allows for the Minister to exercise his authority, especially in a case where the school patron fails to cooperate with regular inspection by the Inspectorate, and to withdraw the recognition of any particular school, school inspections may have a strong functional value of protecting pupils or students from a significant risk of violence or abuse.[925] In its clear wording the *Education Act* 1998 states as a statutory requirement for recognition of a school that the school patron fully agrees to co-operate with the Inspectorate;[926] and as a consequence the school's recognition may be withdrawn by the Minister in a case where such cooperation is not happening in actual practice.[927] At least insofar as the school itself, its management and operation, or one of the teachers or a member of staff is the predominant cause of concern, the functional value of school inspections for prevention and protection against violence and abuse is quite obvious.[928]

Clearly, the Department of Education and Skills has an important oversight role to play in ensuring that children receive the highest quality of care and protection in Irish schools.[929] Equally, the frequency and approach of school inspections, and whether inspections – with or without prior notice – may take place as a matter of course, is one of the aspects to be considered here.[930] As part of the oversight and quality assurance role of the Department, the Inspectorate is required to initiate and perform 'Child Protection and Safeguarding Inspections', being rooted as a public function in Section 13 of the *Education Act* 1998.[931] In some detail the 1998 Act,

---

[924] Ibid.

[925] *Education Act* 1998, s 11 on 'Withdrawal of recognition'.

[926] *Education Act* 1998, s 8 ('school patron').

[927] *Education Act 1998*, s 11, 10(2)(d).

[928] DES *Child Protection Procedures* 2017 (n 936 below) para 9.5 (allegations of abuse directed against members of school personnel).

[929] *Education Act* 1998, s 7 (2)(b), functions of the Minister.

[930] DES *Child Protection Procedures* 2017 (n 936) para 9.13.2.

[931] *Education Act* 1998, s 13(3), functions of an Inspector; DES *Child Protection Proce-*

through its Section 13(3)(a)(i) in particular, elaborates on the list of statutory functions of an inspector who shall visit recognised schools and centres of education on the initiative of the Inspectorate, where the organisation and operation of the school concerned and the quality and effectiveness of the education provided shall be evaluated; where the education standards shall be evaluated; and where the implementation of regulations made by the Minister shall be assessed.[932] Furthermore, the significance of school inspections as an administrative measure for the implementation of children's rights is underlined by the fact that a new offence of obstruction or interference with an Inspector was created and inserted into the law by an amendment to section 13 in the 1998 Act.[933]

As cursorily explained in Ireland's periodic report to the Committee, the Inspectorate of the Department of Education and Skills carries out annual programmes of inspection and evaluation of schools which involve whole-school evaluations (a model for inspection and evaluation that focuses on more than one dimension of the work of a school) of primary and post-primary schools; subject inspections and evaluation of programmes at post-primary level; inspection of the work of individual teachers, including probationary teachers; and focused evaluations of particular aspects of the system.[934] What is designated here as a 'Whole-School Evaluation', in practice encompasses as one among a series of checks, whether the school's Child Safeguarding Statement meets the requirements of the *Child Protection Procedures for Primary and Post-Primary Schools* 2017.[935]

From a treaty implementation perspective what seems to be important about the Inspectorate as a government institution is that substantive obligations to keep children safe from harm as spelled out under the *Children First Act* 2015, are strictly observed and routinely followed in primary and post-primary schools. Accordingly, while Child Protection

---

dures 2017 (n 936) 88 (Child Protection and Safeguarding Inspections as a model of inspection).

932 *Education Act 1998,* s 13 (3)(a)(i), further detailing activities for an inspector.

933 *Education Act* 1998 as amended by *Education (Miscellaneous Provisions) Act* 2007, *Education and Training Boards Act* 2013, s 13.(12A) reads (extract): *'A person who obstructs or interferes with an Inspector … or impedes the exercise by the Inspector … commits an offence …* '.

934 DCYA (2013), *Ireland's Consolidated Third and Fourth Report to the Committee on the Rights of the Child,* para 564.

935 Fn 936 below.

and Safeguarding Inspections are carried out in accordance with section 7(2)(b) and section 13(3)(a)(i) of the *Education Act* 1998, the substance of the Inspectorate's oversight work is widely determined by the *Children First Act* 2015, and its Part 2 (Child Safeguarding Statements) as well as Part 3 (Reporting) in particular. This becomes obvious from the fact that core provisions of the 2015 Act are transposed into the practice of school inspections *via* the Department of Education and Skills' *Child Protection Procedures for Primary and Post-Primary Schools* (2017), a lengthy and complex document which all boards of management are required to formally adopt and implement as part of their respective school's Child Safeguarding Statement.[936] Developed collaboratively as an administrative instrument between, among others, the Department of Education and Skills, the Department of Children and Youth Affairs and CFA/Tusla, these 'Procedures' serve the purpose of giving direction and guidance to school authorities and to school personnel in relation to meeting their (relatively) new statutory obligations under the *Children First Act* 2015; additionally, this instrument fully defines an oversight role for the Department of Education's Inspectorate.[937] As a consequence, the Inspectorate is required, under these *Child Protection Procedures* 2017, to monitor and report on schools' compliance with those same Procedures and its monitoring work serves to ensure that recognised schools and their staff are operating in compliance with the *Children First Act* 2015.[938] Moreover, any inspection work such as school inspections related to a service provided to a child under the *Education Act* 1998 is defined as a 'relevant service' for purposes of the *Children First Act* 2015, implying that core child protection duties as created under that same 2015 Act do equally fall on the Inspectorate as a government institution.[939] Thus, for itself the Inspectorate must equally prepare and display a Child Safeguarding Statement, and as an institutionalised body its

[936] Department of Education and Skills (DES), *Child Protection Procedures for Primary and Post-Primary Schools* 2017 para 1.1.4 (purpose); para 1.1.14 (adoption and implementation); *Inspectorate* DES *A Guide to Child Protection and Safeguardig Inspections* 13 October 2020,2.

[937] DES *Child Protection Procedures* 2017 (n 936) para 9.13.

[938] Ibid para 9.13.1 .

[939] *Children First Act* 2015, s 2 entry 'relevant service' read in conjunction with Schedule 1 Nr 2.

members of staff are collectively obliged to follow all rules and regulations for mandatory reporting as defined under the *Children First* legislation.

Compliance with Statutory Obligations

Looking closer at obligations under the *Children First Act* 2015, just as all registered teachers were found to be mandated persons,[940] all schools and centres of education in Ireland are providing 'relevant services' (section 2 read in conjunction with Schedule 1) implying that, as a provider of services, any such educational organisation must ensure that all school attending children are kept safe from harm, as a matter of statutory obligation.[941]

Moving on to the level of supervision and oversight the picture gets a bit more complex. As mentioned above, all oversight activities functionally performed by the Inspectorate do *per se* come under a statutory definition of 'relevant services' as provided by the *Children First Act* (Schedule 1), meaning that anyone appointed by the Minister to be an Inspector might possibly become subject to reporting obligations under this *Children First* legislation. Clearly, there are additional requirements stated in the law which need to be fulfilled for this to follow: if simultaneously qualified as a psychologist who practises as such (Schedule 2, Nr 7) or as a registered teacher (Schedule 2, Nr 12) he or she will then be seen as a mandated person for purposes of the 2015 Act.[942] In practice, however, school inspectors are, for the most part, unlikely to be mandated persons: the only way for school inspectors to be covered as a 'mandated person' seems to be if they were a former teacher who happened to register with the Teaching Council on their own initiative. In conclusion, seen from a perspective of children claiming their right to non-violent education it makes no sense to have inspection as a 'relevant service' under the *Children First Act* without simultaneously looking at inspectors who do the work of inspection as 'mandated persons' under that same Act. At this point, there is an inconsistency within the law and its schedules, as it stands.

---

[940] Fn 819 and accompanying text.

[941] Fn 825 and accompanying text.

[942] *Education Act* 1998, s 13 (2), qualified psychologists appointed as inspectors.

Conflicts in Practice

In practice, what was found to be problematic is that not all concerns about child protection in a school context will be determined as mandatory reports, only those that fall above a defined threshold of harm; when 'harm' is defined in section 2 of the 2015 Act.[943] On its face this seems to be a matter for mandatory reporting, not school-inspections, as a child protection policy to be clarified *via* ministerial guidance or through case-law handed down by the courts. As the regulatory materials for keeping schoolchildren safe from harm are presently arranged, however, much of the clarifying work in this regard is done from a perspective of administrative monitoring and supervision, and in a context of so-called whole-school inspections in particular.[944] If inspections substantially have to make sure that schools operate in compliance with DES *Child Protection Procedures,* and if, in these *Procedures* the thrust of the matter is about compliance with the requirements of the core aspects of *Children First* legislation, then the work of the Inspectorate essentially consists in finding out if, in this particular school to be inspected, a proper Child Safeguarding Statement is drawn up; and any potential for harm to a child is fully assessed; and also that everyone in the school is absolutely clear about his or her reporting duties. Accordingly, any problem or conflict weighing on teaching personnel who are remaining unclear about how far exactly the extent of their statutorily rooted duties (of safeguarding, reporting and assistance) reaches, must functionally become a problem for inspection as a child protection policy.

Inspectorate's Oversight Role to be Placed on Statutory Footing

As was shown above,[945] an oversight role of the Inspectorate when it comes to child protection and safeguarding in schools, is clearly defined and delineated on a sub-statutory level only, namely through a section in the Department of Education and Skills' 2017 *Procedures.*[946] At this location, in some detail, it is stated-

---

943 Fn 815 and accompanying text.

944 Fn 935 and accompanying text; most practical aspects of the role of the Inspectorate systematically belong to the list of functions of an inspector and should be legislated *via* an amendment to *Education Act* 1998, s 13.

945 Fn 937 and accompanying text.

946 DES *Child Protection Procedures* (n 936) para 9.13

- What the activities of the Inspectorate are:[947] monitoring the compliance of schools with the requirements of the *Procedures* and reporting to Tusla about schools that are not in compliance with Child Safeguarding Statement requirements;
- What models and activities the Inspectorate will rely on:[948] conducting dedicated Child Protection and Safeguarding inspections, among others;
- What will happen after the inspection:[949] the Inspectorate may decide to refer schools that are not compliant to specialist treatment for further observation; and schools visited that have no Child Safeguarding Statement in place will be reported to Tusla; and in an exceptional case of serious deficiencies an immediate referral to specialist treatment may follow;
- What access to documentation will be needed:[950] minutes of board of management meetings that should record the rectification or changed practice directed by the board in a case where non-compliance has been identified;
- What the status and function of the Child Protection Oversight Group is:[951] in a case where the Inspectorate has serious concerns about a school's compliance the case will be referred to this Oversight Group which is comprised of members of the Inspectorate and officials from the Department's (DES) School Division; this Group will manage the engagement of the Department with the board and/or patron of schools where serious weaknesses or systemic failures were identified by the Inspectorate; this Group will also ensure that all cases referred to the Department from CFA/Tusla or from An Garda Síochána will be pursued with the board and/or patron of the school as appropriate;

Clearly, this whole section in the *Procedures* provides for necessary detail regarding most practical aspects of school inspections; whether this is sufficient for the inspection regime to play its part in protecting children from sexual abuse, is less obvious. Here, even a key administrative role for the Child Protection Oversight Group is being created which coordinates the Department's actions in cases of serious concern.

947 Ibid para 9.13.1
948 Ibid para 9.13.2.
949 Ibid para 9.13.3.
950 Ibid para 9.13.4.
951 Ibid para 9.13.5.

Given a plethora of substantive child protection provisions – relating to safeguarding from and reporting of, abuse – being fully developed through statutory legislation and the *Children First Act* 2015 in particular, it is unsatisfactory and adds to conflict and confusion that the Inspectorate's oversight role is not statutorily prescribed at the same level of authority.[952] Even if parliamentary legislation is generally deemed to be for the statement of broad principles only, it is for the protection of basic values and rights, such as the right to non-violent education that an oversight role testing the performance of statutory duties and obligations must equally be secured by means of statutory legislation. Additionally, since obstruction of or interference with school inspections was created as a criminal offence (under the *Education Act* 1998[953]) in the meantime, it must be implied that respective duties and obligations surrounding the Inspectorate's school monitoring activities are statutorily stated in a crystal clear manner, lest the offence becomes toothless and ineffective.

To sum up, the current arrangements for school inspections cannot fully discharge the State's duty to protect the right to non-violent education: seen from a perspective of children's human rights, what needs to be strengthened and detailed by means of parliamentary legislation are the powers and duties of the Inspectorate as an organ of the State. The proper location for such a supervisory authority to be clearly outlined and plainly stated is Section 13 of the *Education Act* 1998 where the functions of the Inspectorate are listed in several items; at this location the Inspectorate should be accorded powers to make provison for (partly) closing down the operation of a school or for suspending teaching qualifications as an emergency measure, as soon as plausible allegations or disclosures about incidents of child sexual abuse are brought to the attention of inspectors. As such the DES Inspectorate clearly has to play a major role for creating a functional link permanently installed between the State and the realities of a schooling life protected from violence and abuse.

Sub-Section (5) – Incorporation of Children's Rights in Ireland

Whereas the four sub-sections just completed essentially came in under 'Protect' for the typology of obligations, the remaining sub-sections fall under the 'Fulfil' component of the RPF typology. In the following, 'In-

[952] CRC/C/IRL/CO/2 para 33 (Social Services Inspectorate).

[953] Fn 933 above.

corporation', 'Inter-Agency Collaboration' and 'Comprehensive Sexuality Education' will be explored as obligations because of their significance for making reality of children's rights within this jurisdiction. Since they are not particularly case-related but require strong and wide-ranging structural efforts, their fulfilment, in fact, remains somewhat patchy and inconsistent.

As was demonstrated earlier an incorporation of its text taken as a catalogue of children's rights replicated literally with immediate effect for the whole jurisdiction is not an obligation under the Convention; as long as every single right elaborated in the treaty is secured in effect to every child living within the jurisdiction.[954] My argument here somewhat deviates from the position taken by the Committee which repeatedly recommended that all necessary measures be taken to fully incorporate the Convention into Irish law.[955]

Ireland's constitutional framework, in effect, constitutes a typical common law jurisdiction built on a written Constitution instrument guaranteeing personal rights explicitly numerated through the text of this instrument, but un-enumerated personal rights also.[956] At the foundation of protection from violence and sexual abuse lies a constitutional right to bodily integrity that enjoys protection as an unenumerated personal right primarily identified in the 1964 Supreme Court case of *Ryan* v *Attorney General*; in a functional context of state reporting to the UN it may easily remain under-developed.[957] In general, Irish courts appear to be rolling back and forth between a position that seems to be willing to accept the CRC as a 'persuasive source' when interpreting legislation and other statutory instruments on the one hand, and a strict observance of Article 29(6) of the Constitution which declares the Oireachtas (Irish parliament) to be the sole location for an incorporation of the Convention as an international treaty, on the other.

Sub-Section (6) – Inter-Agency Cooperation

Introduction

Since the 'Fulfil'-component of the tripartite typology of obligations equally serves a purpose of securing the comprehensiveness of rights-

---

954 Fn 456 and accompanying text.

955 Fn 707 and accompanying text.

956 de Blacam (n 693) 379; Doyle (n 734) chapter 4.

957 Fn 736 and accompanying text.

based child protection in the State,[958] testing against children's rights standards those legally established structures on which Inter-agency collaboration is running, is a requirement for the coherence and consistency of this study. Any act of cooperation between child-concerned agencies in the State should function so as to encourage and enhance a pooling of information and expertise relevant for the protection and vindication of children's rights in practice, and for the right to non-violent education in particular. As stated by Ireland's Special Rapporteur,

> *child protection is an inherently multi-disciplinary space; to work effectively, it requires input at various points from social workers, police, lawyers, judges and court staff, guardians ad litem, a wide range of health care professionals, as well as teachers and education welfare officers and others who come into regular contact with children.*[959]

Just amassing data about child-related offences or convictions for instance, without proper analysis or break-down and disaggregation in order to make discriminations visible, clearly is not in children's best interest. As observed by the UN Special Rapporteur, CFA/Tusla implements its actual strategy which addresses topics, such as inter-agency cooperation, governance, and data and performance, among others;[960] it remains to be seen, however, if this is happening in accordance with children's interests and rights that must be fulfilled.

Practically, since joint working between CFA/Tusla and An Garda Siochána forms an integral part of child protection services in the State, their cooperation and interacting, based on clarity of responsibility, should be made legally binding so as to secure the child's best interest (Article 3 CRC). One of the main recommendations brought forth by *'Ryan'* hints at the need to implement relevant 'guideline' instruments (including protocols) uniformly and consistently throughout the State, which therefore must be placed on a statutory footing.[961] Several studies and reviews of individual cases show that effective inter-agency collaboration gained momentum in inter-agency engagements to develop more effective working; it was also noted, however, that the majority

---

[958] P 134 above.

[959] *Annual Report* 2020 (n 389) 30.

[960] A/HRC/40/51/Add.2 para 54 (UN Special Rapporteur).

[961] *'Ryan'* vol IV para 7–21; Shannon (n 75) para 14–23.

of actions, although on track for implementation, are yet to be completed.[962]

Cooperation Institutionally Consolidated

Prominent as an institution close to the highest level of government, an Interdepartmental Implementation Group was created by force of the *Children First Act* 2015 which outlines membership and functions of this Group in some detail.[963] Thus, comprising representatives from every Government Department, from CFA/Tusla, from the Health Service Executive and from An Garda Síochána, this Group is primarily tasked with a promotion of compliance by Departments of State with their obligations under the *Children First* legislation; equally, as an Implementation Group it shall monitor the implementation by said departments of ministerial child protection guidelines issued in accordance with the 2015 Act.[964] As described by the *Children First* policy document this Group is a forum for members to raise child welfare and protection issues of general concern, or with a cross-departmental or cross-sectoral dimension across the various sectors.[965]

Regrettably, this Group has no authority to make formal assessments about the quality of implementing steps planned for the future, and if such steps as were actually taken by any of the Government Departments may count as an achievement of effective implementation; nor has the Group any authority to create specific performance obligations in a case where it found implementing efforts to be unsatisfactory as yet. For instance, to identify as a potential issue an apparent lack of awareness among private sector organisations providing services to children of the statutory requirement for Child Safeguarding Statements is all this Implementation Group seems capable of achieving.[966]

Furthermore, most of the safeguarding and reporting obligations rooted in the *Children First Act* 2015 are not falling on government

---

962 *Annual Report* 2020 (n 389) 31.

963 *Children First Act* 2015, ss 20–26 in Part 4 'Children First Inter-Departmental Group and Sectoral Implementation Plans'.

964 *Children First Act* 2015, s 22.

965 Department of Children and Youth Affairs, *Children First* National Guidance for the Protection and Welfare of Children (Dublin 2017) 50.

966 Children First Inter-Departmental Implementation Group, *Annual Report* [2019] to the Minister for Children and Youth Affairs para 5.2.

officials (working in Government buildings) but rather fall on school personnel and other private employees performing their educational work duties for and with children in schools and other places qualifying as "relevant services". As a consequence, from a children's rights point of view there is not much use in having an Implementation Group promoting and monitoring an implementation of abstract obligations when, clearly, those obligations are substantially disconnected from children and their daily schooling lives. It, therefore, does not come as a surprise that the UN Special Rapporteur uttered concern about the fragmented nature of the Government's approach to the issue of sexual violence against children; also, she found that the fact that no single government department has ownership of the issue hinders coordination; and that there does not appear to be an evaluative component assessing the actual impact of Government-wide efforts to prevent and respond to child sexual abuse and exploitation.[967]

Joint Working Between Tusla and An Garda Síochána

As mentioned above, for all practical purposes of child protection and abuse prevention any joint working between Tusla and the Gardaí should be made legally binding and structured so as to secure a priority for the consideration of the child's best interests. Joint working between social work and policing services involved in the investigation of child abuse is recognised internationally as providing children with a less traumatic investigation experience and better outcomes where criminal and social care enquiries run in parallel.[968]

Regrettably, between both agencies (Gardaí/Tusla) it is only an administrative protocol that is actually in place which details how they cooperate and interact in dealing with child protection concerns.[969] This protocol specifically covers the formal communication required between the agencies about notifications of child protection concerns, and record keeping about joint working and recording of decisions. Given the practical complexities to be handled in joint specialist interviews this is unsatisfactory

[967] A/HRC/40/51/Add.2 para 56.

[968] *Children First* National Guidance (n 965) 43; as a positive example, see Barnahus/Onehouse model at Fn 901 above.

[969] *Tusla and An Garda Síochána Children First – Joint Working Protocol for Liaison between both Agencies* (2018).

and should be replaced by statutory legislation detailing, clarifying and according respective responsibilities as they are regularly involved. As indicated by the Special Rapporteur's Annual Report there are expert considerations regarding the need for joint specialist training between Tusla and An Garda Síochána to be of the utmost urgency, and this clearly adds further weight to a call for legislative amendment.[970]

Sub-Section (7) – Comprehensive Sexuality Education

As an element to the 'Fulfil' component of the tripartite typology of obligations it was demonstrated that the right to non-violent education encompasses quality education which in a comprehensive manner teaches about human sexuality including its cognitive, emotional, physical and social aspects. It must, therefore, be ensured that sexual health, respectful relationships and consent as a prerequisite to close interpersonal communication are conceptually well understood among young children and adolescents in formal education.[971] As Daly and O'Sullivan explain, *'there is no doubt that the benefits of state provision of comprehensive sexuality education for children and young people are numerous'*; even young children, to whom this aspect of education can be provided in an age-appropriate way, need education about consent and respect to help them protect themselves and others against violence and abuse.[972] Not only may this rights-based approach to sexuality education help a young person to avoid being victimized by abusive behaviour originating from others, but it may also prevent that same person from becoming a perpetrator of sexual offences causing harm and grief to others around him or her. As explained earlier sexual activity among adolescents above 15 years of age may well be covered by criminal offences; some of these offences are expressly stated in statutory legislation recently amended.[973]

Sexuality Education in Ireland

One characteristic feature of the Irish education system seems to be a high percentage of educational institutions which are denominationally

---

970 *Annual Report* 2020 (n 389) 30, 31.
971 Fn 484 and accompanying text.
972 Daly, O'Sullivan (n 475) 835, 838; UNESCO *International Technical Guidance* (n 472) 54.
973 Fn 768 and accompanying text.

anchored and promote their ethos accordingly, meaning that in educational practice most schools are operating under the patronage of an ecclesiastic authority, or are owned and managed by Catholic congregations.[974] The scarcity of non-denominational schools, in the eyes of the Committee, remains a cause for concern from a wider perspective of children's education rights.[975] More specifically, a near monopoly of schools featuring a Catholic ethos remains a problem for children's rights to have access to comprehensive sexuality education, since not a few elements of Catholic teaching on human sexuality are based on a kind of rigid moralism overburdening most adolescents (and adults alike) in their daily lives among family, friends and peers.[976] Developed by the Irish Bishops' Conference a relationships and sexuality education programme stated that Catholic schools ought to be transmitting Gospel values, including: the sacredness of human life; the dignity of the person; integrity; peace; tolerance; justice; honesty and truth; holiness; gentleness and compassion; mercy and forgiveness; purity; respect.[977]

An official understanding about an educational function being spirit and ethos-based of a recognised school is reflected normatively through statutory legislation in *Education Act* 1998, sections 9, 15. Although none of these rules and regulations are particularly narrow or limiting in their approach to comprehensive sexuality education as a curricular requirement, together with the denominational character of the majority of schools they tend to function as a barrier to the actual provision of sexuality education in a manner that takes the right to non-violent education seriously. Not surprisingly, it was found through social science research that if sexuality education is left exclusively to parents or families, there is a risk that family education becomes non-existent.[978] More specifically, research from Ireland documents that when parents discuss sexuality with their children, the emphasis of the education differs according to gender, with parents ass-

---

974 *Nora O'Shiel et al v Minister for Education and Science* [1999] 2 I.L.R.M. 241 at 250; *O'Keeffe v Ireland* (n 1) paras 49–53.

975 CRC/C/IRL/CO/3–4 para 63.

976 Keenan (n 61) 133.

977 Irish Bishops' Conference (2021) *Flourish: An RSE programme for Catholic Primary Schools on the Island of Ireland* 1.

978 A/65/162 para 71, UN Special Rapporteur on the right to education (23 July 2010).

uming that their sons will be sexually active and their daughters not.[979] Generally, in Ireland sexuality education is included as an element belonging to the 'Social, Personal and Health Education' (SPHE) curriculum.[980] In secondary school, a specific 'Relationship and Sexuality Education' (RSE) is incorporated into the SPHE programme for the junior cycle, but RSE also runs in the senior cycle. These lessons, however, are not delivered to students as a matter of legal entitlement, and attendance at these classes is subject to a parental right of withdrawal.

In short, Ireland may appear as having a problem with comprehensive sexuality education to be provided through a national curriculum which includes the topic as a matter of adaptability (to the needs and interests of students) being a core quality aspect of rights-based education.[981] More specifically, failure in rights implementation undermines the protective function of comprehensive sexuality education which necessarily remains underdeveloped as a means at the disposition of children themselves to recognise and protect against sexual violence and abuse. In 2013 already, the Inspectorate noted problems with the provision of sexuality education, including incorrect information being presented, disproportionate focus on abstinence and "a disregard for the rights of students to a comprehensive health education".[982] Since each school individually determines the topics covered in its sexuality education programme in accordance with the mostly Catholic ethos of the school, these negative findings did not come as a surprise.

Committee Recommendations

Already, in its 2016 General Comment on the implementation of rights during adolescence, the Committee widely elaborated on children's rights to basic health and found that adolescents everywhere should have access to free, confidential and non-discriminatory sexual and reproductive health

---

979 Daly, O'Sullivan (n 475) 845.

980 Department of Children and Youth Affairs (2013) *Ireland's Consolidated Third and Fourth Reports to the UN Committee on the Rights of the Child*, para 244; Department of Education (2007), *Relationships and Sexuality Education: Policy Guidelines* 4.

981 Fn 185 above and accompanying text.

982 E Kiely et al, *The Sexualisation and Commercialisation of Children in Ireland: An Explanatory Study* (Dublin; Department of Children and Youth Affairs 2015) 87.

services, information and education.[983] Specifically, this implies that age-appropriate, comprehensive and inclusive sexual and reproductive health education, based on scientific evidence and human rights standards should be part of the mandatory school curriculum; for the development of which adolescents should be asked to collaborate.[984]

Along these lines the Committee, in its Concluding Observations expressed concern at the severe lack of access to sexual and reproductive health education for adolescents; it was recommended that the State adopts a comprehensive sexual and reproductive health policy for adolescents and ensures that sexual and reproductive health education becomes part of the mandatory school curriculum.[985] With particular attention to boys and men measures should be taken to raise awareness of and foster responsible parenthood and sexual behaviour.[986] While no statutory instruments providing for this kind of mandatory education were enacted nationally Ireland developed and installed a set of national Relationship and Sexuality Education programmes which are required at secondary schools throughout the State. There is concern, however, that individual schools or even individual teachers remain free to change the content of programmes designed by the Health Service Executive, possibly reducing its effectiveness. Ireland's implementation obligations in this regard remain unfulfilled with schoolchildren having fewer means available to them to recognise abuse and to protect themselves against it; from this perspective their CRC education rights cannot develop their full effects leaving children at risk of violence and abuse.

Third Section: Conclusions

Quintessentially, my research aims at non-violent education and how, as a core aspect of quality education, this will be secured to children who are attending Catholic schools and similar educational institutions, in Ireland and wherever else governance activities deployed by the Holy See are impacting. Arguably, the preferred means of securing non-violent education to every child is by virtue of according an individualised right to

---

983 CRC/C/GC/20 para 59.

984 CRC/C/GC/20 para 61.

985 CRC/C/IRL/CO/3–4 (2016) para 57, 58

986 CRC/C/IRL/CO/3–4 (2016) para 58.

non-violent education to him or her; according the right, however, is only the beginning of the process. For children to vindicate this right for themselves many more requirements have to be met detailed here in terms of obligations to respect, protect and fulfil their human rights. As international obligations they were shown to be falling on State Parties to the Convention turning them into duty-bearers *vis-a-vis* all children under their jurisdiction.

Addressed as an issue through Article 19 CRC the risk of sexual abuse was brought centre stage here; also, as a well documented reality of child-related violence that risk deserves prioritised vigilance. Therefore, the first part of this study reviews children's fundamental human rights and freedoms: children were found to be lacking in targeted protection against sexual abuse in education although the Convention is according them a wealth of protection rights covering many aspects of their lives in the family-home or in professional care provided by adults in schools. As a response, developed by means of treaty interpretation, the right to non-violent education was designed and delineated as a children's right; its scope and substance were described in terms of freedom from all forms of physical or mental violence, including sexual abuse. Flowing from this right is an entitlement to having access to an acceptable learning environment which, in all its institutional and behavioural aspects, must be kept free from violence and abuse. As an issue for children's rights a definition of 'sexual abuse' was elaborated and 'sexual activities' were more precisely defined for the purpose of going into the wider definition of sexual abuse as a treaty term.

Intermediary Steps

On their way to the final synthesis two different chapters looked first, into the reality of children's lives as experienced and documented in officially published Abuse Reports. Another chapter analysed and interpreted CRC provisions most relevant for protection against violence in education, namely the right to freedom from all forms of violence as stipulated through Article 19 CRC and children's education rights as comprehensively stated in Articles 28, 29 CRC. In order to design and delineate the right to non-violent education I had to undertake an interpretive effort framed by the *Vienna Convention on the Law of Treaties* which lays out principles and rules for an interpretation of human rights treaties such as the Convention.

Here, most prominently features the ordinary meaning rule (Article 31 VCLT) which allows for an interpretation in accordance with the terms of the treaty in their context and in the light of its object and purpose; providing for a legal entitlement to education free from violence and abuse was found to be the object and purpose of Article 19 CRC read in conjunction with Articles 28, 29 CRC. This dissertation's 'rights'-pillar elaborated the right to non-violent education as a synthesis of special protection rights distilled from Article 19 CRC and transposed into the remit of education rights as they are stipulated in Articles 28, 29 CRC. There, not only a general right *to* education is stated in Article 28 CRC but rights *in* education and rights *through* education are proclaimed, through Article 29 CRC, for clarification of core quality aspects any rights-based educational system must have.

Itemized Obligations

This study's second part started with an 'obligations'-pillar built of international obligations exactly matching the right to non-violent education as a children's right, under the heading of 'Duties and Obligations'. Here, the tripartite typology of obligations was brought to detailed application on the right to non-violent education. Accordingly, in three sections an obligation to respect this right was explained and elaborated, as well as an obligation to protect and an obligation to fulfil that same right.

Under an obligation to respect the right to non-violent education it was shown that the State must desist from actively inflicting violence in education; along that same line, the State has to refrain from funding providers of educational services who inflict violence in education. Next, four main obligations were demonstrated to flow from an obligation to protect the right to non-violent education: violence against children must be prohibited and criminalized (1), a State-wide system of mandatory reporting must be established and maintained (2), complaints about child abuse must be fully and thoroughly investigated (3), and a government-controlled system of school inspections must be initiated, properly staffed and funded (4); as handed out to inspectors their legal mandate must include making inquiries into the way schoolchildren are being treated by school personnel in practice.

Finally, to be subsumed under an obligation to fulfil the right to non-violent education it was demonstrated that inter-agency cooperation must be made effective between all government branches and at all levels throughout the State; that an age-adapted program of comprehensive sexuality education must become an element of the general school curriculum; and that children's rights must be disseminated by means of teaching and training in fields such as justice, health and education. Not in full accordance with the Committee's concluding observations I could not find any convincing reason why incorporation of the Convention text should generally be seen as a matter for this type of 'Fulfil' obligation; at least, as long as an implementation of CRC rights is accepted as an obligation under Article 4 CRC.

The Holy See

For my third part things got unusually complicated since the Holy See as a State Party to the Convention continuously raises qualms about fundamental aspects regarding the extent and legal nature of its commitment made by signature and ratification of the Convention. Thus, an elaborate sub-section of this Holy See chapter had to clarify, who exactly made the commitment and on behalf of whom this commitment was made. Therefore, distinguishing the Holy See as a subject of international law from the small territory of Vatican City State and also from the Catholic church as a spiritual worldwide community of millions of believers – minors and adults alike – proved to be a necessary first half-step. Explicitly acting in its capacity as a subject of international law the Holy See signed and ratified the Convention as a legislative treaty out of which an international obligation arises to bring the canon law based internal legal order of the Church in line with the provisions of this treaty. Obviously, the Holy See signed and ratified the Convention on its own behalf and on behalf of Vatican City State thereby establishing some sort of parallelism for further analysis.

Next, as an exercise in treaty law application the Holy See's interpretive declaration and its three reservations entered into when ratifying the Convention were analysed and tested as to their validity under international law. As far as it was claimed that the internal legal order of the Church be deemed exempt from implementing obligations under the Convention neither the Holy See's declaration nor the three reservations made were found to be valid. This dissertation's distinctive effort for determining the legal status of the Holy See as a State Party to the Convention lies in its reference to Canon 113 CIC by which the Catholic Church and the Apostolic (Holy) See are declared to be qualifying as having the status of a "moral person" elevating it to a *per se* higher status compared to other legal entities constituted within the Church.[987] Consequently, acceptance on behalf of that same legal subject of international obligations arising out of a human rights treaty is to be followed through within the Catholic Church and must not be unilaterally renounced later.

Somewhat in contrast to its fundamental opposition regarding international obligations of implementing children's rights the Holy See made remarkable amendments to its internal legal order. However, from a CRC perspective implementing obligations regarding 'Mandatory Reporting' and 'Investigation of Complaints' remained unfulfilled by the Holy See as a State Party to the Convention. Moreover, obligations of inspection were found to exist but were not specific enough so as to identify and mitigate the risk of child sexual abuse in schools governed by ecclesiastic authorities. Although a special unit for child protection (*Pontifical Council for the Protection of Minors*) was set up at the Holy See, coordination among a number of Holy See offices each responsible for partial aspects of clerical sexual abuse remains insufficient for safeguarding children's rights within the Church.

Ireland

From the beginning, Ireland had accepted its CRC obligations unreservedly and had taken its reporting obligations to the Committee quite seriously; accordingly, this dissertation covers five cycles of reporting to the UN treaty body. As a consequence, it may be stated that Ireland successfully discharged its implementing obligations under the Convention but measured against the listing of recommendations set up by the Committee, promises given to children on the basis of their human rights remain partially unfulfilled.

An international obligation of 'criminalization' regarding child sexual abuse and its preparatory activities was widely fulfilled especially as far as criminalizing explicit sexual activities involving children below the age of consent is concerned; however, rules on "honest mistake" regarding circumstances for assuming (age dependent) validity of consent given to

[987] See Fn 544 and accompanying text for Canon 113(1) CIC.

sexual activity were found to be over-generous to the detriment of minors. An international obligation of 'mandatory reporting' was partly fulfilled since certain instances of non-reporting remain unsanctioned but the legislation in either the *Criminal Justice (Withholding Information on Offences Against Children and Vulnerable Persons) Act* 2012 or the *Children First Act* 2015 is not specific enough for clarification of the interplay between these pieces of legislation. Statutory rules drafted for creating a mandate to report based on assessing the legal quality of what had happened to the child are over-complex and might cause blockages against a swift transfer of information, especially for information gathererd from a school context.

An international obligation of 'investigation' was partly fulfilled, since an offer of counselling and support to be made to the child victim or witness is not obligatory in all cases; also, no statutory legislation exists specific enough for supporting an elaborate practice of administrative investigations into complaints about child sexual abuse leading to findings about child abuse and sharing of information. Thus, adverse incentive may be caused to remain passive or desist from leading an investigation to its proper conclusion. An obligation of 'inspection' was partly fulfilled since the principal rules and regulations for school inspections are defined and delineated on a sub-statutory level only. Given the core child protection provisions as laid out through the *Children First Act* 2015 functioning as the substantive standard for school inspections it seems unbalanced and confusing that no corresponding legislation exists for the Inspectorate as a division of the Department of Education and Skills.

An obligation of 'inter-agency cooperation' was found to be partially fulfilled since an Interdepartmental Implementation Group was established by virtue of the *Children First Act* 2015 which operates at a far too remote distance from safeguarding and reporting obligations as they were made obligatory for 'relevant services' in education. Cooperation between agencies for an enforcement of laws on the one hand and agencies providing social care and assistance for families and children on the other, is limited by a lack of resources needed for training rights-aware specialists. What can be achieved in terms of positive collaboration between child protection agencies became evident by looking into the Barnahus/Onehouse model recently introduced *ad experimentum*. An international obligation of 'comprehensive sexuality education' was partially fulfilled since programs for school-based sexuality education were developed and are sporadically put into practice; Ireland, however, may appear as having a problem with comprehensive sexuality education as a topic for fulfilment of CRC protection rights. Since not enough training and teaching on children's rights is being offered for professionals working in the fields of justice, health and education, dissemination of the principles and provisions of the Convention as required by Article 42 CRC remains incomplete.

Holders of the Right to Non-Violent Education

Respecting children in Catholic schools as holders of the right to non-violent education, what is the overall assessment respecting the level of protection achieved by means of implementing childrens' rights? Do the measures undertaken, by either Ireland or the Holy See, prove to be necessary and sufficient for protecting children against the risk of sexual abuse in education when this kind of abuse was wide-spread and well documented historically?

As a State Party to the Convention the Holy See cannot be allowed to abstain from implementing children's rights throughout its canon law-based internal legal order; also in respect of the Church's factual role as a provider of educational and care services to hundreds of millions of children, taking defined measures to implement children's rights proves to be imperative. Even if a reductive reading of its treaty-based obligations should be acceptable to someone, the Church's established responsibilities of aiding and abetting clerical sexual abuse lend urgency to an appeal for taking decisive steps for an immediate and comprehensive realisation of the right to non-violent education.

Reviewing the multitude of measures taken over time by governments in Ireland for combating child abuse what remains is an impression of confusion and over-complexity with not enough inter-agency cooperation being encouraged and facilitated at the same time. Seen through the eyes of children involved it looks more like a labyrinth or a maze what government services have on offer for support and protection in a case of complaints about sexual abuse, especially when an educational setting is concerned.

As an overall conclusion to the whole study, it became evident that a stipulation of the right to non-violent education is clearly missing from catalogues of rights presently available to children as rights-holding individuals. All efforts to combat child sexual abuse of schoolchildren which have started but remain patchy and tokenistic in most environments, will become more consistent and comprehensive as a consequence.

Bibliography

Books

Abramson B, 'Article 2: The Right of Non-Discrimination' in Alen A, Vande Lanotte J, Verhellen E, Ang F, Berghmans E, Verheyde M (eds), A Commentary on the United Nations Convention on the Rights of the Child (Martinus Nijhoff Leiden Boston 2008)

Alen A, Vande Lanotte J, Ang F, Berghmans E, Verheyde M (eds), A Commentary on the United Nations Convention on the Rights of the Child (Martinus Nijhoff Leiden Boston 2005–2012)

Aymans-Mörsdorf-Müller, Kanonisches Recht Band IV (Ferdinand Schöningh 2013)

Aust A, Handbook of International Law (CUP 2005) 55, 83, 79, 81

Beal JP, Coriden JA, Green TJ (eds) New Commentary on the Code of Canon Law (Paulist Press 2000) 957

Besson S, 'The Principle of Non-discrimination in the Convention on the Rights of the Child' in Freeman M (ed), Progress and Perspectives (Mart Nijhoff 2011) 85, 103

Blackburn S, The Oxford Dictionary of Philosophy (OUP 1994)

Boven TV, 'Categories of Rights' in Harris D, Moeckli D, Shah S and Sivakumaran S, International Human Rights Law (3rd ed OUP 2018) 135, 143, 145, 147, 152

Bracken L, Child Law in Ireland (Clarus Press 2018) 147, 211

Bridge C (ed) Family Law Towards the Millennium: Essays for P M Bromley (Butterworths 1997) 203

Buck T, International Child Law (3rd ed Routledge 2014) 353

Byrnes A and Renshaw C, 'Within the State' in Harris D, Moeckli D, Shah S and Sivakumaran S, International Human Rights Law (3rd ed OUP 2018) 482, 483, 488

Cantwell N, 'Are Children's Rights still Human?' in A Invernizzi et al (eds) *The Human Rights of Children* (Ashgate 2011) 37, 41, 43, 53, 54

– – and Holzscheiter A, 'Article 20, Children Deprived of their Family Environment' in Alen A, Vande Lanotte J, Verhellen E, Ang F, Berghmans E, Verheyde M, A Commentary on the United Nations Convention on the Rights of the Child (Leiden 2005) 1

Capps P, Human Dignity and the Foundations of International Law (Hart 2010) 7, 210

Cardinale HE, The Holy See and the International Order (Colin Smythe Ltd 1977) 80, 82, 256, 362

Chinkin C, 'Sources' in Harris D, Moeckli D, Shah S and Sivakumaran S (eds) International Human Rights Law (3rd ed OUP 2018) 63, 65, 68, 75, 78, 79, 81, 105

Cismas I, 'The Child's Best Interests and Religion' in Sutherland E E, MacFarlane LB (eds), Implementing Article 3 of the United Nations Convention on the Rights of the Child: Best Interests, Welfare and Well-being (CUP 2016) 3, 6

Clapham A, Human Rights Obligations of Non-State Actors (OUP 2006) 318

– – 'Non-State Actors' in Harris D, Moeckli D, Shah S and Sivakumaran S, International Human Rights Law (3rd ed OUP 2018) 557, 560

Coomans F, 'Education and Work' in Harris D, Moeckli D, Shah S and Sivakumaran S, International Human Rights Law (3rd ed OUP 2018) 232, 233, 235, 236, 240

Cornwell J, The Dark Box: A Secret History of Confession (Profile Books 2014) 169

Covell K, Howe RB, McGillivray, 'Implementing Children's Rights in Schools' in Ruck MD, Peterson-Badali and Freeman M (eds) Handbook of Children's Rights: Global and Multidisciplinary Perspectives (Routledge 2017) 296, 302

De Blacam M, Judicial Review (3rd ed Bloomsbury Professional 2017) 379, 385

Denza E, 'The Relationship between International and National Law' in M Evans (ed) International Law (4th ed OUP 2014) 412, 416

Detrick S (ed) The United Nations Convention on the Rights of the Child: A Guide to the 'Travaux Preparatoires' (Martinus Nijhoff 1992)

– – 'A Commentary on the UN Convention on the Rights of the Child' (2001)

Doyle O and Hickey T, Constitutional Law: Text, Cases and Materials (Clarus 2008)

Egan S, The United Nations Human Rights Treaty System: Law and Procedure (Bloomsbury Professional 2011)

– – 'Tackling the Rise of Child Labour in Europe' (2015) 64 ICLQ 601, 608

Euart SA, The Catholic Education in Beal JP, Coriden JA, Green TJ, New Commentary on the Code of Canon Law (Paulist Press New York 2000) 960

Ferrari S, 'Concordats' in Max Planck Encyclopedia of International Law (MPEPIL 2006) http://opil.ouplaw.com/

Fitzmaurice M, 'Interpretation of Human Rights Treaties' in Shelton D (ed) The Oxford Handbook of International Human Rights Law (OUP 2013) 739, 742 745, 751, 753

– – 'The Practical Working of the Law of Treaties' in Evans M (ed) International Law (4th ed OUP 2014) 166, 179

Fottrell D, 'Children's Rights' in Hegarty A and Leonard S (eds), Human Rights, An Agenda for the 21st Century (Cavendish 1999) 167, 171

Grabenwarter C, European Convention on Human Rights: Commentary (C.H. Beck 2014) 64, 289, 390, 394

– – 'Zur Frage der Integration der Kinderrechtskonvention in das österreichische Bundesverfassungsrecht', in Berka W, Grabenwarter C, Weber K (eds) Studien zur Kinderrechtskonvention und ihrer Umsetzung in Österreich (BMFJ Wien 2014) 78

Grant J and Barker J, 'Holy See' in Encyclopaedic Dictionary of International Law (3rd ed OUP 2009)

– – 'Lateran Treaty' in Encyclopaedic Dictionary of International Law (3rd ed OUP 2009)

Grover L, Keller H, Ulfstein G, UN Human Rights Treaty Bodies, Law and Legitimacy (CUP 2012) 6

Hamilton C, 'Rights of the Child: A Right to Education and a Right in Education' in Bridge C (ed) Family Law Towards the Millennium: Essays for P M Bromley (Butterworths 1997) 201, 203

Hanly C, An Introduction to Irish Criminal Law (3rd ed Gill Education 2006) 316, 318,328, 332, 333, 335

Harris DJ, Bates E, Buckley C, O'Boyle M, Law of the European Convention on Human Rights (2nd ed OUP 2009) 18, 704, 107, 110

Hausler K, Protecting Education in Insecurity and Armed Conflict: An International Law Handbook (2nd ed BIICL 2012) 17, 18, 27

H F Köck, entry 'Holy See' in Max Planck Encyclopedia of International Law (1992) 866

Hodgkin R, Newell P, UNICEF (ed) Implementation Handbook, E/ICEF(09)I342 (2007) 41, 42, 258, 266, 267, 268, 412, 442, 513, 589, 699, 701

Howe R B and Covel K, 'Miseducating children about their rights' in Kilkelly U and Lundy L (eds), Children's Rights' (Routledge 2017) 245, 247, 248, 250, 255

Huels JM in Beal JP, Coriden JA and Green TJ, New Commentary on the Code of Canon Law (Paulist Press New York 2000) 50, 51

Joseph S and Dipnall S, 'Scope of Application' in Harris D, Moeckli D, Shah S and Sivakumaran S, International Human Rights Law (3rd ed OUP 2018) 110, 111, 114, 115, 130

Kälin W and Künzli J, The Law of International Human Rights Protection (2nd Ed OUP 2009) 77, 78, 81, 96, 97,103

Kaslyn RJ, 'The People of God: Introduction' in Beal JP, Coriden JA, Green TJ, New Commentary on the Code of Canon Law (Paulist Press New York 2000) 247

Keenan M, Child Sexual Abuse and the Catholic Church: Gender, Power and Organizational Culture (OUP 2012) 4, 7, 41, 133, 162, 166, 180, 192, 194, 202, 209

Keller H and Grover L, 'General Comments of the Human Rights Committee and their legitimacy' in Grover L, Keller H Ulfstein G, UN Human Rights Treaty Bodies, Law and Legitimacy (CUP 2012) 116, 131, 261, 264, 311

Kennedy RT, 'Juridic Persons' in Beal JP, Coriden JA, Green TJ, New Commentary on the Code of Canon Law (Paulist Press New York 2000)

Khaliq U and Churchill R, 'The protection of economic and social rights: a particular challenge?' in Grover L, Keller H Ulfstein G, UN Human Rights Treaty Bodies, Law and Legitimacy (CUP 2012) 199, 209, 218, 219, 225

Lenzer G, 'Violence against Children' in Vandenhole W, Desmet E, Reynaert D, Lembrechts S, Routledge International Handbook of Children's Rights Studies (Routledge London New York 2015) 276, 278, 279, 284, 289, 292

Listl J, 'Konkordat' in W Kasper et al (eds) LThK (2009) 263

Lüdicke K, Münsterischer Kommentar zum Codex Iris Canonici (Ludgerus 1987)

Lundy L, 'Mainstreaming Children's Rights In, To and Through Education in a Society Emerging from Conflict' in M Freeman (ed) Progress and Perspectives (Mart Nijhoff 2011) 191

– – 'Children's rights and educational policy in Europe: the implementation of the United Nations Convention on the Rights of the Child' (2012) 38 Oxford Review of Education 393, 395, 404, 405

– – and Bryne B, Kilkelly U 'Incorporation of the United Nations Convention on the Rights of the Child in Law: A Comparative Review' (2013) IJCR 442, 452, 457, 459, 460, 463

– – and Orr K, Shier H, 'Children's Education Rights: Global Perspectives' in Ruck MD, Peterson-Badali M, Freeman M (eds) Handbook of Children's Rights: Global and Multidisciplinary Perspective (Routledge 2017) 364, 365, 366, 367, 369

Lynch K and Baker J, 'The Status of Children' in Lynch K (ed) Equality in Education (Gill & Macmillan 1999) 162, 163, 164, 167

Mathews B, 'Exploring the Contested Role of Mandatory Reporting Laws in the Identification of Severe Child Abuse and Neglect' in Freeman M (ed) Law and Childhood Studies: Current Legal Issues, vol 14 (OUP 2012) 302

– – and Ju Lee X, Norman RE, 'Impact of a New Mandatory Reporting Law on Reporting and Identification of Child Sexual Abuse: A Seven Year Time Trend Analysis' (Epub 2016) 56 Child Abuse & Neglect 62

McAleese M, Quo Vadis (The Columba Press 2012) 103

– – Children's Rights and Obligations in Canon Law: The Christening Contract (Brill Nijhoff, Leiden Boston 2019) 3, 6, 18, 21, 29, 30, 33, 69, 106, 187, 188,

189, 345, 353, 386, 388, 398, 401, 406, 416, 419, 424, 428, 436, 438, 441, 442, 456

McCorquodale R, 'The Individual and the International Legal System' in Evans M, International Law (4th ed OUP 2014) 280, 282

McPartland E, The Best Interests of the Child (2nd ed Gill & Macmillan 2013) 32

Mégret F, 'Nature of Obligations' in Harris D, Moeckli D, Shah S and Sivakumaran S, International Human Rights Law (3rd ed OUP 2018) 86, 88, 97, 99, 278, 285

Michaelis R, 'The Functional Method of Comparative Law' in Reimann M, Zimmermann R (eds) The Oxford Handbook of Comparative Law (OUP 2006)

Mowbray AR, The development of positive obligations under the European Convention on Human Rights by the European Court of Human Rights (Hart Publishing Oxford, Portland Oregon, 2004) 2, 158, 223, 225.

– – Cases, Materials, and Commentary on the European Convention of Human Rights (3rd ed OUP 2012), 145, 155, 156, 157, 159

Muntarbhorn V, 'Article 34: Sexual Exploitation and Sexual Abuse of Children' in Alen A, Vande Lanotte J, Verhellen E, Ang F, Berghmans E, Verheyde M, A Commentary on the United Nations Convention on the Rights of the Child (Leiden 2005)

Nolan A, 'Litigating the Child's Right to a Life free from Violence: Seeking the Prohibition of Parental Physical Punishment of Children through the Courts' in Freeman M, Current Legal Issues: Childhood and Law Studies (OUP 2012) 530

Nowak M, 'A Commentary on the United Nations on the Rights of the Child, Article 6: The Right to Life, Survival and Development' in Alen A, Vande Lanotte J, Verhellen E, Ang F, Berghmans E, Verheyde M, A Commentary on the United Nations Convention on the Rights of the Child (Nijhof Leiden 2005)

Okolo JMT, The Holy See: A Moral Person, The Juridical Nature of the Holy See in the Light of the Present Code of Canon Law (Pontificia Universitas Urbaniana Facultas Iuris Canonici, Romae 1990) 266

O'Malley T, Sexual Offences: Law, Policy and Punishment (Roundhall Dublin 1996) 1, 12, 24, 26, 28

O'Malley T, Criminal Law (Sexual Offences) Act 2017 – The Offence Provisions, Presentation to the 18th Annual National Prosecutors' Conference (2017)

Robertson G, The Case of the Pope (Penguin 2010) 96, 100

Rossetti SJ, 'Learning from Our Mistakes' in Scicluna CJ, Zollner H, Ayotte DJ (eds) Toward Healing and Renewal: The 2012 Symposium on the Sexual Ab-

use of Minors Held at the Pontifical Gregorian University (Paulist Press 2012) 29, 40
Salmon J in Corten O and Klein P (eds), The Vienna Conventions on the Law of Treaties, A Commentary (OUP 2011) 661
Schlütter B, 'Aspects of human rights interpretation by the UN treaty bodies' in Keller H and Ulfstein G (eds) UN Human Rights Treaty Bodies: Law and Legitimacy (CUP 2012) 261, 265, 282
Scicluna CJ, 'The Quest for Truth in Sexual Abuse Cases' in Scicluna CJ, Zollner H, Ayotte DJ (eds) Towards Healing and Renewal: The 2012 Symposium on the Sexual Abuse of Minors (NJ Paulist Press 2012)
– –'Taking Responsibility for Processing Cases of Sexual Abuse Crisis and for Prevention of Abuse', Presentation at the Vatican Meeting 'The Protection of Minors in the Church' (Vatican's New Synod Hall, 21–24 February 2019) 2 https://www.vatican.va/resources/resources_mons-scicluna-protezioneminori_20190221_en.html
Shannon G, Child Law (2nd ed Thomson Reuters Dublin 2010)
– – Fifth Report of the Special Rapporteur on Child Protection: A Report Submitted to the Oireachtas (2011) 9, 10
– – Children and Family Relationships Law in Ireland (Clarus Press 2016)
Shue H, Basic Rights: Subsistence, Affluence, and US Foreign Policy (Princeton University Press 2nd ed 1996)
Steiner HJ, Goodman R, Alston P, International Human Rights in Context (3rd ed OUP 2007) 187, 806
Todres J, Wojcik ME, Revaz, CR (eds) The United Nations Convention on the Rights of the Child: An Analysis of Treaty Provisions and Implications of U. S. Ratification (Transnational Publishers 2006)
– – 'Taking Prevention Seriously: Developing a Comprehensive Response to Child Trafficking and Sexual Exploitation' (2010) 43 Vand.J.Transnat'l L. 1, 3
Van der Vyver JD, 'Sovereignty' in Shelton D, Oxford Handbook of International Human Rights Law (OUP 2013) 379, 383
Verhellen E, 'The Convention on the Rights of the Child' in Vandenhole W, Desmet E, Reynaert D, Lembrechts S (eds) Routledge International Handbook of Children's Rights Studies (Routledge 2015) 43, 55
Wacks R, Law: A Very Short Introduction (OUP 2008) 59
Woodhouse BB, 'The Changing Status of the Child' in Todres J, Wojcik M, Revaz C (eds), The U.N. Convention on the Rights of the Child, An Analysis of Treaty Provisions and Implications of U.S. Ratifications (Transnational Publishers 2006) 51, 61

Studies, Reports and Judicial Inquiries

An Garda Síochána, Gardaí Policy, The Investigation of Sexual Crime, Crimes Against Children, Child Welfare (2nd ed 2013) https://www.garda.ie/en/about-us/publications/policy-documents/policy-on-the-investigation-of-sexual-crime-crimes-against-children-and-child-welfare-.pdf

Annual Report of the Special Rapporteur on Child Protection June 2020 (Dr Conor O'Mahony) https://www.gov.ie/en/collection/51fc67-special-rapporteur-on-child-protection-reports/.

Annual Report of the Special Rapporteur on Child Protection June 2021 (Professor Conor O'Mahony)

Annual Report of the Special Rapporteur on Child Protection 2022 (Professor Conor O'Mahony)

Children First Interdepartmental Implementation Group (CFIDIG), Annual Report (2019) https://www.gov.ie/pdf/?file=https://assets.gov.ie/131179/f29caf6c-0b04--4eab-ad8a-4419f6d1b266.pdf{#}page=null

Child Rights International Network, Child Sexual Abuse and the Holy See: A Preliminary Report (CRIN 2014)

Council of Europe, Explanatory Report to the Council of Europe Convention on the Protection of Children against Sexual Exploitation and Sexual Abuse, Lanzarote 25.X.2007, Council of Europe Treaty Series – No. 201;

ECPAT International (Jaap E Doek chairperson of the Interagency Working Group), *Terminology Guidelines for the Protection of Children from Sexual Exploitation and Sexual Abuse* (Luxembourg 28 January 2016), available from CRC Committee website http://tbinternet.ohchr.org , 1, 3, 5, 12, 13, 16, 19, 24, 25, 77, 78

European Commission for Democracy Through Law (Venice Commission) Report on the Protection of Children's Rights: International Standards and Domestic Constitutions, 98th Plenary Session Opinion no 713/2013 (2014)

European Union Agency for Fundamental Rights (FRA), Handbook on European Law Relating to the Rights of the Child (Luxembourg 2015) 115, 116, 121

Government of Ireland and Department of Children and Youth Affairs (ed), *EAG Discussion Paper* (10 April 2019) Appendix 9: Retrospective Allegations of Child Abuse: The Legal Framework (prepared by Dr Conor O'Mahony) 7, 11

Government of Ireland 'Ireland's Consolidated Third and Fourth Report to the UN Committee on the Rights of the Child (UNRC) on the Rights of the Child (Minister for Children and Youth Affairs 2013)

Government of Ireland 'Combined fifth and sixth periodic reports submitted by Ireland under Article 44 of the Convention, due in 2021' UN document CRC/C/IRL/5–6 (5 September 2022)

International Commission of Jurists, Courts and the Legal Enforcement of Economic, Social and Cultural Rights: Comparative Experiences of Justiciability (Geneva 2008) 7

– – Maastricht Guidelines on Violations of Economic, Social and Cultural Rights (1997) 20 HRQ 691, 693, 694, 698

International Criminal Court, The Office of the Prosecutor, Draft policy on children (2016) https://www.icc-cpi.int/sites/default/files/iccdocs/otp/22.06.2016-Draft-Policy-on-Children_ENG.pdf

Irish Bishops' Conference, Flourish: An RSE programme for Catholic Primary Schools on the Island of Ireland 1 (2021), https://www.cpsma.ie/wp-content/uploads/2021/04/RSE_Catholic-RSE-in-Primary-FINAL.pdf.

Kiely E, Ging D, Kitching K, Leane M, The Sexualisation and Commercialisation of Children in Ireland: An Explanatory Study (Department of Children and Youth Affairs 2015) 87

Murphy FD, Buckley H and Joyce L, The Ferns Report, Presented to the Minister for Health and Children (*'Ferns'*) (Dublin, Government Publications, 2005), 23, 35, 183, 189, 192 196, 197

OSCE Office for Democratic Institutions and Human Rights (Venice Commission), Joint Guidelines on the Legal Personality of Religious or Belief Communities, 99th Plenary Session (Venice 2014)

Rape Crisis Network Ireland, Hearing Every Voice-Towards a New Strategy on Vulnerable Witness in Legal Proceedings (March 2018) 7, 8

Report by the Commission of Investigation into the Catholic Archdiocese of Dublin (2009) (*'Murphy'*), http://www.justice.ie/en/JELR/Pages/PB09000504

Report of the Commission to Inquire into Child Abuse (2009) (Dublin, Government Stationary Office)(*'Ryan'*), http://childabusecommission.ie

Report by the Commission of Investigation into the Catholic Diocese of Cloyne (2011)(*'Cloyne'*), http://www.justice.ie/en/JELR/Pages/Cloyne_Rpt

Fifth Report of the Special Rapporteur on Child Protection 2011 (G Shannon), A Report Submitted to the Oireachtas, wwwgov.ie .

Tusla and Children First, Joint Working Protocol for An Garda Síochána/Tusla-Child and Family Agency Liaison (2018)

World Health Organisation, Krug, EG, Dahlberg LL, Mercy JA, Zwi AB and Lozano R (ed) World Report on Violence and Health (Geneva 2002)

Holy See Materials

All legal-canonical documents issued by the Holy See are available either *via* https://www.vatican.va/ or *via* http://press.vatican.va/ ; all legal-canonical documents issued by the Pontifical Commission for the Protection of Minors are available either *via* http://www.protectionofminors.va/ or *via* https://www.tutelaminorum.org/ .

Dicastery for the Doctrine of the Faith (DDF), 'Vademecum: On Certain Points of Procedure in Treating Cases of Sexual Abuse of Minors Committed by Clerics', Version 2.0 (Vatican 2022) https://www.vatican.va/roman_curia/congregations/cfaith/ddf/rc_ddf_doc_20220605_vademecum-casi-abuso-2.0_en.html

The Holy See, Code of Canon Law ('Codex Iuris Canonici') (1983) https://www.vatican.va/archive/cod-iuris-canonici/cic_index_en.html

– – John Paul II, 'Pastor Bonus', Apostolic Constitution (1988) https://www.vatican.va/content/john-paul-ii/en/apost_constitutions/documents/hf_jp-ii_apc_19880628_pastor-bonus.html

– – Agreement between the Holy See and the Republic of Malta on Church Schools (1991/ rev. 1993) https://www.vatican.va/roman_curia/secretariat_state/archivio/documents/rc_seg-st_19930218_santa-sede-rep-malta-scuole_en.html

– – Catechism of the Catholic Church, popular and definitive edition (Burns & Oates New York 2000)

– – Code of Canon Law (Canon Law Society of America 1983/rev 1999) 193, 361, 363, 805, 806, 1331, 1395, 1717, 1720, 1722

– – Pope John Paul II, Motu Proprio 'Sacramentorum Sanctitatis Tutela', Apostolic Letter, official Latin text of the revised substantial and procedural norms, Acta Apostolicae Sedes (AAS) 102 (2010) 419–430

– – Congregatio Pro Doctrina Fidei: Circular Letter to Assist Episcopal Conferences in 'Developing Guidelines for Dealing with Cases of Sexual Abuse of Minors Perpetrated by Clerics' (2011) https://www.vatican.va/roman_curia/congregations/cfaith/documents/rc_con_cfaith_doc_20110503_abuso-minori_en.html

– – Apostolic Constitution: 'Pascite Gregem Dei' of the Holy Father Francis: Reforming Book VI of the Code of Canon Law (2012) https://www.vatican.va/content/francesco/en/apost_constitutions/documents/papa-francesco_costituzione-ap_20210523_pascite-gregem-dei.html

– – Pope Francis, chirograph 'Institution of the Pontifical Commission for the Protection of Minors', 24 February 2014, Acta Apostolicae Sedes (AAS) 107 (2014) 562–563

– – Legge N.VIII: Norme complementari in materia penale (11 Luglio 2013) https://www.vaticanstate.va/phocadownload/leggi-decreti/normativa-penale/Legge%20n.%20VIII%20-%20Norme%20complementari%20in%20materia%20penale.pdf

– – Comments of the Holy See on the Concluding Observations of the Committee on the Rights of the Child (2014) https://www.vatican.va/roman_curia/secretariat_state/2014/documents/rc-seg-st-20140205_concluding-observations-rights-child_en.html
– – Motu proprio: 'Like a loving mother', Apostolic Letter (2016) https://press.vatican.va/content/salastampa/en/bollettino/pubblico/2016/06/04/160604a.html
– – Pope Francis 'Vos estis lux mundi', Apostolic Letter (2019) https://www.vatican.va/content/francesco/en/motu_proprio/documents/papa-francesco-motu-proprio-20190507_vos-estis-lux-mundi.html
– – Pope Francis, 'Praedicate Evangelium', Costituzione Apostolica (2022) https://www.vatican.va/content/francesco/en/apost_constitutions/documents/20220319-costituzione-ap-praedicate-evangelium.html
– – Pope Francis, Address of his Holiness Pope Francis to the Members of the Pontifical Commission for the Protection of Minors (29 April 2022) https://www.vatican.va/content/francesco/en/speeches/2022/april/documents/20220429-pontcommissione-tutelaminori.html

Academic Articles

Arato J, 'Treaty Interpretation and Constitutional Transformation: Informal Change in International Organizations' (2013) 38 The Yale Journal of International Law 289, 291, 335
Araujo RJ and Lucal JA, 'A Forerunner for International Organizations: The Holy See and Community of Christendom: With Special Emphasis on the Medieval Papacy' 20 JLR 305, 323, 324, 327
– – 'Holy See and Community of Christendom' (2018) 20 Journal of Law & Religion 305, 323, 325
Barbato M, 'A State, a Diplomat, and a Transnational Church: The Multi-Layered Actorness of the Holy See' (2013) 21 Perspectives 27, 36
Buckley R, 'The Children First Bill 2014: A Step in the Right Direction?' (2015) 2 IrJournFamL 34
Buergenthal T, 'Human Rights: From San Francisco to The Hague' (2017) 77 ZaöRV 289, 300
Cahill M, 'McD v L and the Incorporation of the European Convention on Human Rights' 45 Irish Jurist (2010) 221, 223
Daly A, O'Sullivan C, 'Sexuality Education and International Standards: Insisting Upon Children's Rights' (John Hopkins University Press 2020) 42 HRQ 835, 837, 838, 840, 841
De Brabandere E, Non-state Actors, State-Centrism and Human Rights Obligations (2009) 22 LJIL 191, 197

Doek JE, 'The CRC 20 years: An overview of some of the major achievements and remaining challenges' (2009) 33 Child Abuse & Neglect 771, 777, 781

Elkins Z, Ginsburg T and Simmons B, 'Getting to Rights: Treaty Ratification, Constitutional Convergence, and Human Rights Practice' (2013) 54 HarvInternLJ 61, 64, 69

Federle KH, 'Rights flow downhill' (1994) 2 IJCR 343

– – Children and the Law (OUP 2013)

Ferguson L, 'Not merely rights for children but children's rights: The theory gap and the assumption of the importance of children's rights' (2013) 21 IJCR, 177, 179

Fiorvanti CM, Brassard MR, 'Advancing Child Protection through Respecting Children's Rights: A Shifting Emphasis for School Psychology' (2014) 43 School Psychology Review 350

Freeman M, 'The Problem of Secularism in Human Rights Theory' (2004) 26 HRQ 375, 399

– – 'Article 3: The Best Interests of the Child' in: Alen A, Vande Lanotte J, Verhellen E, Ang F, Berghmans E, Verheyde M, A Commentary on the United Nations on the Rights of the Child (Nijhoff Leiden 2007)

– – 'The Value and Values of Children's Rights' in Williams J and Invernizzi A (eds), The Human Rights of Children: From Visions to Implementation (Ashgate 2011) 21, 22, 23, 26, 30

– – and Saunders B J, 'Can we Conquer Child Abuse if we don't outlaw Physical Chastisement of Children?' (2014) 22 IJCR 681, 697

Greenberg J and Sechler MJ, 'Constitutionalism Ancient and Modern: the Contributions of Roman Law, Canon Law and English Common Law' (2013) 34 CardozLRev 1021, 1037

Hailu TG, 'The Holy See: Government of the Catholic Church' (2017) 25 IJCR 779, 784, 789, 792, 800, 801, 807

Hakimi M, 'State Bystander Responsibility' (2010) 21 EJIL 341, 342, 346, 347, 357

Hallermann H, 'Präzisierung und Erleichterung? Die Überarbeitung der Leitlinien zum Umgang mit Sexuellem Missbrauch im Bereich der DBK (2013) KuR 19, 178, 190

Harris-Short S, 'International Human Rights Law: Imperialist, Inept and Ineffective? Cultural Relativism and the CRC' (2003) 25 HRQ 130, 135

Kilkelly U, 'The Best of Both Worlds for Children's Rights? Interpreting the European Convention on Human Rights in the Light of the UN Convention on the Rights of the Child' (2001) 23 HRQ 308, 310, 317, 326

– – 'Article 8: The Right to Respect for Private and Family Life, Home and

Correspondence' in Harris D, O'Boyle M, Bates E, Buckley C M (eds) Law of the European Convention (2nd ed OUP 2007) 361, 382, 384
– – Children's Rights in Ireland: Law, Policy and Practice (Tottel Publishing 2008) 252, 999
– – 'Children's Rights and the Family: Myth and Reality' (2008) 97 Studies 7, 9
– – 'Protecting children's rights under the ECHR: the role of positive obligations' (2010) 61 NILQ 245
– – 'The CRC at 21: Assessing The Legal Impact' (2011) 62 NILQ 143, 147
– – 'Using the Convention on the Rights of the Child in Law and Policy: Two Ways to Improve Compliance' in Williams J and Invernizzi A (eds) The Human Rights of Children: From Visions to Implementation (Ashgate 2011) 179, 180, 183, 185, 191
– – 'Learning lessons from the past: Legal issues Arising from Ireland's Child Abuse Reports' (2012) 12 Irish Journal of Applied Social Studies 8, 11, 12, 15, 16
– – 'Foreword' in Parkes A, Children and IHR Law (Routledge 2013) xix
– – 'The Convention on the Rights of the Child after Twenty-five Years' in Ruck MD, Peterson-Badali M, Freeman M (eds), Handbook of Children's Rights: Global and Multidisciplinary Perspective (Routledge 2017) 80, 87
– – 'The CRC after 25 Years', in Ruck MD, Peterson-Badali M, Freeman M (eds) Handbook of Children's Rights: Global and Multidisciplinary Perspective (Routledge 2017) 80, 87, 88
Kirchner S, 'Das Beichtgeheimnis zwischen staatlichem und kirchlichem Recht' (2012) 19 Jurisprudencija/Jurisprudence 1317, 1326
Kissane B, 'Catholicism and the concept of 'the State' in the Irish (1937) Constitution' (2020) 9 Oxford Journal of Law and Religion 508, 526
Klee SJ and Thalipyal N, 'The Right to Education: The Work of Katarina Tomasevski' (2007) 51 Comparative Education Review 497, 500
Koch I E, 'Dichotomies, Trichotomies or Waves of Duties' (2005) 5 Human Rights Law Review 81, 82, 87
Leblanc LJ, 'Reservations to the Convention on the Rights of the Child: A macroscopic view of state practice' 4 IJCR (1996) 357, 381
Marie J-B, 'International Instruments relating to Human Rights, Classification and status of Ratification as of 1 January 2008' (2008) 29 Human Rights Law Journal 163
Mawhinney A, 'Freedom of religion in the Irish primary school system: a failure to protect human rights?' (2007) 27 Legal Studies 379
McAlinden A-M, 'An inconvenient truth: barriers to truth recovery in the after-

math of institutional child abuse in Ireland' (2013) 33 Legal Studies 189, 191, 193, 195, 202

McCrudden C, 'Legal and Roman Catholic Conceptions of Human Rights' (2012) 1 Oxford Journal of Law and Religion 185, 187

McGorrery P, 'The Philosophy of Criminalisation' (2018) 12 Criminal Law and Philosophy 185, 187, 188

McGowan L, 'Sexual Offence: Constitutionality: CC v Ireland, Attorney-General and Director of Public Prosecutions' [2006] IESC 33 (2006) 70 Journal of Criminal Law 406, 408, 411

McGrogan D, 'The Problem of Causality in International Human Rights Law' (2016) 65 ICLQ 615, 619, 615, 643

McLachlan C, 'Legal Theory: The Principle of Systematic Integration in International Law' (UN Audiovisual Library 2012) United Nations Audiovisual Library of International Law, https://legal.un.org/avl/ls/McLachlan_IL_video_1.html

McManus K, 'The Holy See's Compliance with the United Nations Convention on the Rights of the Child' (2019) 12 DePaul J Soc Just 1

Melnyk RA, 'Pontifical Legation to the United Nations' (2009) 98 Periodica 365, 372, 386

Mullaney M, 'Mandatory Reporting and the Seal of Confession' (2011) 62 The Furrow 62, 523, 524, 525

Murphy Y, 'Clerical Child Abuse: The Irish Experience' (2013) Victoria University Law & Justice Journal 19, 20

Nohilly M, 'Becoming and Being DLP: Designated Liaison Persons' Experience of the Role in the Irish Primary School' (2018) 37 Irish Educational Studies 19, 20, 29

– – 'Child Protection Training for Teachers' (2019) 19 Irish Journal of Applied Social Studies 1, 76

O'Mahony C, 'State liability for abuse in primary schools: systemic failure and O'Keeffe v Hickey' (2009) 28 Irish Educational Studies 315, 316, 321, 324

– – 'The Challenge of Constitutionalising Children's Rights in Ireland' (2009) 11, http://ssrn.com/abstract=1986586

– – 'Falling short of expectations: the 2012 children amendment, from drafting to referendum' (2016) 31 Irish Political Studies 252

– – 'Child Protection and the ECHR: Making Sense of Positive and Procedural Obligations' (2019) 27 IJCR 4, 660, 671

– – and Killkelly U, 'O'Keeffe v Ireland and the Duty of the State to Identify and Prevent Child Abuse' (2014) 36 JSocWelfFamLaw 320, 321, 325, 328

Pellai A, Caranzano-Maitre M, 'Primary prevention of child sexual abuse: Child focused interventions' (2015) 15 Irish Journal of Applied Social Sciences 27, 29

Pietrantonio AM, Wright E, Gibson KN, Alldred T, Jacobson D, Niec A, 'Mandatory reporting of child abuse and neglect: Crafting a positive process for health professionals and caregivers' (2013) 37 Child Abuse & Neglect 102, 103, 107

Rhode U SJ, Relazione giuridiche tra la Chiesa e la Società civile, Typoscript produced for a Canon Law course at Pontificia Università Gregoriana 2022/3 90, 124, wwwulrichrhode.de

Schabas W, 'Reservations to the Convention on the Rights of the Child' (1996) 18 HRQ 472, 479

Shelton D and Gould A, 'Positive and Negative Obligations' in Shelton D (ed) The Oxford Handbook of International Human Rights Law (OUP 2013) 577, 562

Staberock G, 'Human Rights, Domestic Implementation' in Max Planck Encyclopedia of Public International Law (MPEPIL 2011), http://opil.ouplaw.com

Stanley N, Ellis J, Farrelly N, Hollinghurst S, Downe S, 'Preventing domestic abuse for children and young people: A review of school-based interventions' (2015) 59 Children and Youth Service Review 120

Svevo-Cianci K A, Herczog M, Krappmann L, Cook P, 'The new UN CRC General Comment 13: The right of the child to freedom from all forms of violence: Changing how the world conceptualizes child protection' (2011) 35 Child Abuse & Neglect 979, 980, 982

Tobin J, 'Judging the Judges: Are they Adopting the Rights Approach in Matters Involving Children?'(2009) Melbourne University Law Review 579, 610

– – 'Seeking to Persuade: A Constructive Approach to Human Rights Treaty Interpretation' (2010) 23 Harvard Human Rights Journal 1, 7, 10, 16, 22, 41, 49

– –'Understanding a Human Rights Based Approach to Matters Involving Children: Conceptual Foundations and Strategic Considerations' in Williams J and Invernizzi A (eds) The Human Rights of Children: From Visions to Implementation (Ashgate 2011) 61, 62, 67, 69

– –'Justifying Children's Rights' (2013) 21 IJCR 395, 413, 417

– – 'Fixed Concepts but Changing Conceptions: Understanding the Relationship between Children and Parents under the CRC' in Ruck MD, Peterson-Badali M, Freeman M (eds) Handbook of Children's Rights: Global and Multidisciplinary Perspective (Routledge 2017) 53, 65

Todres J, 'Taking Prevention Seriously: Developing a Comprehensive Response to Child Trafficking and Sexual Exploitation' 43 Vand J Transnat'l L 1 (2010) 1

Troy J, '"The Pope's own hand outstretched": Holy See diplomacy as a hybrid mode of diplomatic agency' (2018) 20 British Journal of Politics and International Relations 521, 526

Walsh K, Zwi K, Woolfenden S, Shlonsky A, 'School-Based Education Programmes For The Prevention of Child Sexual Abuse' (2015) Cochrane Database of Systematic Reviews 4 7, 8

Waters M, 'Creeping Monism: The Judicial Trend toward Interpretative Incorporation of Human Rights Treaties' (2007) 107 Columbia Law Review 628, 633, 698

Weckerle C, 'Resilience in the context of child maltreatment: Connections to the practice of mandatory reporting' (2013) 37 Child Abuse and Neglect 93, 94, 95

Westdickenberg G, 'Holy See' in Max Planck Encyclopedia of International Law (MPEPIL 2006)

Media Articles

Department of Education, Minister Foley announces details of Scoping Inquiry to shape Government's response to revelations of historical sexual abuse in schools run by religious orders, March 7, Department of Education (2023), https://www.gov.ie/en/publications/42b7e-education-scoping-inquiry/

McGarry P, Vatican has never Co-Operated with Irish Inquiries into Clerical Child Sex Abuse, August 7, The Irish Times (2018)

O'Brien C, Boarding Schools to be inspected for first time amid concern over gaps in child protection, December 16, The Irish Times (2022)

Royal Irish Academy, Mary McAleese Presents Research into the Catholic Church, Child Protection, Canon Law and the United Nations, YouTube (2018) https://www.youtube.com/watch?v=RbOicUyHfHE

Legislation

Council of Europe, European Convention on Human Rights: As Amended by Protocols Nos. 11, 14, 15 (European Court of Human Rights 1950)

– – 'Convention on the Protection of Children against Sexual Exploitation and Sexual Abuse, adopted by the Committee of Ministers' (2007) Council of Europe Treaty Series (CETS) 201

– – Explanatory Report to the Council of Europe Convention on the Protection of Children Against Sexual Exploitation and Sexual Abuse, CETS 201- Protection of Children against Sexual Exploitation and Sexual Abuse (2007) 7, 10, 18, 32

– – and Gittins C, Violence Reduction in Schools- How to Make a Difference: A Handbook (2006) 12
European Parliament, Directive 2011/93/EU of the European Parliament and of the Council of 13 December 2011 on Combating the Sexual Abuse and Sexual Exploitation of Children and Child Pornography and replacing Council Framework Decision 2004/68/JHA, OJ L 335, 1
European Union Council Framework Decision 2004/68/JHA of 22 December 2003 on Combating the Sexual Exploitation of Children and Child Pornography (2003) L013 44
German Civil Code in the version promulgated on 2 January 2002, last amended by Article 4 para. 5 of the Act of 1 October 2013
Government of Ireland, Offences Against the Person Act, 1861 (1861)
– – Criminal Law (Amendment Act) 1935, Number 6 (1935)
– – Guardianship of Infants Act 1964, Number 7 (1964)
– – Criminal Law (Rape) (Amendment) Act 1990, Number 32 (1990)
– – The Law Reform Commission, Report on Child Sexual Abuse (1990)
– – Child Care Act, Number 17 (1991)
– – Criminal Evidence Act, 1992: Number 12 (1992)
– – Education Act 1998, Number 51 (1998)
– – Sex Offenders Act 2001, Number 18 (2001)
– – Criminal Law (Sexual Offences) Act 2006, Number 15 (2006)
– – Adoption Act, Number 21(2010)
– – Criminal Justice (Withholding of Information on Offences against Children and Vulnerable Persons) Act 2012, Number 24 (2012)
– – Child and Family Agency Act, Number 40 (2013)
– – Children First Act, Number 36 (2015)
– – Criminal Law (Sexual Offences) Act 2017, Number 2 (2017)
– – Criminal Justice (Victims of Crime) Act 2017, Number 28 (2017)
– – Constitution of Ireland: Enacted by the People 1 July 1937 (2020) 101
Government of Ireland, Domestic Violence Act 2018, Number 6 (2018)
– – 'Action Plan for Education', 9 February 2021 (9th Edition) https://www.gov.ie/en/collection/b1330-action-plan-for-education/
– – and Department of Children, Equality, Disability, Integration and Youth, The Report of the Commission to Inquire into Child Abuse (The Ryan Report) (2009)
– – 'Children First: National Guidelines for the Protection and Welfare of Children 2011' (2011 rev/ 2017) 23, 43, 50
Government of Ireland and Department of Education, Relationships and Sexuality

Education: Policy Guidelines 4 (2007) https://www.sess.ie/sites/default/files/rse_policy_guidelines.pdf
Government of Ireland and Department of Education and Skills, Inspectorate, Code of Practice for the Inspectorate (2015)
– – Child Protection Procedures for Primary and Post-Primary Schools 2017 (2017)
– – A Guide to Child Protection and Safeguarding Inspections (13 October 2020) 2
Government of Ireland and Minister McEntee announces Government Approval for the Ratification of the Lanzarote Convention (2020) http://ipo.gov.ie/en/JELR/Pages/PR20000312.
International Court of Justice, Statute of the International Court of Justice, https://www.icj-cij.org/statute
Republik Österreich Bundeskanzleramt, Bundesgesetzblatt für die Republik Österreich, Bundesverfassungsgesetz über die Rechte von Kindern, Teil I (2011)

Case Law

A.S.M.A and Anor v Minister for Justice and Equality and Ors [2013] (30 July 2013) IEHC 381 http://www2.bailii.org/ie/cases/IEHC/2013/H381.html
Airey v Ireland 32 EHRR 305 (ECtHR, 9 October 1979)
Assenov and others v Bulgaria App no 24760/94 (ECtHR, 28 October 1998)
A v UK App no 25599/94 (ECtHR, 23 September 1998)
B v Russia App no 36328/20 (ECtHR, 7 February 2023)
CAS and CS v Romania App no 26692/05 (ECtHR, 20 March 2012)
CC v Ireland and Ors [2006] IESC 33
CD v The Child and Family Agency [2020] IEHC 452
Cook v. Carroll [1945] I.R. 515
Costello-Roberts v UK App no 13134/87 (ECtHR, 25 March 1993)
Dos Santos and Ors v Minister for Justice and Equality & Ors [2015] IECA 210
E and others v UK App no 33218/96 (ECtHR, 26 November 2002)
FG v The Child and Family Agency & Ors [2016] IEHC 156
GS v The Commissioner of An Garda Siochána [2017] IEHC 190 The High Court Judicial Review, No. 225 J.R. (2014)
G v An Bord Uchtála G. Plaintiff and An Bord Uchtala and Other Defendants, Supreme Court (1978 No. 290 Sp.) (1980)
IG v Republic of Moldova App no 53519/07 (ECtHR, 15 May 2012)
International Court of Justice, Reparations for Injuries Suffered in the Service of the United Nations, Advisory Opinion of 11 April 1949, 174, 178

Juppala v Finland App no 18620/03 (ECtHR, 2 December 2008)
McDonnell v Ireland [1998] 1 IR 134, 148
MQ v Gleeson, IEHC 26, 1998, 4 IR 85
O'Donoghue v Minister for Health [1996] 2 IR 20
O'Keeffe v Hickey and Others [2008] IESC 72
O'Keeffe v Ireland App no 35809/10 (ECtHR, 28 January 2014)
O'Shiel and Ors v Minister for Education and Ors [1999] 2 I.L.R.M. 241, 250
P.O'T v Child and Family Agency [2016] IEHC 101
PM v Bulgaria App no 49669/07 (ECtHR, 24 January 2012)
RIP and DLP v Romania App no 27782/10 (ECtHR, 10 May 2012)
Ryan v Attorney General [1965] IR 294, 314
Scozzari and Giunta v Italy, Applications nos. 39221/98 and 41963/98 (ECtHR, 13 July 2000)
Siliadin v France App no 73316/01 (ECtHR, 26 July 2005)
Söderman v Sweden App no 5786/08 (ECtHR, 12 Nov 2013)
X and Y v The Netherlands App no. 8978/80 (ECtHR, 26 March 1985)

UN Materials

All documents issued by the CRC Committee are available *via* the Committee website https://tbinternet.ohchr.org ; they are referenced in the thesis by their UN document number in a format usually beginning with "CRC/C/".
UNESCO, Convention against Discrimination in Education, adopted by the General Conference at its eleventh session, (Paris 1960) ED/2003/CONV/H/1 https://unesdoc.unesco.org/ark:/48223/pf0000132598
-- International technical guidance on sexuality education (2018) 12, 13, 34, 16, 54, 56
-- and UNICEF (Gerison Lansdown drafting), A Human Rights-Based Approach to Education for All (Paris, New York 2007) 27, 39, 75
UNICEF (Hodgkin R, Newell P) Implementation Handbook for the Convention on the Rights of the Child (3rd ed 2007)
United Nations General Assembly, Universal Declaration of Human Rights, resolution 217A (111), adopted 10 December 1948, U.N. doc A/810 (1948).
-- Vienna Convention on the Law of Treaties, pursuant to UNGA resolution 97 (1) (1946), 23 May 1969, Treaty Series (1155) 331.
-- Convention on the Rights of the Child 1989, A/RES/44/25, adopted 20 Nov. 1989, U.N. Treaty Series (1577) 3ff. Optional Protocol on the involvement of children in armed conflict, A/RES/54/263 of 25 May 2000; Optional Protocol on the sale of children, child prostitution and child pornography,

A/RES/54/263 adopted 25 May 2000; Optional Protocol on a communicatioins procedure, A/RES/66/138, adopted 19 December 2011.

Vienna Declaration and Programme of Action (1993) https://www.ohchr.org/en/instruments-mechanisms/instruments/vienna-declaration-and-programme-action

– – Convention on the Rights of Persons with Disabilities (CRPD) (2007) A/RES/61/106

– – Consideration of Reports Submitted by States Parties Under Article 44 of the Convention: Concluding Observations: Democratic Republic of Congo (2009) CRC/C/COD/CO/2 https://documents-dds-ny.un.org/doc/UNDOC/GEN/G09/405/57/pdf/G0940557.pdf?OpenElement

– – The UN Guiding Principles on Business and Human Rights: An Introduction (2011) https://www.ohchr.org/sites/default/files/Documents/Issues/Business/Intro_Guiding_PrinciplesBusinessHR.pdf

– – Consideration of Reports Submitted by States Parties Under Article 44 of the Convention: Second Reports of States parties due in 1997 (2012) CRC/C/VAT/2 https://documents-dds-ny.un.org/doc/UNDOC/GEN/G12/468/09/pdf/G1246809.pdf?OpenElement

– – United Nations, Committee Against Torture, Consideration of Reports Submitted by States Parties Under Article 19 of the Convention: Concluding Observations of the Committee Against Torture (2011) CAT/C/IRL/CO/1 https://documents-dds-ny.un.org/doc/UNDOC/GEN/G11/436/48/PDF/G1143648.pdf?OpenElement

– – Concluding Observations on the Initial Report of the Holy See (2014) CAT/C/VAT/CO/1 https://documents-dds-ny.un.org/doc/UNDOC/GEN/G14/054/05/PDF/G1405405.pdf?OpenElement

United Nations, Committee on Economic, Social And Cultural Rights, General Comment No. 3: The Nature of States Parties' Obligations (Art. 2, Para 1, of the Covenant) (1990) E/1991/23 https://www.ohchr.org/en/documents/general-comments-and-recommendations/e199123-committee-economic-social-and-cultural

– – Draft General Comment No. 9: The Domestic Application of the Covenant (1998) E/C.12/1998/24 https://documents-dds-ny.un.org/doc/UNDOC/GEN/G98/148/36/pdf/G9814836.pdf?OpenElement

– – General Comment No. 11: Plans of Action for Primary Education (Art. 14 of the International Covenant on Economic, Social and Cultural Rights) (1999) E/C.12/1999/4 https://documents-dds-ny.un.org/doc/UNDOC/GEN/G99/422/76/pdf/G9942276.pdf?OpenElement

– – General Comment No. 13: The Right to Education (Art. 13 of the Covenant)

(1999) E/C.12/1999/10 https://documents-dds-ny.un.org/doc/UNDOC/GEN/G99/462/16/pdf/G9946216.pdf?OpenElement

– – General Comment No. 14: The Right to the Highest Attainable Standard of Health (Article 12 of the International Covenant on Economic, Social and Cultural Rights) (2000) E/C.12/2000/4 https://digitallibrary.un.org/record/425041

United Nations, Convention on the Rights of the Child, Consideration of Reports Submitted by States Parties under Article 44 of the Convention: Initial Reports of States Parties Due in 1994: Addendum: Ireland (1996) CRC/C/11/Add 12 https://documents-dds-ny.un.org/doc/UNDOC/GEN/G96/176/23/pdf/G9617623.pdf?OpenElement

– – Consideration of Reports Submitted by States Parties under Article 44 of the Convention: Concluding Observations of the Committee on the Rights of the Child: Ireland (1998) CRC/C/15/Add.85 https://documents-dds-ny.un.org/doc/UNDOC/GEN/G98/152/43/pdf/G9815243.pdf?OpenElement

– – General Comment No. 1, Article 29 (1): The Aims of Education (2001) CRC/GC/2001/1 https://documents-dds-ny.un.org/doc/UNDOC/GEN/G01/412/53/pdf/G0141253.pdf?OpenElement

– – Report on the Thirty-First Session (2002) CRC/C/121 162 https://documents-dds-ny.un.org/doc/UNDOC/GEN/G02/462/70/pdf/G0246270.pdf?OpenElement

– – General Comment No. 4: Adolescent Health and Development in the Context of the Convention on the Rights of the Child (2003) CRC/GC/2003/4 https://documents-dds-ny.un.org/doc/UNDOC/GEN/G03/427/24/pdf/G0342724.pdf?OpenElement

– – General Comment No. 5, General Measures of Implementation of the Convention on the Rights of the Child (2003) CRC/GC/2003/5 https://documents-dds-ny.un.org/doc/UNDOC/GEN/G03/455/14/pdf/G0345514.pdf?OpenElement

– – General Guidelines Regarding the Form and Content of Periodic Reports to the Submitted by States Parties Under Article 44, Paragraph 1(b) of the Convention on the Rights of the Child (2005) CRC/C/58/Rev.1 https://documents-dds-ny.un.org/doc/UNDOC/GEN/G05/452/89/pdf/G0545289.pdf?OpenElement

– – Consideration of Reports Submitted by States Parties Under Article 44 of the Convention: Concluding Observations: Ireland (2006) CRC/C/IRL/CO/2 https://documents-dds-ny.un.org/doc/UNDOC/GEN/G06/450/74/pdf/G0645074.pdf?OpenElement

– – General Comment No. 7: Implementing Child Rights in Early Childhood

(2006) CRC/C/GC/7/Rev. 1 https://documents-dds-ny.un.org/doc/UNDOC/GEN/G06/443/80/pdf/G0644380.pdf?OpenElement
– – General Comment No. 8: The Right of the Child to Protection from Corporal Punishment and other Cruel or Degrading Forms of Punishment (2007) CRC/C/GC/8 https://documents-dds-ny.un.org/doc/UNDOC/GEN/G07/407/71/pdf/G0740771.pdf?OpenElement
– – General Comment No. 12: The Right of the Child to be Heard (2009) CRC/C/GC/12 https://www2.ohchr.org/english/bodies/crc/docs/advanceversions/crc-c-gc-12.pdf https://documents-dds-ny.un.org/doc/UNDOC/GEN/G09/436/99/pdf/G0943699.pdf?OpenElement
– – General Comment No. 13: The Right of the Child to Freedom from all Forms of Violence (2011) CRC/C/GC/13 https://documents-dds-ny.un.org/doc/UNDOC/GEN/G11/423/87/pdf/G1142387.pdf?OpenElement
– – Consideration of Reports Submitted by States Parties under Article 12, Paragraph 1, of the Optional Protocol to the Convention on the Rights of the Child on the Sale of Children, Child Prostitution and Child Pornography: Initial Reports of States Parties Due in 2003: Holy See (2012) CRC/C/OPSC/VAT/1 https://documents-dds-ny.un.org/doc/UNDOC/GEN/G12/471/22/pdf/G1247122.pdf?OpenElement
– – General Comment No. 14: On the Right of the Child to Have His or Her Best Interest Taken As A Primary Consideration (2013) CRC/C/GC/14 https://documents-dds-ny.un.org/doc/UNDOC/GEN/G13/441/89/pdf/G1344189.pdf?OpenElement
– – General Comment No. 15: On the Right of the Child to the Enjoyment of the Highest Attainable Standard of Health (2013) CRC/C/GC/15 https://documents-dds-ny.un.org/doc/UNDOC/GEN/G13/428/14/pdf/G1342814.pdf?OpenElement
– – General Comment No. 16: on the State Obligations regarding the Impact of the Business Sector on Children's Rights (2013) CRC/C/GC/16 https://documents-dds-ny.un.org/doc/UNDOC/GEN/G13/428/21/pdf/G1342821.pdf?OpenElement
– – General Comment No. 17: on the Right of the Child to Rest, Leisure, Play, Recreational Activities, Cultural Life and the Arts (2013) CRC/C/GC/17 https://documents-dds-ny.un.org/doc/UNDOC/GEN/G13/428/28/pdf/G1342828.pdf?OpenElement
– – List of Issues in Relation to the Second Periodic Report of the Holy See (2013) CRC/C/VAT/Q/2 https://documents-dds-ny.un.org/doc/UNDOC/GEN/G13/457/25/pdf/G1345725.pdf?OpenElement
– – Concluding Observations on the Second Periodic Report of the Holy See

(2014) CRC/C/VAT/CO/2 https://documents-dds-ny.un.org/doc/UNDOC/GEN/G14/412/00/pdf/G1441200.pdf?OpenElement
– – Summary Record of the 1852nd Meeting (2014) CRC/C/SR.1852 https://documents-dds-ny.un.org/doc/UNDOC/GEN/G14/402/38/pdf/G1440238.pdf?OpenElement
– – List of Issues in Relation to the Second Periodic Report of the Holy See: Addendum: Replies of the Holy See to the List of Issues (2014) CRC/C/VAT/Q/2/Add.1 https://documents-dds-ny.un.org/doc/UNDOC/GEN/G14/400/83/pdf/G1440083.pdf?OpenElement
– – Concluding Observations on the Combined Third and Fourth Periodic Reports of Ireland (2016) CRC/C/IRL/CO/3–4 https://documents-dds-ny.un.org/doc/UNDOC/GEN/G16/039/97/pdf/G1603997.pdf?OpenElement
– – Concluding Observations on the Combined Fifth and Sixth Periodic Reports of Ireland (2023) CRC/C/IRL/CO/5–6 https://documents-dds-ny.un.org/doc/UNDOC/GEN
– – Concluding Observations on the Fifth Periodic Report of New Zealand: Committee on the Rights of the Child (2016) CRC/C/NZL/CO/5 https://documents-dds-ny.un.org/doc/UNDOC/GEN/G16/236/30/pdf/G1623630.pdf?OpenElement
– – Concluding Observations on the Fifth Periodic Report of the United Kingdom of Great Britain and Northern Ireland (2016) CRC/C/GBR/CO/5 https://documents-dds-ny.un.org/doc/UNDOC/GEN/G16/149/88/pdf/G1614988.pdf?OpenElement
– – General Comment No. 19: on Public Budgeting for the Realization of Children's Rights (art. 4) (2016) CRC/C/GC/19 https://documents-dds-ny.un.org/doc/UNDOC/GEN/G16/162/31/pdf/G1616231.pdf?OpenElement
– – General Comment No. 20: on the Implementation of the Rights of the Child during Adolescence (2016) CRC/C/GC/20 https://documents-dds-ny.un.org/doc/UNDOC/GEN/G16/404/44/pdf/G1640444.pdf?OpenElement
– – General Comment No. 24 on Children's Rights in the Child Justice System (2019) CRC/C/GC/24 https://documents-dds-ny.un.org/doc/UNDOC/GEN/G19/275/57/PDF/G1927557.pdf?OpenElement
United Nations, Economic and Social Council, General Comment No. 12: The Right to Adequate Food (art. 11) (1999) E/C.12/1999/5 https://documents-dds-ny.un.org/doc/UNDOC/GEN/G99/420/12/PDF/G9942012.pdf?OpenElement
– – International Covenant on Economic Social and Cultural Rights, Resolution 2200A (XXI) (1976)
– – Consideration of Reports Submitted by States Parties Under Ar-

ticle 44 of the Convention: Convention on the Rights of the Child: Initial Reports of States Parties Due in 1992: Holy See (1994) CRC/C/3/Add.27 https://documents-dds-ny.un.org/doc/UNDOC/GEN/G94/159/87/pdf/G9415987.pdf?OpenElement
– – Report of the independent expert for the United Nations study of violence against children (2006) A/61/299 https://documents-dds-ny.un.org/doc/UNDOC/GEN/N06/491/05/pdf/N0649105.pdf?OpenElement
– – Report of the Special Rapporteur on Freedom of Religion or Belief, Heiner Bielefeldt: Addendum (2010) A/HRC/16/53 https://digitallibrary.un.org/record/698259?ln=en
– – Report of the International Law Commission (Guide to Practice on Reservations to Treaties) Sixty-sixth Session Supplement No. 10 (2011) A/66/10 Add.1 https://documents-dds-ny.un.org/doc/UNDOC/GEN/N12/203/18/pdf/N1220318.pdf?OpenElement
– – Report of the Working Group on the Universal Periodic Review- Ireland, A/HRC/19/9 (2011) 4 https://www.ohchr.org/sites/default/files/Documents/HRBodies/HRCouncil/RegularSession/Session19/A-HRC-19--9_en.pdf
– – Human Rights Council: Resolution (2011) A/RES/60/251 https://documents-dds-ny.un.org/doc/UNDOC/GEN/N05/502/66/PDF/N0550266.pdf?OpenElement
– – Resolution adopted by the General Assembly on 19 December 2011 (on the report of the Third Committee) (2012) A/RES/66/137, https://documents-dds-ny.un.org/doc/UNDOC/GEN/N11/467/04/PDF/N1146704.pdf?OpenElement
– – Human Rights Council, Report of the Special Rapporteur on the Right to Education, Kishore Singh: Justiciability of the Right to Education (2013) A/HRC/23/35 https://documents-dds-ny.un.org/doc/UNDOC/GEN/G13/135/64/pdf/G1313564.pdf?OpenElement
– – General Comment No. 35, Article 9 (Liberty and security of Person) (2014) CCPR/C/GC/35
– – Report of the Special Rapporteur on the Right to Education, Kishore Singh: Protecting the Right to Education Against Commercialization (2015) A/HRC/29/30 https://documents-dds-ny.un.org/doc/UNDOC/GEN/G15/120/82/pdf/G1512082.pdf?OpenElement
– – The Right to Education: Draft Resolution A/HRC/29/L.14/Rev.1 (2015) https://documents-dds-ny.un.org/doc/UNDOC/LTD/G15/140/10/pdf/G1514010.pdf?OpenElement
– – Human Rights Council, Visit to Ireland: Report of the Special Rapporteur on the Sale and Sexual Exploitation of Children, Including Child Prostitution, Child Pronography and other Child Sexual Abuse Material

(2019) A/HRC/40/51/Add.2 https://documents-dds-ny.un.org/doc/UNDOC/GEN/G19/325/66/pdf/G1932566.pdf?OpenElement

United Nations, International Covenant on Civil and Political Rights, General Assembly Resolution 2200A (XXI) (1966).

United Nations, International Covenant on Civil and Political Rights, General Comment on Issues Relating to the Reservations Made Upon Ratification or Accession to the Covenant or the Optional Protocols thereto, or in Relation to Declaration under Article 41 of the Covenant (1994) CCPR/C/21/Rev.1/Add.6 https://documents-dds-ny.un.org/doc/UNDOC/GEN/G94/199/34/PDF/G9419934.pdf?OpenElement

– – General Comment No. 31 (80): The Nature of the General Legal Obligation Imposed on States Parties to the Covenant (2004) CCPR/C/21/Rev.1/Add.13 https://documents-dds-ny.un.org/doc/UNDOC/GEN/G04/419/56/pdf/G0441956.pdf?OpenElement

– – Legislative History of the Convention on the Rights of the Child (New York and Geneva 2007)

United Nations, Office of the Special Representative of the Secretary General on Violence against Children, Tackling Violence in Schools: A Global Perspective: Bridging the Gap Between Standards and Practice (New York 2012) 1, 29, 39.

ReligionsRecht im Dialog / Law and Religion
hrsg. von Prof. Dr. Adrian Loretan
(Universität Luzern)

Marius Tongendorff
Beichtgeheimnis als Täterschutz?
Ein theologisch-kirchenrechtlicher und staatlich-rechtswissenschaftlicher Vergleich, zugleich ein Beitrag zur Verständigung zwischen Staat und Kirche
Das Beichtgeheimnis wird nicht erst seit den Missbrauchsskandalen in der Katholischen Kirche verdächtigt, (auch) dem Täterschutz zu dienen. Dieses Buch behandelt die Problematik zwischen Geheimnis- und Täterschutz in voller Breite. Es entwickelt Lösungsmöglichkeiten, wie die staatlichen und kirchlichen Interessen ausgeglichen werden können, ohne die Opfer von Straftaten zu vergessen. Das Buch richtet sich nicht nur an Studierende, sondern insbesondere an Praktikerinnen und Praktiker in der Kirche und der staatlichen Verwaltung, in der Politik, in Strafverfolgungsbehörden und an Gerichten. Zugleich ermöglicht es allen Interessierten einen verständlichen Einstieg in die Theologie und das Recht des Beichtsakraments.
Bd. 34, 2025, 368 S., 49,90 €, br., ISBN 978-3-643-80408-2

Adrian Loretan (Hg.)
Machtmissbrauch und sexuelle Gewalt in der Kirche
Beiträge aus Rechtswissenschaften und Theologie von Adrian Loretan, Mary McAleese, Doris Reisinger und Wolfgang Treitler
Die Bekämpfung von Machtmissbrauch und sexueller Gewalt durch Priester verlangt eine Analyse der Machtkonzentration auf zölibatäre Männer. Doch auch Handlungsoptionen sind ins Blickfeld zu rücken: Das Zweite Vatikanische Konzil und die Bischofssynode von 1967 schlagen Menschenrechte als Instrument gegen Machtmissbrauch in der Kirche vor. Mit seiner Kurienreform eröffnet Papst Franziskus 2022 den Frauen den Zugang zu den obersten Leitungsämtern. Der Heilige Stuhl hat die Kinderrechtskonvention ratifiziert. Durch deren Umsetzung wären die Rechte der Kinder in der Kirche geschützt.
Gott steht auf der Seite der Opfer. Die Amtskirche muss diesen Seitenwechsel noch einüben.
Bd. 33, 2023, 214 S., 29,90 €, br., ISBN 978-3-643-80385-6

Merlin Rengith Ambrose
Right of Defense in Marriage Nullity Trials
A Study Based on CIC 1983, DC and MIDI
vol. 32, 2022, 364 pp., 39,90 €, br., ISBN 978-3-643-91509-2

Burkhard Berkmann (Hg.)
Widersprüche zwischen Universal- und Partikularkirchenrecht als Ernstfall von Dezentralisierung in der Kirche?
Ausgewählte Beispiele in Deutschland, Österreich und der Schweiz
Bd. 31, 2022, 228 S., 39,90 €, br., ISBN 978-3-643-15210-7

Paul Schneider
Grundrechte im Ordensrecht am Beispiel der Gleichheit der Personen
Bd. 30, 2021, 328 S., 39,90 €, br., ISBN 978-3-643-80321-4

LIT Verlag Berlin – Münster – Wien – Zürich – London
Auslieferung Deutschland / Österreich / Schweiz: siehe Impressumsseite